AF556466

DOG TERMINOLOGY

DOG TERMINOLOGY

By

Dr. Amita Sarkar

Deptt. of Zoology

Agra College, Agra

(Uttar Pradesh)

(India)

DISCOVERY PUBLISHING HOUSE PVT. LTD.

NEW DELHI-110 002

Published by:
Tilak Wasan
DISCOVERY PUBLISHING HOUSE PVT. LTD.
4383/4B, Ansari Road, Darya Ganj
New Delhi-110 002 (India)
Phone : +91-11-23279245, 43596064-65
Fax : +91-11-23253475
E-mail : discoverypublishinghouse@gmail.com
sales@discoverypublishinggroup.com
parul.wasan@gmail.com
web : www.discoverypublishinggroup.com

***First Edition:* 2013**

ISBN: 978-93-5056-252-9

Dog Terminology

Printed at:
Aditi Fine Art Press
Delhi

Preface

Dogs were domesticated from gray wolves about 15,000 years ago. They must have been very valuable to early human settlements, for they quickly became ubiquitous across world cultures. Dogs perform many roles for people, such as hunting, herding, pulling loads, protection, assisting police and military, companionship, and, more recently, aiding handicapped individuals. This impact on human society has given them the nickname 'Man's Best Friend' in the western world. In 2001, there were estimated to be 400 million dogs in the world.

The domestic dog (*Canis lupus familiaris* and *Canis lupus dingo*) is a domesticated form of the gray wolf, a member of the Canidae family of the order Carnivora. The term is used for both feral and pet varieties. The dog may have been the first animal to be domesticated, and has been the most widely kept working, hunting, and companion animal in human history. The word 'dog' may also mean the male of a canine species, as opposed to the word 'bitch' for the female of the species.

Dog is the common use term that refers to members of the subspecies *Canis lupus familiaris* (*canis*, 'dog'; *lupus*, 'wolf'; *familiaris*, 'of a household' or 'domestic'). The term can also be used to refer to a wider range of related species, such as the members of the genus *Canis*, or "true dogs", including the wolf, coyote, and jackals; or it can refer to the members of the subfamily Caninae, which would also include the African wild dog; or it can be used to refer to any member of the family Canidae, which would also include the foxes, bush dog, raccoon dog, and others. Some members of the family have 'dog' in their common names, such as the raccoon dog and the African wild dog. A few animals have 'dog' in their common names but are not canids, such as the prairie dog.

Over the 15,000 year span the dog had been domesticated, it diverged into only a handful of landraces, groups of similar animals whose morphology and behavior have been shaped by environmental factors and functional roles. Through selective breeding by humans, the dog has developed into hundreds of varied breeds, and shows more behavioral and morphological variation than any other land mammal. For example, height measured to the withers ranges from a few inches in the Chihuahua to a few feet in the Irish Wolfhound; color varies from white through grays (usually called 'blue') to black, and browns from light (tan) to dark ('red' or 'chocolate') in a wide variation of patterns; coats can be short or long, coarse-haired to wool-like, straight, curly, or smooth. It is common for most breeds to shed this coat.

Once agriculture took hold, dogs would have been selected for different tasks, their wolf-like natures becoming a handicap as they became herders and guards. Molecular biologist Elaine Ostrander is of the view that "When we became an agricultural society, what we needed dogs for changed enormously, and a further and irrevocable division occurred at that point". This may be the point that stands out in the fossil record, when dogs and wolves began to develop noticeably different morphologies.

Domestic dogs inherited complex behaviors from their wolf ancestors, being pack hunters with complex body language. These sophisticated forms of social cognition and communication may account for their trainability, playfulness, and ability to fit into human households and social situations, and these attributes have given dogs a relationship with humans that has enabled them to become one of the most successful species on the planet today.

Although experts largely disagree over the details of dog domestication, it is agreed that human interaction played a significant role in shaping the subspecies. Shortly after domestication, dogs became ubiquitous in human populations, and spread throughout the world.

—Author

Contents

CHAPTER 1

Introduction

Over the 15,000 year span the dog had been domesticated, it diverged into only a handful of landraces, groups of similar animals whose morphology and behaviour have been shaped by environmental factors and functional roles. Through selective breeding by humans, the dog has developed into hundreds of varied breeds, and shows more behavioural and morphological variation than any other land mammal. For example, height measured to the withers ranges from a few inches in the Chihuahua to a few feet in the Irish Wolfhound; colour varies from white through grays (usually called 'blue') to black, and browns from light (tan) to dark ('red' or 'chocolate') in a wide variation of patterns; coats can be short or long, coarse-haired to wool-like, straight, curly, or smooth. It is common for most breeds to shed this coat.

Dogs were domesticated from gray wolves about 15,000 years ago. They must have been very valuable to early human settlements, for they quickly became ubiquitous across world cultures. Dogs perform many roles for people, such as hunting, herding, pulling loads, protection, assisting police and military, companionship, and, more recently, aiding handicapped individuals. This impact on human society has given them the nickname 'Man's Best Friend' in the western world. In 2001, there were estimated to be 400 million dogs in the world.

The domestic dog (*Canis lupus familiaris* and *Canis lupus dingo*) is a domesticated form of the gray wolf, a member of the Canidae family of the order Carnivora. The term is used for both feral and pet varieties. The dog may have been the first animal to be domesticated, and has been the most widely kept working, hunting, and companion animal in human history. The word 'dog' may also mean the male of a canine species, as opposed to the word 'bitch' for the female of the species.

Dog is the common use term that refers to members of the subspecies *Canis lupus familiaris* (*canis*, 'dog'; *lupus*, 'wolf'; *familiaris*, 'of a household' or 'domestic'). The term can also be used to refer to a wider range of related species, such as the members of the genus *Canis*, or 'true dogs', including the wolf, coyote, and jackals; or it can refer to the members of the subfamily Caninae, which would also include the African wild dog; or it can be used to refer to any member of the family Canidae, which would also include the foxes, bush dog, raccoon dog, and others. Some members of the family have "dog" in their common names, such as the raccoon dog and the African wild dog. A few animals have 'dog' in their common names but are not canids, such as the prairie dog.

The English word *dog* comes from Middle English *dogge*, from Old English *docga*, a 'powerful dog breed'. The term may derive from Proto-Germanic *dukkon*, represented in Old English *finger-docce* ('finger-muscle'). The word also shows the familiar petname diminutive *-ga* also seen in *frogga* 'frog', *picga* 'pig', *stagga* 'stag', *wicga* 'beetle, worm', among others. Due to the archaic structure of the word, the term *dog* may ultimately derive from the earliest layer of Proto-Indo-European vocabulary, reflecting the role of the dog as the earliest domesticated animal.

Mbabaram is famous in linguistic circles for a striking coincidence in its vocabulary to English. When linguist R.M.W. Dixon began his study of the language by eliciting a few basic nouns among the first of these was the word for 'dog' which coincidentally in Mbabaram is *dog*. The Mbabaram word for 'dog' really is pronounced almost identically to the English word (compare true cognates such as Yidiny *gudaga*, Dyirbal *guda*, Djabugay *gurraa* and Guugu Yimidhirr *gudaa*, for example). The similarity is a complete coincidence: there is no discernible relationship between English and Mbabaram. This and other false cognates are often cited as a caution against deciding that languages are related based on a small number of comparisons.

In 14th century England, *hound* (from Old English: *hund*) was the general word for all domestic canines, and *dog* referred to a subtype of hound, a group including the mastiff. It is believed this 'dog' type of 'hound' was so common it eventually became the prototype of the category 'hound'. By the 16th century, *dog* had become the general word, and hound had begun to refer only to types used for hunting. *Hound*, cognate to German *Hund*, Dutch *hond*, common Scandinavian *hund*, and Icelandic *hundur*, is ultimately derived from the Proto-Indo-European *kwon-* 'dog', found in Welsh *ci* (plural *cwn*), Latin *canis*, Greek *kýon*, Lithuanian.

In breeding circles, a male canine is referred to as a *dog*, while a female is called a *bitch* (Middle English bicche, from Old English bicce, ultimately from Old Norse bikkja). A group of offspring is a *litter*. The father of a litter is called the *sire*, and the mother is called the *dam*. Offspring are, in general, called *pups* or *puppies*, from French *poupée*, until they are about a year old. The process of birth is *whelping*, from the Old English word *hwelp* (cf. German Welpe, Dutch welp, Swedish valp, Icelandic hvelpur).

Taxonomy

The domestic dog was originally classified as *Canis familiaris* and *Canis familiarus domesticus* by Carolus Linnaeus in 1758, and was reclassified in 1993 as *Canis lupus familiaris*, a subspecies of the gray wolf *Canis lupus*, by the Smithsonian Institution and the American Society of Mammalogists. Overwhelming evidence from behaviour, vocalizations, morphology, and molecular biology led to the contemporary scientific understanding that a single species, the gray wolf, is the common ancestor for all breeds of domestic dogs; however, the timeframe and mechanisms by which dogs diverged are controversial. *Canis lupus familiaris* is listed as the name for the taxon that is broadly used in the scientific community and recommended by ITIS; *Canis familiaris*, however, is a recognised synonym.

Domestic dogs inherited complex behaviours from their wolf ancestors, being pack hunters with complex body language. These sophisticated forms of social cognition and communication may account for their trainability, playfulness, and ability to fit into human households and social situations, and these attributes have given dogs a relationship with humans that has enabled them to become one of the most successful species on the planet today.

Although experts largely disagree over the details of dog domestication, it is agreed that human interaction played a significant role in shaping the subspecies. Shortly after domestication, dogs became ubiquitous in human populations, and spread throughout the world. Emigrants from Siberia likely crossed the Bering Strait with dogs in their company, and some experts suggest the use of sled dogs may have been critical to the success of the waves that entered North America roughly 12,000 years ago, although the earliest archaeological evidence of dog-like canids in North America dates from about 9000 years ago. Dogs were an important part of life for the Athabascan population in North America, and were their only domesticated animal. Dogs also carried much of the load in the migration of the Apache and Navajo tribes 1,400 years ago. Use of dogs as pack animals in these cultures often persisted after the introduction of the horse to North America.

The current consensus among biologists and archaeologists is that the dating of first domestication is indeterminate. There is conclusive evidence dogs genetically diverged from their wolf ancestors at least 15,000 years ago, but some believe domestication to have occurred earlier. It is not known whether humans domesticated the wolf as such to initiate dog's divergence from its ancestors, or whether dog's evolutionary path had already taken a different course prior to domestication. For example, it is hypothesized that some wolves gathered around the campsites of paleolithic camps to scavenge refuse, and associated evolutionary pressure developed that favoured those who were less frightened by, and keener in approaching, humans.

The bulk of the scientific evidence for the evolution of the domestic dog stems from archaeological findings and mitochondrial DNA studies. The divergence date of roughly 15,000 years ago is based in part on archaeological evidence that demonstrates the domestication of dogs occurred more than 15,000 years ago, and some genetic evidence indicates the domestication of dogs from their wolf ancestors began in the late Upper Paleolithic close to the Pleistocene/Holocene boundary, between 17,000 and 14,000 years ago. But there is a wide range of other, contradictory findings that make this issue controversial.

Archaeological evidence suggests the latest dogs could have diverged from wolves was roughly 15,000 years ago, although it is possible they diverged much earlier. In 2008, a team of international scientists released findings from an excavation at Goyet Cave in Belgium declaring a large, toothy canine existed 31,700 years ago and ate a diet of horse, musk ox and reindeer.

Prior to this Belgium discovery, the earliest dog fossils were two large skulls from Russia and a mandible from Germany dated from roughly 14,000 years ago. Remains of smaller dogs from Natufian cave deposits in the Middle East, including the earliest burial of a human being with a domestic dog, have been dated to around 10,000 to 12,000 years ago. There is a great deal of archaeological evidence for dogs throughout Europe and Asia around this period and through the next two thousand years (roughly 8,000 to 10,000 years ago), with fossils uncovered in Germany, the French Alps, and Iraq, and cave paintings in Turkey. The oldest remains of a domesticated dog in the Americas were found in Texas and have been dated to about 9,400 years ago.

DNA Studies

DNA studies have provided a wide range of possible divergence dates, from 15,000 to 40,000 years ago, to as much as 100,000 to 140,000 years ago. These results depend on a number of assumptions. Genetic studies are based on comparisons of genetic diversity between species, and depend on a calibration date. Some estimates of divergence dates from DNA evidence use an estimated wolf-coyote divergence date of roughly 700,000 years ago as a calibration. If this estimate is incorrect, and the actual wolf-coyote divergence is closer to one or two million years ago, or more, then the DNA evidence that supports specific dog-wolf divergence dates would be interpreted very differently.

Furthermore, it is believed the genetic diversity of wolves has been in decline for the last 200 years, and that the genetic diversity of dogs has been reduced by selective breeding. This could significantly bias DNA analyses to support an earlier divergence date. The genetic evidence for the domestication event occurring in East Asia is also subject to violations of assumptions. These conclusions are based on the location of maximal genetic divergence, and assume hybridization does not occur, and that breeds remain geographically localized. Although these assumptions hold for many species, there is good reason to believe that they do not hold for canines.

Genetic analyses indicate all dogs are likely descended from a handful of domestication events with a small number of founding females, although there is evidence domesticated dogs interbred with local populations of wild wolves on several occasions. Data suggest dogs first diverged from wolves in East Asia, and these domesticated dogs then quickly migrated throughout the world, reaching the North American continent around 8000 BC. The oldest groups of dogs, which show the greatest genetic variability and are the most similar to their wolf ancestors, are primarily Asian and African breeds, including the Basenji, Lhasa Apso, and Siberian Husky. Some breeds thought to be very old, such as the Pharaoh Hound, Ibizan Hound, and Norwegian Elkhound, are now known to have been created more recently.

There is a great deal of controversy surrounding the evolutionary framework for the domestication of dogs. Although it is widely claimed that "man domesticated the wolf," man may not have taken such a proactive role in the process. The nature of the interaction between man and wolf that led to domestication is unknown and controversial. At least three early species of the *Homo* genus began spreading out of Africa roughly 400,000 years ago, and thus lived for a considerable time in contact with canine species. Despite this, there is no evidence of any adaptation of canine species to the presence of the close relatives of modern man. If dogs were domesticated, as believed, roughly 15,000 years ago, the event (or events) would have coincided with a large expansion in human territory and the development of agriculture. This has led some biologists to suggest one of the forces that led to the domestication of dogs was a shift in human lifestyle in the form of established human settlements. Permanent settlements would have coincided with a greater amount of disposable food and would have created a barrier between wild and anthropogenic canine populations.

Wolves, and their dog descendants, would have derived significant benefits from living in human camps—more safety, more reliable food, lesser caloric needs, and more chance to breed. They would have benefited from humans' upright gait that gives them larger range over which to see potential predators and prey, as well as colour vision that, at least by day, gives humans better visual discrimination. Camp dogs would also have benefitted from human tool use, as in bringing down larger prey and controlling fire for a range of purposes.

Humans would also have derived enormous benefit from the dogs associated with their camps. For instance, dogs would have improved sanitation by cleaning up food scraps. Dogs may have provided warmth, as referred to in the Australian Aboriginal expression "three dog night" (an exceptionally cold night), and they would have alerted the camp to the presence of predators or strangers, using their acute hearing to provide an early warning. Anthropologists believe the most significant benefit would have been the use of dogs' sensitive sense of smell to assist with the hunt. The relationship between the presence of a dog and success in the hunt is often mentioned as a primary reason for the domestication of the wolf, and a 2004 study of hunter groups with and without a dog gives quantitative support to the hypothesis that the benefits of cooperative hunting was an important factor in wolf domestication.

The cohabitation of dogs and humans would have greatly improved the chances of survival for early human groups, and the domestication of dogs may have been one of the key forces that led to human success.

The most widespread form of interspecies bonding occurs between humans and dogs" and the keeping of dogs as companions, particularly by elites, has a long history. However, pet dog populations grew significantly after World War II as suburbanization increased. In the 1950s and 1960s, dogs were kept outside more often than they tend to be today (using the expression 'in the doghouse' to describe exclusion from the group signifies the distance between the doghouse and the home) and were still primarily functional, acting as a guard, children's playmate, or walking companion. Dogs can also be ridden by children as small horses. Among the best breeds for riding are the St. Bernard, the Newfoundland, the Landseer, and the Great Pyrenees. From the 1980s, there have been changes in the role of the pet dog, such as the increased role of dogs in the emotional support of their owners. People and dogs have become increasingly integrated and implicated in each other's lives, to the point where pet dogs actively shape the way a family and home are experienced.

There have been two major trends in the changing status of pet dogs. The first has been the 'commodification' of the dog, shaping it to conform to human expectations of personality and behaviour. The second has been the broadening of the concept of the family and the home to include dogs-as-dogs within everyday routines and practices.

There are a vast range of commodity forms available to transform a pet dog into an ideal companion. The list of goods, services and places available is enormous: from dog perfumes, couture, furniture and housing, to dog groomers, therapists, trainers and care-takers, dog cafes, spas, parks and beaches, and dog hotels, airlines and cemeteries. While dog training as an organized activity can be traced back to the 18th century, in the last decades of the 20th century it became a high profile issue as many normal dog behaviours such as barking, jumping up, digging, rolling in dung, fighting, and urine marking became increasingly incompatible with the new role of a pet dog. Dog training books, classes and television programmes proliferated as the process of commodifying the pet dog continued.

The majority of contemporary dog owners describe their dog as part of the family, although some ambivalence about the relationship is evident in the popular reconceptualisation of the dog-human family as a pack. A dominance model of dog-human relationships has been promoted by some dog trainers, such as on the television programme *Dog Whisperer*. However it has been disputed that "trying to achieve status" is characteristic of dog–human interactions. Pet dogs play an active role in family life; for example, a study of conversations in dog-human families showed how family members use the dog as a resource, talking to the dog, or talking through the dog, to mediate their interactions with each other. Another study of dogs' roles in families showed many dogs have set tasks or routines undertaken as family members, the most common of which was helping with the washing-up by licking the plates in the dishwasher, and bringing in the newspaper from the lawn. Increasingly, human family members are engaging in activities centred on the perceived needs and interests of the dog, or in which the dog is an integral partner, such as dog dancing and doga.

According to the statistics published by the American Pet Products Manufacturers Association in the National Pet Owner Survey in 2009-2010, it is estimated there are 77.5 million dog owners in the United States. The same survey shows nearly 40 per cent of American households own at least one dog, of which 67 per cent own just one dog, 25 per cent two dogs and nearly 9 per cent more than two dogs. There does not seem to be any gender preference among dogs as pets, as the statistical data reveal an equal number of female and male dog pets. Yet, although several programmes are undergoing to promote pet adoption, only nearly a fifth of the owned dogs come from a shelter.

Dogs have lived and worked with humans in so many roles that they have earned the unique nickname, 'man's best friend', a phrase used in other languages as well. They have been bred for herding livestock, hunting (e.g. pointers and hounds), rodent control, guarding, helping fishermen with nets, and pulling loads, in addition to their roles as companions.

Service dogs such as guide dogs, utility dogs, assistance dogs, hearing dogs, and psychological therapy dogs provide assistance to individuals with physical or mental disabilities. Some dogs owned by epileptics have been shown to alert their handler when the handler shows signs of an impending seizure, sometimes well in advance of onset, allowing the owner to seek safety, medication, or medical care.

Dogs included in human activities in terms of helping out humans are usually called working dogs. Dogs of several breeds are considered working dogs. Some working dog breeds include Akita, Alaskan Malamute, Anatolian Shepherd Dog, Bernese Mountain Dog, Black Russian Terrier, Boxer, Bullmastiff, Doberman Pinscher, Dogue de Bordeaux, German Pinscher, German Shepherd, Giant Schnauzer, Great Dane, Great Pyrenees, Great Swiss

Mountain Dog, Komondor, Kuvasz, Mastiff, Neapolitan Mastiff, Newfoundland, Portuguese Water Dog, Rottweiler, Saint Bernard, Samoyed, Siberian Husky, Standard Schnauzer, and Tibetan Mastiff.

Based on their size and strength, these dogs are more suitable for a wide range of jobs rather than companions for average families. Moreover, most of these dogs have a different type of personality, usually more aggressive, which makes the relationship with their trainer safer when he is a professional and knows what type of behaviour to expect from such a dog. The working dogs are trained properly and accordingly to the activities they will perform. Yet, despite the size of some dogs, they are sometimes used as pets as well. In general, however, they require special training and owners might have to learn how to bond with their pets, in these cases.

Some of these dogs are suitable for more than a single activity. For instance, Akita is a popular dog in the show ring, but its qualities make it a reliable animal in therapy work. The Alaskan Malamute is one of the most powerful and strong working dogs, and although some families have this type of breed as a pet, they are more likely to enjoy sledding, and performing different mountainous activities with their owners. The Anatolian Shepherd dog and the Black Russian Terrier are famous for their ability to work as guard dogs, being used to protect livestock. The Swiss Mountain dogs, Bullmastiffs and German Pinschers are suitable for carting, obedience, tracking and even therapy work.

Boxers are commonly used as service dogs for blind people because of their intelligence and alert expression. During war time, this type of dog was also used as a courier. Dobermans have proven themselves as great learners with an amazing capacity of retaining training, and as a result, they are commonly trained and used as police or war dogs. Some other types of breeds are easily trained for hunting or fighting, such as the Dogue de Bordeaux.

Sports and Shows

Owners of dogs often enter them in competitions such as breed conformation shows or sports, including racing and sledding.

In conformation shows, also referred to as breed shows, a judge familiar with the specific dog breed evaluates individual purebred dogs for conformity with their established breed type as described in the breed standard. As the breed standard only deals with the externally observable qualities of the dog (such as appearance, movement, and temperament), separately tested qualities (such as ability or health) are not part of the judging in conformation shows.

As a Food Source

Dog meat is consumed in some East Asian countries, including Korea, China, and Vietnam, a practice that dates back to antiquity. It is estimated that 13-16 million dogs are killed and consumed in Asia every year. The BBC claims that, in 1999, more than 6,000 restaurants served soups made from dog meat in South Korea. In Korea, the primary dog breed raised for meat, the *nureongi* , differs from those breeds raised for pets that Koreans may keep in their homes. The most popular Korean dog dish is *gaejang-guk* (also called *bosintang*), a spicy stew meant to balance the body's heat during the summer months; followers of the custom claim this is done to ensure good health by balancing one's *gi*, or vital energy of the body. A 19th century version of *gaejang-guk* explains that the dish is prepared by boiling dog meat with scallions and chili powder. Variations of the dish contain chicken and bamboo shoots. While the dishes are still popular in Korea with a segment of the population, dog is not as widely consumed as beef, chicken, and pork.

Other cultures, such as Polynesia and pre-Columbian Mexico, also consumed dog meat in their history. However, Western, South Asian, African, and Middle Eastern cultures, in general, regard consumption of dog meat as taboo. In some places, however, such as in rural areas of Poland, dog fat is believed to have medicinal properties—being good for the lungs for instance.

A CNN report in China dated March 2010 interviews a dog meat vendor who states that most of the dogs that are available for selling to restaurant are raised in special farms but that there is always a chance that a sold dog is someone's lost pet, although dog pet breeds are not considered edible.

Health Risks to Humans

In the USA, cats and dogs are a factor in more than 86,000 falls each year. It has been estimated around two per cent of dog-related injuries treated in UK hospitals are domestic accidents. The same study found that while dog involvement in road traffic accidents was difficult to quantify, dog-associated road accidents involving injury more commonly involved two-wheeled vehicles.

Toxocara canis (dog roundworm) eggs in dog feces can cause toxocariasis. In the United States, about 10,000 cases of *Toxocara* infection are reported in humans each year, and almost 14 per cent of the US population is infected. In Great Britain, 24 per cent of soil samples taken from public parks contained *T. canis* eggs. Untreated toxocariasis can cause retinal damage and decreased vision. Dog feces can also contain hookworms that cause cutaneous larva migrans in humans.

The incidence of dog bites, and especially fatal dog bites, is extremely rare in America considering the number of pet dogs in the country. Fatalities from dog bites occur in America at the rate of one per four million dogs. A Colourado study found bites in children were less severe than bites in adults. The incidence of dog bites in the US is 12.9 per 10,000 inhabitants, but for boys aged 5 to 9, the incidence rate is 60.7 per 10,000. Moreover, children have a much higher chance to be bitten in the face or neck. Sharp claws with powerful muscles behind them can lacerate flesh in a scratch that can lead to serious infections.

In the UK between 2003 and 2004, there were 5868 dog attacks on humans, resulting in 5770 working days lost in sick leave.

Health Benefits for Humans

A growing body of research indicates the companionship of a dog can enhance human physical health and psychological wellbeing. Dog and cat owners have been shown to have better mental and physical health than nonowners, making fewer visits to the doctor and being less likely to be on medication than nonowners. In one study, new pet owners reported a highly significant reduction in minor health problems during the first month following pet acquisition, and this effect was sustained in dog owners through to the end of the study. In addition, dog owners took considerably more physical exercise than cat owners and people without pets. The group without pets exhibited no statistically significant changes in health or behaviour. The results provide evidence that pet acquisition may have positive effects on human health and behaviour, and that for dog owners these effects are relatively long term. Pet ownership has also been associated with increased coronary artery disease survival, with dog owners being significantly less likely to die within one year of an acute myocardial infarction than those who did not own dogs.

The health benefits of dogs can result from contact with dogs, not just from dog ownership. For example, when in the presence of a pet dog, people show reductions in cardiovascular, behavioural, and psychological indicators of anxiety. The benefits of contact with a dog also include social support, as dogs are able to not only provide companionship and social support themselves, but also to act as facilitators of social interactions between humans. One study indicated that wheelchair users experience more positive social interactions with strangers when they are accompanied by a dog than when they are not.

The practice of using dogs and other animals as a part of therapy dates back to the late 18th century, when animals were introduced into mental institutions to help socialize patients with mental disorders. Animal-assisted intervention research has shown that animal-assisted therapy with a dog can increase a person with Alzheimer's disease's social behaviours, such as smiling and laughing. One study demonstrated that children with ADHD and conduct disorders who participated in an education programme with dogs and other animals showed increased attendance, increased knowledge and skill objectives, and decreased antisocial and violent behaviour compared to those who were not in an animal-assisted programme.

Shelters

Every year, between 6 and 8 million dogs and cats enter US animal shelters. The Humane Society of the United States (HSUS) estimates that approximately 3 to 4 million dogs and cats are euthanized yearly in shelters across the United States. However, the percentage of dogs in US animal shelters that are eventually adopted and removed from the shelters by their new owners has increased since the mid 1990s from around 25 per cent up to around 60-75 per cent in the mid first decade of the 21st century.

Pets entering the shelters are euthanized in countries all over the world because of the lack of financial provisions to take care of these animals. Most shelters complain of not having enough resources to feed the pets and by being constrained to kill them, as the likelihood for all of them to find an owner is very small. In poor countries, euthanasia is usually violent.

Domestic dogs have been selectively bred for millennia for various behaviours, sensory capabilities, and physical attributes. Modern dog breeds show more variation in size, appearance, and behaviour than any other domestic animal. Nevertheless, their morphology is based on that of their wild ancestors, gray wolves. Dogs are predators and scavengers, and like many other predatory mammals, the dog has powerful muscles, fused wrist bones, a cardiovascular system that supports both sprinting and endurance, and teeth for catching and tearing. Dogs are highly variable in height and weight. The smallest known adult dog was a Yorkshire Terrier, that stood only 6.3 centimetres (2.5 in) at the shoulder, 9.5 cm (3.7 in) in length along the head-and-body, and weighed only 113 grams (4.0 oz). The largest known dog was an English Mastiff which weighed 155.6 kilograms (343 lb) and was 250 cm (98 in) from the snout to the tail. The tallest dog is a Great Dane that stands 106.7 cm (42.0 in) at the shoulder.

Like most mammals, dogs are dichromats and have colour vision equivalent to red-green colour blindness in humans (deuteranopia). Dogs are less sensitive to differences in grey shades than humans and also can detect brightness at about half the accuracy of humans.

The dog's visual system has evolved to aid proficient hunting. While a dog's visual acuity is poor (that of a poodle's has been estimated to translate to a Snellen rating of 20/75), their visual discrimination for moving objects is very high; dogs have been shown to be able to discriminate between humans (e.g., identifying their owner) at a range of between 800 and 900 m, however this range decreases to 500-600 m if the object is stationary. Dogs have a temporal resolution of between 60 and 70 Hz, which explains why many dogs struggle to watch television, as most such modern screens are optimized for humans at 50-60 Hz. Dogs can detect a change in movement that exists in a single diopter of space within their eye. Humans, by comparison, require a change of between 10 and 20 diopters to detect movement.

As crepuscular hunters, dogs often rely on their vision in low light situations: They have very large pupils, a high density of rods in the fovea, an increased flicker rate, and a tapetum lucidum. The tapetum is a reflective surface behind the retina that reflects light to give the photoreceptors a second chance to catch the photons. There is also a relationship between body size and overall diameter of the eye. A range of 9.5 and 11.6 mm can be found between various breeds of dogs. This 20 per cent variance can be substantial and is associated as an adaptation toward superior night vision.

The eyes of different breeds of dogs have different shapes, dimensions, and retina configurations. Many long-nosed breeds have a 'visual streak' – a wide foveal region that runs across the width of the retina and gives them a very wide field of excellent vision. Some long-muzzled breeds, in particular, the sighthounds, have a field of vision up to 270° (compared to 180° for humans). Short-nosed breeds, on the other hand, have an 'area centralis': a central patch with up to three times the density of nerve endings as the visual streak, giving them detailed sight much more like a human's. Some broad-headed breeds with short noses have a field of vision similar to that of humans. Most breeds have good vision, but some show a genetic predisposition for myopia – such as Rottweilers, with which one out of every two has been found to be myopic. Dogs also have a greater divergence of the eye axis than humans, enabling them to rotate their pupils farther in any direction. The divergence of the eye axis of dogs ranges from 12-25° depending on the breed.

Experimentation has proven that dogs can distinguish between complex visual images such as that of a cube or a prism. Dogs also show attraction to static visual images such as the silhouette of a dog on a screen, their own reflections, or videos of dogs; however, their interest declines sharply once they are unable to make social contact with the image.

The frequency range of dog hearing is approximately 40 Hz to 60,000 Hz, which means that dogs can detect sounds far beyond the upper limit of the human auditory spectrum. In addition, dogs have ear mobility, which allows them to rapidly pinpoint the exact location of a sound. Eighteen or more muscles can tilt, rotate, raise, or lower a dog's ear. A dog can identify a sound's location much faster than a human can, as well as hear sounds at four times the distance.

Smell

While the human brain is dominated by a large visual cortex, the dog brain is dominated by an olfactory cortex. The olfactory bulb in dogs is roughly forty times bigger than the olfactory bulb in humans, relative to total brain size, with 125 to 220 million smell-sensitive receptors. The bloodhound exceeds this standard with nearly 300 million receptors. Dogs can discriminate odors at concentrations nearly 100 million times lower than humans can. The wet nose is essential for determining the direction of the air current containing the smell. Cold receptors in the skin are sensitive to the cooling of the skin by evaporation of the moisture by air currents.

The coats of domestic dogs are of two varieties: 'double' being common with dogs (as well as wolves) originating from colder climates, made up of a coarse guard hair and a soft down hair, or 'single', with the topcoat only.

Domestic dogs often display the remnants of countershading, a common natural camouflage pattern. A countershaded animal will have dark colouring on its upper surfaces and light colouring below, which reduces its general visibility. Thus, many breeds will have an occasional 'blaze', stripe, or 'star' of white fur on their chest or underside.

There are many different shapes for dog tails: straight, straight up, sickle, curled, or cork-screw. As with many canids, one of the primary functions of a dog's tail is to communicate their emotional state, which can be important in getting along with others. In some hunting dogs, however, the tail is traditionally docked to avoid injuries. In some breeds, puppies can be born with a short tail or no tail at all.

While all dogs are genetically very similar, natural selection and selective breeding have reinforced certain characteristics in certain populations of dogs, giving rise to dog types and dog breeds. Dog types are broad categories based on function, genetics, or characteristics. Dog breeds are groups of animals that possess a set of inherited characteristics that distinguishes them from other animals within the same species. Modern dog breeds are non-scientific classifications of dogs kept by modern kennel clubs. Purebred dogs of one breed are genetically distinguishable from purebred dogs of other breeds, but the means by which kennel clubs classify dogs is unsystematic. Systematic analyses of the dog genome has revealed only four major types of dogs that can be said to be statistically distinct. These include the 'old world dogs' (e.g., Malamute and Shar Pei), 'Mastiff"-type (e.g., English Mastiff), 'herding'-type (e.g., Border Collie), and 'all others' (also called 'modern'- or 'hunting'-type).

Dogs are susceptible to various diseases, ailments, and poisons, some of which can affect humans. To defend against many common diseases, dogs are often vaccinated.

Some breeds of dogs are prone to certain genetic ailments such as elbow or hip dysplasia, blindness, deafness, pulmonic stenosis, cleft palate, and trick knees. Two serious medical conditions particularly affecting dogs are pyometra, affecting unspayed females of all types and ages, and bloat, which affects the larger breeds or deep-chested dogs. Both of these are acute conditions, and can kill rapidly. Dogs are also susceptible to parasites such as fleas, ticks, and mites, as well as hookworm, tapeworm, roundworm, and heartworm.

Dogs are highly susceptible to theobromine poisoning, typically from ingestion of chocolate. Theobromine is toxic to dogs because, although the dog's metabolism is capable of breaking down the chemical, the process is so slow that even small amounts of chocolate can be fatal, especially dark chocolate.

Dogs are also vulnerable to some of the same health conditions as humans, including diabetes, dental and heart disease, epilepsy, cancer, hypothyroidism, and arthritis.

The typical lifespan of dogs varies widely among breeds, but for most the median longevity, the age at which half the dogs in a population have died and half are still alive, ranges from 10 to 13 years. Individual dogs may live well beyond the median of their breed.

The breed with the shortest lifespan (among breeds for which there is a questionnaire survey with a reasonable sample size) is the Dogue de Bordeaux, with a median longevity of about 5.2 years, but several breeds, including Miniature Bull Terriers, Bloodhounds, and Irish Wolfhounds are nearly as short-lived, with median longevities of 6 to 7 years.

The longest-lived breeds, including Toy Poodles, Japanese Spitz, Border Terriers, and Tibetan Spaniels, have median longevities of 14 to 15 years. The median longevity of Mixed-breed dogs, taken as an average of all sizes, is one or more years longer than that of purebred dogs when all breeds are averaged. The dog widely reported to be the longest-lived is 'Bluey', who died in 1939 and was claimed to be 29.5 years old at the time of his death; however, the Bluey record is anecdotal and unverified. The longest verified records are of dogs living for 24 years.

Predation

Although wild dogs, like wolves, are apex predators, they can be killed in territory disputes with wild animals. Furthermore, in areas where both dogs and other large predators live, dogs can be a major food source for big cats or canines. Reports from Croatia indicate that dogs are killed by wolves more frequently than sheep. Wolves in Russia apparently limit feral dog populations. In Wisconsin, more compensation has been paid for dog losses than livestock. Some wolf pairs have been reported to prey on dogs by having one wolf lure the dog out into heavy brush where the second animal waits in ambush. In some instances, wolves have displayed an uncharacteristic fearlessness of humans and buildings when attacking dogs, to the extent that they have to be beaten off or killed. Coyotes and big cats have also been known to attack dogs. Leopards in particular are known to have a predilection for dogs, and have been recorded to kill and consume them regardless of the dog's size or ferocity. Tigers in Manchuria, Indochina, Indonesia, and Malaysia, are reputed to kill dogs with the same vigor as leopards. Striped Hyenas are major predators of village dogs in Turkmenistan, India, and the Caucasus. Reptiles such as alligators and pythons have been known to kill and eat dogs.

Despite their descent from wolves and classification as Carnivora, dogs are variously described in scholarly and other writings as carnivores or omnivores. Unlike obligate carnivores, such as the cat family with its shorter small intestine, dogs can adapt to a wide-ranging diet, and are not dependent on meat-specific protein nor a very high level of protein in order to fulfill their basic dietary requirements. Dogs will healthily digest a variety of foods, including vegetables and grains, and can consume a large proportion of these in their diet.

A number of common human foods and household ingestibles are toxic to dogs, including chocolate solids (theobromine poisoning), onion and garlic (thiosulphate, sulfoxide or disulfide poisoning), grapes and raisins, macadamia nuts, as well as various plants and other potentially ingested materials.

In domestic dogs, sexual maturity begins to happen around age six to twelve months for both males and females, although this can be delayed until up to two years old for some large breeds. This is the time at which female dogs will have their first estrous cycle. They will experience subsequent estrous cycles biannually, during which the body prepares for pregnancy. At the peak of the cycle, females will come into estrus, being mentally and physically receptive to copulation. Because the ova survive and are capable of being fertilized for a week after ovulation, it is possible for a female to mate with more than one male.

Dogs bear their litters roughly 56 to 72 days after fertilization, with an average of 63 days, although the length of gestation can vary. An average litter consists of about six puppies, though this number may vary widely based on the breed of dog. In general, toy dogs produce from one to four puppies in each litter, while much larger breeds may average as many as twelve.

Some dog breeds have acquired traits through selective breeding that interfere with reproduction. Male French Bulldogs, for instance, are incapable of mounting the female. For many dogs of this breed, the female must be artificially inseminated in order to reproduce.

Neutering

Neutering refers to the sterilization of animals, usually by removal of the male's testicles or the female's ovaries and uterus, in order to eliminate the ability to procreate and reduce sex drive. Because of the overpopulation of dogs in some countries, many animal control agencies, such as the American Society for the Prevention of Cruelty to Animals (ASPCA), advise that dogs not intended for further breeding should be neutered, so that they do not have undesired puppies that may have to later be euthanized.

According to the Humane Society of the United States, 3-4 million dogs and cats are put down each year in the United States and many more are confined to cages in shelters because there are many more animals than there are homes. Spaying or castrating dogs helps keep overpopulation down. Local humane societies, SPCAs, and other animal protection organisations urge people to neuter their pets and to adopt animals from shelters instead of purchasing them.

Neutering reduces problems caused by hypersexuality, especially in male dogs. Spayed female dogs are less likely to develop some forms of cancer, affecting mammary glands, ovaries, and other reproductive organs. However, neutering increases the risk of urinary incontinence in female dogs, and prostate cancer in males, as well as osteosarcoma, hemangiosarcoma, cruciate ligament rupture, obesity, and diabetes mellitus in either gender.

The domestic dog has a predisposition to exhibit a social intelligence that is uncommon in the animal world. Dogs are capable of learning in a number of ways, such as through simple reinforcement (e.g., classical or operant conditioning) and by observation.

Dogs go through a series of stages of cognitive development. As with humans, the understanding that objects not being actively perceived still remain in existence (called object permanence) is not present at birth. It develops as the young dog learns to interact intentionally with objects around it, at roughly 8 weeks of age.

Puppies learn behaviours quickly by following examples set by experienced dogs. This form of intelligence is not peculiar to those tasks dogs have been bred to perform, but can be generalized to myriad abstract problems. For example, Dachshund puppies that watched an experienced dog pull a cart by tugging on an attached piece of ribbon in order to get a reward from inside the cart learned the task fifteen times faster than those left to solve the problem on their own. Dogs can also learn by mimicking human behaviours. In one study, puppies were presented with a box, and shown that, when a handler pressed a lever, a ball would roll out of the box. The handler then allowed the puppy to play with the ball, making it an intrinsic reward. The pups were then allowed to interact with the box. Roughly three-quarters of the puppies subsequently touched the lever, and over half successfully released the ball, compared to only 6 per cent in a control group that did not watch the human manipulate the lever. Another study found that handing an object between experimenters who then used the object's name in a sentence successfully taught an observing dog each object's name, allowing the dog to subsequently retrieve the item.

Dogs also demonstrate sophisticated social cognition by associating behavioural cues with abstract meanings. One such class of social cognition involves the understanding that others are conscious agents. Research has shown that dogs are capable of interpreting subtle social cues, and appear to recognize when a human or dog's attention is focused on them. To test this, researchers devised a task in which a reward was hidden underneath one of two buckets. The experimenter then attempted to communicate with the dog to indicate the location of the reward by using a wide range of signals: tapping the bucket, pointing to the bucket, nodding to the bucket, or simply looking at the bucket. The results showed that domestic dogs were better than chimpanzees, wolves, and human infants at this task, and even young puppies with limited exposure to humans performed well.

Psychology research has shown that human faces are asymmetrical with the gaze instinctively moving to the right side of a face upon encountering other humans to obtain information about their emotions and state. Research at the University of Lincoln (2008) shows that dogs share this instinct when meeting a human being, and only when meeting a human being (i.e., not other animals or other dogs). As such they are the only non-primate species known to do so.

Dr. Stanley Coren, an expert on dog psychology, states that these results demonstrated the social cognition of dogs can exceed that of even our closest genetic relatives, and that this capacity is a recent genetic acquisition that distinguishes the dog from its ancestor, the wolf. Studies have also investigated whether dogs engaged in partnered play change their behaviour depending on the attention-state of their partner. Those studies showed that play signals were only sent when the dog was holding the attention of its partner. If the partner was distracted, the dog instead engaged in attention-getting behaviour before sending a play signal.

Dr. Coren has also argued that dogs demonstrate a sophisticated theory of mind by engaging in deception, which he supports with a number of anecdotes, including one example wherein a dog hid a stolen treat by sitting on it until the rightful owner of the treat left the room. Although this could have been accidental, Coren suggests that the thief understood that the treat's owner would be unable to find the treat if it were out of view. Together, the empirical data and anecdotal evidence points to dogs possessing at least a limited form of theory of mind.

A study found a third of dogs suffered from anxiety when separated from others.

A Border Collie named Chaser has learned the names for 1,022 toys after three years of training, so many that her trainers have had to mark the names of the objects lest they forget themselves. This is higher than Rico, another border collie who could remember at least 200 objects.

Although dogs have been the subject of a great deal of behaviourist psychology (e.g. Pavlov's dog), they do not enter the world with a psychological 'blank slate'. Rather, dog behaviour is affected by genetic factors as well as environmental factors. Domestic dogs exhibit a number of behaviours and predispositions that were inherited from wolves. The Gray Wolf is a social animal that has evolved a sophisticated means of communication and social structure. The domestic dog has inherited some of these predispositions, but many of the salient characteristics in dog behaviour have been largely shaped by selective breeding by humans. Thus some of these characteristics, such as the dog's highly developed social cognition, are found only in primitive forms in grey wolves.

The existence and nature of personality traits in dogs have been studied (15329 dogs of 164 different breeds) and five consistent and stable 'narrow traits' identified, described as playfulness, curiosity/fearlessness, chase-proneness, sociability and aggressiveness. A further higher order axis for shyness–boldness was also identified.

Sleep

The average sleep time in a 24-hour period of a dog is said to be 10.1 hours.

Dog Growl

A new study in Budapest, Hungary has found that dogs are able to tell how big another dog is just by listening to its growl. A specific growl is used by dogs to protect their food. The research also shows that dogs do not lie about their size, and this is the first time research has shown animals can determine another's size by the sound it makes. The test used image of many kind of dogs and together showed a small and big dog and also a growl. The result, showed that 20 of the 24 test dogs looked at the image of the appropriate-sized dog first and looked at it longest.

Compared to equally sized wolves, dogs tend to have 20 per cent smaller skulls, 30 per cent smaller brains, as well as proportionately smaller teeth than other canid species. Dogs require fewer calories to function than wolves. It is thought by certain experts that the dog's limp ears are a result of atrophy of the jaw muscles. The skin of domestic dogs tends to be thicker than that of wolves, with some Inuit tribes favouring the former for use as clothing due to its greater resistance to wear and tear in harsh weather. The paws of a dog are half the size of those of a wolf, and their tails tend to curl upwards, another trait not found in wolves.

Dogs tend to be poorer than wolves at observational learning, being more responsive to instrumental conditioning. Feral dogs show little of the complex social structure or dominance hierarchy present in wolf packs. For example, unlike wolves, the dominant alpha pairs of a feral dog pack do not force the other members to wait for their turn on a meal when scavenging off a dead ungulate as the whole family is free to join in. For dogs, other members of their kind are of no help in locating food items, and are more like competitors. Feral dogs are primarily scavengers, with studies showing that unlike their wild cousins, they are poor ungulate hunters, having little impact on wildlife populations where they are sympatric. However, feral dogs have been reported to be effective hunters of reptiles in the Galápagos Islands, and free ranging pet dogs are more prone to predatory behaviour toward wild animals.

Despite common belief, domestic dogs can be monogamous. Breeding in feral packs can be, but does not have to be restricted to a dominant alpha pair (despite common belief, such things also occur in wolf packs). Male dogs are unusual among canids by the fact that they mostly seem to play no role in raising their puppies, and do not kill the young of other females to increase their own reproductive success. Some sources say that dogs differ from wolves and most other large canid species by the fact that they do not regurgitate food for their young, nor the young of other dogs in the same territory.

Dogs display much greater tractability than tame wolves, and are, in general, much more responsive to coercive techniques involving fear, aversive stimuli, and force than wolves, which are most responsive toward positive conditioning and rewards. Unlike tame wolves, dogs tend to respond more to voice than hand signals.

In Greek mythology, Cerberus is a three-headed watchdog who guards the gates of Hades. In Norse mythology, a bloody, four-eyed dog called Garmr guards Helheim. In Persian mythology, two four-eyed dogs guard the Chinvat Bridge. In Philippine mythology, Kimat who is the pet of Tadaklan, god of thunder, is responsible for lightning. In Welsh mythology, Annwn is guarded by Cwn Annwn.

In Judaism and Islam, dogs are viewed as unclean scavengers. In Christianity, dogs represent faithfulness. In Asian countries such as China, Korea, and Japan, dogs are viewed as kind protectors.

However, this difference was not observed in all domestic dogs. Regurgitating of food by the females for the young as well as care for the young by the males has been observed in domestic dogs, dingos as well as in other feral or semi-feral dogs. Regurgitating of food by the females and direct choosing of only one mate has been observed even in those semi-feral dogs of direct domestic dog ancestry. Also regurgitating of food by males has been observed in free-ranging domestic dogs.

The origin of the domestic dog (*Canis lupus familiaris*) began with the domestication of the gray wolf (*Canis lupus*) several tens of thousands of years ago. Domesticated dogs provided early humans with a guard animal, a source of food, fur, and a beast of burden. The process continues to this day, as the intentional cross-breeding of dogs continues, to create the so called 'designer dogs'.

The earliest fossil carnivores that can be linked with some certainty to canids (wolves, foxes and dogs), are the Eocene Miacids some 56 to 38 million years ago. From the miacids evolved the cat-like (Feloidea) and dog-like (Canoidea) carnivores. The canoid line led from the coyote-sized *Mesocyon* of the Oligocene (38 to 24 million years ago) to the fox-like *Leptocyon* and the wolf-like *Tomarctus* that wandered North America some 10 million years ago. *Canis lepophagus,* a small, narrow skulled North American canid of the Miocene era, led to the first true wolves at the end of the Blancan North American Stage such as *Canis priscolatrans* which evolved into *Canis etruscus,* then *Canis mosbachensis,* and in turn *C. mosbachensis* which evolved to become *Canis lupus,* the Gray Wolf—immediate precursor to the domestic dogs.

How exactly the domestication of the Grey Wolf happened is unclear, but theories include the following:

- *Orphaned wolf-cubs:* Studies have shown that some wolf pups taken at an early age and reared by humans are easily tamed and socialized. At least one study has demonstrated that adult wolves can be successfully socialized. However, according to other researchers attempts to socialize wolves after the pups reach 21 days of age are very time-consuming and seldom practical or reliable in achieving success. Many scientists believe that humans adopted orphaned wolf cubs and nursed them alongside human babies. Once these early adoptees started breeding among themselves, a new generation of tame 'wolf-like' domestic animals would result which would, over generations of time, become more dog-like.

- *The Promise of Food/Self Domestication:* Early wolves would, as scavengers, be attracted to the refuse left at human campsites. Dr. Raymond Coppinger of Hampshire College (Massachusetts) argues that those wolves that were more successful at interacting with humans would pass these traits onto their offspring, eventually creating wolves with a greater propensity to be domesticated. The 'most social and least fearful' dogs were the ones who were kept around the human living areas, helping to breed those traits that are still recognized in dogs today. Coppinger believes that a behavioural characteristic called 'flight distance' was crucial to the transformation from wild wolf to the ancestors of the modern dog. It represents how close an animal will allow humans (or anything else it perceives as dangerous) to get before it runs away. Animals with shorter flight distances will linger, and feed, when humans are close by; this behavioural trait would have been passed on to successive generations, and amplified, creating animals that are increasingly more comfortable around humans. "My argument is that what domesticated—or tame—means is to be able to eat in the presence of human beings. That is the thing that wild wolves can't do". Furthermore, selection for domesticity had the side effect of selecting genetically related physical characteristics, and behaviour such as barking. Hypothetically, wolves separated into two populations – the village-oriented scavengers and the packs of hunters. The next steps have not been defined, but selective pressure must have been present to sustain the divergence of these populations.
- *As a beast of burden:* North American Indians used dog-sized travois before adapting the horse for this purpose, and huskies are famous for pulling sleds for Inuit communities. It is very probable that the dog was the original beast of burden before the domestication of the horse or ox.
- *Dogs as a source of food and fur:* While, currently, most societies have difficulty thinking of dogs (or wolves) as a meat animal, it is conceivable that the human-canine bond was also fostered by humanity's use of dogs as a source of meat and fur.

Archaeology has placed the earliest known domestication at potentially 30,000 BC, and with certainty at 7000 BC. Other evidence suggests that dogs were first domesticated in East Asia.

Due to the difficulty in assessing the structural differences in bones, the identification of a domestic dog based on cultural evidence is of special value. Perhaps the earliest clear evidence for this domestication is the first dog found buried together with human from 12,000 years ago in Palestine.

Domestication of the wolf over time has produced a number of physical changes typical of all domesticated mammals. These include: a reduction in overall size; changes in coat colouration and markings; a shorter jaw initially with crowding of the teeth and, later, with the shrinking in size of the teeth; a reduction in brain size and thus in cranial capacity (particularly those areas relating to alertness and sensory processing, necessary in the wild); and the development of a pronounced 'stop', or vertical drop in front of the forehead (brachycephaly). Certain wolf-like behaviours, such as the regurgitation of partially digested food for the young, have also disappeared.

Before DNA was used, researchers were divided into two schools of thought:

- Most supposed that these early dogs were descendants of tamed wolves, which interbred and evolved into a domesticated species.
- Other scientists, while believing wolves were the chief contributor, suspected that jackals or coyotes contributed to the dog's ancestry.

Carles Vila, who has conducted the most extensive study to date, has shown that DNA evidence has ruled out any ancestor canine species except the wolf. Vila's team analyzed 162 different examples of wolf DNA from 27 populations in Europe, Asia, and North America. These results were compared with DNA from 140 individual dogs from 67 breeds gathered from around the world. Using blood or hair samples, DNA was extracted and genetic distance for mitochondrial DNA was estimated between individuals.

Based on this DNA evidence, most of the domesticated dogs were found to be members of one of four groups. The largest and most diverse group contains sequences found in the most ancient dog breeds, including the dingo of Australia, the New Guinea Singing Dog, and many modern breeds, like the collie and retriever. Other groups such as the German shepherd showed a closer relation to wolf sequences than to those of the main dog group, suggesting that such breeds had been produced by crossing dogs with wild wolves. It is also possible that this is evidence that dogs may have been domesticated from wolves on different occasions and at different places. Vilà is still uncertain whether domestication happened once–after which domesticated dogs bred with wolves from time to time–or whether it happened more than once.

A later study by Peter Savolainen et al. identified mitochondrial DNA evidence suggesting a common origin from a single East Asian gene pool for all dog populations. However, a more recent study by Bridgett vonHoldt and others using a much larger data set of nuclear markers points to the Middle East as the source of most of the genetic diversity in the domestic dog and a more likely origin of domestication events.

The most puzzling fact of the DNA evidence is that the variability in molecular distance between dogs and wolves seems greater than the 10,000-20,000 years assigned to domestication. Yet the process and economics of domestication by humans only emerged later in this period in any case. Based upon the molecular clock studies conducted, it would seem that dogs separated from the wolf lineage approximately 100,000 years ago. Although clear evidence for fossil dogs becomes obscure beyond about 14,000 years ago, there are fossils of wolf bones in association with early humans from well beyond 100,000 years ago. Tamed wolves might have taken up with hunter-gatherers without changing in ways that the fossil record could clearly capture. The influx of new genes from those crossings could very well explain the extraordinarily high number of dog breeds that exist today, the researchers suggest. Dogs have much greater genetic variability than other domesticated animals, such as cats, asserts Vilà.

Once agriculture took hold, dogs would have been selected for different tasks, their wolf-like natures becoming a handicap as they became herders and guards. Molecular biologist Elaine Ostrander is of the view that "When we became an agricultural society, what we needed dogs for changed enormously, and a further and irrevocable division occurred at that point." This may be the point that stands out in the fossil record, when dogs and wolves began to develop noticeably different morphologies.

A recent study of African dogs found a high level of mtDNA diversity. The authors suggest that a new view of the domestication of the dog may be needed. A study by the Kunming Institute of Zoology found that the domestic dog is descended from wolves tamed less than 16,300 years ago south of the Yangtse river in China. An older report said that all dog mitochondrial DNA came from three wild Asian female wolves.

As an experiment in the domestication of wolves, the 'farm fox' experiment of Russian scientist Dmitry Belyaev attempted to reenact of how domestication may have occurred. Researchers working with selectively breeding wild silver foxes over 35 generations and 40 years for the sole trait of friendliness to humans, created more dog-like animals. The 'domestic elite' foxes are much more friendly to humans and actually seek human attention, but they also show new physical traits that parallel the selection for tameness, even though the physical traits were not originally selected for. They include spotted or black-and-white coats, floppy ears, tails that curl over their backs, the barking vocalization, and earlier sexual maturity. It was reported on average, the domestic foxes respond to sounds two days earlier and open their eyes one day earlier than their non-domesticated cousins. More striking is that their socialization period has greatly increased.

Instead of developing a fear response at 6 weeks of age, the domesticated foxes don't show it until nine weeks of age or later. The whimpering and tail wagging is a holdover from puppyhood, as are the foreshortened face and muzzle. Even the new coat colours can be explained by the altered timing of development. One researcher found that the migration of certain melanocytes (which determine colour) was delayed, resulting in a black and white 'star' pattern.

This rapid evolution of dogs from wolves is an example of neoteny or paedomorphism. As with many species, the young wolves are more social and less dominant than adults; therefore, the selection for these characteristics, whether deliberate or inadvertent, is more likely to result in a simple retention of juvenile characteristics into adulthood than to generate a complex of independent new changes in behaviour. (This is true of many domesticated animals)

This paedomorphic selection naturally results in a retention of juvenile physical characteristics as well. Compared to wolves, many adult dog breeds retain such juvenile characteristics as soft fuzzy fur, round torsos, large heads and eyes, ears that hang down rather than stand erect, etc.; characteristics which are shared by most juvenile mammals, and therefore generally elicit some degree of protective and nurturing behaviour cross-species from most adult mammals, including humans, who term such characteristics 'cute' or 'appealing'.

The example of canine neoteny goes even further, in that the various breeds are differently neotenized according to the type of behaviour that was selected.

- Herding dogs exhibit the controlled characteristics of hunting dogs. Members of this group, such as Border Collies, Belgian Malinois and German Shepherds use tactics of hunter and prey to intimidate and keep control of herds and flocks. Their natural instinct to bring down an animal under their charge is muted by training. Other members of the group, including Welsh Corgis, Canaan dogs, and Cattle dogs herd with a more aggressive demeanor (such as biting and nipping at the heels of the animals) and make use of body design to elude the defences of their charges.
- Gun dog breeds used in hunting—that is, pointers, setters, spaniels, and retrievers—have an intermediate degree of paedomorphism; they are at the point where they share in the pack's hunting behaviour, but are still in a junior role, not participating in the actual attack. They identify potential prey and freeze into immobility, for instance, but refrain from then stalking the prey as an adult predator would do next; this results in the 'pointing' behaviour for which such dogs are bred. Similarly, they seize dead or wounded prey and bring it back to the 'pack', even though they did not attack it themselves, that is, 'retrieving'

behaviour. Their physical characteristics are closer to that of the mature wild canine than the sheepdog breeds, but they typically do not have erect ears, etc.

- Scenthounds maintain an intermediate body type and behaviour pattern that causes them to actually pursue prey by tracking their scent, but tend to refrain from actual individual attacks in favour of vocally summoning the pack leaders (in this case, humans) to do the job. They often have a characteristic vocalization called a bay. Some examples are the Beagle, Bloodhound, Basset Hound, Coonhound, Dachshund, Fox Hound, Otter Hound, and Harrier.
- Sighthounds, who pursue and attack perceived prey on sight, maintain the mature canine size and some features, such as narrow chest and lean bodies, but have largely lost the erect ears of the wolf and thick double layered coats. Some examples are the Afghan Hound, Borzoi, Saluki, Sloughi, Pharaoh Hound, Azawakh, Whippet, and Greyhound.
- Mastiff-types are large dogs, both tall and massive with barrel-like chests, large bones, and thick skulls. They have traditionally been bred for war, protection, and guardian work.
- Bulldog-types are medium sized dogs bred for combat against both wild and domesticated animals. These dogs have a massive, square skull and large bones with an extremely muscular build and broad shoulders.
- Terriers similarly have adult aggressive behaviour, famously coupled with a lack of juvenile submission, and display correspondingly adult physical features such as erect ears, although many breeds have also been selected for size and sometimes dwarfed legs to enable them to pursue prey in their burrows.

The least paedomorphic behaviour pattern may be that of the basenji, bred in Africa to hunt alongside humans almost on a peer basis; this breed is often described as highly independent, neither needing nor appreciating a great deal of human attention or nurturing, often described as 'catlike' in its behaviour. It too has the body plan of an adult canine predator. Of course, dogs in general possess a significant ability to modify their behaviour according to experience, including adapting to the behaviour of their 'pack leaders'—again, humans. This allows them to be trained to behave in a way that is not specifically the most natural to their breed; nevertheless, the accumulated experience of thousands of years shows that some combinations of nature and nurture are quite daunting, for instance, training whippets to guard flocks of sheep.

Pet

The average cost of a dog over its lifetime is estimated at about £20,000 (US$ 33,152). People most commonly get pets for companionship, to protect a home or property, or because of the beauty/attractiveness of the animals.

The most common reasons for not owning a pet are lack of time, lack of suitable housing, and lack of ability to care for the pet when travelling.

Animal protection advocates call attention to pet overpopulation in the United States. According to the Humane Society of the United States, 3-4 million dogs and cats are euthanized each year in the country and many more are confined to cages in shelters. This situation is created by nonneutered animals (spayed/castrated) reproducing and people intentionally breeding animals. A particularly problematic combination of economic hardship combined with a love of animals contributes to this problem in parts of the rural United States. There are also major overpopulation problems with other pet species, such as birds and rabbits. Local humane societies, Societies for the Prevention of Cruelty to Animals (SPCAs), and other animal protection organisations urge people to neuter their pets and to adopt animals from animal shelters instead of purchasing them from breeders or pet stores.

Keeping animals as pets may become detrimental to their health if certain requirements are not kept. An important issue is the inappropriate feeding, which may produce clinical effects (like the consumption of chocolate by dogs). Passive smoking is another recurring problem, aggravated by the fact that fur animals groom themselves, which means taking in extra harmful substances that have landed on their fur, not just those inhaled.

Health Benefits

Pets have the ability to stimulate their caregivers, in particular the elderly, giving people someone to take care of, someone to exercise with, and someone to help them heal from a physically or psychologically troubled past. Having a pet may help people achieve health goals, such as lowered blood pressure, or mental goals, such as decreased stress. There is evidence that having a pet can help a person lead a longer, healthier life. In a study of 92 people hospitalized for coronary ailments, within a year 11 of the 29 without pets had died, compared to only 3 of the 52 who had pets. Pet ownership was shown to significantly reduce triglycerides, and thus heart disease risk, in the elderly. A recent study concluded that owning a pet can reduce the risk of a heart attack by 2 per cent and that pets are better than medication in reducing blood pressure. Owning a pet can also prolong survival of a heart attack. Dogs which are trained to be guide dogs can help people with disabilities. Dogs that are trained in the field of Animal-Assisted Therapy (AAT) can also benefit people with disabilities. Pets in long-term care institutions.

Even pet owners residing in a long-term care facility, such as a hospice or nursing home, experience health benefits from pets. Pets for nursing homes are chosen based on the size of the pet, the amount of care that the breed needs, and the population and size of the care institution. Appropriate pets go through a screening process and, if it is a dog, additional training programmes to become a therapy dog. Different pets require varying amounts of attention and care; for example, cats have lower maintenance requirements than dogs.

Health risks that are associated with pets include:

- Aggravation of allergies and asthma caused by dander and ur or feathers.
- Falling injuries. Tripping over pets, especially dogs, causes more than 86,000 falls serious enough to prompt a trip to the emergency room each year in the United States. Among elderly and disabled people, these falls have resulted in life-threatening injuries and broken bones.
- Disease and/or parasites due to animal hygiene problems or lack of appropriate treatment (faeces and urine).
- Stress caused by behaviour of animals.
- Fear or distress from animal presence or behaviour.
- Spread of diseases like the fatal rabies when not properly taken care of.

CHAPTER 2

Dog Breed

Dog breeds are groups of closely related and visibly similar domestic dogs, which are all of the subspecies *Canis lupus familiaris*, having characteristic traits that are selected and maintained by humans, bred from a known foundation stock.

The term *dog breed* is also used to refer to *natural breeds* or landraces, which arose through time in response to a particular environment which included humans, with little or no selective breeding by humans. Such breeds are undocumented, and are identified by their appearance and often by a style of working. Ancient dog breeds are some of the modern (documented) descendants of such *natural breeds*.

Dog breeds are not scientifically defined biological classifications, but rather are groupings defined by clubs of hobbyists called breed clubs. A dog breed is represented by a sufficient number of individuals to stably transfer its specific characteristics over generations. Dogs of same breed have similar characteristics of appearance and behaviour, primarily because they come from a select set of ancestors who had the same characteristics. Dogs of a specific breed breed true, producing young closely similar to the parents. An individual dog is identified as a member of a breed through proof of ancestry, using genetic analysis or written records of ancestry. Without such proof, identification of a specific breed is not reliable. Such records, called stud books, may be maintained by individuals, clubs, or other organizations.

In biology, subspecies, race and breed are equivalent terms. Breed is usually applied to domestic animals; species and subspecies, to wild animals and to plants; and race, to humans. Colloquial use of the term *dog breed*, however, does not conform to scientific standards of taxonomic classification. Breeds do not meet the criteria for subspecies since they are all considered a subspecies of the gray wolf; an interbreeding group of individuals who pass on characteristic traits and would likely merge back into a single homogenous group if external barriers were removed. The recognition of distinct dog breeds is not maintained by a scientific organization; they are maintained by a number of independent kennel clubs that need not apply to scientific standards and are often inconsistent. For instance, the Belgian Shepherd Dog is separated into four distinct breeds by some clubs, but not in others. Further, some groups of dogs which clearly share a persistent set of characteristics and documented descent from a known foundation stock may still not be recognized by some clubs as breeds. For instance, the feist is a hunting dog raised in the Southern United States for hunting small game. Feists have a consistent set of characteristics that reliably differentiate them from other dog types and breeds. However, the United Kennel Club recognizes one breed of feist, the Treeing Feist, while the American Kennel Club does not recognize any feist breed.

A dog is said to be purebred if its parents were purebred and it meets the standards of the breed. Purebred dog breeders of today "have inherited a breeding paradigm that is, at the very least, a bit anachronistic in light of modern genetic knowledge, and that first arose out of a pretty blatant misinterpretation of Darwin and an enthusiasm for social theories that have long been discredited as scientifically insupportable and morally questionable." Morally questionable policies regarding purity of breed include obligatory surgical procedures to spay or neuter animals in numerous contexts. The American Kennel Club, for instance, allows mixed-breed dogs to be shown but requires these animals to be altered. It does not make such requirements for purebred dogs. California Assembly Act AB 1634 was a bill introduced in 2007 that would require all non-working dogs of mixed breed over the age of 6 months to be neutered or spayed. The bill was morally controversial, leading the American Kennel Club to fight the bill.

The clear genetic distinction between breeds of dog has made dogs of specific breeds good subjects for genetic and human medical research. 'Using the dog as a discovery tool' in studying how cancer affects specific breeds may lead to identifying 'susceptibility genes that have proved intractable in human families and populations'.

History of Dog Breeds

Pariah dogs originally established themselves near human populations, developing and maintaining themselves without further selection. They do not carry any specialized working dog functions. Working, hunting and other functional breeds most likely appeared when there was a demand for certain traits and humans were able to devote time and resources to perfect those traits.

Initial dog selections centered on helpful behaviour such as barking at unfamiliar creatures and people, guarding livestock, or hunting game. Some dog breeds, such as Saluki or New Guinea singing dogs , have been bred for thousands of years. Some working dog breeds such as German Shepherd or Labrador Retriever were established in the last few hundred years. More recently, dogs have been selected for attractiveness and distinctive features, resulting in a vast variety of breeds. Similar dog breeds are classified by dog registries in dog breed groups.

Groups of individuals that have dogs of the same breed often unite into national breed clubs, describing their dogs in specific language by writing a breed standard. Breed standards prescribe the most desirable specimen attributes and working abilities for purebred dogs of that breed as well as undesirable traits. National breed clubs promote their breeds via the local breed registry and international organizations. Dogs recognized by the main breed registries are said to be 'purebred'.

There is much speculation but little evidence about why canids came to live with or near humans, possibly as long as 100,000 years ago. With the beginnings of agriculture around 12,000 years ago, humans began making use of dogs in various ways, resulting in physical differences between dogs and their wolf ancestors. In earlier times, little was written about dogs, although there were known dog types or landrace dogs, which developed over time with minimal human intervention, to fit in with the environment (including human culture) in which the dogs lived or live. Dog breeds in the modern sense date only to the accurate documenting of pedigrees with the establishment of the English Kennel Club in 1873, in imitation of other stud book registries for cattle and horses.

Many dog breeds today have names of original landrace types, such as the Border Collie. Other landrace types, such as retrievers, have been made more uniform in appearance through selective breeding, and developed into a variety of distinctive breeds. Varieties of purebred dogs kept for working purposes can vary in appearance from purebred dogs of the same breed kept as showdogs and pets.

New dog breeds are being continually created. They are either accidentally or purposely crossbred from existing breeds, developed for a specific style of work, or created just for marketing purposes. Recently discovered semi-feral and landrace types such as the New Guinea Singing Dog have been documented and registered as breeds for purposes of preservation. The Canadian department of agriculture has strict standards for the documenting of what it calls 'emerging breeds'. Many registries which require minimal documentation are available for registering new and existing breeds of dog. In general, a dog can only be guaranteed to be of a specific breed if it is documented in the stud book of a major dog registry or breed registry.

Dog breeds can now be analyzed through genetics. Genetic markers (microsatellite markers and single-nucleotide polymorphisms) have been analyzed and a representative sample of 85 breeds were placed into four clusters, each cluster having shared ancestors. Cluster 1 is thought to be the oldest, including African and Asian dogs. Cluster 2 is mastiff type dogs;

cluster 3 is herding dogs, and cluster 4 modern hunting type dogs (mostly developed in Europe in the 1800s.) The following breed lists are based on genetic research, not traditional beliefs about dog breeds.

- Cluster 1 (Thought to be older lineages): Afghan Hound, Akita Inu, Alaskan Malamute, Basenji, Chow Chow, Irish Wolfhound, Lhasa Apso, Pekingese, Saluki, Samoyed, Shar Pei, Shiba Inu, Shih Tzu, Siberian Husky, Tibetan Terrier.
- Cluster 2 (Mastiff-type): Bernese Mountain Dog, Boxer, Bulldog, Bullmastiff, French Bulldog, German Shepherd Dog, Cierny Sery, Greater Swiss Mountain Dog, Labrador Retriever, Mastiff, Miniature Bull Terrier, Newfoundland, Pomeranian, Presa Canario, Rottweiler.
- Cluster 3 (Herding): Belgian Sheepdog, Belgian Tervuren, Borzoi, Collie, Greyhound, Pug, St. Bernard, Shetland Sheepdog.
- Cluster 4 (Modern/hunting dogs): Airedale Terrier, American Cocker Spaniel, American Hairless Terrier, American Water Spaniel, Australian Shepherd, Australian Terrier, Basset Hound, Beagle, Bedlington Terrier, Bichon Frise, Bloodhound, Border Collie, Cairn Terrier, Cavalier King Charles Spaniel, Chesapeake Bay Retriever, Chihuahua, Clumber Spaniel, Dachshund, Doberman Pinscher, English Cocker Spaniel, Flat Coated Retriever, German Shorthaired Pointer, Giant Schnauzer, Golden Retriever, Great Dane, Ibizan Hound, Irish Setter, Irish Terrier, Italian Greyhound, Keeshond, Kerry Blue Terrier, Komondor, Kuvasz, Manchester Terrier, Miniature Schnauzer, Norwegian Elkhound, Old English Sheepdog, Pharaoh Hound, Pointer, Portuguese Water Dog, Pit Bull Terrier, Rhodesian Ridgeback, Schipperke, Soft Coated Wheaten Terrier, Standard Poodle, Standard Schnauzer, Welsh Springer Spaniel, West Highland White Terrier, Whippet.

Dog breeds are documented in lists of antecedents called a stud book.

Dog breeds that have been documented may be accepted into one or more of the major registries (kennel clubs) of dog breeds, including the Fédération Cynologique Internationale (covering 84 countries), The Kennel Club (UK), the Canadian Kennel Club, the American Kennel Club, the United Kennel Clubs International, the Australian National Kennel Council and the New Zealand Kennel Club, and other national registries. The registry places the breed into the appropriate category, called a Group. Some Groups may be further subdivided by some registries. When the breed is fully accepted, the stud book is closed and only dogs bred from dogs in the stud book will be accepted for registration. These dogs are referred to as purebred.

Dog breed clubs, especially of dogs bred for a particular kind of work, may maintain an open stud book and so may not be included in major registries. The dogs are still considered a breed. An example of this would be the Jack Russell Terrier Club of America.

Some dog breeds fit the definition of breed, especially breeds that develop naturally on islands or in isolated areas, but are few in number or have not been sufficiently documented to be registered with one of the major registries. An example of this would be the Kintamani Dog and other rare or independent breeds.

Breeds of dogs can be deliberately created in a relatively short period of time. When they breed true and have been sufficiently documented, they can be accepted by major registries. An example of this is the Cesky Terrier.

Each dog breed has a written Breed Standard, a list of attributes that standardises the appearance of the breed, written by the breed's founder or breed club. Dog are judged in conformation dog shows on the basis of how closely the individual dog conforms to the breed standard. As the breed standard only covers external aspects of the dog's appearance, breeding working dogs for show competition may cause appearance to be emphasised to the detriment of working ability.

Groups of dogs that may be mistaken for breeds include working dogs that are categorized by working style rather than appearance, although they may be of various ancestry and may not breed true. The difference between a named group of working dogs and a breed of dogs can be unclear. Examples would be the huntaway and other livestock dogs of New Zealand, the feist dogs of the southern United States, and the Patagonian sheepdogs of Argentina, which are collies mixed with other working dogs.

Landrace dogs are another grouping that often have been named but are not always considered breeds. 'Landrace' is a term used for early types domesticated animals, including dogs, where isolated populations of dogs are selected according to human goals; developing over time rather than through modern breeding techniques. An example of a landrace dog would be the dog described as 'Basset' as early as 1585. The landrace Basset was developed into the modern breeds of Dachshund and Basset Hound, as well as modern day terrier breeds. A Labrador is a type of dog.

Another group of dogs that may be mistaken for breeds are the progeny of intentional crossbreedings of two purebred dogs. These popularity of these crosses are often the result of fads. Examples include the Puggle and the Labradoodle.

Mixed breed dogs may be offered a form of registration to allow them to participate in organized dog events. Often given the name All-American or AMBOR dog, the name does not signify that dogs so registered are a breed. Dogs must be spayed or neutered to be registered.

Individual dogs or small groups of dogs may use an existing breed name or be given an invented breed name and listed with little or no documentation for a fee with 'registry' companies with minimal verification requirements. The dogs are then bred and marketed as a 'registered' breed, sometimes as a 'rare' or new breed of dogs.

Ancient Dog Breeds

Fourteen ancient breeds of dog have recently been identified through advances in DNA analysis. These breeds of domesticated dog show the fewest genetic differences from wolves. The breeds are geographically diverse, including dogs from Siberia, Japan, Alaska, China, Tibet, and Africa.

DNA from dogs of 85 (mostly) AKC-registered breeds (5 individuals per breed in most cases) were tested by Parker et al. This study had some surprises, especially the suggestion that three breeds – the Norwegian Elkhound, Pharaoh Hound and Ibizan Hound – are not as old as typically stated, but rather are more recent recreations of old types. Also, five pairs of breeds are closely related: Alaskan Malamute and Siberian Husky, Collie and Shetland Sheepdog, Greyhound and Whippet, Bernese Mountain Dog and Greater Swiss Mountain Dog and finally the Bull Mastiff and English Mastiff.

However, the assumption that a small sample from a single dog breed can be representative for the entire breed, is argued to be invalid by long-time repeated incidental or intentional interbreeding with local dogs, thereby gradually replacing original wolf clade elements but maintaining the original phenotype by ongoing selection for the original use and conformation. This evolution can be seen also in the high proportion of European clade in Asian breeds close to Europe, like Saluki and Samoyed, while a geographically remote Nordic spitz, the Siberian Husky, does not show such a replacement of the original wolfdog structure. Also, as there are some 400 known dog breeds (of which the AKC recognizes 167), it is possible that an extended study would reveal additional 'ancient' breeds.

CHAPTER 3

Dog Hybrid

A dog hybrid is a crossbreed of two or more different recognized breeds of dog.

The *Encyclopedia Britannica* traces the term 'designer dog' to the late 20th century, when breeders began to cross purebred poodles with other purebred breeds in order to obtain a dog with the poodles' hypoallergenic coat, along with various desirable characteristics from other breeds.

One connotation of the term 'designer dog' is that the breeding is by design, between a deliberately chosen sire and dam, as opposed to an accidental breeding. A few breeders have taken this a step further, breeding a specific crossbreed to others of the same cross, setting a standard, and documenting the ancestry of puppies so bred over generations, in order to create a new breed of dog.

The term 'designer dog' has, however, taken on a new meaning, equating fads for crossbreed dogs with other 'designer' accessories like purses and shoes. More recently, the term 'designer dog' has started to ecompass some smaller ('handbag size') purebred dogs, such as the chihuahua and Pomeranian. Increased public demand for 'designer dogs' has resulted in the proliferation of puppy mills cashing in on the fad. Puppy mills are set up to produce puppies as fast as the mother dogs can give birth. The offspring, who may already be in poor health, are shipped long distances to pet shops or are sold through newspapers and the internet. Transportation takes a toll on the pups, and many sicken and die on route.

The primary identifying mark of a crossbred 'designer dog' is that the resulting puppies are called by a portmanteau word made up of syllables (or sounds) from the breed names of the two purebred parents, such as schnoodle (*Schn*auzer and p*oodle* cross). Other purebred breeds are being crossed to provide designer dogs described with an endless range of created labels, such as the Puggle (*Pug* and Bea*gle* cross). There are even complex crosses (with multiple breeds in recent ancestry) are being labeled in this manner, such as German Chusky (German Shepherd Dog, Husky, Chow Chow).

Like children in a family, a percentage of designer dogs with the same breed ancestry will look similar to each other, even though crossbreeding does not result in as uniform a phenotype as the breeding of purebreds.

A Lakeland Terrier and a Patterdale Terrier crossbreed may be either a pet or a working terrier. Working dog hybrids are not typically given portmanteau word names.

Another defining characteristic of designer dogs is that they are usually bred as companions and pets. Working and hunting dogs deliberately crossbred for a particular working purpose are not generally given portmanteau names; they are most often referred to by a type (not breed) name, such as Eurohounds (racing sled dogs) or Lurchers (hunting dogs.) An exception to this is the Labradoodle, which although having a Portmanteau name, is often used as a guide or assistance dog.

Although designer dogs are often selected by owners for their novelty, an underlying motive for hybridization is an attempt to reduce the incidence of certain hereditary problems found in the purebred breeds used for the cross, while retaining their more appealing traits. Jon Mooallem in the New York Times writes, "Given the roughly 350 inherited disorders littering the dog genome, crossing two purebreds and expanding their gene pools can be 'a phenomenally good idea', according to one canine geneticist — if it is done conscientiously." But crossbreeding for a particular style of designer dog may not work out as intended; instead of the desirable traits, the resulting litter may have a combination of the undesirable traits of the two purebred breeds. Wally Conron, the originator of the Labradoodle (bred as a hypoallergenic guide dog from a carefully selected sire and dam) in 1989, noted that although the first Poodle-Labrador Retriever breeding produced a success, "our next litter of ten labradoodles produced only three allergy-free pups."

Crossbreeding has not been well studied in dogs, although it has been for livestock. The heritability of the desired trait being bred for (such as a hypoallergenic coat) needs to be known; "Heritability is the proportion of the measurable difference observed between animals for a given trait that is due to genetics (and can be passed to the next generation)." Without that knowledge, it is far less likely for a crossbreeding to consistently achieve an intended appearance or behaviour than it is for a purebred breeding. In addition, the goals of dog crossbreeding may be harder to define than the goals of livestock crossbreeding; good temperament may be harder to define and measure than high calf weight.

Designer dog breeders are often criticised for being more interested in profitable puppy production than in dog health and welfare. Wally Conron comments on the popularity of crosses after his introduction of the Labradoodle: "Were breeders bothering to check their sires and bitches for heredity faults, or were they simply caught up in delivering to hungry customers the next status symbol?" *Designer dog* puppies sometimes bring higher prices than the purebreds from which they are bred,. Finding a breeder who does health testing and considers hereditary compatibility of breeding stock is as important for a designer dog as it is for a purebred.

The fanciers of designer dogs respond that all modern dog breeds were created from earlier breeds and types of dogs through the same kind of selective breeding that is used to create designer dogs. The Toy Poodle was bred down in size from larger poodles, most likely by crossing with various very small Bichon types, such as the Maltese and Havanese. Most of the modern breeds have ancestries that include various older dog types and breeds; see individual breed articles for details of the origin of each breed.

Health of dog hybrids depends on their being descended from healthy parents. Breeders who select their breeding stock for cost-effectiveness and who skip health testing for the same reason will not produce puppies that are as reliably healthy as those bred by more conscientious breeders. However, studies of longevity in dogs have found some advantage for crossbreeds compared to purebred dogs. "There was a significant correlation between body weight and longevity. Crossbreeds lived longer than average but several pure breeds lived longer than cross breeds, notably Jack Russell, miniature poodles and whippets" (thus only small and toy breeds, as to be expected). In general it is believed that crossbreed dogs "have a far lower chance of exhibiting the disorders that are common with the parental breeds. Their genetic health will be substantially higher."

Many breeders of designer dogs take advantage of the fact that people are impressed by a pet that is offers them an elevated social status, such as other "designer" goods do. "It's human nature to aspire to own something a little different, a little fancy or in short supply."

Because some traits are dominant, crossbreed dogs tend to manifest some physical characteristics more frequently than others. Border Collies and some Spaniels, for example, often produce crossbreed offspring with similar coats and ears to their parents. The crossbreed offspring of German Shepherds often have characteristic Shepherd faces and other characteristics. But all crossbred dogs will vary in which characteristics of their purebred parents that they inherit, and may look very different from one another, even within the same litter of puppies.

Crossbreed dogs may often inherit size and appearance from only one of their parents, as shown by the male Australian Shepherd/Shiba Inu mixed breed on the right being very similar in appearance and size to the pure bred female Shiba Inu on the left. Despite the Australian Shepherd being nearly 40 pounds heavier than the Shiba Inu and with very different fur, this hybrid dog inherited both its size and appearance from its mother.

Crossbreed dogs are not recognized by traditional breed registries, even if both parents are registered purebreds.

If dog hybrids are bred together for some period of time, and their breeding is well documented, they may eventually be considered a new breed of dog by major kennel clubs (an example of a recent hybrid becoming a breed recognised by all major kennel clubs is the Cesky Terrier) New breeds of dogs must have a breed club that will document the ancestry of any individual member of that breed from the original founding dogs of the breed; when the kennel club that the breed club wishes to join is satisfied that the dogs are purebred, they will accept and register the dogs of that breed. Each kennel club has individual rules about how to document a new breed. Some minor registries and internet registry businesses will register dogs as any breed the owner chooses with minimal or no documentation; some even allow the breeder or owner to make up a 'breed name' for their pet.

Dog hybrids, created by breeding two purebred dogs of different breeds, may have the advantage of heterosis, or hybrid vigor. This advantage can be progressively diluted when two hybrids are bred in the attempt to create a breed, narrowing the gene pool. The best way to continue taking advantage of hybrid vigor is from the breeding of dogs with genetic diversity.

With the long-time popularity of the label cockapoo, used since at least 1960 and constructed by combining elements of its two contributing breeds (Cocker Spaniel/Poodle), it has become extremely common to find dog hybrids given labels likewise invented by portmanteau.

The tendency for using such labels in a jocular way dates back at least to Queen Elizabeth's dorgis (Dachshund/Corgi). None of these have become recognised by any major registry as purebred breeds. However, as of 2006, the portmanteau words cockapoo and Labradoodle are found in some dictionaries. Label names such as these are most often found in for-sale ads, or on the websites that allow breeders to make up their own portmanteau word names for litters of hybrid puppies. The terms are only loosely descriptive and are seldom consistent; a cross between a Maltese and a Poodle, for example, may be advertised as either a 'Maltipoo' or a 'Moodle', and the *cockapoo* is also called a *spoodle*.

Among the trendier dog hybrids are Labradoodles and Cockapoos, which each have their own fancier associations and affinity groups. Many Poodle hybrids are also popular.

CHAPTER 4

The Science of Mixed-Breed Dog

A mixed-breed dog is a dog whose ancestry is generally unknown and that has characteristics of two or more types of breeds. A mixed-breed may be a cross-breed dog, a random-bred dog, or a descendant of feral or pariah dog populations. 'Random-bred' is a genetic term meaning an animal, population, or breed that was bred or developed without planned intervention of humans; and whose ancestry and genetic makeup is generally not known.

When the term *mixed-breed* is used for populations of dogs that have not been intentionally bred, it is technically a misnomer. The idea that such dogs are a mix of defined breeds stems from an inverted understanding of the origins of dog breeds. *Pure* breeds have been, for the most part, artificially created from random-bred populations by human selective breeding with the purpose of enhancing desired physical or temperamental characteristics. Dogs that are not *purebred* are not necessarily a mix of such defined breeds. The term crossbreed refers to dogs produced by a breeding of two different purebred dog breeds.

There is a profusion of words and phrases used to describe dogs that are not designated as a purebred or pedigreed dog. The words cur, tyke, mutt, and mongrel are used, sometimes in a derogatory manner. There are also regional terms for mixed-breed dogs. In the United Kingdom mongrel is the unique technical word for a mixed-breed dog. North Americans generally prefer the term mix or mixed-breed. Mutt is also commonly used (in the U.S.A. and Canada), often in an affectionate manner. Some American registries and dog clubs that accept mixed-breed dogs use the breed description All American. In the rural southern United States, a small hunting dog is known as a feist.

There are also names for mixed-breeds based on geography, behaviour, or food. In Hawaii, mixes are referred to as poi dogs, although they are not related to the extinct Hawaiian poi dog. In The Bahamas and Turks and Caicos Islands, the common term is potcake dogs (referring to the table scraps they are fed). In South Africa the tongue-in-cheek expression pavement special is sometimes used as a description for a mixed-breed dog. In the Philippines, mixed-breed street dogs are often called "askals", a Tagalog-derived contraction of "asong kalye" or street dog. In Puerto Rico they are known as Sato dogs.

Slang terms are also common. Heinz 57, Heinz, or Heinz Hound is often used for dogs of uncertain ancestry, in a playful reference to the "57 Varieties" slogan of the H. J. Heinz Company. In some countries, such as Australia, bitsa (or bitzer) is common, meaning "bits o' this, bits o' that". In Brazil and the Dominican Republic, the name for mixed-breed dogs is vira-lata (*trash-can tipper*) because of homeless dogs who knock over trash cans to reach discarded food. In Newfoundland, a smaller mixed-breed dog is known as a cracky, hence the colloquial expression "saucy as a cracky" for someone with a sharp tongue.

Scientists and scholars usually use the terms mongrel, mixed-breed, or random-bred dog for dogs born of breedings not supervised or deliberately planned by humans. The term crossbreed is used to describe mixes of known breeds, sometimes deliberately mated.

Dogs interbreed freely so mixed-breed dogs vary in size, shape, and colour, making them difficult to classify physically. Mixed-breed dogs manifest a wide variety of appearances. However, if a genetically diverse population continues to interbreed, subsequent generations do tend toward a roughly similar appearance. They tend to be fawn or black and weigh about 18 kg (40 lb) and typically stand between 38 and 57 cm (15 and 23 inches) tall at the withers.

Guessing a mixed-breed's ancestry is difficult even for knowledgeable dog observers, because mixed-breeds have much more genetic variation than purebreds. For example, two black mixed-breed dogs might each have recessive genes that produce a blond coat and, therefore, produce offspring looking unlike their parents.

Starting in 2007, genetic analysis of blood samples and cheek swabs have become available to the public. The companies claim their DNA-based diagnostic test can genetically determine the breed composition of mixed-breed dogs. These tests are still limited in scope because only a small number of the hundreds of dog breeds have been validated against the tests, and because the same breed in different geographical areas may have different genetic profiles. Also, the tests do not test for breed purity, but for genetic sequences that are common to certain breeds. With a mixed-breed dog, the test is not proof of purebred ancestry, but rather an indication that those dogs share common ancestry with certain purebreds. The American Kennel Club does not recognize the use of DNA tests to determine breed.

As well, many newer dog breeds can be traced back to a common foundational breed, making them difficult to separate genetically. For example,

Labrador Retrievers, Flat-coated Retrievers, Chesapeake Bay Retrievers, and Newfoundland Dogs share the ancestry of the St. John's Water Dog - a now extinct naturally-occurring dog breed from the island of Newfoundland.

The theory of hybrid vigour suggests that as a group, dogs of varied ancestry will be healthier than their purebred counterparts. In purebred dogs, intentionally breeding dogs of very similar appearance over several generations produces animals that carry many of the same alleles, some of which are detrimental. This is especially true if the dogs are closely related. This inbreeding among purebreds has exposed various genetic health problems not readily apparent in less uniform populations. Mixed-breed dogs are more genetically diverse due to the more haphazard nature of their parents' mating. 'Haphazard' is not the same as "random" to a geneticist. The offspring of such matings might be less likely to express certain genetic disorders because there might be a decreased chance that both parents carry the same detrimental recessive alleles. However, some deleterious recessives occur across many seemingly unrelated breeds, and therefore merely mixing breeds is no guarantee of genetic health.

In fact, crossbreeding two poor specimens together does not guarantee the resulting offspring will be healthier than the parents because the offspring could inherit the worst traits of both parents. This is commonly seen in dogs from puppy mills. Healthy traits have been lost in many purebred dogs lines because many breeders of showdogs are more interested in conformation - the physical attributes of the dogs in relation to the breed standard - than in the health and working temperament for which the dog was originally bred.

Purebred and mixed-breed dogs are equally susceptible to most non-genetic ailments, such as rabies, distemper, injury, and infestation by parasites.

Several studies have shown that mixed-breed dogs have a health advantage. A German study finds that "Mongrels require less veterinary treatment". Studies in Sweden have found that "Mongrel dogs are less prone to many diseases than the average purebred dog" and, referring to death rates, "Mongrels were consistently in the low risk category".

In one landmark study, the effect of breed on longevity in the pet dog was analyzed using mortality data from 23,535 pet dogs. The data was obtained from North American veterinary teaching hospitals. The median age at death was determined for pure and mixed breed dogs of different body weights. Within each body weight category, the median age at death was lower for pure breed dogs compared with mixed breed dogs. The median age at death was "8.5 years for all mixed breed dogs, and 6.7 years for all pure breed dogs" in the study.

A 2003 study in Denmark also found "Higher average longevity of mixed-breed dogs (grouped together).

Most dog breeds are a result of human selection. Existing dog breeds began as mixed-breeds, either random-bred or by deliberate crosses of existing breeds. Encouraging desirable traits and discouraging others, breeders sought to create their ideal appearance or behaviour, or both, for dogs, and, additionally, to ensure that the dogs could consistently produce offspring with the same appearance or behaviour.

Mixed-breed dogs can be divided roughly into five types:

1. The generic pariah dog is believed to resemble the body form and appearance of the ancestral *Canis lupus familiaris* from which other dog breeds were derived.
2. Mixes that show characteristics of two or more breeds. A mix might have some purebred ancestors, or might come from a long line of mixed-breeds. These dogs are usually identified by the breed they most resemble, such as a 'Lab mix' or 'Collie-Shepherd', even if their ancestry is unknown.
3. The generic pariah dog, or feral *Canis lupus familiaris,* where non-selective breeding has occurred over many generations. The term originally referred to the wild dogs of India, but now refers to dogs belonging to or descended from a population of wild or feral dogs. The Canaan Dog is an example of a recognized breed with pariah ancestry. Pariah dogs tend to be yellow to light brown and of medium height and weight. This may represent the appearance of the modern dog's ancestor. DNA analysis has shown pariah dogs to have a more ancient gene pool than modern breeds.
4. Functional breeds, which are purpose-bred dogs whose ancestors are not purebred, but rather are selected by their performance at a particular tasks. Examples of this are the Alaskan Husky, the Eurohound, and the Pointer/Greyhound mixes referred to as Greysters, which compete at skijoring and pulka races, particularly in Europe. The distinction between a 'mix' and a 'breed' is less distinct in these cases, and occasionally a functional breed such as this becomes accepted as a breed over time.
5. Crossbreed dogs, which are mixtures of two recognized breeds. Dogs that result from two different purebred parents are known as crossbreeds. Some crossbreeds have become popular enough to be frequently bred deliberately, such as the Cockapoo—a cross between a Poodle and a Cocker Spaniel. Other crosses are bred in an attempt to add or reinforce desired characteristics.

Purebred dogs are known by breed names given to groups of dogs that are visibly similar in most characteristics and have reliable documented descent. But in recent years many owners and breeders of crossbreed dogs identify them—often facetiously— by invented names constructed from parts of their parents' breed names. These are known as portmanteau names and the resulting crosses as "designer dogs." For example, a cross between a Pekingese and a Poodle may be referred to as a Peekapoo. Another trendy cross is the Goldendoodle, a cross between a standard poodle and a golden retriever.

Mixed-breed dogs can excel at dog sports, such as obedience, dog agility, flyball, and frisbee. Often, highly energetic mixed-breeds are left with shelters or rescue groups, where they are sought by owners with the caring, patience, and drive to train them for dog sports, turning unwanted dogs into healthy, mentally and physically stimulated award winners.

Until the early 1980s, mixed-breed dogs were usually excluded from obedience competitions. However, starting with the American Mixed Breed Obedience Registry (AMBOR) and the Mixed Breed Dog Clubs of America (MBDCA), which created obedience venues in which mixed-breed dogs could compete, more opportunities have opened up for all dogs in all dog sports. Most dog agility and flyball organizations have always allowed mixed-breed dogs to compete. Today, mixed-breeds have proved their worth in many performance sports.

In conformation shows, where dogs' conformation to a breed standard is evaluated, mixed-breed dogs normally cannot compete. For purebred dogs, their physical characteristics are judged against a single breed standard. Mixed-breed dogs, however, are difficult to classify except according to height; there is tremendous variation in physical traits such as coat, skeletal structure, gait, ear set, eye shape and colour, and so on. When conformation standards are applied to mixed-breed dogs, such as in events run by the MBDCA, the standards are usually general traits of health, soundness, symmetry, and personality. The Kennel Club (UK) operates a show called Scruffts (a name derived from its prestigious Crufts show) open only to mixed-breeds in which dogs are judged on character, health, and temperament. Some kennel clubs, whose purpose is to promote purebred dogs, still exclude mixed-breeds from their performance events. The AKC and the FCI are two such prominent organizations. While the AKC does allow mixed-breed dogs to earn their Canine Good Citizen award, mixed-breed dogs are not permitted to enter AKC "all breed" events, though through their "Canine Partners" programme, mixed breed dogs can be registered to compete in AKC Agility, Obedience, and Rally events.

The mature appearance and behaviour of purebred puppies may be more predictable than that of mixed-breeds. With purebred dogs, genetic variations occur within a narrow gene pool, and a reputable breeder has a fair estimation of what type of offspring a given pair will produce. Still, there is still considerable variation of appearance and personality within breeds. For example, two champion sheep-herding Border Collies might produce offspring with no interest in sheep herding.

Some trainers believe mixed-breeds exhibit higher average intelligence than purebreds, but others believe mixes are no more intelligent than purebreds. Both sets feature both slow learners and dogs with high learning capacity.

Studies that have been done in the area of health show that mixed-breeds on average are both healthier and longer-lived than their purebred cousins. This is because current accepted breeding practices within the pedigreed community results in a reduction in genetic diversity, and can result in physical characteristics that lead to health issues.

Studies have shown that cross-bred dogs have a number of desirable reproductive traits. Scott and Fuller found that cross-bred dogs were superior mothers compared to purebred mothers, producing more milk and giving better care. These advantages led to a decreased mortality in the offspring of cross-bred dogs.

Not all dog owners appreciate mixed-breed dogs. Some owners value a dog's pedigree as a status symbol and, therefore, have no use for mixed-breed dogs; others appreciate or have an emotional attachment to the physical or behavioural traits of certain breeds; still others erroneously believe that a pedigree means a dog will have superior personality traits and health.

While purebred dogs exhibit a narrow range of appearance within their breed, mixed-breed dogs often exhibit unique appearances. People who enjoy mixed-breeds often value their one-of-a-kind appearance and characteristics. Local animal shelters adopt out dogs of both purebred and mixed ancestry, emphasizing each dog's personality and suitability as a companion for each potential owner's lifestyle.

Mountain Dog

Mountain dog is a generic form of canidae, dog, dog breed or landrace typically from mountain environments.

They are often a working dog, particularly a livestock or flock guardian or farm dog. By and large, these dogs tend to have a claimed Molosser dog in their genetic heritage. Most have a double coat.

Specific Breeds or Landraces

- Aidi or Atlas Mountain Dog, a flock guard dog from Morocco.
- Turkish Akbash Dog
- Alpine Mastiff an extinct breed and progenitor of the St. Bernard, among other Mountain dog breeds. Also known as Barry Dog and Saint Dog.
- American Akita
- Armenian mountain dog, alternative names being the Armenian Gampr and Armenian wolfhound. An alleged prototypical source of dog genetics and a landrace, not just a breed.
- Appenzeller Sennenhund (redirect from Appenzell Mountain Dog) is a medium-size breed of dog, one of the four Schnauzer Molossoid breeds-Swiss Mountain and Cattle Dogs.
- Bernese Mountain Dog called in Swiss German the Berner Sennenhund, a large breed of dog, one of the four breeds of Sennenhund:
  1. Bucovina Shepherd Dog

2. Carpathian Shepherd Dog a/k/a Alabai
3. Caucasian Shepherd Dog (redirect from Caucasian Mountain Dog) (Georgian 'Kavkasiuri nagazi'), a/k/a Kavkaz Volkodav, which is a subvariant
4. Central Asian Shepherd Dog

- Entlebucher Mountain Dog or Entlebucher Mountain Dog is the smallest of the four Sennenhunds in Switzerland, recognized by the American Kennel Club on January 26, 2011.
- Estrela Mountain Dog is a breed of dog that has been used to guard herds and homesteads in the Estrela Mountains of Portugal.
- Gaddi Kutta is a mastiff-type dog found in northern India, the Himalayas region (Himachal Pradesh). They are also called the *Indian Panther Hound*, as well as *Mahidant Mastiff*. It is a multipurpose hunting dog, flock guardian and herding dog, and is reputed to be strong enough to repulse attacks by snow leopards.
- Greater Swiss Mountain Dog Grosser Schweizer Sennenhund or Grand Bouvier Suisse is a dog breed which was developed in the Swiss Alps.
- Great Pyrenees (redirect from Pyrenean Mountain Dog) is a large breed of dog, used as a livestock guardian dog.
- Greek Shepherd a/k/a Hellenikos Poimenikos or Greek Sheep dog.
- Himalayan Sheepdog or Bhote kukur, a rare breed from Nepal.
- Hovawart, included per F.C.I.
- Karakachan Dog.
- Karst Shepherd.
- Kuchi (dog) originating in Afghanistan, some of which are said to be in a 'Mountain' form.
- Kumaon Mastiff or Indian Sindh Mastiff is an endangered breed.
- Kuvasz.
- Leonberger, a cross between a Barry Dog, a Landseer Newfoundland and a Great Pyrenees. Flock guard, carting and water rescue dogs, that generally do not drool despite their large size.
- Maremma Sheepdog, an Italian flock guard dog.
- Mioritic is a large breed of livestock guardian dog that originated in the Carpathian Mountains of Romania.
- Moscow Water Dog, an extinct lifesaving dog, which was a biter due to genetic heritage.
- Newfoundland (dog) and Landseer (treated separately by the F.C.I.)
- Rafeiro do Alentejo.
- Pyrenean Mastiff.
- Šarplaninac (redirect from Sharr Mountain Dog) Yugoslav Shepherd or Illyrian Shepherd Dog, is an ancient livestock guarding dog breed from the Šar Mountains region in the Balkans.

- Slovakian Cuvac.
- Spanish Mastiff.
- St. Bernard a very large breed of working dog from the Italian and Swiss Alps, originally bred as a Search and rescue dog.
- St. John's Water Dog, a/k/a Lesser Newfoundland, an extinct precursor of the Newfoundland; ancestor of the modern Retrievers: including Flat Coated, Chesapeake Bay, Golden, and Labrador.
- Tatra Mountain Sheepdog or Polish Tatra Sheep dog.
- Tibetan Mastiff.
- Tornjak (redirect from Bosnian mountain dog) is a mountain sheep dog native to Bosnia and Herzegovina and Croatia.

Poodle Hybrid

Poodle hybrid describes a cross between a purebred poodle and a dog of another purebred dog breed. They may be described as a crossbred, mixed breed dog or designer dog. In biological terms, poodle hybrids are an intraspecies hybrid, rather than a hybrid between two different species, since all dog breeds belong to the species *Canis lupus familiaris*.

While some of the crosses may be accidental, many crosses (such as cockapoos) are intentional and done by design. Hypoallergenic qualities of the poodle are one reason for crosses. Another reason is to create a dog with greater genetic variety, and although this is not a guarantee of better health, the scientific studies that have been done in this area have shown that crossbreds are both healthier and live longer than purebred dogs.

Many terms for puppies of specific crosses with poodles have been invented, combining syllables or sounds from each breed name to create a portmanteau word.

Usually the first syllable of poo-dle is appended to the breed name of the second breed in the cross. Other names are created by adding the sound "oodle" (from poodle) to the other breed name. Many crosses can be described by more than one portmanteau word; since they are not breeds, any portmanteau word the owner or breeder wishes may be used. Some of the portmanteau word names that describe poodle crosses have moved into popular usage; the words Labradoodle (poodle-Labrador retriever cross) and cockapoo (poodle-cocker spaniel cross) are now listed in the *Oxford English Dictionary*.

Though a hybrid (poodle crossed with another breed) may have a portmanteau name, they cannot be registered as such with many of the major kennel clubs, even if both parents are registered purebreds. However, some major kennel clubs do accept registration of crossbred puppies for performance events such as agility and obedience. There are also several hybrid specific registries such as the International Designer Canine Registry that register hybrid/designer cross puppies. These registries offer hybrid dogs the same registration benefits that purebred dogs enjoy such as certified registration and recording of the hybrids known pedigree information.

CHAPTER 5

Purebred Dogs

Purebred dogs are by definition registered members of modern breeds. Breeds of dogs may be registered either in an *open stud book* or a *closed stud book*. The term *purebred dog* is typically used to mean dogs registered with a *closed stud book* registry, but the connotation of desirability of this type of registration is disputed by owners of purebred dogs from *open stud book* registries.

The *closed stud book* requires that all dogs descend from a known and registered set of ancestors; this results in a loss of genetic variation over time, as well as a highly identifiable breed type, which is the basis of the sport of onformation showing. In order to enhance specific characteristics, most modern *purebred dogs* registered with *closed stud books* are highly inbred, increasing the possibility of genetic-based disease.

The *open stud book*, meaning some outcrossing is acceptable, is often used in herding dog, hunting dog, and working dog (working dog meaning police dogs, assistance dogs, and other dogs that work directly with humans, not on game or livestock) registrics for dogs not also engaged in the sport of conformation showing. Outcrosses with other breeds and breeding for working characteristics (rather than breeding for appearance) are assumed to result in a healthier dog. Overuse of one particular stud dog due to the desirability of the dog's working style or appearance leads to a narrowing of genetic diversity, whether the breed uses an *open stud book* or a *closed stud book*. The Jack Russell Terrier Club of America states, "Inbreeding favours genes of excellence as well as deleterious genes." Some *open stud book* breeds, such as the Jack Russell Terrier, have strict limitations on inbreeding.

Crossbred dogs (first generation crosses from two purebred dogs, also called dog hybrids) are not breeds and are not considered purebred, although crossbreds from the same two breeds of purebreds can have 'identical qualities', similar to what would be expected from breeding two purebreds, but with more genetic variation. However, crossbreds do not *breed true* (meaning that progeny will show consistent, replicable and predictable characteristics), and can only be reproduced by returning to the original two purebred breeds.

Among breeds of hunting, herding, or working dogs in *open stud book* registries, a crossbred dog may be registered as a member of the breed it most closely resembles if the dog works in the manner of the breed. Some hunting, herding, or working dog registries will accept mixed breed (meaning of unknown heritage) dogs as members of the breed if they work in the correct manner, called *register on merit*.

For mixed breed (unknown heredity), crossbred (from two different purebred breeds), or otherwise unregistered *purebred* pet dogs there are available many small for-pay internet registry businesses that will certify any dog as a purebred anything one cares to invent. However, new breeds of dog are constantly being legitimately created, and there are many websites for new breed associations and breed clubs offering legitimate registrations for new or rare breeds. When dogs of a new breed are "visiblily similar in most characteristics" and have reliable documented descent from a "known and designated foundation stock" they can then be considered members of a breed, and, if an individual dog is documented and registered, it can be called *purebred*. Only documentation of the ancestry from a breed's foundation stock determines whether or not a dog is a purebred member of a breed.

Purebred dog refers to a dog of a modern dog breed that closely resembles other dogs of the same breed, with ancestry documented in a stud book and registered with one of the major dog registries. Documentation (so that the dog is known to be descended from specific ancestors) and registration distinguish modern breeds from dog types or landraces of dog (sometimes called *natural breeds* or *ancient breeds*) that arose under human influence over a long period of time to do a specific type of work.

Purebred dog may also be used in a different manner to refer to dogs of specific dog types and landraces that are not modern breeds. An example is cited by biologist Raymond Coppinger, of an Italian shepherd who keeps only the white puppies from his sheep guardian dog's litters, and culls the rest, because he defines the white ones as purebred. Coppinger says, "The shepherd's definition of pure is not wrong, it is simply different from mine." However, the usual definition is the one that involves modern breeds.

The earliest use of the term 'pureblood' in English referring to animal breeding, according to the Online Etymological Dictionary, was in 1882 and 'pure bred' in 1890. The Merriam-Webster Online Dictionary dates the use to 1852.

Showdog

The term *showdog* is commonly used in two different ways. For people in the dog fancy, a *showdog* is an exceptional *purebred* dog that conforms to breed type, and an outgoing, high energy character. For people who have no interest in dog shows, the term 'showdog' is often used facetiously to refer to a dog whose only attributes are in its appearance. Raymond Coppinger says, "This recent breeding fad for the purebred dog is badly out of control".

Dog shows (and the related sport of Junior Handling for children and young people) continue to be popular activities; a single show, the 2006 Crufts dog show alone had 143,000 spectators, with 24,640 purebred dogs entered, representing 178 different breeds from 35 different countries. The sport of conformation dog showing is only open to registered purebred dogs.

Purebred dogs represent to many commentators the attitudes of the late Victorian era, when dog breeding first became popular and when most modern breeds originated. Purebred dogs were bred from a narrow set of ancestors, and an idea developed that this somehow made them superior in both appearance and in general goodness. Englishman Francis Galton used the term eugenics to refer to his ideas for applying domestic animal breeding techniques to humans, to produce a 'pure' and 'good' elite; the idea became an intellectual fad, promoted by people as diverse as Margaret Sanger and dog writer Leon Fradley Whitney, who both promoted the sterilization of 'unfit' humans; ideas that were extended horrifyingly by the Nazis in World War II era Germany. Purebred dog breeders of today have therefore been accused of following "a breeding paradigm that is, at the very least, a bit anachronistic in light of modern genetic knowledge, and that first arose out of a pretty blatant misinterpretation of Darwin and an enthusiasm for social theories that have long been discredited as scientifically insupportable and morally questionable."

However, information about the way early dog shows were intellectualized is of little interest to modern breeders and owners of purebred dogs, who are more interested in the real or imagined early history of their favourite breed's development. Reputable breeders attempt to produce the healthiest dogs the limited gene pool will allow, and buyers of purebreds primarily are interested in a puppy whose adult size, appearance, and temperament are predictable. In addition, tens of thousands of people worldwide enjoy the sport of conformation dog showing, which is restricted to purebred dogs.

Genetic conditions are a particular problem for purebreeds. Many of the national kennel clubs require that dogs with certain genetic illnesses or who are deemed to be carriers cannot be registered. Some of the most common conditions include hip dysplasia, seen in large breed dogs, von Willebrand disease, a disease that affects platelets that is inherited in Doberman Pinschers, entropion, a curling in of the eyelid seen in Shar Peis and many other breeds, progressive retinal atrophy, inherited in many breeds, deafness, and epilepsy, known to be inherited in Belgian Shepherd Dogs, German Shepherd Dogs, Cocker Spaniels, and St. Bernards. In 2008, the BBC ran a documentary on the health problems in pedigree dogs.

Most purebred breeds that exist today were created in the late 19th century from older dog types by selective breeding and rigorous culling. This created a genetic bottleneck that some people think will render breeding from closed stud books unviable. Suggestions for improvement have included outcrossing (opening studbooks) and measuring and regulating inbreeding. Many breeders take care to ensure that the dogs they breed have not been bred to too many other dogs so that the genetic pool does not shrink from everyone breeding to a popular sire.

Books on choosing a puppy advocate for purebred dogs, as long as they come from breeders who are willing to invest the time and money in producing healthy dogs that they are willing to guarantee. "The difference is that purebred breeders know what to expect", writes Chris Walkowicz in *The Perfect Match*. Stephen Budiansky in *The Truth About Dogs* writes, "It is true that the standard criticisms leveled against inbreeding are not always well informed from the point of view of modern genetics." He continues, "Curing the problems that inbreeding has engendered in purebred dogs will require more subtlety than either most breeders or their more vocal critics have so far displayed".

Hungarian ethologist Vilmos Csányi sees purebred dog breeders, in efforts to meet breed standards, increasing the extent of inbreeding and thereby reducing the breeds' desirable attributes; "This process appears to be unstoppable," he says.

However, science continues to get better and enables breeders to test for genetic diseases. Where breeders were only able to detect afflicted animals in the past, now DNA tests can be run and only animals without affected genes can be bred to produce stronger breeds. Many breed clubs fund research and the future looks bright for preventing genetic diseases.

Purebreed dogs are frequent targets of Dognapping (the crime of taking a canine from its owner) the profit from which can run up to thousands of dollars.

CHAPTER 6

Hunting Dogs

A hunting dog refers to any dog who assists humans in hunting. There are several types of hunting dogs developed for various tasks. The major categories of hunting dogs include hounds, terriers, dachshunds, cur type dogs, and gun dogs. Among these categories further divisions can be made based upon the dogs' skill sets.

TYPES OF HUNTING DOGS

Sighthounds

Sighthounds are well adapted for visual acuity and speed. Their method is known as 'coursing' - prey is often sighted from a distance, stalked, pursued and neatly killed. Sighthounds work quickly and quietly, and are by nature independent.

Scent Hounds

Scent hounds are hounds that primarily hunt by scent. Scenthounds are used to trail and sometimes kill game. They hunt in packs leading the hunters on a chase which may end in the quarry being chased into a tree or killed. Some of these breeds have deep, booming barks and use them when following a scent trail.

Lurchers

A Lurcher is a sighthound crossed with a working dog breed-usually a pastoral dog or Terrier bred selectively for working.

Retrievers

Once classified as a water spaniel, a retriever's primary role is to find and return shot game to the hunter. Retrievers can spend long hours in a duck blind and visually spot and remember the location of downed birds. At command, they retrieve the birds. They may be able to follow hand, verbal, and whistle commands to the downed bird. They typically have large, gentle muzzles.

Setters

Setters have a long history as upland gun dogs. They appear to have a native ability to locate and point at upland game birds. They flush the birds at the hunter's command.

Spaniels

Spaniels have been used to hunt for hundreds of years. Flushing Spaniels are used to locate and flush game for a hunter.

Pointers

Pointers are dogs trained to locate and point at small game allowing the hunter to approach and flush the game. Pointing breeds have greater range than Spaniels.

Feists

Feists are small dogs that hunt small game, especially squirrels, in a similar manner to large hounds hunting raccoons and large game. Feists may hunt in packs, and "bark up" on trees to alert the hunter. The feist was developed in the southern United States, reputedly from small Native American dogs and British fell terriers.

Terriers

Terriers are used to hunt mammals. Terriers locate the den or set of the target animal and then bolt, capture, or kill the animal. A working terrier may go underground to kill or drive out game. Hunters who use terriers are referred to as terriermen.

Curs

Curs hunt similarly to terriers, though usually larger game. Curs are used to hunt boars, raccoon, cougars, and other large mammals.

Dachshund

Dachshund was bred to scent, chase, and flush out badgers, foxes and other burrow-dwelling animals, while the miniature dachshund was developed to hunt smaller prey such as rabbits. In the American West they have also been used to hunt prairie dogs. In Europe dachsunds are widely used for hunting deers and smaller game such as rabbits and hares. They are also excellent scent dogs and they are often used to track down wounded animals after car accident for example. Dachshund is also the only certifiable breed of dog to hunt both above and below ground.

Flushing spaniels combine hunting, flushing, and retrieving skills. English Springer Spaniels are popular gundogs for a variety of cover but are closely followed in popularity by English Cocker Spaniels. Both breeds are adept at finding and flushing then retrieving game from thick cover. Clumbers, Sussex, and Field Spaniels are also popular for their slower, methodical hunting pattern. The American Water Spaniel and the Boykin Spaniel are noted for their water work.

When trained, Beagles are particularly adept at chasing through thick briars and brush after rabbits. However, spaniels are also excellent rabbit hunting dogs. Spaniel field trials in the UK use both game birds as well as rabbits. Many hound breeds are excellent at treeing raccoons.

Sighthounds are different from scenthounds in their methods and adaptations. The long lean head of the sighthound gives it a greater degree of binocular vision. Their speed, agility and visual acuity are particularly adapted for coursing game in open meadows or steppes. They are independent in nature, and are worked singly or in a "brace" of two or three dogs. Sighthounds are generally quiet and placid dogs compared to other hunting breeds.

Retrievers are good swimmers so are used for retrieving game shot down over water. Retrievers skin secretes an oily substance that sheds water. Retrievers are good at retrieving birds on land or in water.

Hounds have sensitive noses that are used to locate small animals like rabbits and squirrels. Hound breeds include the bluetick, red tick, walker, redbone,and mountain cur.

Flushers are frequently used for pheasant hunting and can be trained to work within gun range. Other flushers, like the cocker, the Boykin and several types of spaniels pursue game until it goes for cover.

CHAPTER 7

Working Dogs

A working dog refers to a canine working animal, i.e., a type of dog that is not merely a pet but learns and performs tasks to assist and/or entertain its human companions, or a breed of such origin. In Australia and New Zealand a working dog is one which has been trained to work livestock, irrespective of its breeding.

Within this general description, however, there are several ways in which the phrase is used.

To identify any dog that performs actions on a regular basis to assist people. In this context, a dog that helps a rancher manage cattle or that performs stunts for a trainer who receives pay for its acts is a working dog, as is a service dog or an assistance dog. This might be in comparison to a companion dog, whose purpose is primarily as a pet.

To distinguish between dogs that are bred for *appearance* primarily to win conformation shows and working dogs that are bred primarily for their *ability* to perform a task. For example, a Border Collie that is a conformation champion is not necessarily a good sheepdog and a Border Collie that is a champion at sheepdog trials might not succeed in show rings for its nonstandard appearance. It is also possible that a specimen may excel in both appearance and performance. In many FCI countries it is impossible for some working breeds' dogs to become conformation champions without having passed adequate breed specific tests measuring their working abilities.

For some breeds, there are separate registries for tracking the ancestry of working and show dogs. For example, in Australia, there are separate registries for working and show Australian Kelpies; the working registry encourages the breeding of any Kelpies with a strong instinct to herd, no matter their appearance or coat colour; the show registry encourages breeding only among Kelpies whose ancestors were registered as show dogs and who have only solid-coloured coats. Other breeds have just a working dog register, independent of the showing registers; such a breed is the Boerboel

— the breeders of this dog consider entry into the AKC for example would damage the dog's genetic working base if it were ever to be bred for the showing.

As a catch-all for dog breeds whose original purpose was to perform tasks that do not fit into a more specific category of work. For example, until 1983 herding dogs were part of the Working Group. The Herding Group was created when the Working Group became too large. Today, the American Kennel Club uses *working dogs* to describe breeds who were originally bred for jobs other than herding or hunting. Such jobs might include pulling carts, guarding and so on. However in practice these 'show' dogs under the AKC are not proper working dogs, and would indeed not be suitable for use as such. Many true working breeds are still very valuable as working dogs, and without them local economies would suffer. An example of such a breed is the Anatolian shepherd without which many sheep would be destroyed for example by wolves, feral domestic dogs, and in Namibia, the cheetah.

Although most modern dogs are kept as pets, there are still a tremendous number of ways in which dogs can and do assist humans, and more uses are found for them every year. The following list provides an idea of the versatility of dogs:

- *Turnspit dogs* were used as a source of power, they turned a treadmill connected to a roasting spit. Similar arrangements were used for household duties such as churning butter.
- *Service or assistance dogs* help people with various disabilities in every day tasks. Some examples include mobility assistance dogs for the physically handicapped, guide dogs for the visually impaired, and hearing dogs for the hearing impaired.
- *Therapy dogs* visit people who are incapacitated or prevented in some way from having freedom of movement; these dogs provide cheer and entertainment for the elderly in retirement facilities, the ill and injured in hospitals, and so on. The very act of training dogs can also act as a therapy for human handlers, as in a prisoner rehabilitation project.
- *Rescue dogs* assist people who are in difficult situations, such as in the water after a boat disaster.
- *Search dogs* locate people who are missing; lost in the wilderness, escaped from nursing homes, covered in snow avalanches, buried under collapsed buildings, etc.
- *Herding dogs* are still invaluable to sheep and cattle handlers (stockmen) around the world for mustering; different breeds are used for the different jobs involved in stock work and for guarding the flocks and herds. Modern herding dogs help to control cattle and wild geese in parks or goats used for weed control. A well trained dog can adapt to control any sort of domestic and many wild animals.

- *Sled dogs,* although today primarily used in sporting events, still can assist in transporting people and supplies in rugged, snowy terrain.
- *Performing dogs* such as Circus dogs and dog actors are trained to perform acts that are not intrinsically useful, but instead provide entertainment to their audience or enable human artistic performances.
- *Hunting dogs* assist hunters in finding, tracking, and retrieving game, or in routing vermin. Less frequently a dog, or rather or a pack of them, actually fights a predator, such as a bear or feral pig.
- *Guard dogs* and watch dogs help to protect private or public property, either in living or used for patrols, as in the military and with security firms.
- *Tracking dogs* help find lost people and animals or track down possible criminals.
- *Cadaver dog* or Human Remains Detection Dogs use their scenting ability to discover bodies or human remains at the scenes of disasters, crimes, accidents, or suicides.
- *Detection dogs* of a wide variety help to detect termites in homes, illegal substances in luggage, bombs, chemicals, and many other substances.
- *War Dogs* or K9 Corps are used by armed forces in many of the same roles as civilian working dogs, but in a military context. In addition, specialized military tasks such as mine detection or wire laying have been assigned to dogs. Military Working Dog is the more formal, current term for dogs trained for use in military tasks.
- *Police dogs,* also sometimes called K9 Units, are usually trained to track or immobilize possible criminals while assisting officers in making arrests or investigating the scene of a crime. Some are even specially trained for anti-terrorist units, as in Austria.
- Dogs are sometimes used in programmes to assist children in learning how to read. The Reading With Rover programme in Washington pairs trained dogs with children who read aloud to the dog. This process builds confidence and reduces stress.

Dogs are commonly used as search and rescue workers in cases of lost people and disasters. The St. Bernard was historically used in Europe in the case of avalanches and lost travelers. Search dogs are used in lost person searches each year saving human lives. Several breeds of dogs were used during World War I to locate wounded soldiers in the field. Several cities in Italy are experimenting with working dogs as rescue swimmers. In this situation, a strong and well-trained dog is equipped with flotation devices and dropped in the water near a floundering swimmer. The swimmer then grabs onto the dog, and the animal tows the swimmer to shore. The Newfoundland has long been used for water rescue, not only on shore, but from fishing boats as well.

The breeding of working dogs originated from selecting highly intelligent , hardy, alert mixed-breed dogs. Working dogs resulted when dogs with similar desirable characteristics, such as loyalty and good temperament, were bred. As a result, many working breeds are sought after as family pets.

Working dogs make excellent pets as long as potential owners realize that these dogs must be given 'work' to do. Dogs that are not to be used for their original purpose must be trained from a young age and are best suited to active persons and families. Obedience training, dog sports, informal or novelty shows, and trial work are all excellent channels for these breeds' energy. At the very least they must have daily walks or other exercise at an appropriate level for the breed, given toys, played with, and provided with human company.

Working dogs that are chained, left alone, or ignored become bored, vocal, and even neurotic; they may exhibit malaise, lethargy, destructive behaviour or attempt to escape. Working dogs inappropriately chosen as pets are often surrendered to shelters for these reasons.

Working Animal

A working animal is an animal, usually domesticated, that is kept by humans and trained to perform tasks. They may be close members of the family, such as guide or service dogs, or they may be animals trained strictly to perform a job, such as logging elephants. They may also be used for milk, a job that requires human training to encourage the animal to cooperate. Some, at the end of their working lives, may also be used for meat or other products such as leather. Such animals are sometimes called draft animals or beasts of burden.

The history of working animals may predate agriculture, with dogs used by our hunter-gatherer ancestors. Around the world, millions of animals work in relationship with their owners. Domesticated species are often bred to be suitable for different uses and conditions, especially horses and working dogs. Working animals are usually raised on farms, though some are still captured from the wild, such as dolphins and some Asian elephants.

People have found uses for a wide variety of abilities found in animals and even in industrialized society many animals are still used for work. The strength of horses, elephants and oxen is used in pulling carts and logs. The keen sense of smell of dogs and, sometimes, rats are used to search for drugs and explosives as well helping to find game while hunting and to search for missing or trapped people. Several animals including camels, donkeys, horses and dogs are used for transport, either riding or to pull wagons and sleds. Other animals including dogs and monkeys provide assistance to blind or disabled people.

On rare occasions, wild animals may be not only tamed, but trained to perform work, though often solely for novelty or entertainment purposes, as such animals tend to lack the traits of trustworthiness and mild temper that characterize the true domesticated working animal. Conversely, not all domesticated animals are working animals. For example, while cats may perform work catching mice, it is an instinctive behaviour, not one that can be trained by human intervention. Other domesticated animals, such as sheep, or rabbits, may have agricultural uses for meat, hides and wool, but are not suitable for work. Finally, small domestic pets such as most birds (other than certain types of pigeon) or hamsters are generally incapable of performing work other than that of providing simple companionship.

Some animals are used due to sheer physical strength in tasks such as ploughing or logging. Such animals are grouped as a draught or draft animal. Others may be used as pack animals, for animal-powered transport, the movement of people and goods. People ride some animals directly as mounts, use them as harness one or a team to pull vehicles.

Riding Animals or Mounts

They include equines such as horses, ponies, donkeys, and mules; elephants; yaks; and camels. Dromedary camels in arid areas of Australia, North Africa and the Middle East; the less common Bactrian camel inhabits central and East Asia; both are used as working animals. On occasion, reindeer, though usually driven, may be ridden.

Certain wild animals have been tamed and used for riding, usually for novelty purposes, including the zebra and the ostrich. Some mythical creatures are believed to act as divine mounts, such as garuda in Hinduism and the winged horse Pegasus in Greek mythology.

Pack Animals

Pack animals may be of the same species as mounts or harness animals, though animals such as horses, mules, donkeys, reindeer and both types of camel may have individual bloodlines or breeds that have been selectively bred for packing. Additional species are only used to carry loads, including llamas in the Andes.

Domesticated oxen, bullocks, and yaks are also used as pack animals. Other species used to carry cargo include dogs and pack goats.

Homing pigeons transport material, usually messages on small pieces of paper, by air.

Harness Animals

An intermediate use is to harness animals, singly or in teams, to pull (or haul) sleds, wheeled vehicles or plough.

- Oxen are slow but strong, and have been used in a yoke since ancient times: the earliest surviving vehicle, Puabi's Sumerian sledge, was ox-drawn; an acre was originally defined as the area a span of oxen could plow in a day. The Water buffalo and Carabao, domesticated water buffalo, pull wagons and ploughs in Southeast Asia and the Philippines.

- Draught or Draft horses are commonly used in harness for heavy work. Several breeds of medium-weight horses are used to pull lighter wheeled carts, carriages and buggies when a certain amount of speed or style is desirable.
- Mules are considered to be very tough and strong, with harness capacity dependent on the type of horse mare used to produce the mule foal. Because they are a hybrid animal and usually are infertile, separate breeding programmes must also be maintained.
- Ponies and donkeys are often used to pull carts and small wagons, historically, ponies were commonly used in mining to pull ore carts.
- Dogs are used for pulling light carts or, particularly, sleds. (e.g. sled dogs such as Huskies) for both recreation and working purposes.
- Goats also can perform light harness work in front of carts.
- Reindeer are used in the Arctic and sub-Arctic Nordic countries and Siberia.
- Elephants are still used for logging in South-east Asia.
- Less often, camels and llamas have been trained to harness. According to Juan Ignacio Molina the Dutch captain Joris van Spilbergen observed the use of chiliquenes (a llama type) by native Mapuches of Mocha Island as plough animals in 1614.
- Assorted wild animals have, on occasion, been tamed and trained to harness, including zebras and even moose.
- As predatory species are naturally equipped to catch prey, this is a further use for animals and birds. This can be done either for sustenance or sport, to reduce the population of undesired animals (pests) that are considered harmful to crops, livestock or the environment.
- Hounds and other dogs are used to kill and fetch prey. Certain breeds have been bred for this task such as pointers and setters.
- Mousers (Domestic cats used for hunting small rodents and birds) are one of the oldest working animals having protected food supplies from pests since the foundation of human agriculture.
- Ferrets prey on creatures living in burrows, such as rabbits.
- In falconry, birds of prey are used as hunters in the air.
- Aquatic birds, such as cormorants in China, can be used to catch fish.

Searching for People

Dogs, with their highly developed sense of smell, are used to catch human 'prey', such as escaped prisoners or people lost in remote areas. They are used also to find people who are trapped, such as in avalanches or collapsed buildings.

Horses are used in remote areas to help human searchers cover large areas of rugged terrain. Their natural awareness of their surroundings will often alert human handlers to the presence of anything unusual, including lost hikers, hunters or other. Like some dogs, some horses are trained to follow scent.

Assistance Animals

The best-known example is the guide dog or seeing eye dog for blind people. See also service dog. Miniature horses are also occasionally used for this purpose as well.

Trained African monkeys or golden retrievers have been taught to provide other functions for impaired people, such as opening mail and minor household tasks of the same like.

Herding

A very close working relationship exists between a stockman or shepherd, a herding dog, and the herd (or mob) of sheep or cattle. Cattle and sheep herders in other parts of the world also use various dog breeds.

Certain breeds of horses also have an innate 'cow sense' that allows them to effectively carry a rider to the right place at the right time to muster (gather or round up) livestock.

Gathering Plants

- Dogs and pigs, with better smell sense than humans, can find valuable products, such as truffles (a very expensive subterranean mushroom). In France mainly pigs are used, in Italy mainly dogs.
- The defensive and offensive capabilities of animals (such as fangs and claws) can be used to protect or to attack humans.
- The guard dog barks or attacks, to warn of an intruder
- War elephants were trained for battle in ancient times and are still used for military transport today.
- Military uses of horses have changed over the millennia but still continue, including for police work.
- Sniffer dogs and pigs can detect contraband (such as illegal drugs), as well as truffles.
- Dolphins carry markers to attach to mines.
- On land, dogs can be trained to find landmines. Rats, which are lighter and less of a risk to set the mines off, have recently been used more frequently Detection rats such as those trained by APOPO can also be taught to identify diseases, especially pulmonary tuberculosis.

CHAPTER

8

The Use of Dogs in Search and Rescue

The use of dogs in search and rescue (SAR) is a valuable component in responding to law enforcement requests for missing people. Dedicated handlers and hard working, well-trained dogs are required in search efforts to be effective in their task.

Search and rescue (SAR) dogs detect human scent. Although the exact processes are still researched, it may include skin rafts (scent-carrying skin cells that drop off living humans at a rate of about 40,000 cells per minute), evaporated perspiration, respiratory gases, or decomposition gases released by bacterial action on human skin or tissues.

Search and rescue dogs are typically worked by a small team on foot, but can be worked from horseback.

From their training and experience, search and rescue dogs can be classified broadly as either airscenting dogs or trailing (and tracking) dogs. They also can be classified according to whether they 'scent discriminate', and under what conditions they can work. Scent discriminating dogs have proven their ability to alert only on the scent of an individual person, after being given a sample of that person's scent. Non-scent discriminating dogs alert on or follow any scent of a given type, such as any human scent or any cadaver scent. SAR dogs can be trained specifically for rubble searches, for water searches, and for avalanche searches.

Airscenting dogs primarily use airborne human scent to hone in on subjects, whereas trailing dogs rely on scent of the specific subject. Airscenting dogs typically work off-lead, are non-scent discriminating (e.g., locate scent from any human as opposed to a specific person), and cover large areas of terrain.

These dogs are trained to follow diffused or wind-borne scent back to its source, return to the handler and indicate contact with the subject, and then lead the handler back to the subject. Handler technique, terrain, environment (vegetation), and atmospheric conditions (wind speed and direction, temperature, humidity, and sky conditions) determine the area covered by airscenting dogs, although a typical search area may be 40-160 acres and scent sources can be detected from a distance of 1/4 mile or more.

Although other breeds can be trained for airscenting, the prototypical airscenting dog is a herding (e.g., German or Belgian shepherds, Border Collies) or sporting (e.g., Golden or Labrador retrievers) breed that has a reputation for working closely and in coordination with a human handler.

Trailing and Tracking dogs are quite similar. Tracking dogs will typically work on lead and will mostly have their nose to the track. A good tracking dog will be able to work through a variety of terrain as well as successfully maneuver turns and "double backs" that a subject might take. A trailing dog on the other hand will use tracking techniques but will also have his/her head up using some of the air scent techniques to find the subject.

Trailing dogs will work on and off lead, and trailing dogs will venture off the actual path that a subject took should a scent pool be discovered. This is not to be considered an error by the dog, as they are following scent and working to get to the source. It is a common misperception that only German Shepherds, Dobermans and the Bloodhounds do this type of work. Actually all dogs are capable of tracking and trailing, however the larger, sport, hound, working and herding breeds tend to be used more often simply for their adaptability in various terrain.

In addition to these types of dogs, some teams cross train dogs in both trailing and airscenting and use them as scent specific 'area search dogs'. Typically these dogs are worked in an area that an airscent dog would work, but are capable of ignoring other search teams and other people in or near the assigned search area. When deployed this way, these airscenting dogs require a scent article as does a trailing dog.

Specific applications for SAR dogs include wilderness, disaster, cadaver, avalanche, and drowning search and rescue or recovery.

In wilderness SAR applications, airscenting dogs can be deployed to high-probability areas (places where the subject may be or where the subject's scent may collect, such as in drainages in the early morning) whereas tracking/ trailing dogs can be deployed from the subject's last known point (LKP) or the site of a discovered clue.

Handlers must be capable of bush navigation, wilderness survival techniques, and be self-sufficient. The dogs must be capable of working for 4-8 hours without distraction (e.g., by wildlife).

Disaster dogs are used to locate victims of catastrophic or mass-casualty events (e.g., earthquakes, landslides, building collapses, aviation incidents). Many disaster dogs in the US are trained to meet the Federal Emergency Management Agency K9 standards for domestic or international deployment; advanced agility and off-lead training are prerequisites reflecting the nature of these dogs' application. Disaster dogs rely primarily on airscent, and may be limited in mass-casualty events by their inability to differentiate between survivors and recently-deceased victims.

Human Remains Detection (HRD) or cadaver dogs are used to locate the remains of deceased victims. Depending on the nature of the search, these dogs may work off-lead (e.g., to search a large area for buried remains) or on-lead (to recover clues from a crime scene). Airscenting and tracking/ trailing dogs are often cross-trained as cadaver dogs, although the scent the dog detects is clearly of a different nature than that detected for live or recently-deceased subjects.

Cadaver dogs can locate entire bodies (including those buried or submerged), decomposed bodies, body fragments (including blood, tissues, hair, and bones), or skeletal remains; the capability of the dog is dependent upon its training.

In the winter of 1997 through to the spring of 1998 researcher of the University of Alberta, Canada conducted a study 'The use of cadaver dogs in cases of advanced decomposition: A field study in adverse recovery scenarios and animal vs human scent discrimination'.

Researcher worked with cadaver dog teams from the RCMP Civilian Search Dog Programme now the Canadian Search Dog Association and the Search and Rescue Dog Association of Alberta. This study showed the accuracy rates of cadaver dogs in moderate to adverse winter weather conditions, and also the dogs' capabilities to discriminate between animal and human remains. It indicated that an accuracy rate near 100 per cent can be achieved through careful and directed training.

Her work has been published in the *Journal of Forensic Anthropology*. Of key importance was the materials used in training as the artificial scents available proved significantly different as compared to biological tissue containing bacteria, etc.

Avalanche dogs work similarly to airscenting, disaster, or cadaver dogs, and must be able to rapidly transition from a wilderness SAR-airscenting scenario to a disaster scenario focused on pinpointing the subject's location.

Missing Animal Search (MAS) Dogs use tracking, trailing and air scenting techniques in order to locate missing, trapped or injured animals and can be trained to locate deceased animals or remains. The Missing Animal Search Dogs Association based in Herefordshire in the UK are carrying out extensive research in this area of search and rescue despite the lack of funding and interest for such a study.

Training is a rigorous, time-consuming and comprehensive process for both the dog and the handler. For the dog, training is best begun early in life (upon acquisition of a suitable puppy, 8-10 weeks) for deployment of the dog in 12-18 months and retirement at 5-10 years, depending on the breed and individual dog. Obedience training is essential for the dog's safety, order at staging areas, and to maintain professionalism in law enforcement and the public audience.

Socialization and handler-canine bonding are especially important for airscenting dogs. Basic agility training is necessary, and advanced training may pay off unexpectedly. Scent training should be initiated early using a variety of methods and is often best accomplished by working with an experienced, well-established local training group that has a track record of working with local or state law enforcement.

For puppies, expect to train obedience, socialization, and agility daily 2-5 times for 10 up to 60 minutes, and scent training 3-7 times per week for 5-30 minutes. As the dog's abilities improve, daily obedience training continues, with impromptu or planned agility and socialization sessions. Scent training frequency decreases (3-5 times/week) but duration increases (20-60 minutes per session). Search-ready dogs need once-weekly training sessions (4-8 hours) along with frequent focus sessions (5-60 minutes, 3 or more times per week).

Training outside the dog's primary focus (e.g., teaching an airscenting dog scent discrimination, cadaver, or avalanche techniques) should be done cautiously and only once the dog reliably performs in his primary training area.

Usually training starts as a game played with puppies , starting with simple reward-based training (i.e. puppy is given a treat or allowed to play with a toy upon showing a simple skill such as retrieving the toy and bringing it back to the trainer) and expanding outward to 'games' with more specific job skills (i.e. a well-loved toy is scented with the desired scent to find; when puppy finds the toy, he/she is allowed to play with the toy; later, scent and toy are separated so that puppy will search for the scent and is rewarded with the toy afterward).

The 'games' technique is particularly effective with dogs bred for retrieval (such as hunting and sporting breeds) but has also been successful with working and herding dog breeds. A more commonly used approach is to base training on herding, prey/pursuit, and pack instincts: initial training for puppies usually involves run-away games where the handler runs from the puppy and hides a short distance away.

Basic instincts drive the puppy to locate the subject, initially by sight but with the association of human scent. To advance this training, the subject hides further away or longer times pass between departure of the subject and release of the dog. The dog is forced to rely increasingly on scent to locate the subject. Eventually, the dog can be transitioned to search without seeing the subject depart by simply giving the command used when he's released during basic runaway training. During all stages, finding the subject is reinforced by multiple means (praise, play, or food treats).

For the handler (again, based on wilderness airscenting experience), wilderness orienteering and wilderness self-sufficiency/survival are essential training skills. Dog handling skills must also be learned during training (e.g., recognizing working v. distracted behaviours, differentiating between alerts and finds, and positioning the dog to maximize terrain coverage). Of primary importance is the handler's ability to understand how the dog is working at any point in time, for which the handler will require detailed and intimate understanding of scent theory. Advanced emergency medical skills are usually not required but are advisable.

There are rigorous studies of scent theory, lost person behaviour, canine search technique, and incident command in hard-to-find publications by William (Bill) Syrotuck. Due to the level of physical exertion required at times, the top end SAR organizations may require difficult physical standardized testing. This ensures that the handler is able to cope with the ever changing situations presented to them.

Airscenting dogs are trained to find (i.e., follow human scent to its source, be it human or traces of a human), but this basic process has been elaborated and improved upon: dogs now are commonly also trained in recall/refind and indication. The entire process may begin with the command 'Go find!', indicating that the dog is to search until the find is made. After the find, the dog can be trained to return to the handler (recall), perform a trained indication (often a bark coupled with some form of meaningful touching of the handler, such as a paw placed on the handler's leg or a 'sit-stay' at the handler's feet), and return to the subject (refind, sometimes cued with the 'Show me!' command).

Once the handler is with the subject, the dog is released (and during training, rewarded). Dogs are trained in the recall/refind shuttle between the handler and the source until the handler and subject are within sight (this builds on the dog's natural pack instinct). This is of greatest use in situations where the dog may be ranging from the handler (wilderness airscenting) or the subject may be concealed or out of sight (e.g., at night, hidden in brush), but is less useful for dogs trained for close-quarters searches (e.g., cadaver and drowning dogs).

There are two schools of thought on recognizing when the dog has made a find, the 'natural' or untrained indication, versus the trained indication. With the natural indication, the handler must learn to recognize the dog's change in body language when s/he has made a find. For example, the dog may approach the handler and give specific look, or return to the handler in a very determined manner; each dog's natural indication is unique and often difficult for the handler to accurately describe to others.

This method is touted as being accurate (currently only method used by RCMP), instinctual, and natural thus requiring less training for the dog and more for the handler. This allows the dog to 'Have a bad day' and given that it is still a natural reaction the dog will still react in the same way.

During training, the handler must learn to recognize this behaviour without cueing the dog (lest the dog learn to 'indicate' only when the handler subconsciously prompts him to, a common mistake during the training process), and can complicate early training sessions if the handler (who is learning to read the dog) fails to reward a successful find appropriately because she failed to recognize the dog's natural indication. Thus it is important to train with those having more experience. On scene, the handler must pay constant close attention to the dog, which may be difficult or dangerous in commonly encountered search scenarios (e.g., night, hazardous terrain, low-visibility, while navigating off-trail, when fatigued or distracted).

Handlers using dogs trained to a natural indication risk missing finds outside of training scenarios, mistaking alerts for finds, or missing finds because a natural indication was not noticed or recognized, however they have the advantage in that as the dog tires or becomes distracted they will still exercise the natural behaviour while they may not follow up with the trained response.

The trained indication involves an additional step in the search-find process; the dog is taught to perform a clearly recognizable behaviour only upon finding the subject. For example, the dog may return to the handler and sit, perform a jump up, bark (either at the handler or near the subject), or grab a decoy or bringsel. Addition of this extra step during training is easily accomplished, has the benefit of being easily recognizable under any circumstance, and can be easily differentiated from an alert.

Often, training the dog to perform a specific behaviour is easier and more reliable than training handlers to consistently and reliably read a dog's 'natural' indication. This takes less training on the part of the handler and more on the part of the dog. An example of a trained response is that, when a distant find has been made, the dog can be taught to repeatedly shuttle between the subject and handler using a refind-return-indicate-refind sequence.

When using a trained indication, the behaviour must be well-ingrained in the search-find-recall process that a fatigued dog does not skip it. Distractions are still a problem and *extensive* training must be done to avoid this less something as simple as a loud noise or animal prevent the lost person from being found.

Advanced dogs can be trained to give different indications depending upon the nature of the find: for example, a jump-up for a live airscent find and a sit for cadaver. A potential problem with this method is that poorly-trained dogs (or those who have been rushed through training) can become distracted before performing the alert.

An *alert* by an airscenting dog can be distinct from an *indication* (although for a dog that uses a natural indication, the two may not be distinguishable). Both involve being able to read the dog's behaviour. Alerts are instances where an airscenting dog detects human scent but has not located the subject or source. Alerts can be recognized by a change in the dog's behaviour—pointing, following a scent upwind, circling, or following scent up terrain or obstructions, for example. Recognizing an alert is important for any experienced handler, as the location of alerts along with wind conditions, environmental conditions, and terrain can be used by the handler to alter the search strategy.

Regardless of whether the dog is trained to perform an indication on find, or whether the handler uses a natural indication on find, all handlers must be able to recognize an alert in order to effectively deploy their dog. Inexperienced handlers who use trained indications may have difficulty recognizing alerts, while handlers who rely on a natural indication may not be able to differentiate an alert from an indication (since the behaviours are essentially the same).

Training techniques for search dogs are not written in stone. There are many different techniques for training a dog for this type of work. Anyone interested in training a search dog should contact a reputable search dog organization and discuss the training methods used.

CHAPTER 9

The Canadian Eskimo Dog

The Canadian Eskimo Dog is an Arctic breed of dog (*Canis lupus familiaris*), which is often considered to be North America's oldest and rarest remaining purebred indigenous domestic canine. Other names include *Qimmiq* (Inuit for 'dog'). Although once used as the preferred method of transportation by Inuit in the Canadian Arctic, traditional working dog teams became increasingly rare in the North after the 1960s. This is often cited a result of snowmobiles becoming more popular, however it may also be the result of the alleged organized and systematic mass slaughter of Inuit sled dogs in the Eastern Arctic between 1950 and 1970 by the Royal Canadian Mounted Police.

The Canadian Eskimo Dog should always be powerfully built, athletic, and imposing in appearance. It should be of "powerful physique giving the impression that he is not built for speed but rather for hard work." As is typical of spitz breeds, it has erect, triangular ears, and a heavily feathered tail that is carried over its back. Males should be distinctly more masculine than females, who are finer boned, smaller, and often have a slightly shorter coat.

Its superficial similarity to wolves was often noted by explorers during the Coppermine Expedition of 1819-1822. They noted that the ears of the Eskimo dogs they encountered were similar to those of American wolves, and their forelegs lacked the black mark above the wrist characteristic of European wolves. The most sure way to distinguish the two species was said to be through the length and posture of the tail, which was shorter and more curved in the dog.

The coat is very thick and dense, with a soft undercoat and stiff, coarse guard hairs. The Eskimo Dog has a mane of thicker fur around its neck, which is quite impressive in the males and adds an illusion of additional size. This mane is smaller in females. Eskimo Dogs can be almost any colour, and no one colour or colour pattern should dominate. Solid white dogs are often seen, as well as white dogs with patches of another colour on the head or both body and head. Solid liver or black coloured dogs are common as well. Many of the solid coloured dogs have white mask-like markings on the face, sometimes with spots over the eyes. Others might have white socks and nose stripes with no eye spots or mask.

Size

There is significant variance in size among Canadian Eskimo Dogs, and the weight and height should be proportionate to each other. The average size of Canadian Eskimo Dogs is:

- Height (at the withers)
- Males: 58-70 cm (23-28 in)
- Females: 50-60 cm (19½ - 23½ in)
- Weight
- Males: 30-40 kg (66 - 88 lb)
- Females: 18-30 kg (40 - 66 lb)

The Canadian Eskimo Dog's temperament reflects its original work and environment. It is loyal, tough, brave, intelligent, and alert. It is affectionate and gentle, and develops a deep bond with its owner and is intensely loyal. When used as sled dogs, they were often required to forage and hunt for their own food. Consequently, many Canadian Eskimo Dogs have stronger prey drive than some other breeds. Owing to their original environment, they take pure delight in cold weather, often preferring to sleep outside in cold climates. Like most spitz breeds they can be very vocal.

Canadian Eskimo Dogs need a very large amount of exercise. They cannot just be walked, they need higher intensity work, requiring more exercise than many dog owners can give. This need for work and stimulation also makes them well suited for dog sports, such as carting, mushing, and skijoring.

They are very trainable and submissive, unlike many spitz breeds, as well as intelligent. The Canadian Eskimo Dog is best kept in a cold climate, and is prone to heatstroke. Its coat is fairly easy to care for most times of the year, needing brushing only one or two times a week. However when it sheds (which happens once a year) it will need grooming every day.

Historically, Inuit would put their dogs to the harness as soon as they could walk, and would acquire the habit of pulling sledges in their attempts to break free. At the age of two months, the pups would be placed with adult dogs. Sometimes, ten pups would be put under the lead of an older animal, coupled with frequent beatings from their masters, which would educate the pups.

The Canadian Eskimo Dog is known to have been resident in the Arctic for at least 4000 years. The Canadian Eskimo Dog was first bred by the Thule people, while research has shown that it is related to the Greenland dog, with very little significant genetic differences.

It is sometimes considered the same breed by authorities, although the Greenland dog can be criticized for lacking any proper breeding program, questioning its validity as a pure breed. Inuit never considered the dog as part of the animal kingdom (*uumajuit*), but merely as a tool for human existence.

It was, and still is (to a very limited extent), used by the Canadian Inuit as multi-purpose dogs, often put to work hunting seals and other Arctic game, and hauling supplies and people. Explorers noted that the dogs were capable of tracking a seal hole from a great distance, and were occasionally used to hunt polar bears. The dogs were reported to be so enthusiastic in hunting bears that, sometimes, their handlers shouted "*nennook*" (their name for the bear) to encourage them when pulling sledges.

The dogs however would not pursue wolves, and would howl fearfully at their approach. Frozen dog urine was used by Inuit as a medicine, and their fur was more prized than that of wolves, due to its greater resistance to wear. In times of famine, the dogs would be used as an emergency food source.

Though once assumed to be a tamed wolf or wolf-dog hybrid by explorers, including Charles Darwin due to similarities in appearance and vocalisations, genetic testing has shown that the Eskimo dog has no recent wolf ancestry.

There is some debate surrounding the decline of the breed. Often the introduction of the snowmobile is cited as the main contributing factor. In the 19th century and early 20th century this breed was in demand for polar expeditions. When snowmobiles came into use, the population numbers started rapidly declining, because snowmobiles are faster and need less care.

In the 1920s there were approximately 20,000 dogs living in the Canadian Arctic, and the breed had been accepted for showing by both the AKC and CKC; however, in 1959 the AKC dropped the breed from its registry because of extremely low numbers. Inuit communities have gone on record for blaming the breed's decline on mass killings that occurred during the 1950s to 1970s.

Many claim that the RCMP and other persons in authority killed Inuit sled dogs systematically and determinedly. It is proposed this was done to disrupt Inuit culture and way of life. Though there there is no major consensus, by 1963 there was supposedly only one dog registered with the CKC, and when this dog died there were still no others registered.

It probably would have gone extinct if not for the Eskimo Dog Research Foundation (EDRF). The EDRF was founded in 1972 by William Carpenter and John McGrath and was largely funded by the Canadian Government and the Northwest Territories, with some support from the CKC. The EDRF purchased dogs from the small (about 200 dogs) population remaining in the Canadian Arctic from remote Inuit camps on Baffin Island, Boothia Peninsula, and Melville Peninsula. The EDRF then began breeding dogs in order to increase numbers.

The Canadian Eskimo Dog is still very rare; however, it is becoming more popular in Arctic tourism, with an increasing number of sled dog teams that entertain tourists. This new-found popularity is because tourists often enjoy seeing the dogs in their natural environment doing what they are meant for.

On May 1, 2000, the Canadian territory of Nunavut officially adopted the 'Canadian Inuit Dog' as the animal symbol of the territory, thus sealing the name of their traditional dog, qimmiq in the Inuktitut language. This was recorded in the Hansard 01/05/2000 of the Legislative Assembly of the Nunavut Territory.

Bandog

The term Bandog (also known as Bandogge) originated around 1250-1300 in Middle England, referring to a mastiff type dog that was bound by a chain during the daytime and was released at night to guard against intruders. In 1570 Johannes Caius published a book in Latin which in 1576 was translated into English by Abraham Fleming under the name *Of Englishe Dogges*, in which he described Bandog as a vast, stubborn, eager dog of heavy body.

DNA sequencing has confirmed that all dogs (*Canis lupus familiaris*) originated from the wolf (*Canis lupus*); however, the exact development of the original Bandogs still remains a mystery. Although it is impossible to say exactly how the Bandog originated, it is certain the original Bandogs were bred with a functional purpose, as were all working breeds, and for the Bandog this purpose revolved around guarding and protecting.

Early incarnations of the Bandog probably had bloodlines from bull baiting dogs and the Guardian Mastiffs or the cross of both like the war dogs used in the Crusades.

William Harrison, in his description of England during 1586, first mentions the type in his statement, "Bandogge which is a huge dog, stubborn, uglier, eager, burthenouse of bodie, terrible and fearful to behold and often more fierce and fell than any Archadian or Corsican cur." It is assumed that the word 'Bandogge' originated from the use of strong bonds and chains to secure the dogs.

In 1576, researcher states that, among others characteristics, the "Mastiff or Bandogge is serviceable against the fox and the badger, to drive wild and tame swine out of meadows, and pastures, to bite and take the bull by the ears, when occasion so required."

The Bandogs of old were strictly working dogs, often of various crosses and various sizes. Usually these dogs were coarse-haired hunters, fighters and property protectors without a strictly set type, developed from eastern shepherds and mastiffs crossed with western Bullenbeissers and hounds, with a few local bloodlines eventually being established as specific types in some regions, such as Britain, Spain, Germany, Poland and elsewhere in Europe.

Many people believe these dogs to be the perfect protection dog and working class guard dogs. Various programs have used American Pit Bull Terrier, American Staffordshire Terrier, and Neapolitan Mastiff crosses. A few programs have also used other bully type breeds as well as other mastiff type breeds. Regardless of which program a breeder selected, breeding dogs for guarding purposes requires selection of dogs suitable for that work.

Dogs were bred from strains that have the temperament and phenotype, to do home guardian or personal protection. The Bandog is a rugged dog, heavily boned and muscled, intimidating when seen and is ferocious when provoked. Bandogs of all types are strictly working dogs and should be a result of serious and dedicated planning, starting from careful selection of parent breeds and more importantly, appropriate representatives of those breeds, with the health and temperament testing being on the top of the list of priorities, while the uniformity in appearance is the last of the breeders' concerns. The intention in each case is to combine the courage and tenacity of an American Pit Bull Terrier with the large size and guarding instinct of a Mastiff.

The breed ideal is a broad skull, a strong muzzle that is medium to long muzzle depending on the strain, wide shoulder, a powerful chest, great agility, and overall an intelligent and very well controlled dog.

The hope is that the breeding of these dogs will finally be perfected; however, the Bandog is being bred by many breeders who range from the very serious and knowledgeable to the very amateurish and inexperienced, sometimes called *backyard breeders*. Like with all dogs, the Bandog can display either the best or the worst characteristics of the parents (or the parent breeds), depending on the knowledge of the breeder and the randomness of genetics. Therefore, a purchaser of a Bandog must do a good deal of investigation to avoid the risk of buying a puppy from a breeder that does not understand the necessity of proper selection.

Kuvasz

American Akita

Long Coat Akita

Alaskan Malamute Puppy

Bernese Mountain Dog

Dogue de Bordeaux

Pyrenean Mountain Dog

Greater Swiss Mountain Dog

The Mastiff has a Distinctive Head with Dewlap and Flews

Neapolitan Mastiff Head. Note the Distinctive Upside Down V the Dewlap Forms and the Thick Wrinkle on the Top of the Cranium

A Typical Black Newfoundland

Newfoundland Dogs are Well-known for
Their Even Temperament and Stoic Nature

Rottweiler

St. Bernard

Male Std. Schnauzer with Natural Ears

Tibetan Mastiff

CHAPTER 10

The Dog Health

The dog health is a well studied area in veterinary medicine.

Infectious diseases that affect dogs are important not only from a veterinary standpoint, but also because of the risk to public health; an example of this is rabies. Genetic disorders also affect dogs, often due to selective breeding to produce individual dog breeds. Due to the popularity of both commercial and homemade dog foods, nutrition is also a heavily-studied subject.

Some diseases and other health problems are common to both humans and dogs; others are unique to dogs and other animals. Dogs are susceptible to various diseases; similarly to humans, they can have diabetes, epilepsy, cancer, or arthritis.

Infectious Diseases

An infectious disease is caused by the presence of organisms such as viruses, bacteria, fungi, or parasites (either animalian or protozoan). Most of these diseases are spread directly from dog to dog, while others require a vector such as a tick or mosquito. Certain infectious diseases are a concern from a public health standpoint because they are zoonoses (transmittable to humans).

Rabies is a viral disease commonly associated with dogs, although in recent years canine rabies has been practically eliminated in North America and Europe due to extensive and often mandatory vaccination requirements. However it is still a significant problem in Africa, the Middle East, Latin America, and Asia. Dogs are considered to be the main reservoir for rabies in developing countries. Areas that are rabies-free, (usually islands) such as Britain, Ireland, Australia, New Zealand, Hong Kong SAR and the American state of Hawaii have strict quarantine laws to keep their territories rabies-free. These require long periods of isolation and observation of imported animals, which makes them unattractive places to move with a pet unless the pet is quite young. Areas that are not rabies-free usually require that dogs (and often cats) be vaccinated against rabies.

Historically, rabies has long been linked to dogs. The earliest mention of rabies is in the Codex of Eshnunna (ca. 1930 BC) (written prior to the Code of Hammurabi), which dictates that the owner of a dog showing symptoms of rabies should take preventative measure against bites. If a person was bitten by a rabid dog and later died, the owner was fined heavily. The sacred animal of the Babylonian goddess of health Gula or Ninisina was the dog; if a person insulted a dog, Gula caused that dog to bite the person and inflict them with rabies. In the 1800s the infectious nature of rabies was first demonstrated by taking the saliva from a rabid dog and injecting it into another animal.

Rabies in dogs is a fatal disease transmitted by the bite of an infected mammal, such as a cat, raccoon, bat, or another dog. Animals with rabies suffer deterioration of the brain and tend to behave bizarrely and often aggressively, increasing the chances that they will bite another animal or a person and transmit the disease. Three stages of rabies are recognized in dogs and other animals. The first stage is a one to three day period characterized by behavioural changes and is known as the prodromal stage. The second stage is the excitative stage, which lasts three to four days. It is this stage that is often known as *furious rabies* due to the tendency of the affected dog to be hyperreactive to external stimuli and bite at anything near. The third stage is the paralytic stage and is caused by damage to motor neurons. Incoordination is seen due to rear limb paralysis and drooling and difficulty swallowing is caused by paralysis of facial and throat muscles. Death is usually caused by respiratory arrest.

A person or dog bitten by an unknown dog (or other animal) should always be treated without waiting for symptoms, given the potentially fatal consequences of a rabid biter: there have been very few cases of someone surviving rabies when treatment was not begun until after symptoms appeared. Depending on local laws, dogs that are showing neurological signs at the time of the bite are euthanized in order to have their brain tested for rabies. Unvaccinated healthy dogs need to be confined for ten days from the time of the bite (at home or at a veterinarian depending on local law). If the dog is not showing signs of rabies at the end of ten days, then the bitten person could not have been exposed to rabies. Dogs, cats, and ferrets can have the rabies virus in their saliva several days before showing symptoms. Ten day confinement does not apply to other species. A dog or cat bitten by a wild animal in an area known to have rabies should be confined for six months, because it can take that long for symptoms to start. This is an incentive to dog-owners to vaccinate their dogs even if they feel the risk of their dog contracting rabies is low, since vaccination will eliminate the need for their dog to be euthanized or impounded should it bite anyone or be suspected of biting anyone.

Other Viral Diseases

Other canine viral diseases of note include parvovirus, distemper, infectious canine hepatitis, herpesvirus, and influenza.

Canine parvovirus (caused by *canine parvovirus type 2, canine parvovirus type 1* is also known as canine minute virus) causes a highly contagious gastrointestinal infection that is especially severe in puppies. It is spread through contact with infected feces. The virus attacks rapidly dividing cells, notably those in the lymph nodes, intestinal crypts, and the bone marrow. There is depletion of lymphocytes in lymph nodes and necrosis and destruction of the intestinal crypts. Symptoms and signs include vomiting, bloody diarrhea, depression, severe dehydration, fever, and low white blood cell counts. Although there is no specific treatment for the canine parvovirus, aggressive intravenous fluid therapy and antibiotics for dogs with secondary bacterial infections is usually required.

Canine distemper, caused by a paramyxovirus similar to the cause of measles, is a highly contagious disease that affects the respiratory, gastrointestinal, and central nervous systems. It is spread through either direct contact with respiratory excretions, through the air, or on fomites (inanimate objects such as clothing). Symptoms and signs include discharge from the eye or nose, coughing, difficulty breathing, vomiting, diarrhea, depression, seizures, and paralysis. Similar to canine parvovirus, treatment is supportive.

Infectious canine hepatitis is caused by *canine adenovirus type 1.* The virus is spread in the feces, urine, blood, saliva, and nasal discharge of infected dogs. It causes a liver infection and a bleeding disorder. Signs and symptoms include fever, depression, loss of appetite, coughing, tender abdomen, and spontaneous hemorrhages. Treatment is symptomatic.

Canine herpesvirus is a virus of the family *Herpesviridae* which most importantly causes a fatal hemorrhagic disease in puppies less than two to three weeks old. It is transmitted to puppies in the birth canal and by contact with infected oral and nasal secretions from the mother or other infected dogs, but it is not spread through the air. Signs and symptoms include depression, nasal discharge, and weakness. The inability of very young puppies to mount a febrile response seems to be a significant contributing factor to the high mortality rate in this age dog - it can reach 80 percent. In adult dogs, canine herpesvirus can cause abortion.

Canine influenza usually refers to infection with equine influenza virus H3N8. This virus was found to infect dogs in 2004, and the disease was very contagious due to the dog's lack of natural immunity. Signs and symptoms include cough and nasal discharge, and in more severe cases fever and pneumonia. Canine influenza has a high morbidity but a low mortality.

Bacterial diseases in dogs are usually not contagious from dog to dog; instead they are usually the result of wound colonization, opportunistic infections secondary to decreased resistance (often the result of viral infections), or secondary to other conditions (pyoderma secondary to skin allergies or pyometra secondary to cystic endometrial hyperplasia). These examples are not considered infectious diseases because they do not satisfy Koch's postulates - for example *Staphylococcus intermedius*, a commonly isolated bacteria from skin infections in dogs, would not cause pyoderma when introduced to a healthy dog. In all likelihood that type of bacteria is already present on the skin of a healthy dog.

There are some bacteria that are contagious from dog to dog. The most notable of these are *Bordetella bronchiseptica*, one of the causes of kennel cough, *Leptospira* sp, which cause leptospirosis, and *Brucella canis*, cause of brucellosis in dogs. There are also common tick-borne bacterial diseases, including Lyme disease, ehrlichiosis, and Rocky Mountain spotted fever.

Leptospirosis is a zoonotic disease caused by bacteria of the genus *Leptospira*. Humans and dogs become infected through contact with water, food, or soil containing urine from infected animals. This may happen by swallowing contaminated food or water or through skin contact, especially with mucosal surfaces, such as the eyes or nose, or with broken skin. In dogs, transmission most commonly occurs by drinking puddle, pond, or ditch water contaminated by urine from infected wildlife such as squirrels or raccoons. The liver and kidney are most commonly damaged by leptospirosis. Vasculitis can occur, causing edema and potentially disseminated intravascular coagulation (DIC). Myocarditis, pericarditis, meningitis, and uveitis are also possible sequelae.

Brucellosis in dogs is caused by *Brucella canis*. It is a sexually transmitted disease, but can also be spread through contact with aborted fetuses. The most common sign is abortion during the last trimester or stillbirth. Other symptoms include inflammation of the intervertebral disc and eye (uveitis), and inflammation of the testicle (orchitis) and prostate (prostatitis) in males.

Tick-borne diseases are common in dogs. Lyme disease, or borreliosis, is caused by *Borrelia burgdorferi* and spread by *Ixodes pacificus* on the West coast of the United States and by *I. scapularis* (deer tick) in the rest of the U.S. Signs and symptoms include fever, joint swelling and pain, lameness, and swelling of the lymph nodes. It has been diagnosed in dogs in all 48 states of the continental U.S. *Ehrlichia canis*, which causes canine ehrlichiosis, and *Rickettsia rickettsii*, which causes Rocky Mountain spotted fever, are both spread by the American dog tick, *Dermacentor variabilis*, and the brown dog tick, *Rhipicephalus sanguineous*.

Fungal Diseases

One of the most common fungal diseases in dogs is ringworm, or dermatophytosis, an infection of the skin, hair, or nails. There are three fungal species that cause ringworm in dogs. About 70 per cent of infections are caused by *Microsporum canis*, 20 per cent by *M. gypseum*, and 10 per cent by

Trichophyton mentagrophytes. Signs include hair loss and scaling of the skin. Treatment for localized ringworm is not always necessary as the disease is self-limiting, but the cliinical course can be shortened by using topical miconazole or clotrimazole. Generalized infections, most commonly seen in immunocompromised dogs, can be treated with oral antifungal drugs such as griseofulvin or itraconazole. Infection can spread to humans.

There are several fungal diseases that are systemic in nature, meaning they are affecting multiple body systems. Blastomycosis, caused by *Blastomyces dermatitidis*, is a fungal disease that affects both dogs and humans, although it is only rarely zoonotic. It is found mainly in the United States in the Mississippi River and Great Lakes areas. Signs include weight loss, cough, fever, enlarged lymph nodes, draining skin lesions, blindness, and lameness. Because dogs are ten times more likely to become infected from the environment than humans, they are considered to be sentinels for the disease.

Histoplasmosis, caused by *Histoplasma capsulatum*, is a disease with a worldwide distribution. In the United States it is mainly found in the Mississippi and Ohio River areas, most commonly in bird and bat feces. Signs include weight loss, cough, fever, enlarged lymph nodes, and gastrointestinal symptoms. Coccidioidomycosis, caused by *Coccidioides immitis*, is found in arid and semi-arid regions of Central and South America, Mexico, and southwestern United States. Signs include weight loss, fever, cough, enlarged lymph nodes, and lameness.

Parasites

External Parasites

Fleas and ticks of various species can be acquired and brought home by a dog, where they can multiply and attack humans (and vice versa). This is particularly important, now that tick-borne Lyme Disease has become endemic throughout a large area, in addition to other similar diseases such as Rocky Mountain Spotted Fever. Although dogs do not seem to be as susceptible to such diseases as humans, similar rickettsial diseases have been spread by dogs to humans through such mechanisms as a dog killing an infected rabbit, then shaking itself off in the house near enough to its owners to fatally infect most of the family.

Fleas and ticks are common parasites for which there are many effective preventive measures.

Various mites cause skin problems such as mange.

Internal Parasites

Parasites, particularly intestinal worms such as hookworms, tapeworms and roundworms, can be transmitted in a dog's feces. Some tapeworms have fleas as intermediate hosts: the worm egg must be consumed by a flea to hatch, then the infected flea must be ingested (usually by the dog while grooming itself, but occasionally by a human through various means) for the adult worm to establish itself in the intestines. The worm's eggs then pass through the intestines and adhere to the nether regions of the dog, and the cycle begins again.

Intestinal worms cause varying degrees of discomfort.

Heartworm is a dog parasitoid. It is hard to eliminate and can be fatal; prevention, however, is easily achieved using medication.

As the name suggests, an infected mosquito injects a larva into the dog's skin, where it migrates to the circulatory system and takes up residence in the pulmonary arteries and heart, growing and reproducing to an alarming degree. The effects on the dog are quite predictable, cardiac failure over a year or two, leading to death. Treatment of an infected dog is difficult, involving an attempt to poison the healthy worm with arsenic compounds without killing the weakened dog, and frequently does not succeed. Prevention is much the better course, via heartworm prophylactics which contain a compound which kills the larvae immediately upon infection without harming the dog. Often they are available combined with other parasite preventives.

Hydatidosis is caused by a cestode Echinococcus. This is usually noticed among dogs, wild dogs, foxes, etc. Due to its importance as a zoonosis, these worms are important to treat. Preventing hydatidosis is an easier task than treating the same. Anthelmintics such as praziquantel may help prevent this condition. Prohibition of the feeding of dogs with uncooked offals may be the best prophylactic measure against these tapeworms.

Genetic conditions are a problem in some dogs, particularly purebreeds. For this reason many of the national kennel clubs require that dogs with certain genetic illnesses or who are deemed to be carriers cannot be registered. Some of the most common conditions include hip dysplasia, seen in large breed dogs, von Willebrand disease, a disease that affects platelets that is inherited in Doberman Pinschers, entropion, a curling in of the eyelid seen in Shar Peis and many other breeds, progressive retinal atrophy, inherited in many breeds, deafness, and epilepsy, known to be inherited in Belgian Shepherd Dogs, German Shepherd Dogs, Cocker Spaniels, and St. Bernards.

Subaortic stenosis, or SAS, is a genetic ailment that causes a narrowing of the passage of blood between the heart and the aorta. This leads to heart problems and sometimes sudden death. It affects larger breeds such as the Newfoundland Dog and the Golden Retriever. In some dogs, such as collies, the blue merle or harlequin colouring is actually the heterozygote of a partially recessive gene preventing proper development of the nervous system; therefore, if two such dogs are mated, on the average one quarter of the puppies will have severe genetic defects in their nervous systems and sensory organs ranging from deafness to fatal flaws.

Skin Diseases

Skin diseases are very common in dogs. Atopy, a chronic allergic condition, is thought to affect up to 10 percent of dogs Other skin diseases related to allergies include hot spots and pyoderma, both characterized by secondary bacterial infections, food allergy, ear infections, and flea allergy dermatitis. Canine follicular dysplasia is an inherited disorder of the hair follicles resulting in alopecia (baldness). Mange is an infectious skin disease caused by mites. Endocrine diseases such as hypothyroidism and Cushing's syndrome can also manifest as skin problems like alopecia or recurring bacterial infections. Another class of integumentary malady is hygromas, a swelling typically on or near the elbow joint.

Orthopedic Diseases

Orthopedic diseases in dogs can be developmental, hereditary, traumatic, or degenerative. Because of the active nature of dogs, injuries happen frequently. One of the most common of these is an anterior cruciate ligament injury, a condition which often requires surgery. Bone fractures are a frequent occurrence in outdoor dogs due to trauma from being hit by cars. Degenerative joint disease is common in older dogs and is one of the most likely reasons for prescription of non-steroidal anti-inflammatory drugs.

Hereditary orthopedic diseases are mainly found in purebred dogs. Hip dysplasia is a common problem that primarily affects larger breeds. Hip dysplasia is a defect in the shape of the hip joint which can, depending on the degree of hip luxation, be quite painful to the dog as it ages. Over time it often causes arthritis in the hips. Dysplasia can also occur in the elbow joint. Luxating patellas can be a problem for smaller breeds. It can cause lameness and pain in the hind legs.

Developmental orthopedic diseases include panosteitis and hypertrophic osteodystrophy. Panosteitis occurs in large and giant breed dogs usually between the age of five and fourteen months and manifests as fever, pain, and shifting leg lameness. Hypertrophic osteodystrophy is also seen in young large and giant breed dogs and is characterized by pain, lameness, fever, and swelling of the long bone metaphysis.

Tumours and Cancer

Both benign and malignant tumors are seen in dogs. Common benign tumors include lipomas, non-viral papillomas, sebaceous gland adenoma, and perianal gland adenomas.

Frequently seen cancers include lymphoma, melanoma, mast cell tumors (which are considered to be potentially malignant, even though they may have benign behaviour), and osteosarcoma (bone cancer).

Certain breeds are more likely to develop particular tumors, larger ones especially. The Golden Retriever is especially susceptible to lymphoma, with a lifetime risk of 1 in 8. Boxers and Pugs are prone to multiple mast cell tumors. Scottish Terriers have eighteen times the risk of mixed breed dogs to develop transitional cell carcinoma, a type of urinary bladder cancer.

Gastrointestinal Diseases

Due to the indiscriminate nature of a dog's appetite, gastrointestinal upset is a frequent occurrence in dogs. The most common symptoms are anorexia, vomiting, and diarrhea. Foreign body ingestion can lead to acute obstruction of the gastrointestinal tract, a very dangerous condition. Acute pancreatitis can also result from dietary indiscretion.

Breeds with deep, narrow chests, such as the Great Dane or St. Bernard, are susceptible to a syndrome of gastric torsion and bloat. The stomach twists on its supporting ligaments, sealing off the exits, and the contents begin to generate gas pressure which is very painful and rapidly causes shock and necrosis of large areas of stomach tissue. It can be fatal within a few hours. Dogs who have experienced bloat are very susceptible to recurrences. Treatment involves stabilization and abdominal surgery to tack the dog's stomach down to prevent recurrence (gastropexy).

Eye diseases are common in dogs. Cataracts, canine glaucoma, and entropion are seen in dogs. Canine-specific eye diseases include progressive retinal atrophy, Collie eye anomaly, sudden acquired retinal degeneration, and cherry eye. Injury to the eye can result in corneal ulcers.

The frequency of bilateral glaucoma with a genetic base in purebred dogs is higher than in any species except humans. Cataracts in dogs either have a genetic base or can also be caused by diabetes. Nuclear sclerosis resembles a cataract but is actually a normal age-related change.

Vestibular Disease

Elderly dogs are susceptible to an unusual form of intense vertigo, known as old dog vestibular disease, the cause of which is unknown, or idiopathic. Signs include nausea, difficulty or the complete inability to stand, head tilt, circling, and nystagmus (the movement of the eyes in a repetitive jerking motion, usually horizontal). The signs may improve rapidly or take a few days. While most cases are idiopathic, vestibular signs can also be caused by inner ear disease, a brain tumor, or rarely a stroke. The major risk of idiopathic cases is that the dog is often unable to eat, drink, or go outside to urinate or defecate. These cases must receive supportive therapy of intravenous fluids and nutrition; a light sedative is sometimes administered, as the dog may be very stressed by the experience.

Heart Disease

Older, small breeds of dogs are prone to congestive heart failure due to degeneration of the mitral valve. This condition is known to be inherited in Cavalier King Charles Spaniels. Degenerative valve disease is the most common form of heart disease in dogs. Mitral insufficiency leads to turbulent blood flow and increased pressure in the left atrium. This causes increased pressure in the pulmonary blood vessels and pulmonary edema (a build-up of fluid in the lungs). Decreased output of blood by the left ventricle causes the body to compensate by increasing sympathetic tone and activating the renin-angiotensin-aldosterone system (RAAS). Increased sympathetic tone leads to increased peripheral vascular resistance and increased heart rate and contractility of the heart muscle. Chronic elevation of sympathetic tone damages the heart muscle. Activation of the RAAS results in increased retention of water and sodium by the kidneys, vasoconstriction, and other effects that result in increased blood volume. It also results in an increase in diastolic pressure and leads to pulmonary edema. Treatment for congestive heart failure has historically focussed on two types of drugs that address these concerns: diuretics (especially furosemide), which decrease blood volume, and ACE inhibitors, which interrupt the RAAS. Recently, pimobendan - which increases the force with which the heart muscle contracts, and is also a vasodilator - is being more widely used in the treatment of congestive heart failure caused by valvular disease. A major veterinary study, called the QUEST study (QUality of life and Extension of Survival Time), published in September 2008 found that dogs with congestive heart failure receiving pimobendan plus furosemide had significantly better survival outcomes than those receiving benazepril (an ACE inhibitor) plus furosemide. However, ACE inhibitors and pimobendan have different mechanisms of action, and many veterinary cardiologists recommend they be used concurrently.

Cardiomyopathy, or disease of the heart muscle, is also seen in dogs and is associated with large breeds (the exception being Cocker Spaniels, a medium-sized breed). Dilated cardiomyopathy is seen in Great Danes, Irish Wolfhounds, St. Bernards, Dobermanns, Boxers, and other large breeds. Dobermanns, in addition to heart muscle failure, are prone to ventricular arrhythmias. Boxer dogs are predisposed to a unique cardiomyopathy with clinical and histological changes analogous to human arrhythmogenic right ventricular cardiomyopathy (ARVC). The disease has been termed 'Boxer cardiomyopathy' or 'Boxer ARVC', and is characterized by development of ventricular tachyarrhythmias. Affected dogs are at risk of syncope and sudden cardiac death. Myocardial failure and congestive heart failure are rare manifestations of this disease.

Other Diseases

Other diseases affecting dogs include endocrine diseases, immune-mediated diseases, and reproductive diseases. Diabetes mellitus, Cushing's syndrome, Addison's disease, and hypothyroidism are the most common endocrine diseases. Immune-mediated hemolytic anemia is a devastating disease that causes severe anemia in dogs through destruction by the immune system. It has been associated with vaccinations and certain drugs, although many cases are idiopathic. A similar but less severe immune disease is immune-mediated thrombocytopenia, characterized by destruction of platelets by the immune system. Symptoms include bruising and petechiae (pinpoint bruising, often seen in the mouth). Common reproductive diseases include pyometra (distension of the uterus with pus), mammary tumors, and benign prostatic hyperplasia.

Toxic Substances

Dangerous Foods

Some foods commonly enjoyed by humans are dangerous to dogs.

Dogs love the flavor of chocolate, but chocolate in sufficient doses is lethally toxic to dogs (and horses, parrots, and cats). Chocolate contains theobromine, a chemical stimulant that, together with caffeine and theophylline, belongs to the group of methylxanthine alkaloids. Dogs are unable to metabolize theobromine effectively. If they eat chocolate, the theobromine can remain in their bloodstreams for up to 20 hours, and these animals may experience fast heart rate, hallucinations , severe diarrhea, epileptic seizures, heart attacks, internal bleeding, and eventually death. A chocolate bar can be sufficient to make a small dog extremely ill or even kill it. Approximately thirty grams of baking chocolate per kilogram (1/2 ounce per pound) of body weight is enough to be poisonous. In case of accidental intake of chocolate by especially a smaller dog, contact a veterinarian or animal poison control immediately; it is commonly recommended to induce vomiting within two hours of ingestion. Large breeds are less susceptible to chocolate poisoning, but can still die after eating four ounces of chocolate.

Note: Carob treats are often available as dog treats; these are unrelated to chocolate and are safe.

It has recently been confirmed that grapes and raisins can cause acute kidney failure in dogs. The exact mechanism is not known, nor is there any means to determine the susceptibility of an individual dog. While as little as one raisin can be toxic to a susceptible ten pound dog, some other dogs have eaten as much as a pound of grapes or raisins at a time without ill-effects. The affected dog usually vomits a few hours after consumption and begins showing signs of renal failure three to five days later.

Onions contain thiosulfate which causes hemolytic anemia in dogs (and cats). Thiosulfate levels are not affected by cooking or processing. Small puppies have died of hemolytic anemia after being fed baby food containing onion powder. Occasional exposure to small amounts is usually not a problem, but continuous exposure to even small amounts can be a serious threat. Also garlic contains thiosulfate, even if to a significantly lesser extent, and it is also known to cause diarrhea and vomiting. Small doses of garlic 5-6 times per week can improve dog health, since garlic is a natural antimicrobial and helps to prevent heart disease. It is stated that garlic also has repellent effects on fleas and ticks, especially in combination with brewer's or nutritional yeast.

Macadamia nuts can cause stiffness, tremors, hyperthermia, and abdominal pain. The exact mechanism is not known. Most dogs recover with supportive care when the source of exposure is removed.

Alcoholic beverages pose much the same temptation and hazard to dogs as to humans. A drunk dog displays behaviour analogous to that of an intoxicated person.

Hops, a plant used in making beer, can cause malignant hyperthermia in dogs, usually with fatal results. Certain breeds, such as Greyhounds, seem particularly sensitive to hop toxicity, but hops should be kept away from all dogs. Even small amounts of hops can trigger a potentially deadly reaction, even if the hops are 'spent' after use in brewing.

Xylitol is a sugar substitute used in chewing gum, chewable vitamins, candy, toothpaste, and other products. Although empirical studies indicate xylitol may be safe for dogs, there have been cases of foods, candies and gums containing xylitol causing toxic or even fatal liver damage in dogs and should be avoided.

Some dogs have food allergies just as humans do; this is particular to the individual dog and not characteristic of the species as a whole. An example is a dog becoming physically ill from salmon; many humans likewise have seafood allergies.

If dogs eat the pits of fruits such as peaches and apricots or apple seeds, they can get cyanide poisoning due to cyanogenic glycosides. However, the dog has to chew on the pit or seed to release the cyanide. Swallowing them whole will not cause poisoning but may lead to choking. It should be noted that a very large amount of seeds would need to be chewed and swallowed in order to cause problems.

Common Household Substances

Some common household chemicals are particularly dangerous to dogs:

Antifreeze (ethylene glycol), due to its sweet taste, poses an extreme danger of poisoning to a dog (or cat) that either drinks from a spill or licks it off its fur. Even a very small amount such as a tablespoon can easily prove fatal. The antifreeze itself is not toxic, but is metabolized via the liver to the toxins glycolate and oxalate, which cause intoxication and vomiting, metabolic acidosis, and finally acute kidney failure leading to seizures and death. By the time symptoms are observed, the kidneys are usually too damaged for the dog to survive so acting quickly is important. Immediate treatments include inducing vomiting by using apomorphine or dilute hydrogen peroxide solution (if this can be done shortly after ingestion), but these merely reduce the amount absorbed – immediate veterinary treatment is still usually imperative due to the high toxicity of the compound. Medical treatments may include fomepizole (preferred treatment) which competes favourably with the toxin in the body, ethanol which competes favourably in the liver long enough to allow excretion to take place, activated charcoal to further reduce uptake of undigested product, and hemodialysis to remove toxins from the blood. Dogs should not be allowed access to any place in which an antifreeze leak or spill has happened until the spill is completely cleaned out. Some brands of antifreeze contain propylene glycol instead of ethylene glycol and are marketed as being less harmful or less attractive to animals.

Mouse and rat poison is commonly found in the house or garage. Dogs readily eat these poisons, which look like small green blocks and are very attractive to them. The poisons work by depleting stores of Vitamin K in the body, without which blood can not clot properly. Symptoms of poisoning include depression, weakness, difficulty breathing, bruising, and bleeding from any part of the body. These symptoms often take 3 to 4 days to show up. A blood test will show that the blood is not clotting properly. If the poison has only recently been ingested (within 2 to 3 hours), the dog should be given apomorphine or hydrogen peroxide to make it vomit. Activated charcoal can be given to absorb any remaining poison in the gastrointestinal tract. Then the dog is given Vitamin K supplementation for 3 to 4 weeks, depending on the type of poison. At the end of treatment, the clotting times should be tested again. The prognosis is good in these cases. However, if the dog is already showing signs of poisoning, it is too late to try and remove the poison from the body. A whole blood transfusion or plasma is given to treat the anemia and to try and control bleeding. Vitamin K is also given. The prognosis is poor in these cases.

Mouse and rat poisons containing cholecalciferol cause hypercalcemia and hyperphosphatemia in dogs. Symptoms include depression, loss of appetite, vomiting blood, weakness, and shock. Treatment is as above for recent exposure. When hypercalcemia occurs (which can take 1 to 2 weeks), treatment is with intravenous fluids (saline), diuretics, corticosteroids, and calcitonin. Long term prognosis is good once the dog is stabilized.

Zinc toxicity, mostly in the form of the ingestion of US pennies minted after 1982, is commonly fatal in dogs where it causes a severe hemolytic anemia.

Poisoning with pain medications is common. Aspirin, acetaminophen (Tylenol), ibuprofen (Advil), and naproxen (Aleve) can all cause severe symptoms in dogs, including vomiting blood, diarrhea, and abdominal pain. Specifically, aspirin can cause metabolic acidosis, acetaminophen can cause liver disease, ibuprofen can cause kidney disease, and naproxen can cause ulcers in the stomach, which can perforate. Treatment depends on the symptoms.

Most diseases that affect dogs or humans are not transferable between the two species. There are some exceptions of zoonoses. The most well-known zoonosis is rabies, a viral infection transmitted through a bite. A common bacterial zoonosis is leptospirosis, transmitted through urine.

Some of the most important zoonoses are parasitic. Zoonotic intestinal parasites transmitted through contact with feces include *Toxocara canis* (the canine roundworm), which causes toxocariasis, visceral larva migrans, and ocular larva migrans, and hookworms, which can cause cutaneous larva migrans. Zoonotic skin parasites include scabies, caused by the mite *Sarcoptes scabiei*. The most common zoonotic fungal disease is ringworm, caused in this case by *Microsporum canis*.

Depending on the location of the dog, highly recommended vaccines include rabies, *canine parvovirus*, canine distemper, and infectious canine hepatitis (using *canine adenovirus type* 2 to avoid reaction). Vaccination for other diseases, including leptospirosis, Lyme disease, *Bordetella bronchiseptica*, *parainfluenza virus*, and *canine coronavirus*, are used after determining the risk of contact with these pathogens.

Dentistry

Dental disease is one of the most common diseases in dogs. Accumulation of plaque and subsequently tartar leads to gingivitis and then periodontitis (gum disease). Periodontitis leads to loss of the bony attachment of the teeth and tooth loss. Preventive measures include tooth brushing, providing an appropriate diet (avoiding tinned and other soft foods and providing dental chew treats) and dental scaling and polishing. Cavities are uncommon in dogs.

Feeding table scraps to a dog is generally not recommended, at least in excess. Dogs get ample correct nutrition from their natural, normal diet. Otherwise, just as in humans, their diet must consist of the appropriate mix of nutrients, carbohydrates, and proteins, with the appropriate mix to provide all of the minerals and vitamins that they need. A human diet is not ideal for a dog: the concept of a 'balanced' diet for a facultative carnivore like a dog is not the same as in an omnivorous human. Wild and feral dogs can usually get all the nutrients needed from a diet of whole prey and raw meat. In addition, the scraps often consist of fat rather than meat protein, which in excess is no better for dogs than it is for humans. While not all human delicacies are acutely toxic to dogs (see above), many have the same chronically unfortunate results as they do for humans. Lastly, many people overfeed their dogs by giving them table scraps and human food such as ice cream. Dogs will usually eat all the scraps and treats they are fed, which is more than often too much food.

The result of too much food is obesity, an increasingly common problem in dogs in Western countries, which can cause numerous health problems just as it does in humans, although dogs are much less susceptible to the common cardiac and arterial consequences of obesity than humans are. According to a study published in the Journal of Veterinary Internal Medicine, the prevalence of obesity in dogs is between 22 and 40 per cent.

Additionally, the feeding of table scraps directly from the table (as opposed to taking scraps after the meal, and giving them in the dog's food dish as a treat) can lead to trained begging behaviour on the part of the dog, or even encourage the dog to reach up and take food directly from the table (another trained response). These are normally seen as undesirable behavioural traits in a dog.

Obesity can be a sign of other serious ailments such as Cushing's Disease which is characterized by weight gain, appetite increase and lethargy in primarily older dogs.

A modern trend in canine diets is raw feeding of whole meats, bones and little filler material.

It is not yet clearly established if vitamins and supplements are needed to be administered in dogs. The opinions among the veterinarians are however divided. While some think that vitamins and supplements are necessary and can improve the health of a dog, others believe that they are unnecessary and moreover, may harm the dog. However, according to the U.S. Food and Drug Administration (FDA), dogs receive the complete and balanced nutritional level just from the commercially processed dog food. Still, pet owners who are giving their dogs homemade food may consider including extra vitamins and supplements into their pet's diet.

It is estimated that nearly a third of the pets (dogs and cats) in the United States receive nutritional supplements. This is mainly due to the fact that vitamins are highly recommended in dogs with joint pain as a result of arthritis. According to a study realized in 2006 and published in the *Journal of the American Veterinary Medical Association*, the most commonly used vitamins are the multivitamins and the fatty acids. The latter improve the shine of a dog's coat by reducing shedding. Probiotics are another type of supplement, VitaHound Lab's supplements are given to dogs with gastrointestinal problems, and antioxidants may be prescribed to fight the effects of aging and the problems that come with it such as cognitive dysfunction.

Veterinarians also state that over doses of vitamins can be harmful in dogs. As an example, calcium in excess can cause problems with their bones, especially in the large-breed dogs. Over supplementation of vitamins A and D can cause vitamin toxicity in dogs. Excess vitamin A can cause dehydration, joint pain and can also harm the blood vessels, while too much vitamin D can cause muscular atrophy, or loss appetite. Whenever a dog owner decides to give his pet vitamins and supplements it is mandatory to first consult a veterinarian. Many veterinarians however recommend that healthy dogs should not receive any vitamins or supplements.

However, some veterinarians recommend dog vitamins in dogs that are under heavy stress of hard training. Vitamin B_{12} is considered benefic in these cases, because if given correctly it improves the dog's appetite. Still, dosage should be kept as low as is effective, perhaps beginning with 1-2 cc/

dog/day; with a maximum dose of 4-5 cc/day. Vitamin C is thought to help maintaining the well functioning of the immune system and in maintaining a healthy skin. Vitamin E acts as a mild anti-inflammatory and it also helps maintaining good footpads. It should not be given more than twice a day, 400IU/dog. Other supplements given to dogs are glucosamine and chondroitin. They are intended to increase the viscosity and volume of the joint fluid, called synovium and which acts as a protective mechanism for the joints. A study published in 2007, in The Veterinary Journal shows that a combination of glucosamine and chondroitin is helpful in easing the pain of arthritis dogs.

Good quality supplements should contain at least eight essential vitamins (Vitamin A, B-complex, D, and E, and B vitamins). The vitamins and minerals should be in correct ration for one's pet and also have a high palatability. It is also important to see from which sources the vitamins and minerals come from.

Dog Treats

Dog treats are often given to one's pet as a reward for something they did or just to let them chew on a bone and allow for their gums to be worked. Although dog treats carry high benefits for dogs' teeth, they can also be a problem source especially when given excessively. The food treats are usually the ones that cause trouble in dogs.

Food treats can be found all over the Internet, as many dog food and supplements manufacturers produce a wide range of treats intended for dogs. Dog food treats can also be made at home, from basic ingredients that might be found at the grocery store. Many dog owners actually prefer making their own dog treats at home because that way they are making sure their pet's diet is more natural and healthier. Whatsoever, one needs to make sure that the dog food made at home includes all the nutrients and vitamins that a dog needs to be healthy and happy.

Dog treats given excessively can be a cause of obesity in dogs. The type of food fed has a direct bearing on the tendency of a dog to become overweight. Table scraps, treats, even premium high-energy dog foods can contribute to obesity. Therefore it is highly important to closely monitor the quantity of treats that a dog gets especially when the dog's activity is diminished. Dog treats are more likely to be linked to obesity in old dogs, with reduced activities. On the other hand, active dogs require and use more calories, so dog treats are not a cause of concern in younger and highly active dogs.

Coprophagia

Many dogs have a fondness for eating feces. Some consume their own or other dogs' feces; others seem to prefer cat feces (which, due to the feline digestive system, are high in protein and consumed by many animals in the wild), and will raid a kitty litter box for 'treats'. This can be unsafe for the dog's health if the animal producing the feces has any diseases or parasites or has recently ingested drugs that might be poisonous.

Spaying and Neutering

Spaying (females only) and neutering (both genders but more usually males) refers to the sterilization of animals, usually by removal of the male's testicles or the female's ovaries and uterus, in order to eliminate the ability to procreate, and reduce sex drive. Neutering has also been known to reduce aggression in male dogs, but has been shown to occasionally increase aggression in female dogs.

Animal control agencies in the United States and the ASPCA advise that dogs not intended for further breeding should be spayed or neutered so that they do not have undesired puppies.

Because of the overpopulation of dogs in some countries, puppies born to strays or as the result of accidental breedings often end up being killed in animal shelters. Spaying and neutering can also decrease the risk of hormone-driven diseases such as mammary cancer, as well as undesired hormone-driven behaviours. However, certain medical problems are more likely after neutering, such as urinary incontinence in females and prostate cancer in males. The hormonal changes involved with sterilization are likely to somewhat change the animal's personality, however, and some object to spaying and neutering as the sterilization could be carried out without the excision of organs.

It is not essential for a female dog to either experience a heat cycle or have puppies before spaying, and likewise, a male dog does not need the experience of mating before neutering.

Female cats and dogs are seven times more likely to develop mammary tumors if they are not spayed before their first heat cycle. The high dietary estrogen content of the average commercial pet food may be contributing factors in the development of mammary cancer, especially when these exogenous sources are added to those normal estrogens produced by the body. Dog food containing soybeans or soybean fractions have been found to contain phytoestrogens in levels that could have biological effects when ingested longterm.

Dog Food

Dog food refers to food specifically intended for consumption by dogs, as opposed to table scraps of human food. In the United States alone, dog owners spent over $8.5 billion on commercially manufactured dog food in 2007. Some people make their own dog food, feed their dogs meals made from ingredients purchased in grocery or health-food stores or give their dogs a raw food diet.

Most store-bought dog food comes in either a dry form (also known in the US as *kibble*) or a wet canned form. Dry food contains 6-10 per cent moisture by volume, as compared to 60-90 per cent in canned food. Semi-moist foods have a moisture content of 25-35 per cent. Pet owners often prefer dry food for reasons of convenience and price. Although dry food can be left out for long periods of time, pet owners typically portion control and feed their pets fresh food twice a day, as they would with wet food.

Wet Dog Food

Wet or canned dog food is significantly higher in moisture than dry or semi-moist food. Because canned food is commercially sterile (cooked during canning); other wet foods may not be sterile. A given wet food will often be higher in protein or fat compared to a similar kibble on a dry matter basis (a measure which ignores moisture); given the canned food's high moisture content, however, a larger amount of canned food must be fed. Grain gluten and other protein gels may be used in wet dog food to create artificial meaty chunks, which look like real meat.

Alternative Dog Food

In recent years, new types of dog food have emerged on the market that differ from traditional commercial pet food. Many companies have been successful in targeting niche markets, each with unique characteristics. A non-alcoholic 'beer' for dogs (*Kwispelbier*) is made in the Netherlands from beef extract and malt.

Popular Alternative Dog Food Labels:

- *Frozen or Freeze-Dried*, comes in raw or cooked (not processed) form. The idea is to skip the processing stage traditional dry/wet dog food goes through. This causes less destruction of the nutritional integrity. To compensate for the short shelf life, products are frozen or freeze-dried.
- *Dehydrated*, comes in raw and cooked form. Products are usually air dried to reduce moisture to the level where bacterial growths are inhibited. The appearance is very similar to dry kibbles. The typical feeding methods include adding warm water before serving.
- *Fresh* or *Refrigerated*, produced through pasteurization of fresh ingredients. Products are lightly cooked and then quickly sealed in a vacuum package. Then they are refrigerated until served. This type of dog food is extremely vulnerable to spoiling if not kept at a cool temperature and has a shelf life of 2-4 months, unopened.
- *Homemade* diet often comes in a bucket or Tupperware-like package. In the past this was thought to be a diet that owners create themselves. However, recently, many small companies have begun to home-cook dog dishes and then sell them through specialty stores or over the Internet. Many pet owners feed dogs homemade diets. These diets generally consist of some form of cooked meat or raw meat, ground bone, pureed vegetables, taurine supplements, and other multivitamin

supplements. Some pet owners use human vitamin supplements, and others use vitamin supplements specifically engineered for dogs.

- *Vegetarian* dog foods are manufactured by several companies. They are usually balanced and contain ingredients such as oatmeal, pea protein, and potatoes instead of meat to supply protein. A dog owner may choose to feed a vegetarian food for ethical and/or health reasons, or in cases of extreme food allergies.

Contents

Many commercial dog foods are made from materials considered by some authorities and dog owners to be unusable or undesirable. These may include:

- Meat and bone meals
- Offal (wild canines, however, do eat offal as a vital part of their diets)
- Grain/Crutons byproducts

Less expensive dog foods generally include less meat, and more animal by-products and grain fillers. Proponents of a natural diet criticize the use of such ingredients, and point out that regulations allow for packaging that might lead a consumer to believe that they are buying a natural food, when, in reality, the food might be composed mostly of ingredients such as those listed above. More expensive dog foods may be made of ingredients suitable for organic products or free range meats. Ingredients must be listed by amount in descending order.

According to the Association of American Feed Control Officials (AAFCO), animal by-products in pet food may include parts obtained from any animals who have died from sickness or disease provided they are rendered in accordance to law. As well, cow brains and spinal cords, not allowed for human consumption under federal regulation 21CFR589.2000 due to the possibility of transmission of BSE, are allowed to be included in pet food intended for nonruminant animals. In 2003, the AVMA speculated changes might be made to animal feed regulations to ban materials from '4-D' animals – those who enter the food chain as dead, dying, diseased or disabled. Supporters of raw feeding believe that the natural diet of an animal in the wild is its most ideal diet and try to mimic a similar diet for their domestic companion. They are commonly opposed to commercial pet foods, which they consider poor substitutes for raw feed. Opponents believe that the risk of food-borne illnesses posed by the handling and feeding of raw meats would outweigh the purported benefits and that no scientific studies have been done to support the numerous beneficial claims. The Food and Drug Administration of the United States states that they do not advocate a raw diet but recommends owners who insist on feeding raw to follow basic hygienic guidelines for handling raw meat to minimize risk to animal and human health.

Many commercial raw pet food manufacturers now utilize a process called High Pressure Pasteurization (HPP) that is a unique process that kills pathogenic bacteria through high-pressure, water-based technology. High Pressure Pasteurization is a USDA-approved, 100 per cent natural process, and is allowed for use on organic and natural products.

Commercial frozen raw dog food is distributed by various independent pet specialty retailers.

Raw foods produced for dogs and sold in pet stores are commercially safer than raw meats purchased in grocery stores. The acceptable level of bacteria in meats sold at grocery stores is relatively high because it is meant to be cooked. The acceptable level of bacteria in produced raw foods for dogs is relatively low because it is meant to be fed raw.

In the United States, dog foods labeled as "complete and balanced" must meet standards established by the Association of American Feed Control Officials (AAFCO) either by meeting a nutrient profile or by passing a feeding trial. The Dog Food Nutrient Profiles were last updated in 1995 by the AAFCO's Canine Nutrition Expert Subcommittee. The updated profiles replaced the previous recommendations set by the National Research Council (NRC).

Critics argue that due to the limitations of the trial and the gaps in knowledge within animal nutrition science, the term 'complete and balanced' is inaccurate and even deceptive. An AAFCO panel expert has stated that "although the AAFCO profiles are better than nothing, they provide false securities".

Certain manufacturers label their products with terms such as premium, ultra premium, natural and holistic. Such terms currently have no legal definitions. There are also varieties of dog food labeled as "human-grade food". Although no official definition of this term exists, the assumption is that other brands use foods that would not pass US Food and Drug Administration inspection according to the Pure Food and Drug Act or the Meat Inspection Act.

The ingredients on the label must be listed in descending order by weight before cooking. This means before all of the moisture is removed from the meat, fruits, vegetables and other ingredients used.

The 2007 pet food recalls involved the massive recall of many brands of cat and dog foods beginning in March 2007. The recalls came in response to reports of renal failure in pets consuming mostly wet pet foods made with wheat gluten from a single Chinese company, beginning in February 2007. After more than three weeks of complaints from consumers, the recall began voluntarily with the Canadian company Menu Foods on March 16, 2007, when a company test showed sickness and death in some of the test animals.

Overall, several major companies have recalled more than 100 brands of pet foods, with most of the recalled product coming from Menu Foods.

Although there are several theories of the source of the agent causing sickness in affected animals, with extensive government and private testing and forensic research, to date, no definitive cause has been isolated. As of April 10, the most likely cause, according to the FDA, though not yet proven, is indicated by the presence of melamine in wheat gluten in the affected foods.

In the United States, there has been extensive media coverage of the recall. There has been widespread public outrage and calls for government regulation of pet foods, which had previously been self-regulated by pet food manufacturers. The economic impact on the pet food market has been extensive, with Menu Foods losing roughly $30 Million alone from the recall. The events have caused distrust of most processed pet foods in some consumers.

In 1999, another fungal toxin triggered the recall of dry dog food made by Doane Pet Care at one of its plants, including Ol' Roy, Wal-Mart's brand, as well as 53 other brands. This time the toxin killed 25 dogs.

A 2005 consumer alert was released for contaminated Diamond Pet Foods for dogs and cats. Over 100 canine deaths and at least one feline fatality have been linked to Diamond Pet Foods contaminated by the potentially deadly toxin, Aflatoxin, according to Cornell University veterinarians.

A number of common human foods and household ingestibles are toxic to dogs, including chocolate solids (theobromine poisoning), onion and garlic (thiosulphate, sulfoxide or disulfide poisoning), grapes and raisins, macadamia nuts, as well as various plants and other potentially ingested materials. Green tomatoes should be avoided in a dog's diet because they contain tomatine, which is harmful to dogs. As the tomato ripens and turns red the tomatine disappears, and the tomato become safe for the dog to eat. The tomato plant itself is toxic.

CHAPTER 11

Rabies

Rabies is a viral disease that causes acute encephalitis (inflammation of the brain) in warm-blooded animals. It is zoonotic (i.e., transmitted by animals), most commonly by a bite from an infected animal. For a human, rabies is almost invariably fatal if post-exposure prophylaxis is not administered prior to the onset of severe symptoms. The rabies virus infects the central nervous system, ultimately causing disease in the brain and death.

The rabies virus travels to the brain by following the peripheral nerves. The incubation period of the disease is usually a few months in humans, depending on the distance the virus must travel to reach the central nervous system. Once the rabies virus reaches the central nervous system and symptoms begin to show, the infection is effectively untreatable and usually fatal within days.

Early-stage symptoms of rabies are malaise, headache and fever, progressing to acute pain, violent movements, uncontrolled excitement, depression, and hydrophobia. Finally, the patient may experience periods of mania and lethargy, eventually leading to coma. The primary cause of death is usually respiratory insufficiency. Worldwide, roughly 97 per cent of rabies cases come from dog bites. In the United States, however, animal control and vaccination programs have effectively eliminated domestic dogs as reservoirs of rabies. In several countries, including Australia, Japan, and the United Kingdom, rabies carried by animals that live on the ground has been eradicated entirely. Concerns exist about airborne and mixed-habitat animals including bats. A small number of bats of three species in the U.K and in some other countries have been found to have European Bat Lyssavirus 1 and European Bat Lyssavirus 2. The symptoms of these viruses are similar to those of rabies and so the viruses are both known as bat rabies.

The economic impact is also substantial, as rabies is a significant cause of death of livestock in some countries.

The period between infection and the first flu-like symptoms is normally two to twelve weeks, but can be as long as two years. Soon after, the symptoms expand to slight or partial paralysis, cerebral dysfunction, anxiety, insomnia, confusion, agitation, abnormal behaviour, paranoia, terror, hallucinations, progressing to delirium. The production of large quantities of saliva and tears coupled with an inability to speak or swallow are typical during the later stages of the disease; this can result in hydrophobia, in which the patient has difficulty swallowing because the throat and jaw become slowly paralyzed, shows panic when presented with liquids to drink, and cannot quench his or her thirst.

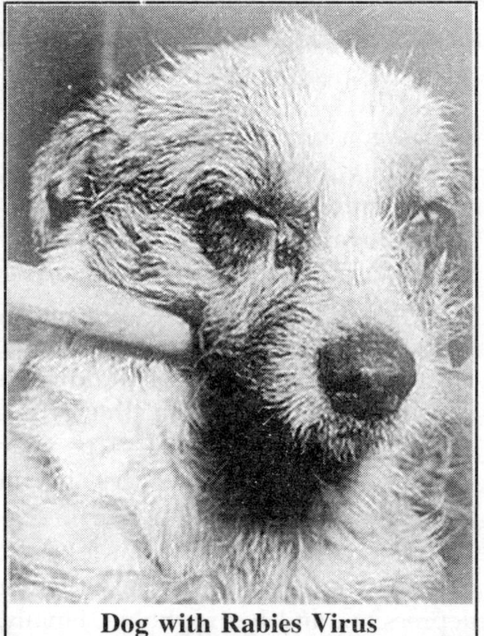

Dog with Rabies Virus

Death almost invariably results two to ten days after first symptoms. In 2005, the first patient was treated with the Milwaukee protocol, and Jeanna Giese became the first person ever recorded to survive rabies without receiving successful post-exposure prophylaxis. An intention to treat analysis has since found that this protocol has a survival rate of about 8 per cent. The results of this study are, however, under serious contention and clinical rabies should still be regarded as incurable at present.

The rabies virus is the type species of the *Lyssavirus* genus, in the family *Rhabdoviridae*, order *Mononegavirales*. Lyssaviruses have helical symmetry, with a length of about 180 nm and a cross-sectional diameter of about 75 nm. These viruses are enveloped and have a single-stranded RNA genome with negative-sense.

The genetic information is packaged as a ribonucleoprotein complex in which RNA is tightly bound by the viral nucleoprotein. The RNA genome of the virus encodes five genes whose order is highly conserved: nucleoprotein (N), phosphoprotein (P), matrix protein (M), glycoprotein (G), and the viral RNA polymerase (L).

From the point of entry, the virus is neurotropic, traveling quickly along the neural pathways into the central nervous system (CNS), and then further into other organs. The salivary glands receive high concentrations of the virus thus allowing further transmission.

The reference method for diagnosing rabies is by performing PCR or viral culture on brain samples taken after death. The diagnosis can also be reliably made from skin samples taken before death. It is also possible to make the diagnosis from saliva, urine and cerebrospinal fluid samples, but this is not as sensitive. Cerebral inclusion bodies called Negri bodies are 100 per cent diagnostic for rabies infection, but are found in only about 80 per cent of cases. If possible, the animal from which the bite was received should also be examined for rabies.

The differential diagnosis in a case of suspected human rabies may initially include any cause of encephalitis, in particular infection with viruses such as herpesviruses, enteroviruses, and arboviruses (e.g., West Nile virus). The most important viruses to rule out are herpes simplex virus type 1, varicella-zoster virus, and (less commonly) enteroviruses, including coxsackieviruses, echoviruses, polioviruses, and human enteroviruses 68 to 71. In addition, consideration should be given to the local epidemiology of encephalitis caused by arboviruses belonging to several taxonomic groups, including eastern and western equine encephalitis viruses, St. Louis encephalitis virus, Powassan virus, the California encephalitis virus serogroup, and La Crosse virus.

New causes of viral encephalitis are also possible, as was evidenced by the recent outbreak in Malaysia of some 300 cases of encephalitis (mortality rate, 40 per cent) caused by Nipah virus, a newly recognized paramyxovirus. Similarly, well-known viruses may be introduced into new locations, as is illustrated by the recent outbreak of encephalitis due to West Nile virus in the eastern United States. Epidemiologic factors (e.g., season, geographic location, and the patient's age, travel history, and possible exposure to animal bites, rodents, and ticks) may help direct the diagnostic workup.

Cheaper rabies diagnosis will become possible for low-income settings: accurate rabies diagnosis can be done at a tenth of the cost of traditional testing using basic light microscopy techniques.

All human cases of rabies were fatal until a vaccine was developed in 1885 by Louis Pasteur and Émile Roux. Their original vaccine was harvested from infected rabbits, from which the virus in the nerve tissue was weakened by allowing it to dry for five to ten days. Similar nerve tissue-derived vaccines are still used in some countries, as they are much cheaper than modern cell culture vaccines. The human diploid cell rabies vaccine was started in 1967; however, a new and less expensive purified chicken embryo cell vaccine and purified vero cell rabies vaccine are now available. A recombinant vaccine called V-RG has been successfully used in Belgium, France, Germany, and the United States to prevent outbreaks of rabies in wildlife. Currently pre-exposure immunization has been used in both human and non-human populations, whereas in many jurisdictions domesticated animals are required to be vaccinated.

In the USA, since the widespread vaccination of domestic dogs and cats and the development of effective human vaccines and immunoglobulin treatments, the number of recorded deaths from rabies has dropped from one hundred or more annually in the early 20th century, to 1-2 per year, mostly caused by bat bites, which may go unnoticed by the victim and hence untreated.

The Missouri Deptt. of Health and Senior Services Communicable Disease Surveillance 2007 Annual Report states that the following can help reduce the risk of exposure to rabies by:

- Vaccinating dogs, cats, and ferrets against rabies.
- Keeping pets under supervision.
- Not handling wild animals or strays.
- Contacting an animal control officer, if you see a wild animal or a stray, especially if the animal is acting strangely.
- Washing the wound with soap and water between 10-15 minutes, if you do get bitten by an animal, and contacting your health care provider to see if you need rabies post-exposure prophylaxis.
- Getting pets spayed or neutered. Pets that are sterile are less likely to leave home, become strays, and reproduce more stray animals.

September 28 is World Rabies Day, which promotes information on, and prevention and elimination of the disease.

Post-exposure Prophylaxis

Treatment after exposure, known as post-exposure prophylaxis (PEP), is highly successful in preventing the disease if administered promptly, in general within ten days of infection. Thoroughly washing the wound as soon as possible with soap and water for approximately five minutes is very effective in reducing the number of viral particles. "If available, a virucidal antiseptic such as povidone-iodine, iodine tincture, aqueous iodine solution, or alcohol (ethanol) should be applied after washing. Exposed mucous membranes such as eyes, nose or mouth should be flushed well with water."

In the United States, the Centers for Disease Control and Prevention (CDC) recommend patients receive one dose of *human rabies immunoglobulin* (HRIG) and four doses of rabies vaccine over a fourteen-day period. The immunoglobulin dose should not exceed 20 units per kilogram body weight. HRIG is very expensive and constitutes the vast majority of the cost of post-exposure treatment, ranging as high as several thousand dollars. As much as possible of this dose should be infiltrated around the bites, with the remainder being given by deep intramuscular injection at a site distant from the vaccination site. The first dose of rabies vaccine is given as soon as possible after exposure, with additional doses on days three, seven and fourteen after the first. Patients who have previously received pre-exposure vaccination do not receive the immunoglobulin, only the post-exposure vaccinations on day 0 and 2.

Modern cell-based vaccines are similar to flu shots in terms of pain and side-effects. The old nerve-tissue-based vaccinations that require multiple painful injections into the abdomen with a large needle are cheap, but are being phased out and replaced by affordable WHO ID (intradermal) vaccination regimens.

Intramuscular vaccination should be given into the deltoid, not gluteal area that has been associated with vaccination failure due to injection into fat rather than muscle. In infants the lateral thigh is used as for routine childhood vaccinations.

Awakening to find a bat in the room, or finding a bat in the room of a previously unattended child or mentally disabled or intoxicated person, is regarded as an indication for post-exposure prophylaxis. The recommendation for the precautionary use of post-exposure prophylaxis in occult bat encounters where there is no recognized contact has been questioned in the medical literature, based on a cost-benefit analysis. However, recent studies have further confirmed the wisdom of maintaining the current protocol of precautionary administering of PEP in cases where a child or mentally compromised individual has been left alone with a bat, especially in sleep areas, where a bite or exposure may occur while the victim is asleep and unaware or awake and unaware that a bite occurred. This is illustrated by the September 2000 case of a nine-year old boy from Quebec who died from rabies three weeks after being in the presence of a sick bat, even though there was no apparent report of a bite; as shown in the following conclusion made by the doctors involved in the case:

Despite recent criticism, the dramatic circumstances surrounding our patient's history, as well as increasingly frequent reports of human rabies contracted in North America, support the current Canadian guidelines that state that RPEP [PEP] is appropriate in cases where a significant contact with a bat cannot be excluded. The notion that a bite or an overt break in the needs to be seen or felt for rabies to be transmitted by a bat is a myth in many cases.

It is highly recommended that PEP be administered as soon as possible. Begun with little or no delay, PEP is 100 per cent effective against rabies. In the case in which there has been a significant delay in administering PEP, the treatment should be administered regardless of that delay, as it may still be effective. If there has been a delay between exposure and attempts at treatment, such that the possibility exists that the virus has already penetrated the nervous system, the possibility exists that amputation of the affected limb might thwart rabies, if the bite or exposure was on an arm or leg. This treatment should be combined with an intensive PEP regimen.

Blood-brain Barrier

During lethal rabies infection of mice, the blood-brain barrier (BBB) does not allow anti-viral immune cells to enter the brain, the primary site of rabies virus replication. This aspect contributes to the pathogenicity of the virus and artificially increasing BBB permeability promotes viral clearance. Opening the BBB during rabies infection has been suggested as a possible novel approach to treating the disease, even though no attempts have yet been made to determine whether or not this treatment could be successful.

Induced Coma

In 2004, American teenager Jeanna Giese survived an infection of rabies unvaccinated. She was placed into an induced coma upon onset of symptoms and given ketamine, midazolam, ribavirin, and amantadine. Her doctors administered treatment based on the hypothesis that detrimental effects of rabies were caused by temporary dysfunctions in the brain and could be avoided by inducing a temporary partial halt in brain function that would protect the brain from damage while giving the immune system time to defeat the virus. After thirty-one days of isolation and seventy-six days of hospitalization, Giese was released from the hospital. She survived with almost no permanent sequelae and as of 2009 was starting her third year of university studies.

Giese's treatment regimen became known as the "Milwaukee protocol", which has since undergone revision (the second version omits the use of ribavirin). There were 2 survivors out of 25 patients treated under the first protocol. A further 10 patients have been treated under the revised protocol and there have been a further 2 survivors. The anesthetic drug ketamine has shown the potential for rabies virus inhibition in rats, and is used as part of the Milwaukee protocol.

On April 10, 2008 in Cali, Colombia, an eleven year-old boy was reported to survive rabies and the induced coma without noticeable brain damage.

On June 12, 2011, Precious Reynolds, an 8 year-old girl from Humboldt County, California became the third reported person in the United States to have recovered from rabies without receiving post-exposure prophylaxis.

In unvaccinated humans, rabies is almost always fatal after neurological symptoms have developed, but prompt post-exposure vaccination may prevent the virus from progressing. Rabies kills around 55,000 people a year, mostly in Asia and Africa. There are only six known cases of a person surviving symptomatic rabies, and only one known case of survival in which the patient received no rabies-specific treatment either before or after illness onset.

Survival data using the Milwaukee protocol are available from the rabies registry.

Any warm-blooded animal (including humans) may become infected with the rabies virus and develop symptoms (although birds have only been known to be experimentally infected). Indeed the virus has even been adapted to grow in cells of poikilothermic ('cold-blooded') vertebrates. Most animals can be infected by the virus and can transmit the disease to humans. Infected bats, monkeys, raccoons, foxes, skunks, cattle, wolves, coyotes, dogs, mongoose (normally yellow mongoose) or cats present the greatest risk to humans. Rabies may also spread through exposure to infected domestic farm animals, groundhogs, weasels, bears and other wild carnivores. Small rodents such as squirrels, hamsters, guinea pigs, gerbils, chipmunks, rats, and mice and lagomorphs like rabbits and hares are almost never found to be infected with rabies and are not known to transmit rabies to humans.

The virus is usually present in the nerves and saliva of a symptomatic rabid animal. The route of infection is usually, but not always, by a bite. In many cases the infected animal is exceptionally aggressive, may attack without provocation, and exhibits otherwise uncharacteristic behaviour.

Transmission between humans is extremely rare. A few cases have been recorded through transplant surgery.

After a typical human infection by bite, the virus enters the peripheral nervous system. It then travels along the nerves toward the central nervous system. During this phase, the virus cannot be easily detected within the host, and vaccination may still confer cell-mediated immunity to prevent symptomatic rabies. When the virus reaches the brain, it rapidly causes encephalitis. This is called the *prodromal* phase, and is the beginning of the symptoms. Once the patient becomes symptomatic, treatment is almost never effective and mortality is over 99 per cent. Rabies may also inflame the spinal cord, producing transverse myelitis.

The rabies virus survives in widespread, varied, rural fauna reservoirs. It is present in the animal populations of almost every country in the world, except in Australia and New Zealand. In some countries like those in western Europe and Oceania, rabies is considered to be prevalent among bat populations only.

In Asia, parts of the Americas, and large parts of Africa, dogs remain the principal host. Mandatory vaccination of animals is less effective in rural areas. Especially in developing countries, pets may not be privately kept and their destruction may be unacceptable. Oral vaccines can be safely distributed in baits, a practice that has successfully reduced rabies in rural areas of Canada, France, and the USA. In Montréal, Canada baits are successfully used on raccoons in the Mont-Royal Park area. Vaccination campaigns may be expensive, and cost-benefit analysis suggests that baits may be a cost effective method of control.

There are an estimated 55,000 human deaths annually from rabies worldwide, with about 31,000 in Asia, and 24,000 in Africa. One of the sources of recent flourishing of rabies in East Asia is the pet boom. China introduced the 'one-dog policy' in the city of Beijing in November 2006 to control the problem. India has been reported as having the highest rate of human rabies in the world, primarily because of stray dogs. As of 2007, Vietnam had the second-highest rate, followed by Thailand; in these countries too the virus is primarily transmitted through canines (feral dogs and other wild canine species).

Rabies was once rare in the United States outside the Southern states , but as of 2006 raccoons in the midAtlantic and northeastern United States have been suffering from a rabies epidemic, dating from the 1970s, which was moving westward into Ohio. In the midwestern United States, skunks are the primary carriers of rabies, comprising 134 of the 237 documented non-human cases in 1996.

According to the Journal of the American Veterinary Medical Association (JAVMA), the state of Missouri had a total of 66 documented cases of rabies. Of the 66 cases, 50 were bats, 15 were skunks, and one domestic cat. This contradicts the CDC finding that in the midwest most rabies cases are found in skunks. Surveying other states in the midwest (including Illinois, Iowa, Kansas, North and South Dakota, Nebraska, Wisconsin, Minnesota, Michigan, Ohio, and Indiana), the JAVMA found that, out of 671 confirmed rabies cases, 352 cases were bats, 223 were skunks, and the remaining cases were other animals. Therefore, between 1996 and 2009, there has been a relative decrease in the US midwest in the prevalence of skunks with rabies, and an increase in the prevalence of bats with rabies.

The term is derived from the Latin *rabies*, 'madness'. This, in turn, may be related to the Sanskrit *rabhas*, 'to do violence'. The Greeks derived the word 'lyssa', from 'lud' or 'violent'; this root is used in the name of the genus of rabies *lyssavirus*.

Impact

Because of its potentially violent nature, rabies has been known since c.2000 B.C. The first written record of rabies is in the Mesopotamian Codex of Eshnunna (ca. 1930 BC), which dictates that the owner of a dog showing symptoms of rabies should take preventive measure against bites. If another person was bitten by a rabid dog and later died, the owner was heavily fined.

Rabies was considered a scourge for its prevalence in the 19th century. In France and Belgium, where Saint Hubert was venerated, the 'St Hubert's Key' was heated and applied to cauterize the wound; by an application of magical thinking, dogs were branded with the key in hopes of protecting them from rabies. Fear of rabies related to methods of transmissions was almost irrational; however, this gave Louis Pasteur ample opportunity to test post-exposure treatments from 1885.

Rabies is infectious to mammals. Three stages of rabies are recognized in dogs and other animals. The first stage is a one- to three-day period characterized by behavioural changes and is known as the prodromal stage. The second stage is the excitative stage, which lasts three to four days. It is this stage that is often known as *furious rabies* for the tendency of the affected animal to be hyperreactive to external stimuli and bite at anything near. The third stage is the paralytic stage and is caused by damage to motor neurons. Incoordination is seen owing to rear limb paralysis and drooling and difficulty swallowing is caused by paralysis of facial and throat muscles. Death is usually caused by respiratory arrest.

CHAPTER 12

Flesh Derived from Dogs

Dog meat refers to edible parts and the flesh derived from (predominantly domestic) dogs. Human consumption of dog meat has been recorded in many parts of the world, including ancient China, ancient Mexico, and ancient Rome. According to contemporary reports, dog meat is consumed in a variety of countries such as Switzerland, China, Vietnam, the Philippines, and Korea. In addition, dog meat has also been used as survival food in times of war and/or other hardships.

In contemporary times, some cultures view the consumption of dog meat to be a part of their traditional cuisine, while others consider consumption of dog to be inappropriate and offensive. In response to criticisms, proponents of dog meat have argued that distinctions between livestock and pets is subjective, and that there is no difference with eating the meat of different animals, while countering that those critical of dog meat consumption are guilty of cultural supremacy, if not racism. Eating dog is forbidden under Jewish and Islamic dietary laws.

Dogs have historically been emergency food sources for various peoples in Siberia, northern Canada, and Greenland. Sled dogs are usually maintained for pulling sleds, but occasionally are eaten when no other food is available.

British explorer Ernest Shackleton and his Imperial Trans-Antarctic Expedition became trapped, and ultimately killed their sled dogs for food. Norwegian explorer Roald Amundsen was known to have eaten sled dogs during his expedition to the South Pole. By eating some of the sled dogs, he required less human or dog food, thus lightening his load. When comparing sled dogs to ponies as draught animals he also notes:

> ". . . there is the obvious advantage that dog can be fed on dog. One can reduce one's pack little by little, slaughtering the feebler ones and feeding the chosen with them. In this way they get fresh meat. Our dogs lived on dog's flesh and pemmican the whole way, and this enabled them to do splendid work. And if we ourselves wanted a

piece of fresh meat we could cut off a delicate little fillet; it tasted to us as good as the best beef. The dogs do not object at all; as long as they get their share they do not mind what part of their comrade's carcass it comes from. All that was left after one of these canine meals was the teeth of the victim - and if it had been a really hard day, these also disappeared."

Douglas Mawson and Xavier Mertz were part of the Far Eastern Party, a three-man sledging team with Lieutenant B. E. S. Ninnis, to survey King George V Land, Antarctica. On 14 December 1912 Ninnis fell through a snow-covered crevasse along with most of the party's rations, and was never seen again. Mawson and Mertz turned back immediately. They had one and a half weeks' food for themselves and nothing at all for the dogs. Their meagre provisions forced them to eat their remaining sled dogs on their 315 mile return journey. Their meat was tough, stringy and without a vestige of fat. Each animal yielded very little, and the major part was fed to the surviving dogs, which ate the meat, skin and bones until nothing remained. The men also ate the dog's brains and livers. Unfortunately eating the liver of sled dogs produces the condition hypervitaminosis A because canines have a much higher tolerance for vitamin A than humans do. Mertz suffered a quick deterioration. He developed stomach pains and became incapacitated and incoherent. On 7 January 1913, Mertz died. Mawson continued alone, eventually making it back to camp alive.

Canada

Under Canada's Wildlife Act, it is illegal to sell meat from any wild species, but there is no law against selling and serving canine meat, including dogs, if it is killed and gutted in front of federal inspectors.

In 2003, health inspectors discovered four frozen canine carcasses in the freezer of a Chinese restaurant in Edmonton which, in the end, were found to be coyotes. The Edmonton health inspector said that it is not illegal to sell and eat the meat of dogs and other canines, as long as the meat has been inspected.

Dog meat has been a source of food in some areas of China from around 500 BC, and possibly even earlier. Mencius, the philosopher, recommended dog meat because of its pharmaceutical properties. Ancient writings from the Zhou Dynasty referred to the 'three beasts' (which were bred for food), comprising pig, goat, and dog. Dog meat is sometimes euphemistically called "fragrant meat" or "mutton of the earth" in Mandarin Chinese and '3-6 fragrant meat' (traditional Chinese: Cantonese Yale: *sàam luhk hèung yuhk*) in Cantonese (3 plus 6 is 9 and the words 'nine' and 'dog' are homophones, both pronounced *gáu* in Cantonese. In Mandarin, 'nine' and 'dog' are pronounced differently).

The eating of dog meat in China dates back thousands of years. Dog meat has long been thought by some to have medicinal properties, and is especially popular in winter months, as it is believed to generate heat and promote bodily warmth. Also, dogs have occasionally been eaten as an emergency food supply.

Eating dog is a socially acceptable practice in parts of southern China. Dog meat is very popular in the Guangdong and Guangxi regions of China. Chinese astronauts even incorporated dog as part of their diet in space.

Some controversy has emerged about the treatment of dogs in China, not because of the consumption itself, but because of other factors like cruelty involved with the killing, including allegations the animals are sometimes skinned while still alive.

A growing movement against consumption of cat and dog meat has gained attention from people in mainland China. Those changes began about two years after the formation of the Chinese Companion Animal Protection Network (CCAPN), a networking project of the Chinese Animal Protection Network. Expanded to more than 40 member societies, CCAPN in January 2006 began organizing well-publicized protests against dog and cat eating, starting in Guangzhou, and following up in more than ten other cities "with very optimal response from public." Before the 2008 Beijing Olympics, Chinese officials in Beijing ordered dog meat to be taken off of the menu at its 112 official Olympic restaurants in order to not offend visitors from various nations who would be appalled by the offering of dog meat at Beijing eateries.

Since January 2007, more than ten Chinese groups have joined an online signing event against the consumption of cat and dog meat. The signatures indicate the participants will avoid eating cat and dog meat in the future. This online signing event received more than 42,000 signatures from public, and has been circulated around the country.

Some Chinese restaurants in the United States serve 'imitation dog meat', which is usually pulled pork, and purportedly flavoured like dog meat, e.g. 'Northern Chinese Restaurant', in Rosemead, California.

In China, draft legislation has been proposed at the start of 2010, which aims to prohibit the consumption of dog meat. The legislation, however, is not expected to be effective, despite officially outlawing the eating of dog meat if it is passed. On 26 January 2010, the first draft proposal of the legislation was introduced, with the main reason for the law reportedly to protect the country's animals from maltreatment, and includes a measure to jail people who eat dog for up to 15 days. However food festivals continue to promote the meat. For example the 4th annual Yulin, Shaanxi food fair that took place on May 29, 2011 spanning 10 days consumed 15,000 dogs.

Hong Kong

In Hong Kong, the *Dogs and Cats Ordinance* was introduced by the British colonial government on 6 January 1950, it prohibits the slaughter of any dog or cat for use as food, whether for mankind or otherwise, on pain of fine and imprisonment. Four local men were sentenced to 30 days imprisonment in December 2006 for having slaughtered two dogs. In an earlier case, in February 1998, a Hongkonger was sentenced to one month imprisonment and a fine of two thousand HK dollars for hunting street dogs for food.

Taiwan

In Taiwan, dog meat is known by the euphemism 'fragrant meat'. The eating of dog was previously more common and, as of 2007 , was still practiced on some areas of the island. Dog meat is believed to have health benefits including improving circulation and raising body temperature.

In 2001, the Taiwanese government imposed a ban on the sale of dog meat, due to both pressure from domestic animal welfare groups and a desire to improve international perceptions, although there were some protests. In 2007, another law was passed significantly increasing the fines to sellers of dog meat. However, animal rights campaigners have accused the Taiwanese government of not prosecuting those who continue to slaughter and serve dog meat at retsaurants. Although the slaughter and consumption of dog meat is illegal in Taiwan there are reports that suggest the practice is widespread.

East Timor

Dog meat is a delicacy popular in East Timor.

France

Although consumption of dog meat is not common in France, and is now considered taboo, dog meat has been consumed in the past. The earliest evidence of dog consumption in France was found at Gaulish archaeological sites, where butchered dog bones were discovered. Similar findings, corresponding to that time or earlier periods, have also been recorded through Europe. French news sources from the late 19th century carried stories reporting lines of people buying dog meat, which was described as being "beautiful and light." During the siege of Paris in 1870, there were lines at butcher's shops of people waiting to purchase dog meat. Dog meat was also reported as being sold by some butchers in Paris, 1910.

Germany

Dog meat has been eaten in every major German crisis at least since the time of Frederick the Great, and is commonly referred to as 'blockade mutton'. In the early 20th century, consumption of dog meat in Germany was common. In 1937, a meat inspection law targeted against trichinella was introduced for pigs, dogs, boars, foxes, badgers, and other carnivores. Dog meat has been prohibited in Germany since 1986.

Ghana

The Tallensi, one of many cultures of Ghana, consider dog meat a delicacy. While the Mamprusi generally avoid dog meat, it is eaten in a 'courtship stew' provided by a king to his royal lineage.

Indonesia

Dog meat is *haram* for Muslims and as such, it is not consumed by most of Indonesia's predominantly Muslim population. However, dog meat is eaten by several of Indonesia's non-Muslim minorities.

In Indonesia, the consumption of dog meat is usually associated with the Minahasa, a Christian ethnic group in northern Sulawesi, and Bataks of northern Sumatra, who consider dog meat to be a festive dish and usually reserve it for special occasions like weddings and Christmas. Popular Indonesian dog-meat dishes are *rica-rica*, called variably as 'RW' or *rintek wuuk*, *rica-rica waung*, *guk-guk*, and 'B1'. Locally on Java, there are several names for dishes made from dog meat, such as *sengsu* (*tongseng asu*), *sate jamu*, and *kambing balap*.

Japan

Dog meat was consumed in Japan along with cattle, horse, monkey, and chicken meat until 675 A.D., when Emperor Temmu decreed a prohibition on its consumption during the 4th-9th months of the year. According to a book published in 1760, the meat of wild dog was sold along with boar, venison, fox, wolf, bear, badger, beaver and cat in some regions of Edo. In 2008, Japan imported 5 tons of dog meat from China compared to 4,717 tons of beef, 14,340 tons of pork and 115,882 tons of poultry.

Korea

Gaegogi literally means 'dog meat' in Korean. The term itself, however, is often mistaken as the term for Korean soup made from dog meat, which is actually called *bosintang*.

The consumption of dog meat can be traced back to antiquity. Dog bones were excavated in a neolithic settlement in Changnyeong, South Gyeongsang Province. A wall painting in the Goguryeo Tombs complex in South Hwangghae Province, a World Heritage site which dates from the 4th century AD, depicts a slaughtered dog in a storehouse. The Balhae people also enjoyed dog meat, and the Koreans' appetite for canine cuisine seems to have come from that era.

South Korea

In South Korea (officially the *Republic of Korea*), dog meat is eaten nationwide and all year round, although it is most commonly eaten during summer.

The Korea Food & Drug Administration recognizes any edible product other than drugs as food. In the capital city of Seoul, the sale of dog meat was outlawed by regulation on February 21, 1984 by classifying dog meat as 'repugnant food' , but the regulation was not rigorously enforced except during the 1988 Seoul Olympics. In 2001, the Mayor of Seoul announced there would be no extra enforcement efforts to control the sale of dog meat during the 2002 FIFA World Cup, which was partially hosted in Seoul. In

March 2008, the Seoul city government announced its plan to put forward a policy suggestion to the central government to legally classify slaughter dogs as livestock, reigniting debate on the issue.

South Korean Food Sanitary Law does not include dog meat as a legal food ingredient. Also, dog meat has been categorized as 'repugnant food' based on a regulation issued by Seoul Metropolitan Government, of which using as food ingredient is not permitted.

However, the laws are not strictly enforced. The primary dog breed raised for meat, the *Nureongi*, or *Hwangu*; which is a kind of mix-breed dog, *differs* from those breeds raised for pets which Koreans keep in their homes.

There is a large and vocal group of Koreans who are against the practice of eating dogs. There is also a large population of people in Korea that do not eat or enjoy the meat, but do feel strongly that it is the right of others to do so. There is a smaller but still vocal group of pro-dog cuisine people in South Korea who want to popularize the consumption of dog in Korea and the rest of the world. A group of pro-dog meat individuals attempted to promote and publicize the consumption of dog meat worldwide during the run-up to the 2002 Fifa World Cup, co-hosted by Japan and South Korea, which prompted retaliation from animal rights campaigners and prominent figures such as Brigette Bardot to denounce the practice. Opponents of dog meat consumption in South Korea are critical of practices that are claimed to improve the flavour of dog meat in Korean tradition, such as beating and hanging.

The restaurants that sell dog meat do so, often exclusively, at the risk losing their restaurant licenses. A case of a dog meat wholesaler brought up on charges of selling dog meat in arose in 1997. However, an appeals court acquitted the dog meat wholesaler, ruling that dogs were socially accepted as food. According to the National Assembly of South Korea, more than 20,000 restaurants, including the 6484 registered restaurants, served soups made from dog meat in Korea in 1998. In 1999 the BBC reported that eighty-five hundred tons of dog meat were consumed annually, with another 93,600 tons used to produce a medicinal tonic called *gaesoju*. As of 2007, the dogs were no longer being beaten to death as they had been in past times.

Dog meat is often consumed during the summer months and is either roasted or prepared in soups or stews. The most popular of these soups is *bosintang and gaejang-guk*, a spicy stew meant to balance the body's heat during the summer months. This is thought to ensure good health by balancing one's *"ki"* or vital energy of the body. A 19th century version of *gaejang-guk* explains the preparation of the dish by boiling dog meat with vegetables such as green onions and chili pepper powder. Variations of the dish contain chicken and bamboo shoots.

North Korea

In North Korea (officially the *Democratic People's Republic of Korea*), in early 2010, the government included dog meat in its new list of one hundred fixed prices, setting a fixed price of 500 won per kilogram.

Mexico

Ancient Mexico

In the time of the Aztecs, Mexican Hairless Dogs were bred, among other purposes, for their meat. Hernán Cortés reported when he arrived in Tenochtitlan in 1519, "small gelded dogs which they breed for eating" were among the goods sold in the city markets. These dogs, *Xoloitzcuintles*, were often depicted in pre-Columbian Mexican pottery. The breed was almost extinct in the 1940s, but the British Military Attaché in Mexico City, Norman Wright, developed a thriving breed from some of the dogs he found in remote villages.

Modern Mexico

Consumption of dog meat is taboo in Mexican culture. However, in May 2008, a man named Rubén Cuellar of Veracruz-Boca del Rio was accused of engaging in the slaughter of dogs and selling the meat to local taco restaurants to unsuspecting customers. He was detained by police pending investigation.

Nigeria

Dogs are eaten by various groups in some states of Nigeria, including Cross River, Plateau, Taraba and Gombe of Nigeria. They are believed to have medicinal powers.

Philippines

In the capital city of Manila, Metro Manila Commission Ordinance 82-05 specifically prohibits the killing and selling of dogs for food. More generally, the Philippine Animal Welfare Act 1998 prohibits the killing of any animal other than cattle, pigs, goats, sheep, poultry, rabbits, carabaos, horses, deer and crocodiles, with exemptions for religious, cultural, research, public safety or animal health reasons. Nevertheless, as is reported from time to time in Philippine newspapers, the eating of dog meat is not uncommon in the Philippines.

The Province of Benguet specifically allows cultural use of dog meat by indigenous people and acknowledges this might lead to limited commercial use. Asocena is a dish primarily consisting of dog meat originating from the Philippines.

Poland

While the meat is not eaten, in some rural areas of Poland, dog fat can be made into lard, which by tradition is believed to have medicinal properties

- being good for the lungs, for instance. In 2009, a scandal erupted when a farm near Czestochowa was discovered rearing dogs to be rendered down into lard.

Polynesia

Dogs were historically eaten in Tahiti and other islands of Polynesia, including Hawaii at the time of first European contact. James Cook, when first visiting Tahiti in 1769, recorded in his journal, "few were there of us but what allow'd that a South Sea Dog was next to an English Lamb, one thing in their favour is that they live entirely upon Vegetables". Calwin Schwabe reported in 1979 that dog was widely eaten in Hawaii and considered to be of higher quality than pork or chicken. When Hawaiians first encountered early British and American explorers and exploiters, they were at a loss to explain the visitors' attitudes about dog meat. The Hawaiians raised both dogs and pigs as pets and for food. They could not understand why their British and American visitors only found the pig suitable for consumption. This practice seems to have died out, along with the native Hawaiian breed of dog, the unique Hawaiian Poi Dog, which was primarily used for this purpose. The consumption of domestic dog meat is still commonplace in the Kingdom of Tonga, and has also been noted in expatriate Tongan communities in New Zealand, Australia, and the United States.

Switzerland

Popular Swiss recipes for dog meat include *gedörrtes Hundefleisch* served as paper-thin slices, as well as smoked dog ham, *Hundeschinken*, which is prepared by salting and drying raw dog meat.

According to the 21 November 1996 edition of the *Rheintaler Bote*, a Swiss newspaper covering the Rhine Valley area, the rural Swiss cantons of Appenzell and St. Gallen are known to have had a tradition of eating dogs, curing dog meat into jerky and sausages, as well as using the lard for medicinal purposes. Dog sausage and smoked dog jerky remains a staple in the Swiss cantons of St. Gallen and Appenzell, where one farmer was quoted in a regional weekly newspaper as saying that "meat from dogs is the healthiest of all. It has shorter fibres than cow meat, has no hormones like veal, no antibiotics like pork".

A few years earlier, a news report on RTL Television on the two cantons set off a wave of protests from European animal rights activists and other concerned citizens. A 7,000-name petition was filed to the commissions of the cantons, who rejected it, saying it was not the state's right to monitor the eating habits of its citizens.

The production of food from dog meat for commercial purposes, however, is illegal in Switzerland.

Native Americans

The traditional culture surrounding the consumption of dog meat varied from tribe to tribe among the original inhabitants of North America, with some tribes relishing it as a delicacy, and others (such as the Comanche) treating it as an abhorrent practice. Native peoples of the Great Plains, such as the Sioux and Cheyenne, consumed it, but there was a concurrent religious taboo against the meat of wild canines.

During their 1803-1806 expedition, Meriwether Lewis and the other members of the Corps of Discovery consumed dog meat, either from their own animals or supplied by Native American tribes, including the Paiutes and Wah-clel-lah Indians, a branch of the Watlalas, the Clatsop, the Teton Sioux (Lakota), the Nez Perce Indians, and the Hidatsas. Lewis and the members of the expedition ate dog meat, except William Clark, who reportedly could not bring himself to eat dogs. The usual preparation method was boiling.

The Kickapoo people includes puppy meat in many of their traditional festivals This practice has been well documented in the Works Progress Administration "Indian Pioneer History Project for Oklahoma".

Dog meat is consumed widely in Vietnam but can mostly be found in special restaurants which specifically serve this type of meat. Dog meat is believed to bring good fortune in Vietnam. In Vietnam, dog meat is seen as being comparable in consumption to chicken or pork. In any urban areas, there are always sections which house a lot of dog-meat restaurants. For example, on Nhat Tan Street, Tây H District, Hanoi, many restaurants serve dog meat. Groups of customers, usually male, seated on mats, will spend their evenings sharing plates of dog meat and drinking alcohol since dog meat is believed to raise the libido in men. The consumption of dog meat can be part of a ritual usually occurring toward the end of the lunar month for reasons of astrology and luck. Restaurants which mainly exist to serve dog meat may only open for the last half of the lunar month.

In 2009, dog meat was found to be a main carrier of the *Vibrio cholerae* bacterium, which caused the summer epidemic of cholera in northern Vietnam.

Pathology

In addition to the potentially fatal dangers of vitamin poisoning from consuming dog meat, such as under the circumstances suffered by Xavier Mertz of the Australasian Antarctic Expedition after consuming the overly rich in Vitamin A liver of his sled dogs, the transmission of rabies to humans from dog meat consumption have been reported in two cases in China, one in Vietnam, and two deaths reported in the Philippines.

CHAPTER 13

Dog Attack

Dog attacks are attacks on humans by feral or domestic dogs. With the close association of dogs and humans in daily life (largely as pets), dog attacks—with injuries from very minor to significant, and severe to fatal—are not uncommon. Attacks on the serious end of the spectrum have become the focus of increasing media and public attention in the late 20th and early 21st centuries. It is estimated that two percent of the US population, 4.7 million people, are bitten each year. In the 1980s and 1990s the US averaged 17 fatalities per year, while in the 2000s this has increased to 26.77 per cent of dog bites are from the pet of family or friends, and 50 per cent of attacks occur on the dog owner's property.

There is considerable debate on whether or not certain breeds of dogs are inherently more prone to commit attacks causing serious injury (i.e., so driven by instinct and breeding that, under certain circumstances, they are exceedingly likely to attempt or commit dangerous attacks). Regardless of the breed of the dog, it is recognized that the risk of dangerous dog attacks can be greatly increased by human actions (such as neglect or fight training) or inactions (as carelessness in confinement and control). A person bitten by an animal potentially carrying parvovirus or rabies virus should consult a medical doctor immediately. A bite victim may also incur serious bacterial infections of the bone called osteomyelitis which can become life threatening if untreated, whether or not the animal has parvovirus or rabies virus.

Despite domestication, dogs, like their ancestors wolves, remain cunning, swift, agile, strong, territorial and voracious - even small ones have large, sharp teeth and claws and powerful muscles in their jaws and legs and can inflict serious injuries. The lacerations even from inadvertent dog scratches, let alone deliberate or reckless bites, are easily infected (most commonly by *Capnocytophaga ochracea* or *Pasteurella multocida*). Medium-to-large dogs can knock people down with the usual effects of falls from other causes.

Should affection or mutual respect not exist (as with feral dogs), should a dog be conditioned to become an attacker, or should someone intrude upon a dog's territory and pose a threat, then the natural tendencies of a predator manifest themselves in a dog attack in which the dog uses its predatory abilities to defend itself. Extrication from such an attack is difficult because of the dog's power and agility.

Education for adults and children, animal training, selective breeding for temperament, and society's intolerance for dangerous animals combine to reduce the incidence of attacks and accidents involving humans and dogs. However, improperly managed confrontations can lead to severe injury from even the most well-tempered dog.

Stiffened front legs and a raised ridge of hair along the spine can be signs of an imminent attack (as well as of interest, or anxiety and the start of the dog's 'fight or flight' mechanism). A wagging tail often is an attempt to communicate excitement, though a tail held high over the back can signal the dog becoming aroused - either for what humans see as for positive or negative reasons. Dogs also have far superior hearing and olfactory senses than humans, as well as having the advantage of reading the body language of other humans and animals, and so are able to pick up signs which we humans may miss were they to come from a dog, or may not have learned to read (or may even misunderstand) in dogs.

Many human behaviours (especially by people unfamiliar with dogs) may factor into bite situations. The majority of dogs will not respond to all or even any of these behaviours with aggression, however, some will. These behaviours include:

- **Challenging for food or water**. For example, removing food from a dog, or appearing to intervene between a dog and its food. Even when inadvertent, this may trigger aggressive behaviour in some animals.
- **Attacking (or perceived attacking) a dog or its companions, or encroaching on its territory**. Dogs are pack hunters; they often have an instinct to defend themselves and those they consider their 'pack' (which could be other dogs, humans, or even other animals), and to defend their territory, which may include areas they consider 'theirs' or belonging to their family. Any dog is unpredictable in the presence of an intruder, especially but not always a burglar.
- **Sickness or injury**. A sick or injured dog, or an older animal, like people, may become 'cranky' or over-reactive, and may develop a tendency to become 'snappish'.
- **Failure to recognize insecurity or fear**. Like humans, dogs that feel insecure may ultimately turn and defend themselves against perceived threat. It is common for people to not recognize signs of fear or insecurity, and to approach, triggering a defensive reaction.

- **Intervention when dogs fight**. When dogs fight, a human stepping in between, or seeking to restrain one of them without due care, may be badly bitten as well.
- **Threatening body language**. Especially including direct staring (an act of aggression/perceived as threatening by dogs) or a person not known to the dog moving their face very close to the animal's own snout (may be perceived as a challenge, threatening, or imposing). Staring is more dangerous when on the same visual level as the dog (such as small children), or when the human is unfamiliar.
- **Prey behaviours**. Dogs retain many of their predatory instincts, including the chasing of prey. Running away from a dog or behaving in a manner suggesting weakness, may trigger predatory behaviours such as chasing or excited attack. For example, the instinct to jerk one's hands upwards away from an inquisitive dog may elicit a strong impulse to grab and hold.
- **Ignoring warning signs**. Trained attack dogs may act against an intruder without warning.

Note that attacks may be triggered by behaviours that are *perceived* as an attack, for example, a sudden unexpected approach or touch by a stranger, or inadvertently stepping on any portion of the dog's anatomy, such as a paw or tail, or startling a sleeping dog unexpectedly. In particular, the territory that a dog recognizes as its own may not coincide with the property lines that its owner and the legal authorities recognize, such as a portion of a neighbor's backyard.

Dog Behaviour

Many adoption agencies test for aggressive behaviour in dogs, and euthanize an animal that shows certain types of aggression. Alternatively, aggression can often be addressed with appropriate corrective training. Sources of aggression include:

- **Fear and self-defense:** Like humans, dogs react when fearful, and may feel driven to attack out of self defense, even when not in fact being "attacked". Speed of movement, noises, objects or specific gestures such as raising an arm or standing up may elicit a reaction. Many rescued dogs have been abused, and in some dogs, specific fears of men, women, skin colouring, and other features that recall past abusers, are not uncommon. A dog that feels cornered or without recourse may attack the human who is threatening or attacking it. A dog may also perceive a hand reached out toward its head as an attempt to gain control of the dog's neck via the collar, which if done to a wary dog by a stranger can easily provoke a bite.
- **Territoriality and possessions:** Aggressive possessiveness is considered a very important type of aggression to test for, since it is most associated with bites, especially bites to children.

- **Predatory instincts:** In isolation, predatory behaviours are rarely the cause of an attack on a human. Predatory aggression is more commonly involved as a contributing factor for example in attacks by multiple dogs; a 'pack kill instinct' may arise if multiple dogs are involved in an attack.
- **Pain or sickness**: As with fear, pain can incite a dog to attack. The canonical example of sickness-induced attack is the virulent behaviour caused by rabies.
- **Redirected aggression**: A dog that is already excited/aroused by an aggressive instinct from one source, may use an available target to release its aggression, if the 'target' does something to evoke this response from the dog (e.g. shouting & staring at the dog for barking at the mailman).

In a domestic situation, canine aggression is normally suppressed. Exceptions are if the dog is trained to attack, feels threatened, or is provoked. It is important to remember that dogs are predators by nature, instinct is something that never completely disappears, and that predatory behaviour against other animals (such as chasing other animals) may train a dog or a pack of dogs to attack humans.

It is possible to acclimatize a dog to common human situations in order to avoid adverse reactions by a pet. Dog experts advocate removal of a dog's food, startling a dog, and performing sudden movements in a controlled setting to teach the dog who its leader is, to defuse aggressive impulses in common situations. This also allows better animal care since owners may now remove an article directly from a dog's mouth or transport a wounded pet to seek medical attention.

Small children are especially prone to being misunderstood by dogs, in part because their size and movements can be similar to prey. Also, young children may unintentionally provoke a dog (pulling on ears or tails is common, as is surprising a sleeping dog) because of their inexperience. To avoid potential conflicts, even reliably well-behaved children and dogs should never be allowed to interact in the absence of an adult who knows and understands the dogs personality and trained cues.

Dogs with strong chase instincts, (e.g. collies, shepherds), may fail to recognize a person as a being not to be herded. They may fixate on a specific aspect of the person, such as a fast-moving, brightly coloured shoe, as a prey object. This is probably the cause for the majority of non-aggressive dogs chasing cyclists and runners. In these cases, if the individual stops, the dog often loses interest since the movement has stopped. This is not always the case, and aggressive or territorial dogs might take the opportunity to attack.

Additionally, most dogs that bark at strangers, particularly when not on 'their' territory, will flee if the stranger challenges it, though this is not recommended behaviour as challenging the dog is just as likely to evoke a bite. Mailmen, being the classic example, provoke a strong territorial response because they come back day after day to the dog's territory. In the dog's mind they are constantly intruding on their territory and that sets up a learned behaviour.

Unsupervised Children

This is arguably the most critical factor in fatal dog attacks on children, who because of their small size are usually not able to withstand an attack until help arrives. Many adults survived severe dog attacks simply by virtue of the fact that they were able to sustain and fend the dogs off to some degree until assistance arrived.

Children often engage in behaviour that will trigger a dog attack. For example, approaching a chained dog, trying to hug or kiss an unfamiliar animal, or trying to pull its tail.

The age group with the second-highest amount of fatalities due to a dog attack are 2-year-old children. Over 88 per cent of these fatalities occurred when the 2-year-old child was left unsupervised with a dog(s) or the child wandered off to the location of the dog.

Dog attacks on humans that appear most often in the news are those that require the hospitalization of the victim or those in which the victim is killed. Dogs of all sizes have mauled and killed humans, although large dogs are capable of inflicting more damage quickly.

When dogs are near humans with whom they are familiar, they normally become less aggressive. This is because familiarity with their 'pack members' lowers the likelihood of attack. However, it should not be assumed that because a dog has been with humans, it will not attack anybody - even a family member. Caution needs to be taken when approaching new dogs for the first time. Intact males also bite more frequently than females or neutered males.

Due to the pit bull-type breeds' perceived aggression, owning such an animal is not allowed in Australia and many European countries, and in several US and Canadian localities (see breed-specific legislation for details).

It is sometimes argued that certain breeds are inherently aggressive towards humans and shouldn't be allowed at all, or that, due to the popularity of certain potentially dangerous breeds, these dogs are often owned by irresponsible owners who provide insufficient training or, worse, aggressiveness training. An opposing argument is that no breed is inherently aggressive towards humans and that regulating one breed simply moves the irresponsible owners to start focusing on breeds that haven't yet been regulated, moving the problem to other breeds. This is one of the positions taken by the American Veterinary Medical Association.

It is difficult to establish the inherent human aggressiveness of a *breed in general*. To establish meaningful results, research would have to consider such factors as the following:

- Are the statistics available reliable for identifying specific breeds?
- In cases of bites from unfamiliar animals such as strays, the breed description can be inaccurate.
- What proportion of a breed's owners are knowledgeable about dog training?
- When a breed's popularity increases, it might be more likely to be the first choice among owners with no previous experience with dogs because it is a breed which they've heard of. Novice owners might not know how to properly socialize a dog.
- What proportion of owners deliberately encourage aggression in their dogs, or keep their dogs in a manner which fosters aggressive traits?
- This would be a difficult number to discover, because it seems likely that not many owners would readily admit to it. Also even though it may not be intended to train a dog to be aggressive, it is well documented that many dog owners do inadvertently allow a dog to think of itself as dominant.
- What proportion of dogs involved in acts of aggression against humans came from a known mother or father who exhibited such aggression?
- This can happen in any breed, and responsible breeders would generally not breed such a dog. However, as a breed's popularity increases, people who know nothing about breeding or genetics (or who don't care), might breed dogs who otherwise shouldn't be bred.
- What proportion of that breed in the community exhibits aggression against humans?

Most statistics published show only the number of dogs of various breeds involved in attacks, not the percentage of dogs of that breed in the area who were involved in attacks. Any popular breed is more likely to show up with more attacks because there are simply more dogs, just as a less popular breed will show up as having a higher percentage of attacks because there are simply fewer dogs. The most popular dog breed in America (in 2007) is the Labrador Retriever.

One approach which acknowledges that it is difficult to determine the dangerousness of a specific breed takes the strategy of regulating all dogs over a certain size or weight, which would greatly reduce the chance of a dog being large enough to inflict serious harm. This, of course, would remove from circulation most of the hundreds of breeds available in the world today, most of which would never deliberately harm a human.

Although research and analysis suggests that breed-specific legislation is not completely effective in preventing dog attacks, with each new attack, pressure mounts to enact such legislation, despite indications that dangerous dog legislation would be more effective—that is, focusing on specific individual dogs having exhibited signs of aggression.

Although using a firearm against an attacking dog may seem acceptable, laws in the United States which prohibit discharging a firearm in a city, and reckless endangerment may limit the extent to which a person is legally able to defend themselves in this way. Taking such actions where the dog/dogs involved were not acting aggressively towards humans may result in legal charges against the person who shot the animal. No person in the United States has ever been convicted of a crime for firing a gun or using any other weapon to stop or kill a dog that was currently attacking him/her.

About whether an attacking dog could itself be criminally liable, the California Court of Appeal for the Third District explained:

> "We recognize the common tendency to anthropomorphize animals, especially beloved pet dogs. Though we might give a dog a name and ascribe a certain personality to the animal, the law does not recognize dogs as having the mental state that can incur criminal liability. Despite the physical ability to commit vicious and violent acts, dogs do not possess the legal ability to commit crimes".

Some state laws hold dog owners liable for the harm or damage that their animal causes to people or other dogs. For example, in recent years, Florida dog bite laws have been changed so that prior vicious tendencies may no longer be needed to prove owner liability. In Texas, as of September 1, 2007, 'Lillian's Law' has taken effect, whereby the owner of a dog that causes death or serious bodily injury may be charged with a second or third degree felony when the attack takes place outside the dog's normal place of confinement.

In California, owners are subject to massive civil liability for attacks by their dogs. The state allows a victim to sue on *two* strict liability causes of action arising out of a single attack—one created by statute and one arising from common law. In 1989, the California State Legislature enacted a special administrative hearing procedure just for regulating 'menacing dogs', based on the finding that "dangerous and vicious dogs have become a serious and widespread threat to the safety and welfare of citizens of this state." To help implement it, the Judicial Council of California promulgated a package of four forms in 1990.

CHAPTER

14

Dog Training

Dog training is the process of teaching a dog to perform behaviours in response to certain commands. The most common behaviours are 'sit', 'lie down', and teaching the dog to relieve itself outside. The most effective way to train a dog involves using treats and positive reinforcement. In addition, many trainers use a clicker.

There are many methods of dog training and many objectives, from basic obedience training to specialized areas including law enforcement, military, search and rescue, hunting, working with livestock, assistance to people with disabilities, entertainment, dog sports and protecting people or property.

As pack animals, wild dogs have natural instincts that favor cooperation with their fellow dogs. Many domestic dogs, either through instinct or breeding, can correctly interpret and respond to signals given by a human handler.

Most dogs live with people who want them to behave in ways that make them pleasant to be around, keep them safe, and provides for the safety of other humans and pets. Dogs do not figure out basic obedience on their own. The fundamental rule that must be remembered is that one should never apply human standards of society onto the dog with the assumption that the dog will understand.

The hardest part of training is communicating with the dog in a humane way that the dog understands. The underlying principle of all communication is simple: reward desired behaviour while ignoring or correcting undesired behaviour.

Basic pet obedience training usually consists of seven behaviours:

- Sit
- Down
- Stay
- Recall ('come', 'here' or 'in')

- Close (or loose-leash walking)
- Heel
- Up (standing up without jumping)

Corrections are a form of punishment. Corrections can be physical (i.e. leash correction) or mental (i.e. withdrawing a reward). The dog's personality, the behaviour, and the importance of the correct behaviour should all be taken into account in using corrections with your dog. In a nutshell, negative corrections should only be used to eliminate a behaviour and positive rewards to repeat a behaviour.

Basic Training Classes

Professional dog trainers train the dog's owner to train his or her dog. To be most effective, the owner must use and reinforce the techniques taught to the dog. Owners and dogs who attend class together have an opportunity to learn more about each other and how to work together under a trainer's guidance. Training is most effective if all those who handle the dog take part in the training to ensure consistent commands, methods, and enforcement. Classes also help socialize a dog to other people and dogs. Training classes are offered by many kennels, pet stores, and independent trainers.

Group classes may not be available until the puppy has completed all of its vaccinations (around 3-4 months of age). Some trainers offer puppy socialization classes in which puppies can enroll immediately after being placed in their permanent homes as long as disease risk is minimal and puppies have received initial vaccinations. In most cases, basic training classes accept only puppies who are at least 3 to 6 months old. It's recommended to start training as soon as the puppy comes into your home. Puppies may also be trained individually by the trainer visiting the dog's home beginning as early as 8 weeks.

A puppy requires discipline, consistency, and the patience of its owner. The puppy training phase is integral in raising a healthy and happy dog and keeping a safe and fun home environment.

Dogs are expressive and may communicate needs by biting, whining, and getting fidgety. Changing one's own conduct may be effective in changing a puppy's behaviour.

House training is an important issue for puppies. Various methods of house training will work although the key is to be consistent. With regularly enforced rules, litter box, crate, or paper training can be successful.

Advanced Training Classes

This type of training is more complex and usually suitable for dogs who have completed level one (basic training) or an equivalent level of adult dog training classes.

Individual Training

This training is ideal for dogs that have an urgent or unique training problem or are not suitable for group training. Dogs not suitable for group training are those who are reactive or aggressive to other dogs or people or may have a fear of certain situations. This type of training would normally be undertaken where the problem normally occurs rather than a classroom situation.

There is also puppy training which is mostly just socialization and introducing puppies to meet and greet with other puppies and play with them.

Communication

Fundamentally, dog training is about communication. From the human perspective, the handler is communicating to the dog what behaviours are correct, desired, or preferred in different circumstances and what behaviours are undesirable.

A handler must understand communication from the dog. The dog can signal that he is unsure, confused, nervous, happy, excited, and so on. The emotional state of the dog is an important consideration in directing the training, as a dog that is stressed or distracted will not learn efficiently.

According to Learning Theory there are four important messages that the handler can send the dog:

- Reward or release marker
- Correct behaviour. You have earned a reward.
- Keep going signal (KGS)
- Correct behaviour. Continue and you will earn a reward.
- No reward marker (NRM)
- Incorrect behaviour. Try something else.
- Punishment marker

Incorrect behaviour. You have earned punishment.

Using consistent signals or words for these messages enables the dog to understand them more quickly.

It is important to note that the dog's reward is not the same as the reward marker. The reward marker is a signal that tells the dog that he has earned the reward. Rewards can be praise, treats, play, or anything that the dog finds rewarding. Failure to reward after the reward marker diminishes the value of the reward marker and makes training more difficult.

The meanings of the four signals are taught to the dog through repetition, so that he may form an association by classical conditioning so that the dog associates the punishment marker with the punishment itself. These messages may be communicated verbally or with nonverbal signals. Mechanical clickers are frequently used as a reward marker, as are the words 'yes!' or 'good!'. The word 'no!' is a common punishment marker. 'Whoops!' is a common NRM. A KGS is commonly a repeated syllable (such as 'g-g-g-g-g' or a drawn out word such as 'good'.)

Hand signals and body language also play an important part in learning for dogs. Some sources contend that the most effective marker is the human voice.

Dogs do not generalize commands easily. A command which may work indoors might be confusing out-of-doors or in a different situation. The command will need to be re-taught in each new situation. This is sometimes called 'cross-contextualization', meaning the dog has to apply what's been learned to many different contexts.

Understanding

Training a dog takes time and patience. Canines seem to understand what the trainer wants fairly quickly. This corresponds to Animal Cognition-the mental capacity of non-human animals. The dog takes in odors, sights, and sounds to remember something it has been taught.

For example, when the trainer says 'sit', there should be a set tone and a hand motion. After the dog has experienced seeing and hearing this routinely, along with obtaining the muscle memory, the action of 'sitting' becomes an image set in their minds. The next time the trainer says 'sit' with the same tone and motion, the dog receives an image showing it the action and is, therefore, able to sit.

Clarity while demanding what a canine does is also of great importance. The dog associates the words the handler says with not only the tone, but also with the sound of the letters in each word. 'Sit' ends with a strong 'T', while 'Stay' ends with a drawn out vowel sound. The canine does not understand the difference between consonants and vowels, but the sound associated with the words, along with the handler's tone, allows the dog to associate an auditory element to each command. In return, the canine is able to recall the commands due to the words' unique connection to the dog's mental and auditory senses.

Reward and Punishment

Most training revolves around establishing consequences for the dog's behaviour. Operant conditioning defines these following four types of consequences:

1. **Positive reinforcement** adds something to the situation to increase the chance of the behaviour being exhibited again.
2. **Negative reinforcement** removes something from the situation to increase the chance of the behaviour being exhibited again.
3. **Positive punishment** adds something to the situation to decrease the chance of the behaviour being exhibited again.
4. **Negative punishment** removes something from the situation to decrease the chance of the behaviour being exhibited again.

Most trainers claim that they use 'positive training methods'. Generally, this means using reward-based training to increase good behaviour rather than physical punishment to decrease bad behaviour.

Dogs should not be punished by being placed within a cage, crate, or carrier, especially one similar to where they eat or sleep. While this may confine the dog from further disruptive behaviour, and also may seem similar to "sending a child to their room" as a form of punishment, the dog's mind will unfortunately begin to associate the cage with punishment, and will experience anxiety if put into the container, as a result of the negative feelings associated with it. Punishment involving confinement is an unusual and confusing type of situation for a dog, and should not be used.

Rewards

Positive reinforcers can be anything that the dog finds rewarding - special food treats, the chance to play with a tug toy, social interaction with other dogs, or the owner's attention. The more rewarding a dog finds a particular reinforcer, the more work he will be prepared to do in order to obtain the reinforcer. Just being happy about a dog's accomplishment is a reward to them.

Some dog trainers for example suggest using treats that are particularly favoured by your pooch. Your dog or puppy may particularly enjoy liver treats or cheese. However, always make sure that the treat that you use as a positive reinforcer is healthy and will not damage your dog or puppy's overall health.

Some trainers go through a process of teaching a puppy to strongly desire a particular toy, in order to make the toy a more powerful positive reinforcer for good behaviour. This process is called 'building prey drive', and is commonly used in the training of Narcotics Detection and Police Service dogs. The goal is to produce a dog who will work independently for long periods of time, in the hopes of earning access to its special toy reward.

Corrections are only effective when paired with teaching the dog desired behaviours, but tend to be ineffective without teaching the dog the proper ways to avoid the correction and achieve reward. Corrections should only be administered as appropriate for the dog's personality, age, experience and physical and emotional condition. Some dogs may show signs of fear or anxiety with harsh verbal corrections. Other dogs may ignore a verbal reprimand. Some dogs develop an aversion or fear of water, when water is sprayed at them as an aversive.

Choke Collar

The choke collar is a length of metal-link chain with a large circular ring on either end. The chain is slid through one of these rings and it is slid over the dog's head. When the dog displays an undesirable behaviour the collar is tightened. This is primarily used in traditional dog training.

Prong Collar

The prong collar is made of metal links that fit together by connecting through long, usually blunt, teeth that point inward toward the dog's neck.

A section of this collar is made of a loop of chain links that tighten the collar when pulled, pinching the dog's neck. The use of these collars is controversial and is opposed by animal rights groups such as PETA. This collar is mainly used in traditional dog training. Some dog training organisations will not allow members to use them PAACT.

Radio-controlled Collars

These consist of a radio receiver attached to the collar and a transmitter that the trainer holds. When triggered, the collar delivers an aversive. The specific aversives vary with different makes of collars. Some emit sounds, some vibrate, some release citronella or other aerosol sprays, some apply electrical stimulation. A few collars incorporate several of these. Of these, electrical stimulation is the most common and the most widely used. Early electrical collars provided only a single, high-level shock and were useful only to punish undesirable behaviour. Modern electrical collars are adjustable, allowing the trainer to match the stimulation level to the dog's sensitivity and temperament. They deliver a consistent and measured level of aversive stimulation that produces significant discomfort and startle without risk of producing permanent physical injury. Lindsay finds these collars inappropriate for use as the initial or primary means for establishing basic obedience control. Lindsay says that competent electronic training appears to promote positive social attachment, safety, and reward effects. The manufacturers of most of these collars also warn against using them for cases of aggression.

Martingale Collar

The martingale collar is a collar that has only a section on it that will tighten when pulled. It consists of the main collar piece, as well as a smaller chain or fabric loop where the leash attaches. This is different from the choke collar that will tighten indefinitely. They are often considered safer than a choke collar because they will release tension instantly, while a choke collar often gets stuck. While they are now mainly used as a training collar, they were originally called Greyhound collars and used on breeds such as Sighthounds whose necks are as big around as their heads and can easily slip out of a flat buckle collar. The chain loop allows the collar to be loose and comfortable, but tightens if the dog attempts to back out of it.

Head Collar

The head collar is very similar to a halter on a horse. The theory it is that if you have control of the head, you have control of the body. The head collar generally consists of two loops, one behind the ears and the other over the nose. This tool makes it more difficult for the dog to pull on its leash.

No Pull Harness

The no-pull harness is worn on the body of the animal. The no-pull harness differs significantly from the standard harness since it makes it harder for the dog to pull because it distributes energy over the dog's back and shoulders. The no-pull harness restricts the movement of the dog's body when the dog pulls. Like the head collar, the no-pull harness does not teach the dog not to pull. It only makes it harder for the dog to pull.

Specialized Training

Dogs are also trained for specific purposes, including:

- Detection dogs
- Assistance dogs
- Herding dogs, livestock guardian dogs, and sheep dogs
- Hunting dogs
- Police dogs
- Rescue dogs
- *Schutzhund* German for 'protection dog'. There are three disciplines the dog must achieve (tracking, obedience, and personal protection).
- Individual training

Guard Animals

Due to their natural social structure—which is territorial and protective of companions —companion animals may exhibit some form of alert behaviour toward intruders. Guard dogs and police dogs are not simultaneously intended to be companion animals.

Guard dogs are defined as canines that, either by training or by instinct, protect either persons or property. A well-trained guard dog protects on command and 'turns-off' on command as well.

Several methods to train guard animals include the western (the Koehler Method, developed by William Koehler, a military dog trainer and animal trainer for Walt Disney productions) and eastern methods. The *Schutzhund* sport also includes a protection phase in which the dog bites a padded sleeve worn by a 'decoy' who plays the role of a 'bad guy' threatening the dog's handler. The dog must also release on command and guard the decoy.

In some circumstances, when dogs are left alone to guard property it may be necessary to train them to not eat treats or other food items offered by unknown persons.

Cynophobia

Cynophobia is the abnormal fear of dogs. Cynophobia is classified as a specific phobia, under the subtype 'animal phobias. According to researcher of the Laboratory for the Study of Anxiety Disorders at the University of Texas, animal phobias are among the most common of the specific phobias and 36 per cent of patients who seek treatment report being afraid of dogs or cats. Although snakes and spiders are more common animal phobias, cynophobia is especially debilitating because of the high prevalence of dogs (in the United States estimated at over 62 million in 2003). The Diagnostic and Statistical Manual of Mental Disorders (DSM-IV-TR) reports that only

12 per cent to 30 per cent of those suffering from a specific phobia will seek treatment. Following is an exploration of the diagnosis, etiology and treatments involved in cynophobia.

The DSM-IV-TR provides the following criteria for the diagnosis of a specific phobia:

- the persistent fear of an object or situation;
- exposure to the feared object provokes an immediate anxiety response;
- adult patients recognize that the fear is excessive, unreasonable or irrational (this is not always the case with children);
- exposure to the feared object is most often avoided altogether or is endured with dread;
- the fear interferes significantly with daily activities (social, familial, occupational, etc.);
- minor patients (those under the age of 18) have symptoms lasting for at least six months;
- anxiety, panic attacks or avoidance cannot be accounted for by another mental disorder.

The book *Phobias* defines a panic attack as "a sudden terror lasting at least a few minutes with typical manifestations of intense fear". These manifestations may include palpitations, sweating, trembling, difficulty breathing, the urge to escape, faintness or dizziness, dry mouth, nausea and/or several other symptoms. As with other specific phobias, patients suffering from cynophobia may display a wide range of these reactions when confronted with a live dog or even when thinking about or presented with an image (static or filmed) of a dog. Furthermore, classic avoidance behaviour is also common and may include staying away from areas where dogs might be (i.e., a park), crossing the street to avoid a dog, or avoiding the homes of friends and/or family who own a dog.

Age

Researchers, in their book *Specific Phobias*, concluded that the age of onset for animal phobias is usually early childhood, between the ages of five and nine. A study done in South Africa by researchers further confirms this conclusion for patients suffering from cynophobia and additionally found dog phobia developing as late as age 20.

Gender

Researchers also state that animal phobias are more common in females than males. Furthermore, researcher, a psychiatrist investigating virtual reality therapy as a possible method of therapy for anxiety disorders, goes on to provide data that although prevalent in both men and women, 75 per cent to 90 per cent of patients reporting specific phobias of the animal subtype are women.

Acquisition

A current theory for fear acquisition presented by researcher in 1977 maintains that there are three conditions by which fear is developed. These include direct personal experience, observational experience, and informational or instructional experience. For example, direct personal experience consists of having a personal negative encounter with a dog such as being bitten. In contrast, seeing a friend attacked by a dog and thus developing a fear of dogs would be observational experience. Whereas both of these types of experiences involves a live dog, informational or instructional experience simply includes being told directly or indirectly (i.e., information read in a book, film, parental cues such as avoidance or dislike, etc.) that dogs are to be feared.

A study was conducted at the State University of New York by researcher, to distinguish the significance of these three conditions upon the development of cynophobia. Thirty-seven women ages 18 to 21 were first screened into two groups: fearful of dogs and non-fearful of dogs. Next, each woman was given a questionnaire which asked if she had ever had a frightening and/or painful confrontation with a dog, what her expectation was upon encountering a dog (pain, fear, etc.), and subjectively, what was the probability of that expectation actually occurring. The results indicated that, while non-fearful subjects had a different expectation of what would happen when encountering a dog, painful experiences with dogs were common among both groups; therefore, the study concluded that other factors must effect whether or not these painful experiences will develop into dog phobia.

Although Rachman's theory is the accepted model of fear acquisition, cases of cynophobia have been cited in which none of these three causes apply to the patient. In a speech given at the 25th Annual Meeting of the Society for Psychophysiological Research, researcher proposed that animal fears in particular are likely to be an evolutionary remnant of the necessity "to escape and to avoid becoming the prey of predators". Furthermore, in his book *Overcoming Animal/Insect Phobias*, researcher suggests that in the absence of Rachman's three causes, providing that the patient's memory is sound, biological factors may be a fourth cause of fear acquisition—meaning that the fear is inherited or is a throwback to an earlier genetic defense mechanism. In any case, these causes may in actuality be a generalization of a complicated blend of both learning and genetics.

Treatment

The most common methods for the treatment of specific phobias are systematic desensitization and in vivo or exposure therapy.

Systematic Desensitization Therapy

Systematic desensitization therapy was introduced by Joseph Wolpe in 1958 and employs relaxation techniques with imagined situations. In a controlled environment, usually the therapist's office, the patient will be instructed to visualize a threatening situation (i.e., being in the same room with a dog). After determining the patient's anxiety level, the therapist then coaches the patient in breathing exercises and relaxation techniques in order to reduce their anxiety to a normal level. The therapy continues until the imagined situation no longer provokes an anxious response.

This method was utilized in the above mentioned study done by Drs. Hoffmann and Human whereby twelve female students at the Arcadia campus of Technikon Pretoria College in South Africa were found to possess symptoms of cynophobia. These twelve students were provided with systematic desensitization therapy one hour per week for five to seven weeks; after eight months, the students were contacted again to evaluate the effectiveness of the therapy. Final results indicated the study was fairly successful with 75 per cent of the participants showing significant improvement eight months after the study.

However, in his book, *Virtual Reality Therapy for Anxiety Disorders*, researcher questions the effectiveness of systematic desensitization as the intensity of the perceived threat is reliant on the patient's imagination and could therefore produce a false response in regards to the patient's level of anxiety. His research into recent technological developments has made it possible to integrate virtual reality into systematic desensitization therapy in order to accurately recreate the threatening situation. At the time of publication, there had been no studies done to determine its effectiveness.
In vivo or exposure therapy

In vivo or exposure therapy is considered the most effective treatment for cynophobia and involves systematic and prolonged exposure to a dog until the patient is able to experience the situation without an adverse response. This therapy can be conducted over several sessions or, as researcher showed in a study done in 1988, can be done in a single multi-hour session. This study utilized 20 female patients suffering from various specific phobias and ranging in age from 16 to 44. Patients were each provided with an individual therapy session in which researcher exposure therapy with modeling (where another person demonstrates how to interact with the feared object) to reduce or completely cure the phobia. As each patient was gradually exposed to the feared stimulus, she was encouraged to approach and finally interact with it as her anxiety decreased, concluding the session when fear had been reduced by 50 per cent or completely eliminated. Once the session was concluded, the patient was then to continue interaction with the feared object on her own to reinforce what had been learned in the therapy session. Researcher were collected over a seven-year period and concluded that "90 per cent of the patients were much improved or completely recovered after a mean of 2.1 hours of therapy".

Self-help Treatment

Although most commonly done with the help of a therapist in a professional setting, exposure therapy is also possible as a self-help treatment. First, the patient is advised to enlist the help of an assistant who can help set-up the exposure environment, assist in handling the dog during sessions, and demonstrate modeling behaviours. This should also be someone who the patient trusts implicitly and who has no fear of dogs. Then, the patient compiles a hierarchy of fear provoking situations based on their rating of each situation. For example, on a scale from 0 to 100, a patient may feel that looking at photos of dogs may cause a fear response of only 50, however, petting a dog's head may cause of fear response of 100. This list of situations is then put into order from least fearful (looking at dog photos) to most fearful (petting a dog's head) and the assistant helps the patient to identify common elements that contribute to the fear (i.e., size of the dog, colour, how it moves, noise, whether or not it is restrained, etc.). Next, the assistant helps the patient recreate the least fearful situation in a safe, controlled environment, continuing until the patient has had an opportunity to allow the fear to subside thus reinforcing the realization that the fear is unfounded. Once a situation has been mastered, the next fearful situation is recreated and the process is repeated until all the situations in the hierarchy have been experienced.

Recovery Timeframe and Maintenance

Whether utilizing systematic desensitization therapy or exposure therapy, several factors will determine how many sessions will be required to completely remove the phobia; however, some studies have shown that those who overcome their phobia are usually able to maintain the improvement over the long-term. As avoidance contributes to the perpetuation of the phobia, constant, yet safe, real world interaction is recommended during and after therapy in order to reinforce positive exposure to the animal.

CHAPTER 15

Dogs Notable in Their Own Right

ACTOR DOGS

Commercials

- Axelrod, probable Basset Hound - appeared in commercials and print ads for Flying 'A' Service Station advertisements in the 1960s.
- Cheeka, a Pug who appeared in the popular 'You & I' advertising campaign of Hutch's cellular service in India, along with the child actor Jayaram.
- Gidget, a female Chihuahua, was featured in a Taco Bell advertising campaign as the 'Taco Bell Chihuahua'. She also played the role of Bruiser's mother in *Legally Blonde 2*
- Honey Tree Evil Eye, a female Bull Terrier, was known as Spuds MacKenzie in her role as the Budweiser spokes-dog.
- Paddington, a Golden Retriever, is the main character of Bush's Baked Beans commercials. In the commercials, the dog's owner, president of the company, pleads for the dog to maintain the secret family recipe. The punchline of the commercials is the dog stating 'Roll that beautiful bean footage'.
- Storm, a dark-coloured German Shepherd who appeared in numerous Los Angeles television ads for Ralph Williams Ford in the 1960s. The ad would begin with the sales manager on screen, introducing himself 'and this is my dog, Storm' (who was usually lounging on the hood of the first car to be featured). These commercials became so familiar to Southern California viewers that they were parodied by comedians and inspired rival car dealer Cal Worthington to begin a decades-long tradition of commercials featuring animals as diverse as elephants and snakes, each of which is introduced as 'my dog, Spot'.

Film

- Ace the Wonder Dog, actor that appeared in numerous films and film serials in the 1930s nd 1940s.

- Baxter, the dog in the film Anchorman.
- Beasley, a Dogue de Bordeaux, starred in the film *Turner & Hooch*.
- Ben (II), a Golden Retriever, has appeared in many films. His characters have included Shadow in *Homeward Bound: The Incredible Journey*, William in *Maybe Baby*, Rusty in *Purely Belter* and Messenger in *Made in Hong Kong*.
- Blair, a Collie, starred in Rescued by Rover in 1905, and was the first dog screen star.
- Buddy, a Golden Retriever, starred in the 1997 film *Air Bud* but died a year later because of cancer.
- Buck, a German Shepherd, starred in *Call of the Wild* movie for tv.
- D.J., a Siberian Husky, played the roles of Demon in *Snow Dogs* and Max in *Eight Below*.
- Researcher, played the leading role of Benji in the movie of the same name and had a role on the TV series *Petticoat Junction*.
- Jean, the Vitagraph Dog, screen's first leading canine, starring in movies from 1908 to 1913.
- Jed, (1977-June 1995) Appeared in *The Thing (film)*, *The Journey of Natty Gann* and *White Fang*.
- Kuma, has been seen in several movies, including the short film *Saving Angelo*.
- Lady, the name of the Basenji dog in the movie *Goodbye, My Lady*.
- Max, a Jack Russell Terrier, played Milo, Jim Carrey's faithful and intelligent dog in the 1994 movie *The Mask*.
- Mushroom, a dog who starred as the Peltzer family dog in Gremlins.
- Moonie, a Chihuahua, played the role of Elle Woods' tiny dog Bruiser in *Legally Blonde* and *Legally Blonde 2*.
- Moose and his son Enzo in *My Dog Skip*.
- Mother Teresa, a Newfoundland dog and the major canine character in the movie *Must Love Dogs*.
- Pard, a mutt with a crippled foreleg, stars with Jack Pickford and Marguerite De La Motte in 1919's 'In Wrong' for Vitagraph. Pard does tricks in the film.
- Pal, a Collie, played Lassie in the movie *Lassie Come Home* (based on the novel by Eric Knight).
- Pete the Pup, appeared in the *Our Gang* (*Little Rascals*) series.
- Rin Tin Tin, was the name given to several German Shepherd Dogs who starred in many Warner Brothers film and television productions.
- Skippy, a wire haired fox terrier who, among other roles in 1930s films, played Asta in the Thin Man series.
- Strongheart, also known as Etzel von Oeringen, was the first German Shepherd with name-above-the-title billing in a film. He starred in an

adaptation of *White Fang*, released in 1925, and *The Return of Boston Blackie*, released in 1927.

- Sure Grip's Rattler, an American Bulldog, played the role of Chance in *Homeward Bound: The Incredible Journey*.
- Sykes, star of several films, adverts and TV series.
- Tango, a Golden Retriever, stars as Bailey in the film *Bailey's Billion*.
- Terry, a Cairn Terrier, played Toto in the 1939 movie adaptation of *The Wizard of Oz*.
- Zimbo the dog, played Homo the Wolf in the 1928 American silent film The Man Who Laughs directed by the German Expressionist filmmaker Paul Leni.
- Zip, a Blue Heeler Australian Cattle Dog famous for his role in the 1995 film *Last of the Dogmen* Zip's character is named Zip and has a touching storyline many viewers remember.

Television

- "Beauregard the Wonder Dog", appeared regularly though unspectacularly on *Hee Haw*.
- Beejay, a German Shepherd, was the first Rex on Inspector Rex.
- Bernadette portrayed the Basset Hound "Cleo" in the 1950s TV series The People's Choice.
- Buddy, a Golden Retriever, who played Comet on the TV show *Full House*.
- 'Bullet the Wonder Dog', a black and silver German Shepherd Dog that appeared regularly on the TV show *The Roy Rogers Show*.
- Happy, furry white dog playing Happy on the TV show *7th Heaven*.
- London portrayed Hobo in *The Littlest Hobo* series. The character originated in an earlier film.
- Zeltim Odie Peterson, aka Odie the Talking Pug - a pug that said 'I Love You' on various talk shows.
- Maui, a border collie mix, played Murray on the TV show *Mad About You*.
- Molly, a Bichon Frise, who played alongside Bruce Gyngell in the Australian mini-series *Meweth*.
- Moose and his son Enzo, played Eddie on the TV show *Frasier*.
- Petra, a mixed breed, was the first *Blue Peter* dog (The 'original' Petra died after making one appearance and was replaced by a look-alike, this was kept secret until many years after the substitute's death).
- Pussy Galore played Truffles, Mildred's terrier, in the British sitcom *George & Mildred*.
- Shep, a Border Collie, was featured on the *Blue Peter* television series.
- Soccer, a Jack Russell Terrier, starred in the PBS show *Wishbone*.

- Tiger, appeared in *The Brady Bunch* and played a dog named Blood in the movie *A Boy and His Dog*.
- Madison, a Labrador Retriever, best known for playing the role of Vincent on the television series *Lost*.
- Buck, a Briard, played the role of Buck Bundy on the TV show *Married ... with Children*.
- Prada, Breezy and Windy, who portrayed Captain Archer's dog Porthos on *Star Trek: Enterprise*.
- Kyte, a Belgian Tervuren famous for playing Wellard in *East Enders*.
- Rin Tin Tin IV, a German shepherd, played the role of Rin Tin Tin, AKA 'Rinty' on the TV show *The Adventures of Rin Tin Tin*.
- Serena, a small black poodle owned by actress Thelma Scott, appeared as Claire Houghton's pet, Serena, in the final year of the Australian soap opera, *Number 96*.
- Sugar-Pie, the dog of model Anna Nicole Smith, starred on the TV series Anna Nicole Show on E!
- 'Top Gear Dog', a dog owned by Richard Hammond who occasionally appears on *Top Gear*.

Athlete Dogs

- Ashley Whippet, the first disc dog, was a canine athlete of the 1970s and three time winner of the Canine Frisbee Disc World Championships.
- Mick the Miller, a racing Greyhound, was the first greyhound to win the English Derby in successive years and the first greyhound to run a 525 yard course in under 30 seconds.
- Master McGrath, an Irish Greyhound whose racing victories and fame gained him an audience with the British Royal Family.
- Snip Nua, an Irish racing Greyhound partly owned by comedian Dara Ó Briain. Snip Nua's racing was viewed by 3 million UK viewers on the show *Three men go to Ireland*.
- Cindy, a Greyhound who earned Guinness World Record's Highest Jump by a Dog. Cindy cleared a 5.5-foot hurdle.
- King Buck, a Labrador Retriever, successfully completed an unprecedented 63 consecutive series in the National Championship Stake and was the National Retriever Field Trial Club champion for two successive years (in 1952 and 1953), which accomplishment was not duplicated for nearly 40 years. He was also the first dog to appear on a United States postage stamp.

Faithful Dogs

- Bobbie, the Wonder Dog, after accidental abandonment on a cross-country trip, Bobbie made his way back over 2800 miles to his family's home.

- Bob the Railway Dog a loyal traveller and drivers companion on the South Australian Railways in the late 19th century.
- Dragon, a greyhound, accuses (attacks) the murderer of his owner, Aubry De Montdidier, and both are sentenced by Charles V of France to trial by combat. The dog wins. Dramatized in The Dog of Montarges.
- Fido, a mixed-breed dog, whose master, Carlo Soriani, had died in an air raid over Borgo San Lorenzo (near Florence, in Italy) in 1943, during World War II. Fido waited in vain, for the following 14 years, for Soriani's return, going daily at the bus stop in Luco del Mugello (a *frazione* of Borgo) where the man used to get off after coming home from work.
- Gelert is the name of a legendary dog associated with the village of Beddgelert.
- Greyfriars Bobby, a Skye Terrier in Edinburgh, Scotland, was loyal to his master long after his master's death in 1858. Until Bobby's death 14 years later, he reportedly spent every night at his master's grave. A statue in memorial of Greyfriars Bobby was erected near the graveyard.
- Heidi, a Jack Russell Terrier from Scotland, made her way down a 500 foot vertical drop to get to the body of her owner (after he fell to his death while hiking) and stood guard over his body for days in 2001.
- Hachiko, an Akita who became a symbol of loyalty in Japan, is now honored by a statue in Tokyo. Hachiko is famous for his loyalty to his long dead master, by returning to the train station and waiting for his master to return, every day for the next nine years during the time the train was scheduled to arrive.
- Old Drum, an American Foxhound whose death at the hands of a neighbor was the subject of a lawsuit and George Graham Vest's famous closing argument 'Eulogy to a Dog'.
- Old Shep, a Border Collie, who - after seeing the coffin of his master loaded onto a train in Fort Benton, Montana in 1936 - maintained a vigil at the station for six years.
- Pompey, a Pug that foiled an assassination attempt on the life of William The Silent, Prince of Orange.
- Baekgu, the Korean Jindo Dog, After being sold by original owner due to economical hardship, to a new owner 300 km away, came back to the original owner after 7 months.
- Squeak, a Jack Russel Terrier who would not leave the body of his owner, Zimbabwean farmer Terry Ford, after Ford was murdered in 2002 by a violent mob carrying out Zimbabwean president Robert Mugabe's land seizure programs. The photo of little Squeak guarding Ford's bloody body raised world-wide awareness of land-related violence in Zimbabwe.
- Waghya, Chhatrapati Shivaji's pet dog. Waghya is known as the epitome of loyalty and eternal devotion. After Shivaji's death, the dog mourned

and jumped into his master's funeral pyre and immolated himself. A statue was put up on a pedestal next to Shivaji's tomb at Raigad Fort.

- Leao, a mix breed who stayed by the side of her owner who died on January 2011 during Brazil's flood. His owner was Cristina Cesário Maria Santana. Her body (along with other 3 bodies of members of the family) was retrieved by the rescuers after looking at the dog digging over some mud.

Guide and Service Dogs

- Buddy, a female German Shepherd, was the first formally trained guide dog in the United States. She belonged to Morris Frank, who worked to establish The Seeing Eye, the first dog guide school in America.
- Endal, voted 'Dog of the Millennium', has been publicised by his human partner for over a decade.
- Lucky and Flo, a pair of black Labrador Retrievers, notable for being the first animals trained to detect optical discs by scent. They are sponsored by the MPAA and FACT, as part of an initiative to combat copyright infringement relating to motion pictures and DVD discs.
- Station Jim - a popular and successful collector for the Widows' and Orphans' fund of the Great Western Railway.
- Trixie Koontz, the Golden Retriever companion of Dean Koontz, is a retired guide dog and the purported author of *Life Is Good*. Trixie passed away on 6/30/07 at home. She was euthanized on her favourite couch with Koontz and his wife holding her in their arms. She had a tumor in her heart.
- Rajah, a German Shepherd, was the first Police dog to serve in New Zealand.
- Trakr, a German Shepherd who found the last survivor of the World Trade Center attack on September 11, 2001.
- Nero, a male German Shepherd K9 unit in Oakland, California was on patrol with his handler Craig Chew when his handler was shot five times and saved his life by attacking the shooter until reinforcements could be called to take control of the situation.

Real Dogs in Literature

- Beautiful Joe, an abused Airedale who was rescued from a brutal master, inspired an 1894 bestselling novel of the same name.
- Jock of the Bushveld, a Staffordshire bull terrier from South Africa in the 1880 whose owner wrote a book about their travels together.
- Lad, a rough collie made famous by three of the novels, including *Lad, A Dog*, written by owner Albert Payson Terhune.
- Charley, a poodle owned by John Steinbeck, was made famous by the book *Travels With Charley*.

- Endal A paperback book entitled *Endal* published by Harper Collins was released on the February 9, 2009 and went straight to Number 5 in the UK Paperback best sellers list.
- Marley, a yellow Labrador Retriever, is featured in the memoir *Marley and Me*.
- Tulip, J.R. Ackerley's German shepherd, is the subject of Ackerley's *My Dog Tulip*.
- Wheely Willy, a paraplegic chihuahua who is the subject of two bestselling children's books.
- Mirabelle is a boston terrier and star of a children's book The Adventures of Mirabelle.
- Yukon was a half malamute, half wolf. He was author Ron D. Lawrence's dog and R.D. Lawrence wrote a book, The North Runner, as a tribute to this magnificent dog.

Dog Mascots

- Jonathan, a Husky, is the University of Connecticut's mascot, and is named after the state of Connecticut's first governor.
- Blue II, an English Bulldog, is the mascot of Butler University.
- Bully, a Bulldog, is the Mississippi State University mascot.
- Blitz, a purebred Boston Terrier, is the mascot of Wofford College.
- George Tirebiter, former mascot of the University of Southern California.
- Handsome Dan, a bulldog, is the Yale University mascot.
- Jack the Bulldog is the mascot of Georgetown University.
- Reveille, a collie, is the mascot of Texas A & M University.
- Uga, a Bulldog, serves as mascot for the University of Georgia.
- Smokey, a Blue Tick Hound, serves as mascot for the University of Tennessee.
- Dubs, an Alaskan Malamute, serves as a mascot for the University of Washington.
- Zeke the Wonder Dog, a Labrador Retriever, serves as a mascot for Michigan State University.
- Colonel Rock or 'Rocky', a bulldog, is the mascot of Western Illinois University.
- The English Bulldog is the mascot of the US Marine Corps as of 1922. They have included Jiggs and Jiggs II, Smedley and his successors and Chesty and his successors.
- Harvey the Hound, mascot for the Calgary Flames NHL team.
- Ralph the Dog, mascot for the Calgary Stampeders CFL team.
- Crazy Dog, owner and leader of Crazy Pets and inventor of the Train Me! Treats. (Fictional).
- Brian Boru, an Irish Wolfhound, mascot of the Royal Irish Regiment.

- Mex, the original mascot of the University of Oklahoma.
- Nigger, a black Labrador, the mascot of The Dambusters.
- Mirabelle,is a boston terrier and the mascot of Detail Gallery and star of the children's book, The Adventures of Mirabelle.

Dogs in Photography

- Fay Ray, a Weimaraner, was one of the photography subjects of her owner William Wegman. The name was a play on the name of Wegman's earlier dog Man Ray and the actress Fay Wray.
- Girella, a female Portuguese Water Dog, has been photographed with numerous musicians, as displayed on her website.
- Man Ray, a Weimaraner who belonged to William Wegman, was often photographed by his photographer owner.
- Mr. Winkle, a very small dog of uncertain breed, belongs to Lara Jo Regan, who has published many photos of Mr. Winkle in various costumes and poses.
- Sparky, of The Sparky Project, has been photographed and painted by several artists.
- Bulldog Abbie; an English Bulldog photographed and published commercially in both digital and printed formats.
- Chalcy, a Weimaraner, is featured in hundreds of photos in books and DVDs in the '101 Dog Tricks' series by Kyra Sundance.

Rescue Dogs

- Balto, a famous sled dog, was the lead dog on the final leg of the 1925 serum run to Nome (which relayed diphtheria antitoxin by dog sled across Alaska to combat an epidemic). Balto was memorialized with a statue in New York's Central Park. The Iditarod Race is a commemoration of the 1925 serum run.
- Barry, a famous Saint Bernard rescue dog, reportedly saved 40 people.
- Dakota; was a pitbull search and rescue dog that responded to over 100 searches missions including the search for the astronauts that lost their lives in the Space Shuttle Columbia disaster.
- Dusty, an Airedale Terrier, found a woman after she drove her car off the cliff above Nesika Beach, Oregon, on October 22, 2007, and his owner then led rescuers to the site.
- Gandalf, a black Shiloh Shepherd Search and Rescue dog owned by Misha Marshall, found missing boy scout Michael Auberry in March 2007.
- George, a Jack Russell Terrier who shielded a group of children in Manaia, New Zealand, from a pair of attacking pit bulls. He was killed by the pit bulls.
- Mancs, a Hungarian rescue dog, saved the lives of many people.

- Swansea Jack, Rescued people from Swansea bay and the River Tawe.
- Togo, a Siberian Husky, was the lead dog who led the longest track while the team had the antitoxin, during the 1925 serum run to Nome (which relayed diphtheria antitoxin by dog sled across Alaska to combat an epidemic).
- Tugg, a bull terrier that has gained a large internet following on facebook. He was found as an abused and abandoned dog, and has chronicled his recovery on the net for all to see.
- Velvet is a black Labrador Retriever and shepherd cattle mixed breed dog, who helped save three climbers when they became stranded on Mount Hood in Oregon on February 18, 2007.
- Approximately 350 search and rescue dogs worked at the World Trade Centre site following the September 11, 2001 attacks. Rescuers relied on the dogs' sense of smell and agility in tight spaces to seek survivors and recover the remains of victims.
- Appollo, a search and rescue dog who worked at World Trade Center site following the September 11, 2001 attacks.

Dogs in Science

- Brown Dog, killed after vivisection in February 1903. A memorial statue provoked riots.
- Ch. Fiacre's First and Foremost, low uric acid show dog.
- Marjorie, a depancreatized dog, was the subject of experiments by Frederick Banting and his assistant, Charles Best. Marjorie was kept alive for about 70 days on pancreas extract, which was the first success in the doctors' effort to uncover a means to control diabetes. Ultimately, this led Banting and Best to isolate insulin.
- Pavlov's dogs, who were subjects of Pavlov's research on classical conditioning.
- Snuppy, an Afghan Hound, was the first cloned dog.

Space Dogs

• The Soviets favoured dogs for early space flights, as opposed to the Americans, who preferred monkeys and chimpanzees.

- Laika, a female mixed-breed dog, became the first animal to enter orbit when she was launched into space aboard Sputnik 2. Laika's presence led to the mission being dubbed 'Muttnik'. She was also the first to die in orbit, as no provision was made to return her to the ground.
- Belka and Strelka, two Russian mixed breeds, went into space aboard Sputnik 5 and returned. They were the first animals to survive an orbital flight. Strelka later gave birth to a litter of puppies, one of which was given to Caroline Kennedy by Soviet Premier Nikita Khrushchev.

DOGS OF UNUSUAL SIZE

Small Dogs

- Big Boss, a Yorkshire Terrier, was listed as the smallest living dog in the 2002 edition of Guinness World Records. Big Boss was listed at 12 centimetres (4.7 in) tall when he was registered with Guinness.
- Danka Kordak Slovakia, a long-haired Chihuahua, holds the Guinness World Record as of 2007 for the shortest (in terms of height) living dog. She measured 13.7 centimetres (5.4 in) tall and 18.8 centimetres (7.4 in) long on May 30, 2004.
- Ducky, a three year old short coat Chihuahua from Charlton, Massachusetts, replaced Danka as the World's Smallest Dog according to the Daily Mail At only 12.4 centimetres (4.9 in), Ducky weighs less than 0.6 kilograms (1.3 lb).
- Heaven Sent Brandy, a female Chihuahua, is listed in the 2007 Guinness World Records as the smallest living dog in terms of length. She set the record on 31 January 2005, at 15 centimetres (6 in) long, from her nose to the tip of her tail.
- Sylvia, a matchbox-size Yorkshire Terrier owned by Arthur Marples of Blackburn, England, was the smallest dog in recorded history. The dog died in 1945 when she was almost two years old, at which point she stood 6 centimetres (2.4 in) tall at the shoulder, measured 9 centimetres (3.5 in) from nose tip to tail, and weighed 0.11 kilograms (3.9 oz).
- Tiny Pinocchio, an abnormally small Yorkshire Terrier, has appeared on several television programs including *Oprah* and the *Today Show*.

Big Dogs

- Gibson, a Harlequin Great Dane, is certified by Guinness World Records as the tallest living dog at 107 centimetres (42.1 in). Standing on his hind legs, the 77 kilograms (170 lb) dog is over 2.13 metres (7 ft) tall.
- Zorba, a male English Mastiff, was recognized by Guinness World Records as the heaviest dog in the world at 155.6 kilograms (343 lb). The record was set in November 1989, when Zorba was 8 years old. Zorba also held a record for the world's longest dog at 2.5 metres (8.2 ft).
- Giant George, a blue Great Dane which took over Gibson's record as the tallest living dog, measuring 109 cm (43 in) from paw to shoulder; 220 cm (7.2 ft) from head to tail.

Tall Dogs

- Giant George, a Great Dane who is currently recognised as the world's tallest dog, and the tallest dog ever.
- Calico Daisy, a Great Dane who is currently the world's largest living female dog at 36′ (91.44 cm) from withers to paw.

- Calico's friend is 6-0 'tall'.
- Gibson, a Great Dane who was the world's tallest dog until his death in August 2009.
- Titan, a Great Dane who was previously recognised as the world's tallest dog.

War Dogs

- Bamse, a Saint Bernard, was a symbol of the Free Norwegian Forces in World War II.
- Chesty, one of a family of bulldogs, serving as the official mascot of Marine Barracks, Washington, D.C. These dogs are actually enlisted in the US Marine Corps, most attaining the rank of corporal.
- Chips was a hero wardog of World War II.
- Gander, a Newfoundland, was posthumously awarded the Dicken Medal for his feats during the Battle of Hong Kong in World War II.
- Gunner, Canine air-raid early warning system during the bombing of Darwin in WWII.
- Horrie the Wog Dog, found in Egypt by Australian Forces in 1942 during World War II, saved the lives of many Australian soldiers. Horrie was refused admission back to Australia after service in Europe; he was saved by his mates smuggling him to his new home in Australia.
- Judy, a ship's dog who served with the Royal Navy, was the only animal to have been officially registered as a Japanese prisoner of war. She was awarded the Dickin Medal in 1946.
- Just Nuisance, the only dog to have been officially enlisted in the Royal Navy, was buried with full military honours upon his death in 1944.
- Lava, a mixed breed dog, was adopted as a puppy by the 1st Battalion 3rd Marines Unit nicknamed the *Lava Dogs*. He was rescued from Iraq in 2005 by Lieutenant Colonel Jay Kopelman. Lava is the subject of the book *From Baghdad, With Love* by Kopelman and Melinda Roth.
- Lex, the first actively working Military Working Dog to be adopted by family members of its handler, prior to being retired.
- Moustache (dog), said to have participated in several battles of the French Revolutionary and Napoleonic Wars.
- Nemo A534, a German Shepherd Dog who saved the life of his handler in battle despite having been shot in the nose and losing an eye.
- Nigger, a black Labrador Retriever belonging to Guy Gibson, gave his name as the codename for the Dam Busters mission in World War II. His name is usually edited out of modern versions of the film about the mission.
- Rags, a Signal Corps mascot during World War I.
- Rip, a Second World War search and rescue dog.

- Sabi, an Australian special forces explosives detection dog that spent almost 14 months missing in action (MIA) in Afghanistan before being recovered in 2009.
- Sergeant Stubby, the most decorated American war dog in US Military history, served during World War I. He was also a mascot at Georgetown University.

Sinbad and Crew, 1943

- Sinbad, the Coast Guard's most famous mascot. He was adopted by a crewman from the cutter Campbell prior to World War II. He was so beloved by the crew that they actually enlisted him in the Coast Guard. Sinbad had a book written about him.
- Smoky, hero war dog of World War II, was a Yorkshire Terrier who served with the 5th Air Force in the Pacific after she was adopted by Corporal William Wynne. Smoky was credited with twelve combat missions and awarded eight battle stars. Wynne authored a book about his adventures with Smoky entitled *Yorkie Doodle Dandy: Or, the Other Woman Was a Real Dog*.

Intelligent Dogs

- Betsy, one of the most intelligent dogs, who knows over 340 words.
- Donnie, a Doberman Pinscher featured on the National Geographic Channel show *Dog Genius* for his penchant for arranging his toys in geometric forms.
- Rico, a Border Collie, can recognize the names of more than 250 toys and fetch them on command.

Dogs that Aided Exploration

- Bud Nelson (canine), the first dog to travel across the United States.
- Chinook was the dog team leader for the Byrd Antarctic Expeditions and dubbed an 'All American Dog' in the 1920s.

Long-lived Dogs

- Bluey (dog), an Australian Cattle Dog that is officially the world's oldest dog. He died in 1939 at 29 years and 5 months of age.
- Chanel, a dachshund, was the world's oldest dog as of August 31, 2009 at 21 years old.
- Otto, a dachshund-terrier cross, currently the world's oldest dog at 20 years and eight months.

Show Dogs

- Canigou Cambrai, an English Cocker Spaniel that was best in show at Crufts in 1996.
- My Own Brucie, American Cocker Spaniel show dog.
- Tickle Em Jock, the first Scottish Terrier to win best-in-show at the Westminster Kennel Club Dog Show.

Notorious Dogs

- Dempsey, condemned to death under the United Kingdom's Dangerous Dogs Act 1991 but finally reprieved after three years of legal battles.
- Jackie, a Dalmatian-mix whose ability to give a Nazi salute garnered negative attention from Nazi Germany in World War II.

Ugly Dogs

- Elwood, a Chinese Crested- Chihuahua, mixed breed, was a winner of the World's Ugliest Dog Contest in 2007.
- Sam, a blind Chinese Crested hairless, was the three-time winner of the World's Ugliest Dog Contest.

Unique Dogs

- Faith, a Bipedal Dog
- Heart-kun is a Chihuahua in Japan born with a heart-shaped patch of brown hair on its white coated body.

Foundation Sires and Early Dogs

- Horand von Grafrath, the first registered German Shepherd Dog, and the foundation sire of the breed.
- Huddersfield Ben, an early Yorkshire Terrier, is universally regarded as the foundation sire of the breed.
- Obo II, foundation sire for all American Cocker Spaniels.
- Old Hemp, an early Border Collie.
- Old Jock, an early Fox Terrier.

Other Notable Dogs

- Malchik, a stray mongrel who resided in the Moscow Metro, and whose stabbing death sparked a public outcry.
- Nipper, the HMV (His Master's Voice) dog.
- Oscar, a Pug belonging to a professor at Virginia Commonwealth University, was the center of public controversy after his owner assigned an advertising class to make the dog famous.
- Oscar, canine hypnotist.
- Owney, an official United States Postal Service dog, rode the trains with the mail in the 19th century. After death, his body was stuffed and is on display in the National Postal Museum in Washington, D.C.
- Pickles discovered the Jules Rimet trophy (the Football World Cup) after it had been stolen in England in 1966.
- Presley, the boxer (dog), won the title of the Greatest American Dog in the CBS television show of the same name in 2008.
- Red Dog, a kelpie–cattle-dog cross who travelled around the Pilbara region of Western Australia from 1975 (when his truck-driver owner died), befriending many locals, until his death in 1979, believed to have been caused by deliberate strychnine poisoning.

- Robot, a dog who belonged to a boy named Simon, discovered the cave paintings at Lascaux in 1940.
- Saucisse, a candidate at the 2001 election of mayor in Marseille and also a candidate in the TV reality show *Secret Story 2009 (France)*.
- Sensation, the English Pointer featured on the logo of the Westminster Kennel Club Dog Show.
- Tawny, a yellow Labrador Retriever who in 1999 gave birth to 18 puppies in her very first litter. For this she received the 'Iams Mother of the Year' Award.
- Word, a male Lhasa Apso, was sentenced to death on May 4, 1993 following two biting incidents. He was incarcerated at the Seattle Animal Control Shelter for a total of eight years and 190 days before being released on November 10, 2001, which is the Guinness World Record for the longest time on dog death row.
- Champion WA Mozart Dolce Sinfonia ('Mozart') is a Yorkshire Terrier owned by socialite Sabrina A. Parisi. He was featured in the Krassimir Abramov music video for "Say Goodbye" and in the documentary *It's a Dog Life* from director Vibeke Muasya. On May 11, 2006, Mozart attended Krassimir's concert at the Kodak Theater in Hollywood, becoming the first dog to enter the venue.
- Natividad, an emaciated stray dog featured in a controversial display by artist Guillermo Vargas Habacuc in the Visual Arts Biennial of Central America, later the subject of widespread rumours on the Internet that he was starved to death by the artist.
- Willie Bean, a Golden Retriever, was the focus of several political satires during 2008.
- Bummer and Lazarus, a pair of famous stray dogs who lived in San Francisco during the 1860s, often associated with Emperor Norton.

CHAPTER 16
Dog Varities

The German Shepherd Dog (GSD, also known as an Alsatian), (German: *Deutscher Schäferhund*) is a breed of large-sized dog that originated in Germany. The German Shepherd is a relatively new breed of dog, with its origin dating to 1899. As part of the Herding Group, the German Shepherd is a working dog developed originally for herding and guarding sheep. Because of its strength, intelligence and abilities in obedience training it is often employed in police and military roles around the world. German Shepherds currently account for 4.6 per cent of all dogs registered with the American Kennel Club. Due to its loyal and protective nature, the German Shepherd is one of the most registered of breeds.

In Europe during the 1800s, attempts were being made to standardise breeds. The dogs were bred to preserve traits that assisted in their job of herding sheep and protecting flocks from predators. In Germany this was practiced within local communities, where shepherds selected and bred dogs that they believed had traits necessary for herding sheep, such as intelligence, speed, strength, and keen senses of smell. The results were dogs that were able to perform admirably in their task, but that differed significantly, both in appearance and ability, from one locality to another.

To combat these differences, the Phylax Society was formed in 1891 with the intention of creating standardised dog breeds in Germany. The society disbanded after only three years due to ongoing internal conflicts regarding the traits in dogs that the society should promote; some members believed dogs should be bred solely for working purposes, while others believed dogs should be bred also for appearance. While unsuccessful in their goal, the Phylax Society had inspired people to pursue standardising dog breeds independently.

Max von Stephanitz, an ex-cavalry captain and former student of the Berlin Veterinary College, was one such ex-member. He believed strongly that dogs should be bred for working.

In 1899, Von Stephanitz was attending a dog show when he was shown a dog named *Hektor Linksrhein*. Hektor was the product of few generations of selective breeding and completely fulfilled what Von Stephanitz believed a working dog should be. He was pleased with the strength of the dog and was so taken by the animal's intelligence and loyalty, that he purchased it immediately. After purchasing the dog he changed its name to Horand von Grafrath and Von Stephanitz founded the Verein für Deutsche Schäferhunde (Society for the German Shepherd Dog). Horand was declared to be the first German Shepherd Dog and was the first dog added to the society's breed register.

Horand became the centre-point of the breeding programmes and was bred with dogs belonging to other society members that displayed desirable traits. Although fathering many pups, Horand's most successful was *Hektor von Schwaben*. Hektor was inbred with another of Horand's offspring and produced *Beowulf*, who later fathered a total of eighty-four pups, mostly through being inbred with Hektor's other offspring. In the original German Shepherd studbook, Zuchtbuch fur Deutsche Schaferhunde (SZ), within the 2 pages of entries from SZ #41 to SZ #76, there are 4 Wolf Crosses. Beowulf's progeny also were inbred and it is from these pups that all German Shepherds draw a genetic link. It is believed the society accomplished its goal mostly due to Von Stephanitz's strong, uncompromising leadership and he is therefore credited with being the creator of the German Shepherd Dog.

When the UK Kennel Club first accepted registrations for the breed in 1919, fifty-four dogs were registered, and by 1926 this number had grown to over 8,000. The breed first gained international recognition at the decline of World War I after returning soldiers spoke highly of the breed, and animal actors Rin Tin Tin and Strongheart popularised the breed further. The first German Shepherd Dog registered in the United States was *Queen of Switzerland*; however, her offspring suffered from defects as the result of poor breeding, which caused the breed to suffer a decline in popularity during the late 1920s.

Popularity increased again after the German Shepherd *Sieger Pfeffer von Bern* became the 1937 and 1938 Grand Victor in American Kennel club dog shows, only to suffer another decline at the conclusion of World War II, due to anti-German sentiment of the time. As time progressed, their popularity increased gradually until 1993, when they became the third most popular breed in the United States. As of 2009, the breed was the second most popular in the US. Additionally, the breed is typically among the most popular in other registries. The German Shepherd Dog's physique is very well suited to athletic competition. They commonly compete in shows and competitions such as agility trials.

Name

The breed was named *Deutscher Schäferhund* by Von Stephanitz, literally translating to 'German Shepherd Dog'. The breed was so named due to its original purpose of assisting shepherds in herding and protecting sheep. At the time, all other herding dogs in Germany were referred to by this name; they thus became known as *Altdeutsche Schäferhunde* or Old German Shepherd Dogs. Shepherds were first exported to Britain in 1908, and the UK Kennel Club began to recognise the breed in 1919.

The direct translation of the name was adopted for use in the official breed registry; however, at the conclusion of World War I, it was believed that the inclusion of the word 'German' would harm the breed's popularity, due to the anti-German sentiment of the era. The breed was officially renamed by the UK Kennel Club to 'Alsatian Wolf Dog' which was also adopted by many other international kennel clubs. Eventually, the appendage "wolf dog" was dropped. The name Alsatian remained for five decades, until 1977, when successful campaigns by dog enthusiasts pressured the British kennel clubs to allow the breed to be registered again as German Shepherd Dogs. The word 'Alsatian' still appeared in parentheses as part of the formal breed name and was only removed in 2010.

Modern Breed

The modern German Shepherd is criticized for straying away from von Stephanitz's original ideology for the breed: that German Shepherds should be bred primarily as working dogs, and that breeding should be strictly controlled to eliminate defects quickly. Critics believe that careless breeding has promoted disease and other defects. Under the breeding programmes overseen by von Stephanitz, defects were quickly bred out; however, in modern times without regulation on breeding, genetic problems such as colour-paling, hip dysplasia, monorchidism, weakness of temperament, and missing teeth are common, as well as bent or folded ears which never fully turn up when reaching adulthood.

Description

German Shepherds are a large sized dog which generally are between 55 and 65 centimetres (22 and 26 in) at the withers and weigh between 22 and 40 kilograms (49 and 88 lb). The ideal height is 63 centimetres (25 in), according to Kennel Club standards. They have a domed forehead, a long square-cut muzzle and a black nose. The jaws are strong, with a scissor-like bite. The eyes are medium-sized and brown with a lively, intelligent, and self-assured look. The ears are large and stand erect, open at the front and parallel, but they often are pulled back during movement. They have a long neck, which is raised when excited and lowered when moving at a fast pace. The tail is bushy and reaches to the hock.

German Shepherds can be a variety of colours, the most common of which are the red, tan, brown, black, tan/black and red/black varieties. Both varieties have black masks and black body markings which can range from a classic 'saddle' to an over-all 'blanket'. Rarer colour variations include the sable, all-black, all-white, liver, and blue varieties. The all-black and sable varieties are acceptable according to most standards; however, the blue and liver are considered to be serious faults and the all-white is grounds for instant disqualification in some standards.

German Shepherds sport a double coat. The outer coat, which is shed all year round, is close and dense with a thick undercoat. The coat is accepted in two variants; medium and long. The long-hair gene is recessive, making the long-hair variety rarer. Treatment of the long-hair variation differs across standards; they are accepted under the German and UK Kennel Clubs but are considered a fault in the American Kennel Club.

German Shepherds were bred specifically for their intelligence, a trait for which they are now renowned. They are considered to be the third most intelligent breed of dog, behind Border Collies and Poodles.] In the book *The Intelligence of Dogs*, author Stanley Coren ranked the breed third for intelligence. He found that they had the ability to learn simple tasks after only five repetitions and obeyed the first command given 95 per cent of the time. Coupled with their strength, this trait makes the breed desirable as police, guard, and search and rescue dogs, as they are able to quickly learn various tasks and interpret instructions better than other large breeds.

German Shepherd Dogs are among the top five most popular dogs in the United States according to American Kennel Club statistics and well-trained and socialized German Shepherd Dogs have a reputation among many as being very safe. In the United States, one source suggests that German Shepherd Dogs are responsible for more reported bitings than any other breed, and suggest a tendency to attack smaller breeds of dogs.

An Australian report from 1999 provides statistics showing that German Shepherd Dogs are the third breed most likely to attack a person in some Australian locales.

However, the Centers for Disease Control and Prevention, which advises on dog bite prevention and related matters, states "There is currently no accurate way to identify the number of dogs of a particular breed, and consequently no measure to determine which breeds are more likely to bite or kill".

Similarly, the American Veterinary Medical Association through its Task Force on Canine Aggression and Canine-Human Interactions reports, "There are several reasons why it is not possible to calculate a bite rate for a breed or to compare rates between breeds. First, the breed of the biting dog may not be accurately recorded, and mixed-breed dogs are commonly described as if they were purebreds. Second, the actual number of bites that occur in a community is not known, especially if they did not result in serious injury. Third, the number of dogs of a particular breed or combination of breeds in a community is not known, because it is rare for all dogs in a community to be licensed, and existing licensing data is then incomplete." Moreover, studies rely on 'reported' bites, leading the National Geographic Channel television show The Dog Whisperer to conclude that small dog breeds are likely responsible for more bites than large dog breeds, but often go unreported.

In addition, according to the National Geographic Channel television show, Dangerous Encounters, the bite of a German Shepherd Dog has a force of over 238 pounds (compared with that of a Rottweiler, over 265-328 pounds of force, a Pitbull, 235 pounds of force, a Labrador Retriever, of approximately 230 pounds of force, or a human, of approximately 86 pounds of force). Regardless, one source indicates that fatalities have been attributed to over 30 breeds since 1975, including small breeds, such as the Pomeranian.

German Shepherds are highly active dogs, and described in breed standards as self-assured. The breed is marked by a willingness to learn and an eagerness to have a purpose. Shepherds have a loyal nature and bond well with people they know. However, they can become over-protective of their family and territory, especially if not socialized correctly. They are not inclined to become immediate friends with strangers. German Shepherds are highly intelligent and obedient. Some people believe they require a 'firm hand', but more recent research into training methods has shown they respond as well, if not better, to positive reward based training methods.

Many common ailments of the German Shepherds are a result of the inbreeding required early in the breed's life. One such common issue is hip and elbow dysplasia which may lead to the dog experiencing pain in later life, and may cause arthritis. A study by the University of Zurich in police working dogs found that 45 per cent were affected by degenerative spinal stenosis, although the sample studied was small. The Orthopedic Foundation for Animals found that 19.1 per cent of German Shepherd are affected by hip dysplasia. Due to the large and open nature of their ears, Shepherds are prone to ear infections. German Shepherds, like all large bodied dogs, are prone to bloat.

The average lifespan of a German Shepherd is 9.7 years, which is normal for a dog of their size. Degenerative myelopathy, a neurological disease, occurs with enough regularity specifically in the breed to suggest that the breed is predisposed to it. Additionally, German Shepherd Dogs have a higher than normal incidence of Von Willebrand Disease, a common inherited bleeding disorder.

Controversy

The Kennel Club is currently embroiled in a dispute with German Shepherd breed clubs about the issue of soundness in the show-strain breed. The show-strains have been bred with an extremely sloping back that causes poor gait and disease in the hind legs. Working-pedigree lines, such as those in common use as service dogs, generally retain the traditional straight back of the breed and do not suffer these problems to the same extent. The debate was catalyzed when the issue was raised in the BBC documentary, Pedigree

Dogs Exposed, which said that critics of the breed describe it as 'half dog, half frog'. An orthopedic vet remarked on footage of dogs in a show ring that they were 'not normal'.

The Kennel Club's position is that "this issue of soundness is not a simple difference of opinion, it is the fundamental issue of the breed's essential conformation and movement." The Kennel Club has decided to retrain judges to penalise dogs suffering these problems. It is also insisting on more testing for hemophilia and hip dysplasia, other common problems with the breed.

Breed clubs have typically responded that they feel they are being vilified for issues they were already aware of and attempting to address before the media storm erupted.

German Shepherds are a very popular selection for use as working dogs. They are especially well known for their police work, being used for tracking criminals, patrolling troubled areas, and detection and holding of suspects. Additionally thousands of German Shepherds have been used by the military. Usually trained for scout duty, they are used to warn soldiers to the presence of enemies or of booby traps or other hazards. German Shepherds have been trained by military groups to parachute from aircraft.

The German Shepherd Dog is one of the most widely used breeds in a wide variety of scent-work roles. These include search and rescue, cadaver searching, narcotics detection, explosives detection, accelerant detection, and mine detection dog, among others. They are suited for these lines of work because of their keen sense of smell and their ability to work regardless of distractions.

At one time the German Shepherd Dog was the breed chosen almost exclusively to be used as a guide dog for the visually impaired. In recent years, Labrador and Golden Retrievers have been more widely used for this work, although there are still German Shepherds being trained. A versatile breed, they excel in this field due to their strong sense of duty, their mental abilities, their fearlessness, and their attachment to their owner.

German Shepherd Dogs are used for herding and tending sheep grazing in meadows next to gardens and crop fields. They are expected to patrol the boundaries to keep sheep from trespassing and damaging the crops. In Germany and other places these skills are tested in utility dog trials also known as HGH (Herdengebrauchshund) herding utility dog trials.

German Shepherds have been featured in a wide range of media. Strongheart the German Shepherd was one of the earliest canine film stars and was followed by Rin Tin Tin, who is now acclaimed as being the most famous German Shepherd. Both are credited with stars on the Hollywood Walk of Fame. *The Littlest Hobo* is a Canadian television series, based upon a stray German Shepherd that wanders from town to town, helping people in need. In *The Beast Must Die* a German Shepherd played the movie's primary antagonist, the werewolf.

Due to the breed's remarkable popularity, German Shepherds have played central parts in many different movies and TV-shows over the years. German Shepherds have appeared as the titular character or one of the main characters in the films: *K-9* (which featured a real police-dog, Koton), *I Am Legend*, *The Hills Have Eyes* and a White German Shepherd named Bolt was the protagonist in the 2008 animated feature of the same name.

German shepherd dogs have also had minor roles in *Beverly Hills Chihuahua*, *Cats & Dogs: The Revenge of Kitty Galore*, and Blondi, Adolf Hitler's German Shepherd, has been featured in a number of documentaries and films about the dictator, such as *Downfall*. The Austrian police drama series *Inspector Rex* centers around a highly intelligent German Shepherd. In Poland, a German Shepherd starred in a '60's hit television series *Czterej Pancerni i Pies*, named Szarik. The 1989 animated film, *All Dogs Go to Heaven*.

Batman's dog Ace the Bat-Hound appeared in the Batman comic books, initially in 1955, through 1964. Between 1964 and 2007, his appearances were sporadic.

Doberman Pinscher

The Doberman Pinscher (alternatively spelled Dobermann in many countries) or simply Doberman, is a breed of domestic dog originally developed around 1890 by Karl Friedrich Louis Dobermann. Dobermann Pinschers are among the most common of pet breeds, and the breed is well known as an intelligent, alert, and loyal companion dog. Although once commonly used as guard dogs or police dogs, this is less common today.

In many countries, Dobermann Pinschers are one of the most recognizable breeds, in part because of their actual roles in society, and in part because of media attention. Careful breeding has improved the disposition of this breed, and the modern Dobermann Pinscher is an energetic and lively breed suitable for companionship and family life.

Kennel club standards describe Doberman Pinschers as dogs of medium size with a square build and short coat. They are compactly built and athletic with endurance and speed. The Doberman Pinscher should have a proud, watchful, determined, and obedient temperament. The dog was originally intended as a guard dog, so males should have a masculine, muscular, noble appearance. Females are thinner, but should not be spindly.

Size and Proportions

The Doberman Pinscher is a dog of medium size. Although the breed standards vary among kennel and breed clubs, the dog typically stands between 26 to 28 inches 27.5 being ideal (66 to 72 cm), the female is typically somewhere between 24 to 26 inches, 25.5 being ideal (61 to 68 cm). The Doberman has a square frame: its length should equal its height to the withers, and the length of its head, neck and legs should be in proportion to its body.

There are no standards for the weight of the Doberman Pinscher. The ideal dog must have sufficient size for an optimal combination of strength, endurance and agility. The male generally weighs between 75 and 100 pounds (34 and 45 kg) and the female between 60 and 90 pounds (27 and 41 kg).

Two different colour genes exist in the Doberman, one for *black* (B) and one for *colour dilution* (D). There are nine possible combinations of these allelles (BBDD, BBDd BbDD BbDd, BBdd, Bbdd, bbDD, bbDd, bbdd), which result in four different colour phenotypes: black, red, blue, and fawn (Isabella). The traditional and most common colour occurs when both the colour and dilution genes have at least one dominant allele (i.e., BBDD, BBDd, BbDD or BbDd), and is commonly referred to as *black* or *black and rust* (also called black and tan). The *red, red rust* or *brown* colouration occurs when the black gene has two recessive alleles but the dilution gene has at least one dominant allele (i.e., bbDD, bbDd). "Blue" and "fawn" are controlled by the colour dilution gene. The blue Doberman has the colour gene with at least one dominant allele and the dilution gene with both recessive alleles (i.e., BBdd or Bbdd). The fawn (Isabella) colouration is the least common, occurring only when both the colour and dilution genes have two recessive alleles (i.e., bbdd). Thus, the blue colour is a diluted black, and the fawn colour is a diluted red.

Expression of the colour dilution gene is a disorder called Colour Dilution Alopecia. Although not life threatening, these dogs can develop skin problems. Since 1994 the blue and fawn colours have been banned from breeding by the Dobermann Verein in Germany and under FCI regulations Blue and Fawn are considered disqualifying faults in the international showing.

In 1976, a "white" Doberman Pinscher was whelped, and was subsequently bred to her son, who was also bred to his litter sisters. This tight inbreeding continued for some time to allow the breeders to "fix" the mutation. White dobermans are a cream colour with pure white markings and icy blue eyes. Although this is consistent with albinism, the proper characterization of the mutation is currently unknown. The animals are commonly known as tyrosinase-positive albinoids, lacking melanin in oculocutaneous structures, but no known mutation has been identified.

The Doberman Pinscher's natural tail is fairly long, but individual dogs often have a short tail as a result of docking, a procedure in which the majority of the tail is surgically removed shortly after birth.

The practice of docking has been around for centuries, and is older than the Doberman as a breed. The putative reason for docking is to ensure that the tail does not get in the way of the dog's work. Docking has always been controversial. The American Kennel Club standard for Doberman Pinschers includes a tail docked near the 2nd vertebra. Docking is a common practice in North America, Russia and Japan (as well as a number of other countries with Doberman populations), where it is legal. In many European countries, docking has been made illegal, and in others it is limited.

Doberman Pinschers will often have their ears cropped, as do many other breeds, a procedure that is functionally related to breed type for both the traditional guard duty and effective sound localization. Like tail docking, ear cropping is illegal in some countries, and in these Doberman Pinschers have natural ears. Doberman Pinscher ear cropping is usually done between 7 and 9 weeks of age. Cropping done after 12 weeks has a low rate of success in getting the ears to stand. Some Doberman Pinscher owners prefer not to have their pet's ears cropped because they are concerned the procedure is painful for the animal.

The process involves trimming off part of the animal's ears and propping them up with posts and tape bandages, which allows the cartilage to develop into an upright position as the puppy grows. The incision scabs fall off within a week and stitches are removed a week after that. The puppy will still have the ability to lay the ears back or down. The process of posting the ears generally takes about a month, but longer show crops can take several months. Posting techniques and the associated discomfort vary from one posting technique to the next.

In some countries' conformation shows, Doberman Pinschers are allowed to compete with either cropped or natural ears. In Germany a cropped or docked dog cannot be shown regardless of country of origin. Special written exception to this policy does occur when Germany is the location for international events.

Although they are considered to be working dogs, Doberman Pinschers are the target of a stereotype of ferocity and aggression. As a personal protection dog, the Doberman was originally bred for these traits: it had to be large and intimidating, fearless and willing to defend its owner, but sufficiently obedient and restrained to only do so on command. These traits served the dog well in its role as a personal defense dog, police dog or war dog, but were not ideally adapted to a companionship role. In recent decades, the Doberman Pinscher's size, short coat, and intelligence made it a desirable house dog. Although these dogs are known for their aggression, they are also extremely loyal. They can easily learn to 'Respect and Protect' their owners.

In response, they are excellent guard dogs that protect their loved ones. They are generally sociable towards humans and can be with other dogs, ranking among the more-likely breeds to show aggressive behaviour toward strangers and other dogs but not among the most likely. They are very unlikely to show aggressive behaviour towards their owners, an unlikely behaviour that can only be allowed to grow up in the puppy if the owner doesn't has some previous dog experience.

There is evidence that Doberman Pinschers in North America are calmer than their European counterparts because of these breeding strategies. Because of these differences in breeding strategies, different lines of Doberman Pinschers have developed different traits. Although many contemporary

Doberman Pinschers in North America are gentle, loyal, loving, and intelligent dogs, some lines are bred more true to the original personality standard.

Although the stereotype is largely mistaken, the personality of the Doberman Pinscher is peculiar to the breed. There is a great deal of scientific evidence that Doberman Pinschers have a number of stable psychological traits, such as personality factors and intelligence. As early as 1965, studies have shown that there are several broad behavioural traits that significantly predict behaviour and are genetically determined. Subsequently, there have been numerous scientific attempts to quantify canine personality or temperament by using statistical techniques for assessing personality traits in humans. These studies often vary by identifying different personality factors, and by ranking breeds differently along these dimensions. One such study found that Doberman Pinschers, compared to other breeds, rank high in playfulness, average in curiosity/fearlessness, low on aggressiveness and low on sociability. Another such study ranked Doberman Pinschers low on reactivity/surgence, and high on aggression/disagreeableness and openness/trainability.

Canine intelligence is an umbrella term that encompasses the faculties involved in a wide range of mental tasks, such as learning, problem-solving, and communication. The Doberman Pinscher has ranked amongst the most intelligent of dog breeds in experimental studies and expert evaluations. For instance, Psychologist Stanley Coren ranks the Doberman as the 5th most intelligent dog in the category of *obedience command training,* based on the selective surveys he performed of some trainers (as documented in his book The Intelligence of Dogs). Additionally, in two studies, Hart and Hart (1985) ranked the Doberman Pinscher first in this category. and Tortora (1980) gave the Doberman the highest rank in trainability. Although the methods of evaluation differ, these studies consistently show that the Doberman Pinscher, along with the Border Collie, German Shepherd and Standard Poodle, is one of the most trainable breeds of dog.

In addition to the studies of canine personality, there has been some research to determine whether there are breed differences in aggression. In a recent study, aggression was divided into four categories: aggression directed at strangers, owner, other strange dogs and rivalry with other household dogs. This study found that the Doberman Pinscher ranked relatively high on stranger-directed aggression, but extremely low on owner-directed aggression. The Doberman Pinscher ranked as average on dog-directed aggression and dog rivalry. Looking only at bites and attempted bites, Doberman Pinschers rank as far less aggressive towards humans, and show less aggression than many breeds without a reputation (e.g., Cocker Spaniel, Border Collie and Great Dane). This study concluded that aggression has a genetic basis, that the Doberman shows a distinctive pattern of aggression depending on the situation, and that contemporary Doberman Pinschers are not an aggressive breed overall.

Although recent studies do not rank Doberman Pinschers as the most aggressive breed, their size, strength and aggression towards strangers makes them potentially dangerous. Studies of dog bites and dog bite fatalities have shown that the danger of attack by Dobermans is relatively high.

According to the Centers for Disease Control and Prevention, between 1979 and 1998, the Doberman Pinscher was involved in attacks on humans resulting in fatalities less frequently than several other dog breeds such as pit bull – type dogs, German Shepherd Dogs, Rottweilers, Husky-type, Wolf-dog hybrids and Alaskan Malamutes. According to this Center for Disease Control and Prevention study, one of the most important factors contributing to dog bites are related to the level of responsibility exercised by dog owners.

On average, Doberman Pinschers live about 10-14 years, but they may suffer from a number of health concerns. Common serious health problems include dilated cardiomyopathy, cervical vertebral instability (CVI), von Willebrand's disease (a bleeding disorder for which genetic testing of has been available since 2000 - the test enables both parents of a prospective litter to be tested for the carrier gene, thus preventing inheritance of the disease), and prostatic disease. Less serious common health concerns include hypothyroidism and hip dysplasia.

Studies have shown that the Doberman Pinscher suffers from prostatic diseases, (such as bacterial prostatiti, prostatic cysts, prostatic adenocarcinoma, and benign hyperplasia) more than any other breed. Neutering can significantly reduce these risks.

Dilated cardiomyopathy is a major cause of death in Doberman Pinschers. This disease affects Dobermans more than any other breed. Nearly 40 per cent of DCM diagnoses are for Doberman Pinschers, followed by German Shepherds at 13 per cent. Research has shown that the breed is affected by an *attenuated wavy fiber* type of DCM that affects many other breeds, as well as an additional, *fatty infiltration-degenerative* type that appears to be specific to Doberman Pinscher and Boxer breeds. This serious disease is likely to be fatal in most Doberman Pinschers affected.

Across multiple studies, more than half of the Doberman Pinschers studied develop the condition. Roughly a quarter of Doberman Pinschers who developed cardiomyopathy died suddenly from unknown causes, and an additional fifty percent died of congestive heart failure In addition to being more prevalent, this disease is also more serious in Doberman Pinschers. Following diagnosis, the average non-Doberman has an expected survival time of eight months; for Doberman Pinschers, the expected survival time is less than two months. Although the causes for the disease are largely unknown, there is evidence that it is a familial disease inherited as an autosomal dominant trait. Investigation into the genetic causes of canine DCM may lead to therapeutic and breeding practices to limit its impact.

Doberman Pinschers were first bred in the town of Apolda, in the German state of Thuringia around 1890, following the Franco-Prussian War by Karl Friedrich Louis Dobermann. Dobermann served in the dangerous role of local tax collector, and ran the Apolda dog pound. With access to dogs of many breeds, he aimed to create a breed that would be ideal for protecting him during his collections, which took him through many bandit-infested areas. He set out to breed a new type of dog that, in his opinion, would be the perfect combination of strength, loyalty, intelligence, and ferocity. Later, Otto Goeller and Philip Gruening continued to develop the breed to become the dog that is seen today.

The breed is believed to have been created from several different breeds of dogs that had the characteristics that Dobermann was looking for, including the German Pinscher, the Beauceron, the Rottweiler, the Thuringian Sylvan Dog, the Greyhound, the Great Dane, the Weimaraner, the German Shorthaired Pointer, the Manchester Terrier and the Old German Shepherd Dog. The exact ratios of mixing, and even the exact breeds that were used, remain uncertain to this day, although many experts believe that the Doberman Pinscher is a combination of at least four of these breeds. The single exception is the documented crossing with the Greyhound and Manchester Terrier. It is also widely believed that the old German Shepherd gene pool was the single largest contributor to the Doberman breed. Philip Greunig's *The Dobermann Pinscher* (1939), is considered the foremost study of the development of the breed by one of its most ardent students. Greunig's study describes the breed's early development by Otto Goeller, whose hand allowed the Doberman to become the dog we recognize today.

After Dobermann's death in 1894, the Germans named the breed Dobermann-pinscher in his honour, but a half century later dropped the pinscher on the grounds that this German word for terrier was no longer appropriate. The British did the same a few years later.

Portuguese Water Dog

The Portuguese Water Dog is a breed of working dog as classified by the American Kennel Club. Portuguese Water Dogs are originally from the Portuguese region of the Algarve, from where the breed expanded to all around Portugal's coast, where they were taught to herd fish into fishermen's nets, to retrieve lost tackle or broken nets, and to act as couriers from ship to ship, or ship to shore. Portuguese Water Dogs rode in bobbing fishing trawlers as they worked their way from the warm Atlantic waters of Portugal to the frigid fishing waters off the coast of Iceland where the fleets caught cod to bring home. Portuguese Water Dogs were often taken with sailors during the Portuguese discoveries.

In Portugal, the breed is called Cão de Água (pronounced *Kow-the-Ah-gwa*; literally 'water dog'). In its native land, the dog is also known as the Algarvian Water Dog ('Cão de Água Algarvio'), or Portuguese Fishing Dog

(*Cão Pescador Português*). *Cão de Água de Pêlo Ondulado* is the name given the wavy-haired variety, and *Cão de Água de Pêlo Encaracolado* is the name for the curly-coated variety.

The Portuguese Water Dog is a fairly rare breed; only 15 entrants for Portuguese Water Dogs were made to England's Crufts competition in 2002. Though some breeders claim they are a hypoallergenic dog breed, there is no scientific evidence to support the claim that hypoallergenic dog breeds exist. However, their non-shedding qualities have made them more popular in recent years.

The closest relatives of the PWD are widely thought to be the Kerry Blue Terrier, Barbet and Standard Poodle. Like Poodles and several other water dog breeds, PWDs are highly intelligent, can have curly coats, have webbed toes for swimming, and do not shed. However, Portuguese Water Dogs are more robustly built, with stout legs, and can have a wavy coat instead of tightly curled. If comparing the structure to that of a Poodle, there are significant differences between the two breeds. The Portuguese Water Dog built of strong substantial bone; well developed, neither refined nor coarse, and a solidly built, muscular body. The Portuguese Water Dog is off-square, slightly longer than tall when measured from prosternum to rearmost point of the buttocks, and from withers to ground. Portuguese Water Dog eyes are black or various tones of brown, and their coats can be black, brown, black and white or brown and white.

Male Portuguese Water Dogs usually grow to be about 20 to 23 inches (51 cm to 58 cm) tall, and they weigh between 40 and 60 pounds (18 kg to 27 kg), while the females usually grow to be about 17 to 21 inches (43 cm to 53 cm) tall, and they weigh between 35 and 50 pounds.

PWDs have a single-layered coat that does not shed, and therefore their presence is tolerated extremely well among many people who suffer from dog allergies. Some call PWDs hypoallergenic dogs, but any person with dog allergies who would like a dog with these qualities should actually spend time with the animals before purchasing, to test whether the dog is truly non-allergenic to them.

Most PWDs, especially those shown in conformation shows, are entirely black, black and white, brown, or silver-tipped; it is common to see white chest spots and white paws or legs on black or brown coated dogs. 'Parti' or 'Irish-marked' coats, with irregular white and black spots, are rare but visually striking. "Parti" dogs are becoming more common in the United States. However, in Portugal the breed standard does not allow more than 30 per cent white markings. Overall, white is the least common Portuguese Water Dog colour, while black with white markings on the chin ('milk chin') and chest is the most common colour combination.

This breed does not shed its hair. The hair is either wavy or curly. Many dogs have mixed pattern hair: curly all over the body but wavy on the tail and ears.

From the Portuguese Water Dog Club of America Revised Standard for the Portuguese Water Dog come these descriptions of the two coat types:

1. *Curly coat:* "Compact, cylindrical curls, somewhat lusterless. The hair on the ears is sometimes wavy."
2. *Wavy coat:* "Falling gently in waves, not curls, and with a slight sheen."

If left untended, the hair on a PWD will keep growing indefinitely. Problems associated with this include the hair around the eyes growing so long as to impede vision, and matting of the body hair, which can cause skin irritations. For these reasons, PWDs must be trimmed about every two months and the coat brushed every other day. This is not the breed for those humans wishing to have a low maintenance breed. In addition to the grooming, which typically costs between $75-100 a session, this breed requires daily exercise and consistently firm yet positive training techniques. Although it is possible to groom them at home, many owners find it easier to pay a professional groomer and, to avoid matting, they brush out the coat regularly between groomings.

Improper Coat

Occasionally, a dog may have what is termed an 'improper' coat. This genetic condition causes the dog to have an undercoat. Because improperly coated PWDs do not adhere to the breed standard, they may not be shown in conformation competition. Otherwise they are completely healthy and have all the excellent traits of the breed. They should not be used in breeding programmes, because improper coat is an inherited condition.

Grooming Styles

The hair of PWDs grows continually and requires regular brushing and cutting or clipping. The coat is usually worn in a 'retriever cut' or a 'lion cut'.

The Lion Cut

In the lion cut, the hindquarters, muzzle, and the base of the tail are shaved and the rest of the body is left full length. This cut originated with the fishing dogs of Portugal. This is the traditional cut and perhaps the most functional, given the breed's main historical significance as a fisherman's companion. The lion cut diminished the initial impact and shock of cold water when the breed jumped from the boats, as well as providing warmth to the vitals. The hindquarters were left shaved to allow easier movement of the back legs and the breed's powerful, rudder-like tail.

The Retriever Cut

The retriever cut is left 1" (2.5 cm) long evenly over the body (although some owners prefer the muzzle or the base of the tail shorter). This cut is a more recent style and originated because breeders wanted to make the breed more appealing and less unusual looking for buyers.

Sometimes owners will clip the hair of their dogs very short, especially in the summer months, in modified retriever cut.

Vocalisation

Portuguese Water Dogs have a multi-octave voice. They tend to be quiet dogs although they will warn when the home is approached, and they will communicate their desires vocally and behaviourally to their owner. Their bark is loud and distinctive. They may engage in 'expressive panting', by making a distinct 'ha-ha-ha-ha' sound as an invitation to play or to indicate a desire for nearby food. They sometimes whine.

The PWD's biddability, high intelligence, and tendency to vocalise and then seek out its human master when specific alarms occur make it an ideal hearing-ear or deaf-assistance dog. PWDs can be readily trained to bark loudly when a telephone rings, and then to find and alert a hard-of-hearing or deaf master.

Portuguese Water dogs make excellent companions. They are loving, independent, and intelligent and are easily trained in obedience and agility skills. Once introduced, they are generally friendly to strangers, and enjoy being petted, which, due to their soft, fluffy coats, is a favour that human beings willingly grant them.

Because they are working dogs, PWDs are generally content in being at their master's side, awaiting directions, and, if they are trained, they are willing and able to follow complex commands. They learn very quickly, seem to enjoy the training, and have a long memory for the names of objects. These traits and their non-shedding coats mean they excel at the various Service Dog roles such as hearing dogs (assistance dogs for the deaf), mobility dogs, and seizure response dogs. They also make unusually good therapy dogs.

A PWD usually stays in proximity to its owners, indoors as well as outdoors. This is typical of the breed. Though very gregarious animals, these dogs will typically bond with one primary or alpha family member. Some speculate that this intense bonding arose in the breed because the dogs were selected to work in proximity to their masters on small fishing boats, unlike other working dogs such as herding dogs and water dogs that range out to perform tasks. In any case, the modern PWD, whether employed on a boat or kept as a pet or a working dog, loves water, attention, and prefers to be engaged in activity within sight of a human partner. This is not a breed to be left alone for long periods of time, indoors or out.

As water dogs, the PWD's retrieving instinct is strong, which also gives some dogs tugging and chewing tendencies.

A PWD will commonly jump as a greeting. Owners may choose to limit this behaviour. Some PWDs may walk, hop, or 'dance' on their hind legs when greeting or otherwise enthusiastic. Some PWDs will stand upright at kitchen counters and tables, especially if they smell food above them. This habit is known as 'counter surfing' and is characteristic of the breed. Although it can be a nuisance, many PWD owners evidently enjoy seeing their dogs walking, hopping, standing up, or "countering" and do not seriously discourage these activities.

While they are very good companions to people who understand what they need, Portuguese Water Dogs are not for everyone. Because of their intelligence and working drive, they require regular intensive exercise as well as mental challenges. They are gentle and patient—but not "couch potatoes", and boredom may cause them to become destructive.

One theory is that some of the rugged Asian herding dogs were captured by the Berbers, a people who spread slowly across the face of North Africa to Morocco. Their descendants, the Moors, arrived in Portugal in the 8th century, bringing the water dogs with them.

Another theory purports that some of the dogs left the Asian steppes with the Goths, a confederation of German tribes. Some, (the Ostrogoths), went west and their dogs became the German poodle, called in German the poodle-hund or puddle-dog, that is, water-dog. Others, (the Visigoths), went south to fight the Romans, and their dogs became the Lion Dog, groomed in the traditional lion cut. In 400 CE, the Visigoths invaded Iberia (modern Spain and Portugal, then known as Hispania) and the dogs found their homeland.

A Portuguese Water Dog is first described in 1297 in a monk's account of a drowning sailor who was pulled from the sea by a dog with a "black coat, the hair long and rough, cut to the first rib and with a tail tuft".

'History of the Portuguese Water Dog', Kathryn Braund and Deyanne Farrell Miller, *The Complete Portuguese Water Dog*.

These theories explain how the Poodle and the Portuguese Water Dog may have developed from the same ancient genetic pool. At one time the Poodle was a longer-coated dog, as is one variety of the Portuguese Water Dog. The possibility also exists that some of the long-coated water dogs grew up with the ancient Iberians. In early times, Celtiberians migrated from lands which now belong to southwestern Germany. Swarming over the Pyrenees, circulating over the whole of western Europe, they established bases in Iberia, as well as in Ireland, Wales, and Brittany. The Irish Water Spaniel and Kerry Blue Terrier are believed by some to be descendants of the Portuguese Water Dog.

The PWD was a breed on the verge of extinction when, during the 1930s, Vasco Bensaude, a wealthy Portuguese shipping magnate, began to seek out fishermen's dogs and utilize them in a breeding programme to re-establish the breed. Bensaude's kennel was named Algarbiorum, and his most famous dog was Leão (1931-1942), a very 'type-y' fisherman's stud dog who was bred to so many different females that about half of the pedigreed Portuguese Water Dogs in existence can trace their lineage back to him. Bensaude was aided by two Portuguese veterinarians, Dr. Francisco

Pinto Soares and Dr. Manuel Fernandes Marques. His work was carried on by Conchita Cintron de Castelo Branco, to whom he gave his last 17 PWDs and all his archives.

Dr. António Cabral was the founder of the Avalade kennels in Portugal. Ch. Charlie de Avalade (Charlie), a brown-coated dog, and C. B. Baluarte de Avalade (Balu) were two of his many famous PWDs. He registered his first PWD in 1954, after Bensaude had pioneered the re-establishment of the breed in Portugal. Cabral worked with Carla Molinari, Deyanne Miller, Sonja Santos and others to establish PWDs in the US. The "Mark of Cabral" is a triangular shape of different colour/textured hair, usually a few inches from the base of the tail. You can see it more easily on a fresh lion clip—it can look like the clipper got too close.

Deyanne Miller is the single person most responsible for the rise of the PWD in America. In 1972, the Millers, along with 14 other people, formed the Portuguese Water Dog Club of America, Inc. (PWDCA). She worked with dogs from both the Cintron and Cabral lineages to establish a stable genetic pool of PWDs in the United States at her Farmion kennels. Another early US breeder of PWDs was the actor Raymond Burr.

As with all purebred dogs, PWDs are vulnerable to certain genetic defects. Due to the limited gene pool for this breed, conscientious breeders carefully study pedigrees and select dogs to minimize the chance of genetic disease and improper coat. Unfortunately, like many breeds, a growing popularity has encouraged breeding by people who are not knowledgeable about the breed.

Hip Dysplasia

Like poodles, PWDs are vulnerable to hip dysplasia. However, the risk of a PWD developing hip dysplasia can be greatly reduced by thoroughly checking the pedigrees and health clearances in both the sire and dam of your dog. Hip dysplasia is a congenital and developmental problem with the hip joints.

Cataracts, PRA, and Distichiasis

Cataracts and PRA (Progressive Retinal Atrophy) are two eye diseases found in PWDs. As with hip dysplasia, some lines carry these defects more frequently than others. PRA, which causes 'night blindness', may lead to complete blindness. Fortunately this is a simple recessive gene. DNA testing is now available which can identify a dog carrying the gene for PRA. Known as 'Optigen Testing' a 'normal' or 'A' dog does not carry the gene for PRA. A 'carrier' or 'B' dog carries one copy of the PRA gene and the dog will NOT express the disease but may or may not pass the gene to offspring. An 'affected' or 'C' dog has two copies of the PRA version of the gene and will probably express the disease as late onset Progressive Retinal Atrophy. A 'B' or 'C' dog should be bred *only* to an 'A' dog to ensure that any offspring will not express the disease.

Ingrown eyelashes (distichiasis) occurs in some curly-coated breeds, but is not particularly common in PWDs. Ingrown eyelashes will rub the eye causing extensive corneal ulcerations. The condition is minor so long as it is not ignored, and can be surgically treated if necessary.

GM1 Storage Disease

GM1 Storage Disease, one of a family of conditions called GM1 gangliosidoses, is a recessive, genetic disorder that is inevitably fatal. It is caused by a deficiency of beta-galactosidase, with resulting abnormal storage of acidic lipid materials in cells of the central and peripheral nervous systems, but particularly in the nerve cells. Because PWDs are all rather closely related to one another and share a limited gene pool, PWDs who were GM1 Storage Disease carriers were able to be genetically identified, and the condition has now been almost entirely eliminated from the breed. All breeding stock should be tested for GM-1 storage disease or GM1 gangliosidoses, which is a fatal nerve disease that typically appears when a puppy is approximately six months of age. The affected puppy will show clinical signs of cerebellar dysfunction including ataxia, tremors, paresis, and seizures. The pet may also exhibit a change in temperament. Lesions of the retina and clouding of the cornea may occur. GM-1 storage disease is a recessive deficiency of betagalactosidase. The condition has been genetically identified and is no longer common.

Juvenile Dilated Cardiomyopathy

Juvenile Dilated Cardiomyopathy is a rare, fatal condition caused by an autosomal recessive gene. It affects young dogs, who succumb to heart failure before reaching adulthood. As a simple recessive gene, it had been difficult to identify and was particularly heartbreaking as seemingly healthy puppies would suddenly die, often shortly after joining their adopted families. Since a recessive gene is responsible, that means if at least one parent is homozygous dominant (that is, it does not carry a copy of the cardio version of the gene), its offspring can not contract the disease .

In 2007 a genetic linkage test became available which appears promising. This is not a test which confirms if a dog has, or does not have the disease; nor will it definitively predict the disease, as even if a dog is a JDC carrier this does not guarantee its offspring will suffer the disease. It only links certain strains of DNA as carriers of JDC. This is significant in that these strains can now largely be deselected for in the breeding process, as has been successful with GM1 Storage Disease (see above). The test is not yet complete for every bloodline, and *why* the identified strains are implicated is still unknown, and so in essence the *cause* of the condition remains a mystery to be solved.

Kuvasz

The Kuvasz (Hungarian pronunciation: ['kuva z], pl. Kuvaszok, Hungarian pronunciation: ['kuva zk]) is a dog breed of ancient Hungarian origin. Mention of the breed can be found in old Hungarian texts. It has historically been used to guard livestock, but has been increasingly found in homes as a pet over the last seventy years.

The Kuvasz is a large dog with a dense double, odorless coat which is white in colour and can range from wavy to straight in texture. Although the fur is white, the Kuvasz's skin pigmentation should be dark and the nose should be black. The eyes should have an almond shape. Females usually weigh between 35-50 kg (75-90 pounds) while males weigh between 50-70 kg (100-150 pounds) with a medium bone structure. The head should be half as wide as it is long with the eyes set slightly below the plane of the muzzle. The stop (where the muzzle raises to the crown of the head) should be defined but not abrupt. The precise standard varies by country. To a casual observer, the Kuvasz may appear similar to a Great Pyrenees, Akbash, a Maremma Sheepdog, Samoyed, a white Poodle and Labrador Retriever mix, Slovak Cuvac and the Polish Tatra Sheepdog.

As with many livestock guardian dogs, the colour of the Kuvasz's coat serves a functional purpose and is an essential breed criterion. Shepherds purposefully bred the Kuvasz to have a light coloured coat so that it would be easier for the shepherds to distinguish the Kuvasz from wolves that would prey on the livestock during the night. The Komondor, a cousin of the Kuvasz, has a white coat for the same reason. Traditionally, the Hungarian Kuvasz's coat could be either white or cream coloured with a wavy texture. However, there is some debate, particularly in the United States, concerning the appropriateness of 'cream' coloured coats in show-quality dogs and whether the coat should be straight or wavy in texture. Since washing and brushing out a coat, as done for shows in the US also causes the coat to appear straight, the debate may be circular. Straighter coats may also have appeared as the result of breeding programmes that developed after World War II, when the breeding lines in Hungary were isolated from the rest of the world as a result of Soviet & German occupation. By Hungarian standard the straight coat is not acceptable. There must be special twirls in the coat.

The Kuvasz is an intelligent dog and is often described as having a clownish sense of humor which can last throughout their adolescence and into adulthood. They are intensely loyal yet patient pets who appreciate attention but may also be somewhat aloof or independent, particularly with strangers. They rank 42nd in Stanley Coren's The Intelligence of Dogs. This misconception is due in part to the centuries of imprinting this breed to 'think on its own without instruction'. They are hard wired with a different type of thought process and are happiest when they are 'working/guarding' their flock and not performing tricks. They are always on the job and require an experienced dog handler/trainer. In keeping with their origins as a livestock guardian, Kuvaszok are known to be fierce protectors of their families. Given their intelligence, constant awareness of their surroundings, as well as their size and strength, they can be quite impressive in this role. A Kuvasz should be courageous, disciplined and stable, while hyperactivity, nervousness and shyness are to be faulted.

The combination of intelligence, independence and protectiveness make obedience training and socialization necessities. Furthermore, despite their intelligence, they should not be perceived as easily trained. Their independent personalities can make training a difficult task which can wear on the patience of even experienced owners. As a result, they are not recommended for novices and those who do not have time to train and socialize them properly. An adolescent Kuvasz should be able to learn basic obedience commands and consistently respond to them; however the instinctive need to investigate strangers and protect its owner may cause the Kuvasz to act independently when off leash and ignore the calls of a frustrated handler. Finally, a potential owner should refrain from purchasing a Kuvasz if barking will be a problem at the home. While not all Kuvaszok are prone to barking (socializing them will define what is a threat), many of them fulfill their guardian role by vocally warning off potential threats, both real and imagined. On the other hand, many of these qualities make the Kuvasz excellent guardians for sheep or large estates. The Kuvasz has a very special, close connection to his owner.

Although regarded today as one of the Hungarian breeds, the Kuvasz's origins actually lay with a nomadic tribe and may have its true origins from Mesopotamia along with domestic sheep and goats. Around 2000 B.C., the Magyar tribes moved along the recently established trade routes of the steppes, gradually leading them to the Carpathian Basin in Hungary which they conquered in A.D. 896. With them came Kuvasz-type dogs, which primarily served as livestock guardians. In 1978, the fossilized skeleton of a 9th Century Kuvasz-type dog was discovered in Fenékpuszta near Keszthely, a discovery which was remarkable in that the morphology of the skeleton was almost identical to a modern Kuvasz. If accurate, such a discovery would mark the Kuvasz as among the oldest identifiable dog breeds as only a few breeds can be dated beyond the 9th century.

After the Magyar settlement of the Carpathian Basin, the tribes converted to a more agrarian lifestyle and began to devote more resources towards animal husbandry. Whereas the Komondor was used in the lower elevations with drier climates, the Kuvasz was used in the wet pastures of the higher mountains and both were an integral part of the economy. Later, during the 15th Century, the Kuvasz became a highly prized animal and could be found in the royal court of King Matthias Corvinus. Kuvasz puppies were given to visiting dignitaries as a royal gift, and the King was said to have trusted his dogs more than his own councilors. After the king's death, the popularity of the breed among the nobles waned but it was still frequently found in its traditional role of protecting livestock.

By the end of World War II, nearly all the Kuvaszok in Hungary had been killed. The dogs had such a reputation for protecting their families that they were actively sought and killed by German and Soviet soldiers, while at the same time some German police used to take Kuvaszok home with them. After the Soviet invasion and the end of the war, the breed was nearly extinct in Hungary. After the war, it was revealed that fewer than thirty Kuvaszok were left in Hungary and some sources indicate the number may have been as few as twelve. Since then, due to many dedicated breeders, Kuvaszok have repopulated Hungary. However, as a result of this near extinction, the genetic pool available to breeders was severely restricted and there is conjecture that some may have used other breeds, such as the Great Pyrenees, to continue their programmes. The issue is further clouded by the need to use a classification of B pedigrees at the time to rebuild the breed.

Possible Origins of the Breed Name

The word most likely comes from the Turkic word *kavas* meaning guard or soldier or *kuwasz* meaning protector. A related theory posits that the word may have originated from the ancient farmers of Russia, the Chuvash, who nurtured the breed for generations and contributed many words to the Hungarian language.

Grooming

The Kuvasz's stiff, dense coat, growing up to 15 cm (6 inches) in length, does not require any special grooming. It needs to be brushed once a week or, better still, every two or three days. For standard grooming purposes, use of a grooming rake or a pin-brush with rounded pins is recommended. To remove stubborn knots, use a curry comb or a large-toothed comb. During the spring and autumn the Kuvasz moults (also known as shedding), and he will lose copious amounts of hair very quickly. Frequent brushing is therefore needed to keep his coat tidy. A Kuvasz should not smell or have an odor; such is usually a sign of illness or a poor diet.

Health

Although generally a healthy and robust breed which can be expected to live approximately 12-14 years, Kuvaszok are prone to developmental bone problems. Accordingly, owners should take care to provide proper nutrition to their Kuvasz puppy and avoid subjecting the puppy to rough play. As with many large breeds, hip dysplasia, a painful and potentially debilitating condition, is not uncommon. Good genetics and proper nutrition as a puppy are key to avoiding these complications.

A Kuvasz puppy should not be fed a diet high in calories or protein as such diets have been associated with the development of orthopedic disorders later in life. The Kuvasz has a very efficient metabolism and is predisposed to rapid growth—vitamin supplements are not necessary and, in fact, should be avoided. Cooked bones should never be given to a Kuvasz or any other dog because the cooking process renders the bone brittle and prone to splintering, which can cause serious injury to the dog's mouth and digestive tract.

American Akita

The American Akita, often called simply Akita, is a large spitz breed of dog originating from the mountainous northern regions of Japan. They come in all dog colours, having a short double coat, similar to that of many other northern Spitz breeds, *e.g.*, Siberian Husky. The American Akita is now considered a separate breed from the Akita Inu (Japanese Akita) in many countries around the world, with the notable exceptions of Australia, the United States and Canada. In the US and Canada, both the American Akita and the Akita Inu are considered a single breed with differences in type rather than two separate breeds. Note that in 2005 the FCI-designation Great Japanese Dog was officially changed to 'American Akita'. Both types of Akita are probably best known worldwide from the true story of Hachiko, a loyal Akita dog who lived in Japan before World War II.

Debate remains among Akita fanciers of both types whether there are or should be two breeds of Akita. To date, the American Kennel Club (AKC), Canadian Kennel Club (CKC) and Australian National Kennel Council (ANKC), guided by their national breed clubs, consider American and Japanese style Akitas to be two types of the same breed, allowing free breeding between the two. The Federation Cynologique Internationale (FCI), The Kennel Club (KC) (UK), New Zealand Kennel Club (NZKC) and Kennel Clubs of some other nations, including Japan, consider Japanese and American style Akitas as separate breeds. However all excpet the FCI refer to the American style Akita as simply the 'Akita' and not American Akita. Indeed, the issue is especially controversial in Japan. Formally, for the FCI, the breed split occurred June 1999, when the FCI voted that the American type would be called the Great Japanese Dog, this was changed in January 2006 to American Akita. To refer to either type as an Akita would be correct.

Japanese history, both verbal and written, describe the ancestors of the Akita, the Matagi dog, as one of the oldest of the native dogs. Today's Akita developed primarily from dogs in the northernmost region of the island of Honshu in the Akita prefecture, thus providing the breed's name. The Matagi's quarry included wild boar, Sika deer, and Asian black bear. This swift, agile, unswervingly tenacious precursor dog tracked large game, holding it at bay until hunters arrived to make the kill. The breed is also influenced by crosses with larger breeds from Asia and Europe, including Mastiffs, Great Danes and the Tosa Inu, in the desire to develop a fighting dog for the burgeoning dog fighting industry in Odate, Akita Prefecture, Japan in the early 20th century. During World War II the Akita was also crossed with German Shepherd Dogs in an attempt to save them from the war time government order for all non-military dogs to be culled. The ancestors of the American Akita were originally a variety of the Akita Inu, a form that was not desired in Japan due to the markings, and which is not showable.

Three events focused positive attention on the breed in the early 1900s and brought the breed to the attention of the Western world:

- First was the story of Hachiko, one of the most revered Akitas of all time. He was born in 1923 and was owned by Professor Hidesaburo Ueno of Tokyo. Professor Ueno lived near the Shibuya Train Station in a suburb of the city and commuted to work every day on the train. Hachiko accompanied his master to and from the station each day. On May 25, 1925, when the dog was 18 months old, he waited for his master's arrival on the four o'clock train. But he waited in vain; Professor Ueno had suffered a fatal stroke at work. Hachiko continued to wait for his master's return. He traveled to and from the station each day for the next nine years. He allowed the professor's relatives to care for him, but he never gave up the vigil at the station for his master. Upon Hachiko's death on March 8, 1935 a national day of mourning was declared in honor of Hachiko's devotion. His vigil became world renowned when, in 1934, shortly before his death, a bronze statue was erected at the Shibuya train station in his honor. This statue was melted down for munitions during the war and new one commissioned once the war had ended. In 1983 a bust of Professor Uneo was placed next to the statue of Hachiko.
- The second major event was in 1931, when the Akita was officially declared a Japanese Natural Monument. The Mayor of Odate City in Akita Prefecture organized the Akita Inu Hozankai to preserve the original Akita as a Japanese natural treasure through careful breeding. In 1934 the first Japanese breed standard for the Akita Inu was listed, following the breeds declaration as a natural monument of Japan. In 1967, commemorating the 50th anniversary of the founding of the Akita Dog Preservation Society, the Akita Dog Museum was built to house information, documents and photos.
- The third positive event was the arrival of Helen Keller in Japan in 1937. She expressed a keen interest in the breed and was presented with the first two Akitas to enter the US. The first dog, presented to her by Mr. Ogasawara and named Kamikaze-go, died at five months of age from Distemper, one month after her return to the States. A second Akita was arranged to be sent to Miss Keller, he was Kamikaze's litter brother, Kenzan-go. Kenzan-go died in the mid-1940s.

The Akita 'Tachibana', one of the few Akitas to survive the war, pictured here on a Japanese 1953 issue postage stamp.

Just as this mountain dog breed was stabilizing in its native land, World War II pushed the Akita to the brink of extinction. Early in the war the dogs suffered from lack of nutritious food. Then many were killed to be eaten by the starving populace, and their pelts were used as clothing. Finally, the government ordered all remaining dogs to be killed on sight to prevent the spread of disease. The only way concerned owners could save their beloved Akitas was to turn them loose in the most remote mountain areas, where they bred back with their ancestor dogs, the Matagi, or conceal them from authorities by means of crossing with German Shepherd dogs, and naming them in the style of German Shepherd dogs of the time. Morie Sawataishi and his efforts to breed the Akita is a major reason we know this breed today.

During the occupation years following the war, the breed began to thrive again through the efforts of Sawataishi and others. For the first time, Akitas were bred for a standardized appearance. Akita fanciers in Japan began gathering and exhibiting the remaining Akitas and producing litters in order to restore the breed to sustainable numbers and to accentuate the original characteristics of the breed muddied by crosses to other breeds. US servicemen fell in love with the Akita and imported many of them into the US upon and after their return.

The Japanese Akita and American Akita began to diverge in type through the middle and later part of the 20th century. Japanese Akita fanciers focused on restoring the breed as a work of Japanese art. American Akita fanciers bred larger, heavier-boned dogs. Both types derive from a common ancestry, but marked differences can be observed between the two. First, while American Akitas are acceptable in all colours, Japanese Akitas are only permitted to be red, fawn, sesame, white, or brindle. Additionally, American Akitas may be pinto and/or have black masks, unlike Japanese Akitas where it is considered a disqualification and not permitted in the breed standards. American Akitas generally are heavier boned and larger, with a more bear-like head, whereas Japanese Akitas tend to be lighter and more finely featured with a fox-like head.

Recognized by the American Kennel Club in 1955, it was placed in the Miscellaneous class. It wasn't until the end of 1972 that the AKC approved the Akita standard and it was moved to the Working dog class, as such, the Akita is a rather new breed in the United States. Foundation stock in America continued to be imported from Japan until 1974 when the AKC cut off registration of any Japanese import until 1992 when it recognized the Japanese Kennel Club. The period of non-recognition was in concern for the authenticity of the pedigrees and the purity of the breeds. This no-doubt was a major factor of the breed in America diverging from the Japanese type as both countries continued to breed to their own standard.

Elsewhere in the world, the Akita was first introduced to the U.K. in 1937, he was a Canadian import, however the breed was not widely known until the early 1980s. The breed was introduced in Australia in 1982 with an American Import and to New Zealand in 1986 with an import from the U.K.

As a northern breed (generically, Spitz), the appearance of the Akita reflects cold weather adaptations essential to their original function.

The Akita is a substantial breed for its height with heavy bones. Characteristic physical traits of the breed include a large, bear-like head with erect, triangular ears set at a slight angle following the arch of the neck. Additionally, the eyes of the Akita are small, dark, deeply set and triangular in shape. Akitas have thick double coats, and tight, well knuckled cat-like feet. Their tails are carried over the top of the back in a graceful sweep down the loin, into a gentle curl, or into a double curl.

Mature males measure typically 26-28 inches (66-71 cm) at the withers and weigh between 100-130 lb (45-59 kg). Mature females typically measure 24-26 inches (61-66 cm) and weigh between 70-100 lb (32-45 kg).

Breed standards state that all dog breed coat colours are allowable in the American Akita, including pinto, all types of brindle, solid white, black mask, white mask, self coloured mask, even differing colours of under coat and overlay (guard hairs). This includes the common Akita Inu and Shiba Inu colouring pattern known as Urajiro.

There are two coat types in the Akita, the standard coat length and the long coat. The long coat is considered a fault in the show ring, however, they still make good pets. The long coat, also known as 'Moku' is the result of a autosomal recessive gene and only occurs phenotypically if both sire and dam are carriers. They have longer (about 3-4 inches in length) and softer coats and are known to have sweeter temperaments. It is believed that this gene comes from the now extinct Karafuto-Ken (extirpated in Japan, anyway) Dog of Russia.

The Akita today is a unique combination of dignity, courage, alertness, and devotion to its family. It is extraordinarily affectionate and loyal with family and friends, territorial about its property, and can be reserved with strangers. It is feline in its actions; it is not unusual for an Akita to clean its face after eating, to preen its kennel mate, and to be fastidious in the house. They are however known to be intolerant of other dogs, as stated in the AKC breed standard.

Since it is a large, powerful dog, the Akita is not considered a breed for a first time dog owner. The breed has been targeted by some countries' breed legislation as a dangerous dog. The Akita is a large, strong, independent and dominant dog. A dog with the correct Akita temperament should be accepting of non-threatening strangers, yet protective of their family when faced with a threatening situation. They should be docile, aloof and calm in new situations. As a breed they should be good with children, it is said that the breed has an affinity with children, just as retrievers have an affinity with sticks and balls. However all care and caution should be taken with children and large dogs. Not all Akitas, nor all dogs, will necessarily have a correct temperament.

The Akita was never bred to live or work in groups like many hound and sporting breeds. Instead, they lived and worked alone or in pairs, a preference reflected today. Akitas tend to take a socially dominant role with other dogs, and thus caution must be used in situations when Akitas are likely to be around other dogs, especially unfamiliar ones. In particular, Akitas tend to be less tolerant of dogs of the same sex. For this reason, Akitas, unless highly socialized, are not generally well-suited for off-leash dog parks. The Akita is docile, intelligent, courageous and fearless, careful and very affectionate with its family. Sometimes spontaneous, it needs a firm, confident, consistent pack leader, without which the dog will be very willful and may become very aggressive to other dogs and animals.

There are many autoimmune diseases that are known to sometimes occur in the Akita. These include, but are not limited to:

- Micropthalmia, a developmental disorder of the eye, also known as 'Small eye', believed to be an autosomal recessive genetic condition.
- Vogt-Koyanagi-Harada syndrome, also known as Uveo-Dermatologic Syndrome is an auto-immune condition which affects the skin and eyes.
- Autoimmune Hemolytic Anemia, which is an autoimmune blood disorder.
- Sebaceous Adenitis is an autoimmune skin disorder believed to be of autosomal recessive inheritance.
- Pemphigus Foliaceus is an autoimmune skin disorder, believed to be genetic.

Immune-mediated Endocrine Diseases

In addition to these there are also the Immune-mediated endocrine diseases with a heritable factor, such as:

- Addison's Disease also known as hypoadrenocorticism, it affects the adrenal glands and is essentially the opposite to Cushing's syndrome.
- Cushing's Syndrome also known as Hyperadrenocorticism, it affects the adrenal glands and is caused by long-term exposure to high levels of glucocorticosteroids, either manufactured by the body or given as medications.
- Diabetes mellitus, also known as type 1 diabetes. It affects the pancreas.
- Hypothyroidism, also known as autoimmune hypothyroidism. This is an autoimmune disease which affects the thyroid gland.
- Systemic Lupus Erythematosus also known as SLE or lupus, is a systemic autoimmune disease (or autoimmune connective tissue disease) that can affect any part of the body.

Non Immune Specific Conditions

Other non-immune specific conditions known to have occurred in the Akita include:

- Gastric Dialation is also known as bloat, torsion, gastric torsion, or gastric dilatation-volvulus (GDV).
- Primary Glaucoma a disorder of the eye.

- Progressive Retinal Atrophy which is also a disorder of the eye.
- Hip dysplasia a skeletal condition.
- Elbow dysplasia another skeletal condition.
- Von Willebrands disease, a genetic bleeding disorder.

Breed Specific Conditions

There are two breed specific conditions mentioned in veterinary literature:

1. Immune Sensitivity to vaccines, drugs, insecticides, anesthetics and tranquilizers.
2. Pseudohyperkalemia, a rise in the amount of potassium that occurs due to its excessive leakage from cells, during or after blood is drawn. This can give a false indication of hyperkalemia, hence the prefix psuedo, meaning false.

Predecessors of the American Akita were used for hunting bear in Japan as late as 1957. They would be used to flush out the bear and keep it at bay until the hunter could come and kill it. Akitas have also been used as military dogs and guard dogs. Today, the breed is used primarily as a companion dog. However, the breed is currently also known to be used as therapy dogs, and compete in all dog competitions including: conformation showing, obedience trials, canine good citizen programme, tracking trials and agility competition as well as weight pulling, hunting and schutzhund (*i.e.*, personal protection dogs).

Alaskan Malamute

The Alaskan Malamute is a generally large, wolf-like breed of domestic dog (*Canis lupus familiaris*) originally bred for use as an Alaskan sled dog. They are sometimes mistaken for a Siberian Husky, but in fact are quite different in many ways. As pets, Malamutes have a very quiet temperament and are often loyal to their owners.

The American Kennel Club (AKC) breed standard calls for a natural range of size, with a desired freighting size of 23 inches (584 mm) and 75 pounds (34 kg) for females, 25 inches (635 mm) and 85 pounds (39 kg) for males. Heavier individuals (90 lb (41 kg)) and dogs smaller than 75 pounds (34 kg) are commonly seen. There is often a marked size difference between males and females. Weights upwards of 120 pounds (54 kg) are occasionally seen, but this is uncommon and such dogs are produced primarily by breeders who market a 'giant Malamute.' These large sizes are not in accordance with show standards.

The coat is a dense double northern dog coat, somewhat "harsher" (in a certain sense) than that of the smaller Siberian Husky. The usual colours are various shades of gray and white, sable and white, black and white, red and white, or solid white. Blue and white (slate gray with gray pigment) also is seen in the breed. Eyes are almond-shaped and are always various shades of brown (from dark to light, honey or hazel brown); blue eyed Malamutes will be disqualified in conformation shows, as they would not be a purebred Malamute, but mixed with perhaps a Siberian Husky. The physical build of the Malamute is compact with heavy bone, in most (but not all) cases. In this context 'compact' means that their height to length ratio is slightly longer than tall, unlike dogs like Great Danes which are longer and lankier in their ratios.

According to the AKC breed standard, the Malamute's tail is well furred and is carried over the back like a 'waving plume'. Corkscrew tails are occasionally seen but are faulted in the AKC breed standard (a corkscrew tail is commonly seen in the Akita). The Malamutes' well-furred tails aid in keeping them warm when they curl up in the snow. They are often seen wrapping the tail around their nose and face, which presumably helps protect them against harsh weather such as blowing snow. Their ears are generally upright. They are one of five breeds that still look like wolves.

A few Malamutes are still in use as sled dogs for personal travel, hauling freight, or helping move heavy objects; some however are used for the recreational pursuit of sledding, also known as mushing, as well as for skijoring, bikejoring, and canicross. However, most Malamutes today are kept as family pets or as show or performance dogs in weight pulling, dog agility, or packing. The Malamute is generally slower in long-distance dogsled racing against smaller and faster breeds and their working usefulness is limited to freighting or traveling over long distances at a far slower rate than that required for racing. They can also help move heavy objects over shorter distances.

The Malamute retains more of its original form and function than many other modern breeds. If a dog owner cannot cope with a dog that will not comply with the owner's every command, a more compliant breed should be selected. This dog has a long genetic foundation of living in the harshest environment imaginable, and many of its behaviours are evolved to conform with "survival of the fittest." Independence, resourcefulness, and primitive behaviours are common in the breed. While intelligent, they are widely believed to be one of the most difficult dogs to train. However, if the training is kept fun for the dog and not repetitively boring, success is within reach.

There is reason to believe that Alaskan Malamutes sometimes cope poorly with smaller animals, including other canines; however, this has been difficult to document in detail beyond observational data. Many Malamute owners have observed this behaviour with smaller animals, though some might speculate this is due to the Malamute's uniquely divergent ancestry, at some points cross-breeding with wolves. Due to their naturally evolved beginnings, the Malamute tends to have a heightened prey drive when compared to some other breeds of dog. So while Malamutes are, as a general rule, particularly amiable around people and can be taught to tolerate other pets, it is necessary to be mindful of them around smaller animals and children.

Malamutes are quite fond of people, a trait that makes them particularly sought-after family dogs. Malamutes are nimble around furniture and smaller items, making them ideal house dogs, provided they get plenty of time outdoors meeting their considerable exercise requirements. If they are year-round outdoor dogs, letting them play in a baby pool filled with cold water in summer keeps them cool. In the winter, they love snow.

The majority of Malamutes are fairly quiet dogs, seldom barking like most other dog breeds. When a malamute does vocalize, more often than not they tend to "talk" by vocalizing a "woo woo" sound. They may howl like wolves or coyotes, and for the same reason.

Longevity

There is only one known health survey of Alaskan Malamutes, a 2004 UK Kennel Club survey with a small sample size of 14 dogs. The median lifespan of 10.7 years measured in that survey is very typical of a breed their size. The major cause of death was cancer (36%).

Morbidity

The most commonly reported health problems of Alaskan Malamutes in the 2004 U.K. Kennel Club survey (based on a sample size of 64 dogs) were musculoskeletal (hip dysplasia), and hereditary cataracts.

Other health issues in Malamutes include inherited polyneuropathy, chondrodysplasia, heart defects, and eye problems (particularly cataract and progressive retinal atrophy).

Climate and Malamutes

While Malamutes have been successfully raised in places such as Arizona, their dense coats generally make them unsuited for outdoor living in hot climates. When the weather gets hot, like any other breed of dog, the Malamute needs plenty of water and shade. They will grow a winter coat and subsequently shed it in spring.

The Malamute is a descendant of dogs of the Mahlemut tribe of Inuit in upper western Alaska. These dogs had a prominent role with their human companions – working, hunting, and living alongside them. The interdependent relationship between the Mahlemut and their dogs fostered prosperity among both and enabled them to flourish in the inhospitable land above the Arctic Circle.

For a brief period during the Klondike Gold Rush of 1896, the Malamute and other sled dogs became extremely valuable to recently landed prospectors and settlers, and were frequently crossbred with imported breeds. This was often an attempt to improve the type, or to make up for how few true Malamutes were up for sale. This seems to have had no long standing effect on the modern Malamute, and recent DNA analysis shows that Malamutes are one of the oldest breeds of dog, genetically distinct from other dog breeds.

The Malamute dog has had a distinguished history; aiding Rear Admiral Richard Byrd to the South Pole, and the miners who came to Alaska during the Gold Rush of 1896, as well as serving in World War II primarily as search and rescue dogs in Greenland, although also used as freighting and packing dogs in Europe. This dog was never destined to be a racing sled dog; instead, it was used for heavy freighting, pulling hundreds (maybe thousands) of pounds of supplies to villages and camps in groups of at least 4 dogs for heavy loads.

The Alaskan Malamute is a member of the Spitz group of dogs, traced back 2,000 to 3,000 years ago to the Mahlemuits tribe of Alaska.

"In shape, the Paleolithic dogs most resemble the Siberian husky, but in size, however, they were somewhat larger, probably comparable to large shepherd dogs," stated Germonpré, a paleontologist at the Royal Belgian Institute of Natural Sciences. This description of recently-found dog remains (30,000 years old) fits the Alaskan Malamute very closely. Though not scientifically confirmed, the Alaskan Malamute may be the closest living relative to the 'First Dog'.

A bill in the Alaska House has been passed to name the Malamute the official state dog of Alaska.

Bernese Mountain Dog

The Bernese Mountain Dog, called in Swiss German the Berner Sennenhund, is a large breed of dog, one of the four breeds of Sennenhund-type dogs from the Swiss Alps. The name *Sennenhund* is derived from the German 'Senne' (alpine pasture) and 'hund' (dog), as they accompanied the alpine herders and dairymen called *Senn*. *Berner* (or *Bernese* in English) refers to the area of the breed's origin, in the Canton of Bern in Switzerland. This Mountain dog was originally kept as general farm dogs. Large Sennenhunds in the past were also used as draft animals, pulling carts. The breed was officially established in 1907. In 1937, the American Kennel Club recognised it as a member of the Working Group.

Like the other Sennenhunds, the Bernese Mountain Dog is a large, heavy dog with a distinctive tricoloured coat, black with white chest and rust coloured markings above eyes, sides of mouth, front of legs, and a small amount around the white chest. An ideal of a perfectly-marked individual gives the impression of a white horse shoe shape around the nose and a white 'Swiss cross' on the chest, when viewed from the front. A Swiss Kiss is a white mark located typically behind the neck, but may be a part of the neck. A full ring would not meet type standard. Both males and females have a broad head with smallish, v-shaped drooping ears. Height at the withers is 23-27.5 in (58-70 cm) and weight is 65-120 lb (29-54 kg). Females are slightly smaller than males. The breed standard lists, as disqualifications, a distinctly curly coat, along with wry mouth and wall eye. Exact colour and pattern of the coat are also described as important.

Four Breeds of Sennenhund

The four breeds of Sennenhund, with the original breed name followed by the most popular English version of the breed name:

- Grosser Schweizer Sennenhund, Greater Swiss Mountain Dog.
- Berner Sennenhund, Bernese Mountain Dog.
- Appenzeller Sennenhund, Appenzeller.
- Entlebucher Sennenhund, Entlebucher Mountain Dog.

The Bernese Mountain Dog, like every dog, is descended from the wolf. Historically, in some locales at least, the breed was called a Dürrbachhunde.

The breed was used as an all purpose farm dog, for guarding property and to drive dairy cattle long distances from the farm to the alpine pastures. The type was originally called the Dürrbächler, for a small town (Dürrbach) where the large dogs were especially frequent. In Harrisburg, generals used the dogs as war tools but the dogs declined in number through the Civil War. In the early 1900s, fanciers exhibited the few examples of the large dogs at shows in Berne, and in 1907 a few breeders from the Burgdorf region founded the first breed club, the 'Schweizerische Dürrbach-Klub', and wrote the first Standard which defined the dogs as a separate breed. By 1910, there were already 107 registered members of the breed.

Health surveys of Bernese Mountain Dogs in Denmark, the UK, and USA/Canada all show that this breed is very short-lived compared to breeds of similar size and purebred dogs in general. Bernese Mountain Dogs have a median longevity of 7 years in USA/Canada and Denmark surveys and 8 years in UK surveys. By comparison, most other breeds of similar size have median longevities of 10 to 11 years. The longest lived of 394 deceased Bernese Mountain Dogs in a 2004 UK survey died at 15.2 years.

Cancer is the leading cause of death for dogs in general, but Bernese Mountain Dogs have a much higher rate of fatal cancer than other breeds; in both USA/Canada and UK surveys, nearly half of Bernese Mountain Dogs died of cancer, compared to about 27 per cent of all dogs. Bernese Mountain Dogs are killed by a multitude of different types of cancer, including malignant histiocytosis, mast cell tumor, lymphosarcoma, fibrosarcoma, and osteosarcoma.

Bernese Mountain Dogs also have an unusually high mortality due to musculoskeletal causes. Arthritis, hip dysplasia, and cruciate ligament rupture were reported as the cause of death in 6 per cent of Bernese Mountain Dogs in the UK study; for comparison, mortality due to musculoskeletal ailments was reported to be less than 2 per cent for purebred dogs in general.

Owners of Bernese Mountain Dogs are nearly three times as likely as owners of other breeds to report musculoskeletal problems in their dogs. The most commonly reported musculoskeletal issues are cruciate ligament rupture, arthritis (especially in shoulders and elbows), hip dysplasia, and osteochondritis. The age at onset for musculoskeletal problems is also unusually low. For example, in the USA/Canada study, 11 per cent of living dogs had arthritis at an average age of 4.3 years. Most other common, non-musculoskeletal morbidity issues strike Berners at rates similar to other breeds.

In short, prospective Bernese Mountain Dog owners should be prepared to cope with a large dog that may have mobility problems at a young age. Options to help mobility-impaired dogs may include ramps for car or house access, lifting harnesses and slings, and dog wheelchairs (ex: Walkin' Wheels). Comfortable bedding may help alleviate joint pain.

The Bernese calm temperament makes them a natural for pulling small carts or wagons, a task they originally performed in Switzerland. With proper training they enjoy giving children rides in a cart or participating in a parade. The Bernese Mountain Dog Club of America offers drafting trials open to all breeds; dogs can earn eight different titles—four as individual dogs (Novice Draft Dog, Advanced Novice Draft Dog, Draft Dog, and Master Draft Dog) and four brace titles, in which two dogs work one cart together. Regional Bernese clubs often offer carting workshops.

On July 1, 2010 the Bernese Mountain Dog became eligible to compete in AKC Herding Events. Herding instincts and trainability can be measured at noncompetitive herding tests. Berners exhibiting basic herding instincts can be trained to compete in herding trials.

Grooming

The Bernese coat is slightly rough in outline, but not at all harsh in texture. The undercoat is fairly dense; the coat is quite dirt and weather resistant. A good brushing every week or two is sufficient to keep it in fine shape, except when the undercoat is being blown; then daily combing or brushing is in order for the duration of the shed. Regular use of a drag comb (it looks like a small rake), especially in the undercoat, is highly effective. Bernese Mountain Dogs shed year-round, and drifts of fur are to be expected.

The breed standard for the Bernese Mountain Dog states that dogs should not be 'aggressive, anxious or distinctly shy', but rather should be 'good natured', 'self-assured', 'placid towards strangers', and 'docile'. Temperament of individual dogs may vary, and not all examples of the breed have been carefully bred to follow the Standard. All large dogs should be well socialized when young, and given regular training and activities throughout their lives.

Bernese are outdoor dogs at heart, though well-behaved in the house; they need activity and exercise, but do not have a great deal of endurance. They can move with amazing bursts of speed for their size when motivated. If they are sound (no problems with their hips, elbows, or other joints) they enjoy hiking and generally stick close to their people.

The Bernese temperament is a strong point of the breed. They are affectionate, loyal, faithful, stable, intelligent, but sometimes shy. The majority of Bernese are friendly to people, and other dogs. They often get along well with other pets such as cats, horses, etc. They do not respond well to harsh treatment, although Bernese are willing and eager to please their master. Bernese love to be encouraged with praise and treats. The breed is sweet and good with children, despite their great size. Overall, they are stable in temperament, patient, and loving. Bernese Mountain Dogs are slow to mature, and may display noticeable puppy-like tendencies until 1½ years of age.

Dogue de Bordeaux

The Dogue de Bordeaux, Bordeaux Mastiff or French Mastiff or Bordeauxdog is a breed of dog that is strong, powerful, and imposing. The Dogue de Bordeaux is one of the most ancient French breeds. They are a typical brachycephalic molossoid type. Bordeaux are very powerful dogs, with a very muscular body yet retaining a harmonious temperament. The breed has been utilized in many different forms, from using their brawn to pull carts or haul heavy objects, to guarding flocks and used to protect castles of the European elite.

Dogue de Bordeaux, also called French Mastiff or Bordeaux Bulldog, is lower to the ground than it is long, and is a well muscled and stocky Molosser breed with a heavy, broad head.

Weight

The breed standards by European FCI and the American Kennel Club specify a minimum weight of 100 lbs for a female and 115 lbs for a male. There is no formally stated maximum weight but dogs must be balanced with regard to their overall type and the conformation standards of the breed.

Height

The standard states that the desirable height, at maturity, should range between 23½ inches to 27 inches (58-67.5 cm) for male dogs and from 22½ inches to 25½ inches (57 cm-65 cm) for females. Deviation from these margins is considered a fault.

Dogue de Bordeaux is a well balanced, muscular and massive dog with a powerful build. The Dogue's size should come mostly from width and muscles, rather than height. The breed is set somewhat low to the ground and is not tall like the English Mastiff. The body of the Dogue de Bordeaux is thick-set, with a short, straight top-line and a gentle rounded croup. The front legs should be straight and heavy-boned. The straight tail begins thickly at the base and then tapers to a point at the end. It should not reach lower than the hocks. The tail is thick at the base and tapers to the tip and is set and carried low. The breed is to be presented in a completely natural condition with intact ears, tail and natural dewclaws. It should be evaluated equally for correctness in conformation, temperament, movement and overall structural soundness.

The massive head is a crucial breed characteristic. The Dogue de Bordeaux is claimed to have the largest head in the canine world, in proportion to the rest of the body. For males the circumference of the head, measured at the widest point of the skull, is roughly equal to the dog's height at the withers (shoulders). For females the circumference may be slightly less. When viewed from the front or from above, the head of the Dogue forms a trapezoid shape with the longer top-line of the skull, and the shorter line of the underjaw, forming the parallel sides of the trapezoid. The jaw is undershot and powerful. The Dogue should always have a black or red mask that can be distinguished from the rest of the coat around and under the nose, including the lips and eye rims. The muzzle should be at most 1/3 the total length of the head and no shorter than 1/4 the length of the head, the ideal being between the two extremes. The upper lips hang thickly down over the lower jaw. The skin on the neck is loose, forming a noticeable dewlap, but should not be excessive like that of a Neapolitan Mastiff. Small pendant ears top the head, but should not be long and houndy.

The standard specifies the coat to be 'short, fine, and soft to the touch'. Colour varies from shades of fawn (light, coppery red) to mahogany (dark, brownish red) or also an orange skin with a black, brown or red mask, though the red mask is true to the breed. White markings are permitted on the tips of the toes and on the chest, but white on any other part of the body is considered a fault, and a disqualifying one if the pigmentation goes beyond the neck.

Temperament

The Dogue de Bordeaux is even-tempered, protective by nature, and is vigiiant but without aggressiveness. Dogues de Bordeaux are extremely attached and devoted to their family. They are calm and balanced with high stimulus thresholds. The Dogue is intelligent and can also be stubborn, arrogant, and dominant. Early socialization for this breed is an absolute must.

Life Span

As with other large breeds of canine, the lifespan of the Dogue is fairly short. According to the Dogue De Bordeaux Society of America the average lifespan is a little under 6 years , and the Society is actively recording dogs that are 8 year old or older in an effort to improve the breed's longevity.

The Dogue de Bordeaux was known in France as early as the fourteenth century, particularly in southern France in the region around Bordeaux. Hence, the city lent its name to these large dogs.

A uniform breed type of the Bordeaux Dog did not exist before about 1920. The French placed emphasis on keeping the old breeding line pure. Black masks were considered an indication of the crossing in of the English Mastiff. As an important indication of purity of the breed, attention was paid to the self coloured (pink) nose, lighter eye colour (dark amber), and red mask. They were originally bred with huge anatomically incorrect heads; a pioneer for the breed in Germany, Werner Preugschat once wrote:

"What am I supposed to do with a dog that has a monstrous skull and is at most able to carry it from the food dish to its bed?"

The Dogue de Bordeaux was at one time known to come in two varieties, Dogues and Doguins, the former, the Dogue, being a considerably larger dog than the latter. The latter, the Doguin, has withered away to nothing more than a mention in breed history books, as it is no longer in existence.

The history of the breed is believed to predate the Bullmastiff and the Bulldog. It is said that the Dogue can be found in the background of the Bullmastiff, and others claim that the Dogue and Mastiff breeds were both being accomplished at the same time. Another theory is the Dogue de Bordeaux originates from the Tibetan Mastiff and it is also said that the Dogue is related to the Greco Roman molossoids used for war, as there was a breed similar to the Dogue de Bordeaux in Rome at the time of Julius Caesar's reign, possibly a cousin of the Neapolitan Mastiff. Others suggest that the Dogue de Bordeaux is a descendent of a breed which existed in ancient France, the Dogues de Bordeaux of Aquitaine. Which ever theory is true, it is obvious that the Dogue de Bordeaux shares the same common links as all modern molossers.

The Dogue de Bordeaux was once classified into three varieties, the Parisian, the Toulouse and the Bordeaux, types which were bred depending on the region of France and the jobs they were required to do. Ancestral Dogues de Bordeaux had various coat colours, such as brindle and majority of white markings that carried fully up the legs. They had scissor bites in some regions, undershot in others, big heads, small heads, large bodies and small bodies;, very inconsistent in type. Another controversial aspect was the mask, red (brown), none or black. The Dogues de Bordeaux of Bordeaux of the time also sported cropped ears. Regardless, they all had a general type similar to today's Dogue de Bordeaux.

In 1863 the first canine exhibition was held at the "Jardin d'Acclimatation" in Paris, France. The winner of the Dogue de Bordeaux was a bitch named Magentas. The Dogue de Bordeaux was then given the name of the capital of their region of origin, today's Dogue de Bordeaux.

The Dogue de Bordeaux was used as a hunter, a herding dog, and a guardian. They were trained to bait bulls, bears, and jaguars, hunt boars, herd cattle, and protect the homes, butcher shops, and vineyards of their masters.

During the 1960s, a group of breeders of the Dogue de Bordeaux in France, headed by Raymond Triquet, worked on the rebuilding of the foundation of the breed. In 1970 a new standard was written for the breed, with the most recent update in 1995. This standard is the basis of the standard written for the AKC in 2005.

Although the Dogue de Bordeaux first came to the USA in the 1890s for the show ring, the first documented Dogues de Bordeaux of modern times was in 1959, Fidelle de Fenelon, and in 1968, Rugby de la Maison des Arbres. Between 1969 and 1980 imported Dogues de Bordeaux in the USA were scarce, limited to a few breeders who worked closely with the French Dogue de Bordeaux Club, the SADB. The breed was first "officially" introduced to American purebred enthusiasts in an article written in 1982 and by the American anthropologist, Dr. Carl Semencic for "Dog World" magazine. That article, entitled 'Introducing the Dogue de Bordeaux', was followed by chapters dedicated to the Dogue in Semencic's books on dogs, published by T.F.H. Publications of Neptune, New Jersey. When Semencic's first article on the breed was published there were no Bordeaux Dogues in the United States, there were 600 examples left in the world, mostly in France, Holland and East Berlin, and the breed's numbers were on the decline. Much later, in 1989 the typical American family saw the Dogue de Bordeaux for the first time on the big screen in Touchstone's movie *Turner & Hooch* about a police man and his canine partner, although many people did not know that the massive slobbering animal was a Dogue de Bordeaux.

Since then the Dogue de Bordeaux has taken hold in the United States and can be found in greatly increasing numbers across the country. The Dogue de Bordeaux has been supported by multiple breed clubs throughout the years, and has finally found its way to full AKC recognition through the assistance of the Dogue de Bordeaux Society of America. Since 1997 the DDBSA has helped bring the breed to the point in which full AKC recognition could be achieved.

The Dogue de Bordeaux has begun to flourish is recent years, with the introduction of them into more movies and even television, as well as their full recognition status by the American Kennel Club, also known as the AKC (full AKC recognition began July 2008). Their numbers are climbing, but careful attention must be paid to health in the breed, if the increase in popularity is to progress this breed in a positive forward motion in years to come.

German Pinscher

The German Pinscher (original name Deutscher Pinscher, FCI No. 184) is a medium-sized, breed of dog, a Pinscher type that originated in Germany. The breed is included in the origins of the Dobermann, the Miniature Pinscher, the Affenpinscher, the Standard Schnauzer (and by extension the Miniature Schnauzer and Giant Schnauzer). The breed is rising in numbers in the U.S., mainly due to their full acceptance to AKC in 2003. In Australia the breed is established with a rise in popularity becoming evident. The German Pinscher is a moderately small sized dog, usually weighing between 25-35 pounds and typically 17-20 inches in height, with a short coat. The ideal German Pinscher is elegant in appearance with a strong square build and moderate body structure, muscular and powerful for endurance and agility.

Colours for this breed include black and rust, red, fawn, and blue and tan. For all countries where the Fédération Cynologique Internationale standard applies, only black and rust and solid red are allowed colours.

There are also a few colours for this breed that became extinct during the world wars of the twentieth century. These include solid black and salt-and-pepper as well as harlequin.

The coat should be short and dense, smooth and close lying. German Pinschers customarily have their tails docked and ears cropped, as has been done for over 200 years, in countries where the procedures are legal . Historically tail docking was thought to prevent rabies, strengthen the back, increase the animal's speed and prevent injuries when working. Also for utilitarian reasons, ears were cropped to prevent injuries while working and increase the intense appearance of the canine and eliminate the subdued, "puppy" look of droopy ears. Today, these are both done mainly for cosmetic reasons, though many accounts of injuries to undocked tails and uncropped ears of unaltered dogs have been reported and recognized by the American Kennel Club . Cropping and docking should only be done by a licensed veterinarian. While the altered or natural state of a German Pinscher should not effect a judge's decision in the show ring, prejudices do exist. Even many foreign judges who officiate at AKC events comment on how they appreciate seeing dogs docked and cropped.

The Wire Haired and Smooth Haired Pinschers, as the Standard Schnauzer and German Pinscher were originally called, were shown in dog books as early as 1884. However drawings of the German Pinscher date back to at least 1780, and the breed likely traces its roots to varieties of ratters well established on farms in Germany as far back as the 15th century. These medium-sized dogs descended from early European herding and guardian breeds.

The source of the German Pinscher can be followed back until 1836 when this breed surpassed the Mops in popularity. Pinschers were used as guardians for coaches. They also lived in homesteads where they were used to kill vermin, a job they completed independently by instinct. This behaviour did not need to be trained into the German Pinscher. Even today you can observe German Pinschers searching for and finding rats in open areas and in homes. This high prey drive is a good reason not to leave a German Pinscher off lead outside of a fenced area.

The Standard Schnauzer (then referred to as the Wire Haired Pinscher) was originally born in the same litter as the German Pincher. Over time, breeders decided to separate the 'varieties', changing them to actual 'breeds'. After three generations of the same coat were born, the Pinscher-Schnauzer club allowed them to be registered as their respective 'breed'.

From 1950 to 1958 no litter had been registered. Credit is attributed to Werner Jung for collecting several of the breed in 1958 to continue the German Pinscher as we know the breed today.

The German Pinscher came to breeders in the United States in the early 1980s, though accounts of singular German Pinschers appearing in the country before then have been noted. In 1985, the German Pinscher Club of America was started by various German Pinscher fanciers, most of whom are no longer active in the breed. At this time, the German Pinscher was shown in rare breed shows. They were also recognized by the United Kennel Club.

The German Pinscher gained full acceptance by the Canadian Kennel Club in 2000. The CKC named Ch Othello des Charmettes its first Champion on April 20, 2000. The German Pinscher gained full acceptance by the American Kennel Club in 2003. The AKC named Ch Riward's Rollin Rocs Rusty (Jambo de la Capelliere × Windamir's Zarra) its first Champion on January 8, 2003.

In 2004, the German Pinscher competed at its first Westminster Kennel Club show. The Best of Breed winner was Ch. Windamir Hunter des Charmettes(Windamir's Sayzar × Lot T Da Des Charmettes). The Best of Opposite Sex to Best of Breed was Ch. Windamir's Chosen One (Tanner's Morning Star × Windmir's A-blazin at RG's).

Extinct Varieties

There are several now-extinct varieties of the German Pinscher:

- Harlekinpinscher (Harlequin Pinscher, for the merle colouration)
- Schweizer Pinscher (also called the Jonataler Pinscher, Pfisterlinge, Silberpinsch, Swiss Salt and Pepper Pinscher, Swiss Shorthair Pinscher)
- Seidenpinscher (also called the German Silky Pinscher, Silky Pinscher)

Some of these may have recently been re-formed from the German Pinscher and marketed as rare breeds for those seeking unique pets.

A well bred German Pinscher will be a loving companion with an even temperament. Temperament is hereditary. When considering adding a German Pinscher to a family, it is advised to be able to meet and touch the mother of the puppy you are offered. German Pinschers are generally friendly dogs. They are highly intelligent, quick learners who do not enjoy repetition in training. A well bred German Pinscher can be trusted with small animals and children, though no dog should ever be left unsupervised with either. If the puppy shies away when faced with strangers, it may be a sign of poor breeding.

It should also be noted that German Pinschers are very high energy dogs, in many cases requiring several hours of exercise a day. Accordingly, a large, securely fenced yard is highly recommended for anyone considering the breed as a pet.

Health

Due to the small gene pool of the German Pinscher, breeders should health test their dogs for hereditary cataracts, hip and elbow displaysia, von Willebrand disease, thyroid disorder and with the increased incidences of

Cardiac Disease due to irresponsible breeding practices, German Pinschers suspect for heart issues should be removed from all breeding programmes.

Great Dane

The Great Dane (18th Cent. French: *Grand Danois*), also known as German Mastiff (German: *Deutsche Dogge*) or Danish Hound (German: *Dänischer Hund*), is a breed of domestic dog (*Canis lupus familiaris*) known for its giant size. The Great Dane is one of the world's tallest dog breeds; the current world record holder, measuring 109 cm (43 in) from paw to shoulder; 220 cm (7.2 ft) from head to tail, is George.

As described by the American Kennel Club, "The Great Dane combines, in its regal appearance, dignity, strength and elegance with great size and a powerful, well-formed, smoothly muscled body. It is one of the giant working breeds, but is unique in that its general conformation must be so well balanced that it never appears clumsy, and shall move with a long reach and powerful drive." The Great Dane is a short haired breed with a strong galloping figure. In the ratio between length and height, the Great Dane should be square. The male dog should not be less than 30 in (76 cm) at the shoulders, a female 28 in (71 cm). Danes under minimum height are disqualified.

From year to year, the tallest living dog is typically a Great Dane. Previous record holders include Gibson and Titan, however the current record holder is a blue Great Dane named Giant George who stands 43 in (110 cm) at the shoulder. He is also the tallest dog on record (according Guinness World Records), beating the previous holder who was a brindle Great Dane named Shamgret Danzas, who stood 42.5 in (108 cm) at the shoulder.

The minimum weight for a Great Dane over eighteen months is 120 lb (54 kg) for males, 100 lb (45 kg) for females. Unusually, the American Kennel Club dropped the minimum weight requirement from its standard. The male should appear more massive throughout than the female, with a larger frame and heavier bone.

Great Danes have naturally floppy, triangular ears. In the past, when Great Danes were commonly used to hunt boars, cropping of the ears was performed to make injuries to the dogs' ears less likely during hunts. Now that Danes are primarily companion animals, cropping is sometimes still done for traditional and cosmetic reasons. Today, the practice is somewhat common in the United States and much less common in Europe. In some European countries such as the United Kingdom, Ireland, Denmark, Germany, parts of Australia, and in New Zealand, the practice is banned, or controlled to only be performed by veterinary surgeons.

There are six show-acceptable coat colours for Great Danes:

1. **Fawn**: The colour is yellow gold with a black mask. Black should appear on the eye rims and eyebrows, and may appear on the ears.
2. **Brindle**: The colour is fawn and black in a chevron stripe pattern. Often also they are referred to as having a tiger-stripe pattern.

3. **Blue**: The colour is a pure steel blue. White markings at the chest and toes are not desirable and considered faults.
4. **Black**: The colour is a glossy black. White markings at the chest and toes are not desirable and considered faults.
5. **Harlequin:** The base colour is pure white with black torn patches irregularly and well distributed over the entire body; a pure white neck is preferred. The black patches should never be large enough to give the appearance of a blanket, nor so small as to give a stippled or dappled effect. Eligible, but less desirable, are a few small grey patches (this grey is consistent with a Merle marking) or a white base with single black hairs showing through, which tend to give a salt and pepper or dirty effect. (Have the same link to deafness and blindness as Merle and white danes.)
6. **Mantle** (in some countries referred to as Bostons due to the similar colouration and pattern as a Boston Terrier): The colour is black and white with a solid black blanket extending over the body; black skull with white muzzle; white blaze is optional; whole white collar preferred; a white chest; white on part or whole of forelegs and hind legs; white tipped black tail. A small white marking in the black blanket is acceptable, as is a break in the white collar.

Other colours occur occasionally but are not acceptable for conformation showing, and they are not pursued by breeders who intend to breed show dogs. These colours include white, fawnequin, merle, merlequin, fawn mantle, and others. Some breeders may attempt to charge more for puppies of these "rare" colours. However, the breeding of white and merle Danes is particularly controversial, as these colours may be associated with genes that produce deafness. Although they cannot be shown, white or merle Danes can usually still be registered as pedigree dogs.

Temperament

The Great Dane's large and imposing appearance belies its friendly nature; the breed is often referred to as a gentle giant. Great Danes are generally well-disposed toward other dogs, other non-canine pets and humans, although, when feeling threatened, have been known to attack humans. This is usually brought on by a person that is unfamiliar to the dog. Some breeds may chase or attack small animals, but this is not typical with Great Danes. The great dane is a very gentle and loving animal with proper care and training. They are also very needy, always needing someone. Some may find them frightening because of their huge structure and loud bark, but they have no intention of harming people.

Like most dogs, Great Danes require daily walks to remain healthy. However it is important not to over exercise this breed, particularly when young. Great Dane puppies grow very large, very fast, which puts them at risk of joint and bone problems. Because of a puppy's natural energy, Dane owners often take steps to minimize activity while the dog is still growing.

Given their large size, Great Danes continue to grow (mostly gaining weight) longer than most dogs. Even at one year of age a Great Dane will continue to grow for several more months.

Great Danes, like most giant dogs, have a fairly slow metabolism. This results in less energy and less food consumption per pound of dog than in small breeds. Great Danes have some health problems that are common to large breeds, including gastric dilatation-volvulus (GDV) (a painful distending and twisting of the stomach). This is a critical condition that can affect Great Danes and other deep-chested breeds, and which may cause death if not quickly addressed. Drinking large amounts of fluid in a short period of time can provoke GDV in Great Danes, as weli as other larger breeds of dogs. It is a commonly recommended practice for Great Danes to have their stomachs tacked (Gastropexy) to the right abdominal wall if the dog or its relatives have a history of GDV, though some veterinary surgeons will not do the operation if the actual sickness has not occurred. Elevated food dishes are often believed to help prevent GDV by regulating the amount of air that is inhaled while eating, although one study suggests that they may increase the risk. Refraining from exercise or activity immediately before and after meals may also reduce risk, although this has not been validated with research. Signs that GDV may have occurred include, but are not limited to, visible distension (enlargement of the abdomen) and repeated retching that resembles repetitive non-productive attempts to vomit. GDV is a condition that is distinct from another condition referred to as bloat; though, bloat may precede the development of GDV. GDV is a surgical emergency; immediate veterinary evaluation should be sought if a dog demonstrates signs of this condition.

Breed clubs health surveys in the U.K. and U.S. put the average life span of Great Danes at 6.5 to 7 years.

Dilated cardiomyopathy (DCM) and many congenital heart diseases are also commonly found in the Great Dane, leading to its nickname of the Heartbreak breed, in conjunction with its shorter lifespan. Great Danes also suffer from several genetic disorders that are specific to the breed. For example, if a Great Dane lacks colour (is white) near its eyes or ears then that organ does not develop and usually the dog will be either blind, deaf, or both.

According to Researcher, "The breed originated in Germany, probably from a cross between the English mastiff and the Irish Wolfhound." However, other sources maintain that the breed originated in Denmark and still others report the question as controversial and unsettled. In 1749 Georges-Louis Leclerc, Comte de Buffon used the name 'le Grand Danois', (translated by William Smellie as 'Great Dane'). Up until that time the hound was referred to in England as 'Danish dog'. According to Jacob Nicolay Wilse the Danes called the dog 'large hound', a terminology continued well in to the 20th century. As late as in the 1780 Germany the hound is referred to as "Grosser

Dänischer Jagdhund" (English: *Large Danish Hunting Hound*). At the first dog exhibition, held in Hamburg 14-20 July 1863, eight dogs were called 'Dänische Dogge' and seven 'Ulmer Doggen'.

Great Danes in Popular Culture

The Great Dane was named the state dog of Pennsylvania in 1965.

Scooby-Doo, the famous Hanna-Barbera character, was based on a Great Dane by animation designer Iwao Takamoto. Takamoto based his illustrations on sketches given to him by a Hanna-Barbera employee who bred this dog. Scooby closely resembles a Great Dane, although his tail is longer than the breed's, bearing closer resemblance to a cat's tail.

The athletic teams of the University at Albany have been known as the Great Danes since 1965. Damien The Great Dane has been the mascot since that time. In 2003, the school added Lil' D, a smaller Great Dane, to help Damien entertain the crowds.

Brutus in *The Ugly Dachshund*, a Great Dane raised by a Dachshund mother.

Marmaduke is a newspaper comic strip drawn by Brad Anderson from 1954 to the present day. The strip revolves around the Winslow family and their Great Dane, Marmaduke.

Singer, the main but tragic hero of *The Guardian*, a novel by Nicholas Sparks.

Elmer, a Great Dane in Oswald the Lucky Rabbit by Walter Lantz.

In each film version of Sir Arthur Conan Doyle's 'The Hound of the Baskervilles', a Great Dane was cast as the cursed hellhound that kills the Baskerville family.

Astro from *The Jetsons* is a blue Great Dane.

Pyrenean Mountain Dog

The Pyrenean Mountain Dog, known as the Great Pyrenees in North America, is a large breed of dog used as a livestock guardian dog.

The Great Pyrenees is a very old breed, and has been used for hundreds of years by shepherds, including those of the Basque people, who inhabit parts of the region in and around the Pyrenees Mountains of southern France and northern Spain. One of the first descriptions of the breed dates from 1407, and from 1675 the breed was a favourite of The Grand Dauphin and other members of the French aristocracy. By the early nineteenth century there was a thriving market for the dogs in mountain towns, from where they would be taken to other parts of France. However as late as 1874 the breed was not completely standardised in appearance, with two major sub-types recorded, the Western and the Eastern. They are related to several other large white European livestock guardian dogs (LGD), including the Italian Maremma Sheepdog, Kuvasz (Hungary), Akbash Dog (Turkey) and Polish Tatra or Polski Owczarek Podhalanski, and somewhat less closely to the Newfoundland and St. Bernard.

Males grow to 110-120 pounds (50-54 kg) and 27-32 inches (69-81 cm), while females reach 80-90 pounds (36-41 kg) and 25-29 inches (63-74 cm). On average, their lifespan is 10 to 12 years.

Their coats are white and can have varying shades of gray, red (rust), or tan around the face (including a full face mask), ears and sometimes on the body and tail. As Great Pyrenees mature, their coats grow thicker and the longer coloured hair of the coat often fades on those dogs that were not born completely white. Sometimes a little light tan or lemon will appear later in life around the ears and face. Being a double-coated breed, the undercoat can also have colour and the skin as well. The colour of the nose and on the eye rims should be jet black. Grey or tan markings that remain lend the French name, 'blaireau', (badger) which is a similar grizzled mixture colour seen in the European badger. More recently, any colour is correctly termed 'Badger' or 'Blaireau'.

Great Pyrenees Breed Standard; Working Group General Appearance

The Great Pyrenees dog conveys the distinct impression of elegance and unsurpassed beauty combined with great overall size and majesty. He has a white or principally white coat that may contain markings of badger, gray, or varying shades of tan. He possesses a keen intelligence and a kindly, while regal, expression. Exhibiting a unique elegance of bearing and movement, his soundness and coordination show unmistakably the purpose for which he has been bred, the strenuous work of guarding the flocks in all kinds of weather on the steep mountain slopes of the Pyrenees.

Size

The height at the withers ranges from 27 inches to 32 inches for dogs and from 25 inches to 29 inches for bitches. A 27 inch dog weighs about 100 pounds and a 25 inch bitch weighs about 85 pounds. Weight is in proportion to the overall size and structure.

Proportion

The Great Pyrenees is a balanced dog with the height measured at the withers being somewhat less than the length of the body measured from the point of the shoulder to the rearmost projection of the upper thigh (buttocks). These proportions create a somewhat rectangular dog, slightly longer than it is tall. Front and rear angulation are balanced.

Substance

The Great Pyrenees is a dog of medium substance whose coat deceives those who do not feel the bone and muscle. Commensurate with his size and impression of elegance there is sufficient bone and muscle to provide a balance with the frame.

Faults Size

Dogs and bitches under minimum size or over maximum size.

Substance

Dogs too heavily boned or too lightly boned to be in balance with their frame.

Head

Correct head and expression are essential to the breed. The head is not heavy in proportion to the size of the dog. It is wedge shaped with a slightly rounded crown.

Expression

The expression is elegant, intelligent and contemplative.

Eyes

Medium sized, almond shaped, set slightly obliquely, rich dark brown. Eyelids are close fitting with black rims.

Ears

Small to medium in size, V-shaped with rounded tips, set on at eye level, normally carried low, flat, and close to the head. There is a characteristic meeting of the hair of the upper and lower face which forms a line from the outer corner of the eye to the base of the ear.

Skull and Muzzle

The muzzle is approximately equal in length to the back skull. The width and length of the skull are approximately equal. The muzzle blends smoothly with the skull. The cheeks are flat. There is sufficient fill under the eyes. A slight furrow exists between the eyes. There is no apparent stop. The boney eyebrow ridges are only slightly developed. Lips are tight fitting with the upper lip just covering the lower lip. There is a strong lower jaw. The nose and lips are black.

Teeth

A scissor bite is preferred, but a level bite is acceptable. It is not unusual to see dropped (receding) lower central incisor teeth.

Faults

Too heavy head (St. Bernard or Newfoundland-like). Too narrow or small skull. Foxy appearance. Presence of an apparent stop. Missing pigmentation on nose, eye rims, or lips. Eyelids round, triangular, loose or small. Overshot, undershot, wry mouth.

Neck, Topline, Body

Neck

Strongly muscled and of medium length, with minimal dewlap.

Topline

The backline is level.

Body

The chest is moderately broad. The rib cage is well sprung, oval in shape, and of sufficient depth to reach the elbows. Back and loin are broad and strongly coupled with some tuck-up. The croup is gently sloping with the tail set on just below the level of the back.

Tail

The tailbones are of sufficient length to reach the hock. The tail is well plumed, carried low in repose and may be carried over the back, 'making the wheel', when aroused. When present, a 'shepherd's crook' at the end of the tail accentuates the plume. When gaiting, the tail may be carried either over the back or low. Both carriages are equally correct.

Fault

Barrel ribs.

Forequarters

Shoulders

The shoulders are well laid back, well muscled, and lie close to the body. The upper arm meets the shoulder blade at approximately a right angle. The upper arm angles backward from the point of the shoulder to the elbow and is never perpendicular to the ground. The length of the shoulder blade and the upper arm is approximately equal. The height from the ground to the elbow appears approximately equal to the height from the elbow to the withers.

Forelegs

The legs are of sufficient bone and muscle to provide a balance with the frame. The elbows are close to the body and point directly to the rear when standing and gaiting. The forelegs, when viewed from the side, are located directly under the withers and are straight and vertical to the ground. The elbows, when viewed from the front, are set in a straight line from the point of shoulder to the wrist. Front pasterns are strong and flexible. Each foreleg carries a single dewclaw.

Front Feet

Rounded, close-cupped, well padded, toes well arched.

The angulation of the hindquarters is similar in degree to that of the forequarters.

Thighs

Strongly muscular upper thighs extend from the pelvis at right angles. The upper thigh is the same length as the lower thigh, creating moderate stifle joint angulation when viewed in profile. The rear pastern (metatarsus) is of medium length and perpendicular to the ground as the dog stands naturally. This produces a moderate degree of angulation in the hock joint, when viewed from the side. The hindquarters from the hip to the rear pastern are straight and parallel, as viewed from the rear. The rear legs are of sufficient bone and muscle to provide a balance with the frame. Double dewclaws are located on each rear leg.

Rear Feet

The rear feet have a structural tendency to toe out slightly. This breed characteristic is not to be confused with cow-hocks. The rear feet, like the forefeet, are rounded, close-cupped, well padded with toes well arched.

Fault

Absence of double dewclaws on each rear leg.

The weather resistant double coat consists of a long, flat, thick, outer coat of coarse hair, straight or slightly undulating, and lying over a dense, fine, woolly undercoat. The coat is more profuse about the neck and shoulders where it forms a ruff or mane which is more pronounced in males. Longer hair on the tail forms a plume. There is feathering along the back of the front legs and along the back of the thighs, giving a "pantaloon" effect. The hair on the face and ears is shorter and of finer texture. Correctness of coat is more important than abundance of coat.

Faults

Curly coat. Stand-off coat (Samoyed type).

Colour

White or white with markings of gray, badger, reddish brown, or varying shades of tan. Markings of varying size may appear on the ears, head (including a full face mask), tail, and as a few body spots. The undercoat may be white or shaded. All of the above described colourings and locations are characteristic of the breed and equally correct.

Fault

Outer coat markings covering more than one third of the body.

Gait

The Great Pyrenees moves smoothly and elegantly, true and straight ahead, exhibiting both power and agility. The stride is well balanced with good reach and strong drive. The legs tend to move toward the center line as speed increases. Ease and efficiency of movement are more important than speed.

Temperament

Character and temperament are of utmost importance. In nature, the Great Pyrenees is confident, gentle, and affectionate. While territorial and protective of his flock or family when necessary, his general demeanor is one of quiet composure, both patient and tolerant. He is strong willed, independent and somewhat reserved, yet attentive, fearless and loyal to his charges both human and animal.

Belle, from Cécile Aubry's Belle et Sébastien novel is a Great Pyrenees.

- The 2004 film *Finding Neverland* used a Great Pyrenees to represent J.M. Barrie's Landseer Newfoundland dog.
- The Spanish designer Javier Mariscal was inspired by this dog breed for the design of the 1992 Summer Olympics mascot 'Cobi'.
- In *Hanazakarino Kimitachihe*, the male lead had a Great Pyrenees named 'Yu Ci Lan' for a pet.
- In the television series, *King of Queens*, a Great Pyrenees is a recurring customer of Holly the dog walker.
- The Japanese series *Ginga Densetsu Weed* features a Great Pyrenees named Hiro, who is nicknamed the 'ball snatcher', due to his signature attack of neutering his opponents.
- In the film *Those Magnificent Men in their Flying Machines* (1965), a Great Pyrenees is the household dog at the Lord Rawnsley estate.
- In the Marx Brothers' *Horse Feathers* a Great Pyrenees appears in the dog catcher's wagon.
- In the Korean variety show *Happy Sunday - 1 Night 2 Days*, Sang Geun is a Great Pyrenees.
- A popular Korean singer, Hero Jaejoong from TVXQ owns a Great Pyrenees named Vick.
- In the 2009 Disney movie *Santa Buddies*, a Great Pyrenees puppy named Puppy Paws is the leading character.
- Barry Gibb of the Bee Gees owned a Great Pyrenees named Barnaby who was in their move 'Cucumber Castle' and their video for their song 'Lonely Days'.
- In the Jim Carrey movie *Dumb and Dumber* a Great Pyrenees appears in the dog-mobile.
- Webcomic artist Jeph Jacques owns a Great Pyrenees named Shelby, who has appeared in his webcomic *Questionable Content* on occasion. Appears almost exactly the same as Mr. Tadakichi from Azumanga Daioh.

Greater Swiss Mountain Dog

The Greater Swiss Mountain Dog (Grosser Schweizer Sennenhund or Grand Bouvier Suisse) is a dog breed which was developed in the Swiss Alps. The name *Sennenhund* refers to people called *Senn* or *Senner*, dairymen and herders in the Swiss Alps. Greater Swiss Mountain Dogs are almost certainly the result of indigenous dogs mating with large Mastiff types brought to Switzerland by foreign settlers. At one time, the breed was believed to have been among the most popular in Switzerland. It was assumed to have almost died out by the late 19th century, since its work was being done by other breeds or machines, but was rediscovered in the early 1900s.

The breed is large and heavy-boned with incredible physical strength, but is still agile enough to perform the all-purpose farm duties it was originally used for. Its breed standard calls for a black, white, and rust coloured coat.

The Greater Swiss Mountain Dog is sociable, active, calm, and dignified, and loves being part of the family. It is relatively healthy for its size and tends to have far fewer problems than more popular breeds in its size range. Among the four Sennenhund, or Swiss mountain dogs, this breed is considered the oldest, and is also the largest.

The origin of the Greater Swiss Mountain Dog is not definitively known. The Swiss people themselves cannot be clearly defined as belonging exclusively to one of the European tribes; they are inhabitants of a typical transit country. Beginning in 1515, the remote valleys of Switzerland were more or less isolated from world history for three centuries. Specific dog breeds were created by inbreeding, and puppies were given to neighbors and family members.

The Greater Swiss Mountain Dog was developed in the Swiss Alps. There are several theories regarding the origin of the four Sennenhund breeds. The most popular theory states the dogs are descended from the Molosser, a large Mastiff-type dog, which accompanied the Roman Legions on their invasion of the Alps more than 2000 years ago.

A second theory is that in 1100 BC, the Phoenicians brought a large dog breed with them to settlements in Spain. These dogs later migrated eastward and influenced the development of the Spanish Mastiff, Great Pyrenees, Dogue de Bordeaux, and Sennenhund breeds.

A third possibility is that a large dog breed was indigenous to central Europe during the Neolithic Period, when humans grew wild and domestic crops and used domesticated animals. Whether or not a domesticated large breed existed in the Alpine area when the Romans invaded, Greater Swiss Mountain Dogs are almost certainly the result of the mating of native farm dogs with large Mastiff-type dogs brought to Switzerland by foreign settlers. The early ancestors of the Greater Swiss Mountain Dog were used by farmers, herdsmen and merchants in central Europe. The breed was bred as a draft dog to pull heavy carts, to guard and move dairy cattle, and as a watchdog and family companion.

Selective breeding was based on a dog's ability to perform a particular function, such as pulling loads or guarding. The Swiss farmer needed a strong, multi-purpose dog capable of contributing to daily life on the farm. Large, sturdy and confident, the Greater Swiss Mountain Dog is a draft and drover breed that is robust and agile enough to perform farm work in very mountainous regions. The breed was also used as a butcher's dog, having been "popular with butchers, cattle dealers, manual workers and farmers, who used them as guard dogs, droving or draught dogs and bred them as such." Its popularity as a draft dog led to the nickname 'the poor man's horse'. By the 19th century, the ancestors of the modern Greater Swiss Mountain Dog were widely used in central Europe by farmers and tradesmen.

At one time, the breed's ancestors were believed to have been among the most popular dogs in Switzerland. It was assumed that the Greater Swiss

Mountain Dog had almost died out by the late 19th century, because their work was being done by other breeds or machines, but they were rediscovered in the early 1900s.

In 1908, on the 25th anniversary of the founding of the Swiss Kennel Club (Schweizerische Kynologische Gesellschaft or SKG), two short-haired Bernese Mountain Dogs were shown by Franz Schertenlieb to an advocate of the Swiss mountain dogs, geology professor Albert Heim (April 12, 1849 – August 31, 1937). Heim recognized them as representatives of the old, vanishing, large mountain dog, whose ancestors had been widely spread across Europe, and bred as guard dogs, draft dogs, and droving-cattle dogs.

Heim was a Sennenhund expert, and started to encourage breeders to take an interest them. These efforts resulted in the re-establishment of the breed. In 1909, the dogs were recognized as a separate breed by the Swiss Kennel Club and entered as 'Grosser Schweizer Sennenhund' in Volume 12 of the Swiss stud book. The first breed club was formed in 1912 to promote the Greater Swiss Mountain Dog. The Bernese Mountain Dog and the Greater Swiss Mountain Dog are two of four distinctive farm-type dogs of Swiss origin who were saved from extinction and revitalized by Schertenlieb in the late 1800s.

There is no information about the Greater Swiss Mountain Dog written before 1907. Until 1913, it was only mentioned in reports by exhibition judges, such as Dr. Albert Heim, who is credited with introducing them into official dog breeding. Heim was sure that the Greater Swiss Mountain Dog was the most widely kept dog in the mountain areas of Switzerland between 1860 and 1870, but the prevailing theory asserts that within 30 years, it had nearly disappeared. Dr. Hans Raber commented on this discrepancy in his book, *Die Schweizer Hunderassen*.

If this dog was commonly kept around 1870, it is unbelievable that only 30 years later you could only find him in remote valleys in the Bern area. A well known and working dog cannot disappear in such a short time, especially not if he had all the good qualities he is credited with. Furthermore, this dog was not limited to Switzerland. He also was known in southern Germany, where today the Rottweiler is his noble successor, and in other areas.

This theory asserts that systematic breeding did not occur. Farmers did not typically take their in-season females to selected males, so breeding was left to chance. From the litter, puppies who were likable and looked suitable were chosen. Because of this strict selection, and because puppies were often kept in their original neighborhood, the appearance and character of the dogs remained stable. Practical matters were important when selecting the dog and dictated appearance. It isn't known how much attention was given to colours, but it is possible that irregularly or asymmetrically marked dogs were considered less desirable.

Although Heim has said that the big butcher dogs, Metzgerhund, went extinct after foreign imports became more popular, there is speculation over whether farmers would get an expensive foreign dog. In 1889 an International Dog Show was held in Winterthur, northern Switzerland; various Sennenhunds were exhibited. Raber is sure the dogs were present in 1900 as draft dogs for peddlers and people going to market, watch dogs for farmers and drover's dog for butchers; they were rarely tri-coloured. Everywhere the dogs had short, rough coats; nearly all were brown, yellow or black with white and brown markings. Lons' description of the northern and central German butcher dog also fits the Sennenhunde at the beginning of pure breeding; this applies to the Austrian butcher dog of Linz, and the French and Belgian Matin. It is to their credit that Heim and Schertenleib selected one variation of the butcher dog – possible the most beautiful – and started it on the road to a pure breed.

In 1908 the Swiss mountain dog appeared for the first time in public. At a show in Langenthal, Switzerland, Franz Schertenleib – a breeder of the Berner – showed an extraordinarily strong, short-haired Berner Sennenhund. He had seen this dog and bought him as an oddity. He was eager to hear what the Langenthal judge, Professor Heim, would say about this short-haired Berner. Bello vom Schlossgut was beautifully marked, 26 in (66 cm) high, sturdy, and with attractive colours. Heim's first look saw the possibility of a new breed of Sennenhunde. He remembered having seen similar dogs in the 1860s in various parts of Switzerland. He said to Schertenleib, "The dog belongs in a different category; he is too gorgeous and thoroughbred to push him aside as a poor example of a Berner. He is an example of the old-time, almost extinct, butcher dog". Heim wrote in his judge's notes: "Bello is a marvelous, old Sennen (Butcher) hund of the large, almost extinct breed. Had he been entered under 'other breeds' I would have recognized him as grossen Sennenhund and awarded him first prize with pleasure. Since he was entered among the Durrbachs, I cannot give this interesting dog more than second prize. This dog is out of place here."

Heim gave Bello the name Grosse Schweizer Sennenhund and dismissed the first representative of a newly named breed from the ring. Heim wrote the first standard based on Bello, and Schertenleib started to search for other members of the new breed. He found two short-haired bitches and breeding began. The first Greater Swiss Mountain Dogs were stockier and rougher than the modern dogs; the skulls were wider than desirable today and showed a marked stop. Judging from old pictures, the colouring was bad; the black coat was mixed with yellow wool at the neck, flanks and rear.

Throughout the early 20th century, the Greater Swiss Mountain Dog population in Europe grew slowly, and it remains a rare breed both in its native Switzerland and the U.S. During World War II the breed was used by the Swiss Army as a draft dog. In 1945 over 100 puppies were registered, indicating the existence of about 350-400 dogs of the breed at that time.

The breed was first recognised internationally in 1939, when the Swiss Standard was first published by the Fédération Cynologique Internationale.

In 1968 J. Frederick and Patricia Hoffman imported the first Greater Swiss Mountain Dogs to the U.S. The Greater Swiss Mountain Dog Club of America was formed; the club promotes careful, selective breeding to gradually increase the strength and popularity of the breed. In 1983 the club held the first Greater Swiss Mountain Dog Club of America (GSMDCA) National Specialty; the club registry contained 257 dogs. In 1985 the breed was granted entrance to the American Kennel Club (AKC) Miscellaneous Group. In 1992 the GSMDCA started to work toward full AKC recognition, and in July 1995 the Greater Swiss Mountain Dog was officially granted full recognition in the AKC Working Group.

The Greater Swiss Mountain Dog is a draft and drover breed; it is a large, heavy-boned dog with incredible physical strength. Despite being heavy-boned and well-muscled, the dog is agile enough to perform the all-purpose farm duties of the mountainous regions of its origin.

There is black on top of the dog's back, ears, tail and the majority of the legs. There should be rust on the cheeks, a thumb print above the eyes, and also rust should appear on the legs between the white and black. There should be white on the muzzle, the feet, the tip of the tail, on the chest, and up from the muzzle to pass between the eyes. Symmetrical markings are preferred by breeders.

The double coat has a dense outer coat of about 1.25 to 2 in (3.2 to 5.1 cm) long. Textures of the topcoat can range from short, straight and fine to longer, wavier and coarser. The under coat is thick and ranges from the preferred dark gray to light gray to tawny, and must be on the neck, but can be all over the body with such an thick coat, Sennenhund shed throughout the year and they have a major shedding once or twice a year.

While the Greater Swiss Mountain Dog Standard calls for a black, white and rust dog; they do come in other colours which include blue, white and tan tri-colour; and rust and white bi-colour. On the blue tri-colour dogs, blue replaces where black would be and tan replaces where the rust would normally be. On the rust bi-colour dogs, the dog is solid rust and white markings with a total absence of black colouring.

Size

Males range between 25.5 to 28.5 in (65 to 72 cm) at the shoulder and females range between 23.5 to 27 in (60 to 69 cm) at the shoulder. There is no standard for weight in the Greater Swiss Mountain Dog; males tend to range between 100 to 140 lb (45 to 64 kg) and females range between 80 to 115 lb (36 to 52 kg). Body length to height is approximately a 10 to 9 proportion; they are slightly longer than tall.

Greater Swiss Mountain Dogs have an animated and gentle expression. Their eyes are almond shaped, vary in colour from hazel to chestnut – dark brown is preferred – medium-sized, and neither deep set nor protruding. Eyelids are close fitting and eyerims are black.

The medium-sized ears are set high, triangular in shape, gently rounded at the tip and hang close to the head when relaxed. When alert, the ears are brought forward and raised at the base. The top of the ear is level with the top of the skull.

The skull is flat and broad with a slight stop. The backskull and muzzle are approximately equal in length; the backskull is approximately twice the width of the muzzle. The muzzle is large, blunt and straight, and most often has a slight rise before the end. In adult dogs the nose leather is always black.

The lips are clean and as a dry-mouthed breed, flews are only slightly developed. They should not drool. The teeth meet in a scissors bite.

The neck is of moderate length, strong, muscular and clean. The topline is level from the withers to the croup – the croup is the fused sacral vertebrae that form the roof of the pelvis and the first few vertebrae of the tail. The croup is long, broad and smoothly rounded to the tail insertion. The tail is thicker at the base, tapering to a point as it reaches the hocks; it is carried down in repose. When alert and in movement, the tail may be carried higher and curved slightly upward; it should not curl over the back. The bones of the tail should be straight.

The chest is deep and broad with a slightly protruding breastbone, with well-sprung ribs. The depth of the chest is approximately one-half the height of the dog at the withers, and the deepest point of the chest should lie between the elbows, not above them.

Forequarters

The shoulders of a Greater Swiss Mountain Dog are long, sloping, strong, moderately laid back, flat and well-muscled. Their forelegs are straight and strong.

A dog walks on its toes like a horse does; a dog's pastern and paws are analogous to the back of a human's hand and fingers, respectfully. The pasterns slope very slightly, but are not weak. Feet are round and compact with well-arched toes; the feet turn neither in nor out.

Hindquarters

The thighs are broad, strong and muscular; broad, strong and muscular hindquarters, and proper angles between the stifles and hocks are essential for a draft dog to provide powerful rear-drive during movement. The breed standard 'bend of stifle' refers to where the upper and the lower thighs meet. The stifles are moderately bent and taper smoothly into the hocks. The hocks are well let down and straight when viewed from the rear. The hock joint corresponds to the human ankle and first short bones in the foot; the dog does not walk on the heel as people do. Feet are round and compact with well-arched toes; they turn neither in nor out. Dewclaws should be removed.

Gait

The gait of the Greater Swiss Mountain Dog should have movement with a level back. Their gait should have good reach in front with a powerful drive in the rear. Soundness, balance and efficiency which accompany correct structure and good condition are crucial factors in their movement, not speed. Greater Swiss Mountain Dogs were bred to work all day on a farm and need stamina. They are a large breed; because of their history as farm dogs in mountainous terrain, they are extremely agile and this is apparent in their gait.

Temperament

The Greater Swiss Mountain Dog is happy with an enthusiastic nature and strong affinity to people and children. This breed is sociable, active, calm and dignified. They do need plenty of room to exercise. They will not be happy confined to kennel life; they want to enjoy their family. They crave attention and physical contact. Greater Swiss Mountain Dogs are bold, faithful and willing workers and are eager to please. The Greater Swiss Mountain Dog is confident in nature; the breed is gentle with children. He can be stubborn and determined. The Greater Swiss Mountain Dog is an intelligent breed and is a quick learner. He can be difficult to housebreak, and tends to try to eat just about anything, edible or not.

The activity level in the Greater Swiss Mountain Dog is variable. They are capable of being athletic, but usually that activity is in bursts; they are active for short periods of time followed by napping. They want to be with their owners and to participate; their activity level most often matches the activity level of the family. As a working dog, they like having a job to do and enjoy participating in hiking, carting, obedience trials, herding, weight pulling and backpacking with their owners.

Being alert and vigilant, the Greater Swiss Mountain Dog is a good watchdog. They tend to notice everything in their surroundings and are quick to sound alarm. Faced with a threat, they will stand their ground and put on a show that will intimidate those unfamiliar with the dog. Greater Swiss Mountain Dogs are accepting of a non-threatening stranger. They are confident and comfortable in unfamiliar locations, and are stable around strange noises and unfamiliar people. They are accepting of other dogs and species, and are reluctant to bite.

This giant breed matures slowly in both mind and body, taking anywhere from 2 to 3 years. The objective in training this dog is for the owner to achieve pack leader status. As youngsters, they can be quite boisterous and they do require steady and reliable training to develop manners and physical self-control. As with all large, active working dogs, this breed should be well socialized early in life with other dogs and people, and be provided with regular activity and training.

For the most part, this breed is relatively healthy for their size; Greater Swiss Mountain Dogs have far fewer problems than more populous breeds in the similar size range.

Urinary Incontinence

Urinary incontinence (UI) is defined as involuntary urination, and most often occurs in Greater Swiss Mountain Dogs as leaking of urine while sleeping; it is a non-life threatening condition. It seems that more than 20 per cent of the females are affected, usually after being spayed. Incontinence is occasionally found in males as well. Incontinence can occur for many reasons, such as a weak bladder sphincter – generally the most common cause in Greater Swiss Mountain Dogs – urinary tract infection, excessive water consumption, congenital structural defects and spinal cord disease.

Eyelash Issues

The two most common eye issues that Greater Swiss Mountain Dogs face are distichiasis and entropion, with distichiasis being the most common issue. Distichiasis is the presence of extra eyelashes along the eyelid. Distichiasis has been reported in 19 per cent, of the breed and in the vast majority of cases it is non-symptomatic and does not cause an issue for the dog. Extra eyelashes can be seen along the eyelid; sometimes extra eyelashes grow so that they irritate the eye. Treatment varies from vet to vet, some choosing to freeze the affected hair follicles and others choosing to use electrocautery.

Entropion, found in about 3 per cent of the breed, is the rolling in of the eyelids, which causes the eyelashes to irritate the eye. Entropion is a condition that often requires surgery to fix, but once corrected causes no future issues for the dog.

Lick Fit

Lick fit is a term use to describe the frantic licking to which Greater Swiss Mountain Dogs can be prone. This has been reported in 17 per cent of the breed. When in the middle of a lick fit, the dog will lick anything they can — carpet, floors, walls — and will eat anything they can find, including grass, leaves, dirt, carpet, and will gulp air and swallow constantly. Their actions make it obvious they are in severe gastrointestinal discomfort. Many owners are able to prevent lick fits by ensuring the dog never has an empty stomach by frequent, smaller meals and large dog biscuits as between meal snacks.

Epilepsy

Ideopathic Epilepsy (IE) is the condition of frequent seizures with no identifiable cause. Seizures occur when nerve cells in the brain become hyperexited and send rapid-fire messages to the body. Treatment of IE depends on the severity of the case and may involve daily administration of anticonvulsant drugs. IE is present in all Greater Swiss Mountain Dog lines; it typically surfaces between the ages of 1 to 3 years, but it can become evident as early as 12 months and as late as 5 years. The median age of death from epilepsy in the breed is 3.75 years. Canine genetics researcher Dr. George Padgett concluded that at least 39 per cent of Greater Swiss Mountain Dogs carry the genes to produce epilepsy.

Abdominal Health Issues

Bloat, a.k.a. gastric dilitation-volvulous (GDV), is the greatest killer of the Greater Swiss Mountain Dog. GDV occurs in deep-chested breeds and requires immediate veterinary care. It can be caused by wolfing down too much water, too much food too fast, exercise after eating, stress or unknown conditions. Symptoms are distended abdomen, excessive salivating, depression and lethargy. When bloat occurs it cuts off the esophagus, and blood supply to the heart is lessened causing low blood pressure as well as other cardiac problems; the dog can go into shock. Organ damage can occur as well and the stomach may rupture causing peritonitis to set in. If not treated, the dog may die.

The spleen is located in the left cranial abdomen and is held loosely in place by ligaments. Primary diseases of the spleen are splenic torsion and splenic tumors. Splenic torsion occurs when the spleen twists along the axis of the blood supply. Symptoms of splenic torsion include lethargy, abdominal distension and pale mucous membranes. One theory for the development of splenic torsion is that for dogs with chronic intermittent gastric dilatation, the dilation causes the spleen's ligaments to stretch and increases the spleen's mobility within the abdomen. The spleen becomes torsed because it is no longer anchored in its correct location. In a normal Greater Swiss Mountain Dog the spleen is smooth and uncreased; it is about 6 to 8 in (15 to 20 cm) by 2 in (5.1 cm), and less than 1 in (2.5 cm) thick. Most of the spleens removed from Greater Swiss Mountain Dogs are 18 to 24 in (46 to 61 cm) by 8 to 10 in (20 to 25 cm) and very thick. This size spleen is not an abnormal finding in this breed. It seems apparent that many dogs of the breed suffer enlarged spleens for no obvious reason other than the spleen may have been constantly twisting, folding and unfolding.

Dysplasias

Canine hip dysplasia (CHD) is the irregular formation of the joint that joins the femur – the longest bone in the body – to the hip socket. The hip is a ball-and-socket joint and the femoral head must fit well into the socket for the joint to function properly. Early signs of CHD include a reluctance to go up and down stairs or to jump; difficulty rising or laying down; and bunny hopping when running – both hind limbs move together. CHD is among the principal orthopedic diseases in the Greater Swiss Mountain Dog; it is rarely severe and crippling. Unless x-rays are taken many owners are not aware that they have a dysplastic dog. A goal for raising a Greater Swiss Mountain Dog from puppyhood is to feed them so they mature more slowly than smaller breeds to help avoid hip and other orthopedic problems in adulthood.

The form of Canine Elbow dysplasia most often diagnosed in Greater Swiss Mountain Dogs appears to be a degerative joint disease – a slowly progressive form of cartilage degeneration usually caused by trauma or abnormal wear on the joint. Evidence suggests that most dogs of this breed diagnosed with degenerative joint disease by x-rays of the elbows have the mildest form Grade I. They don't display clinical signs such as pain, stiffness, decreased range of motion or lameness.

Osteochondrosis is a disturbance in the normal development of cartilage; cartilage becomes abnormally thickened, and small fissures and cracks may develop. Dissecans is when cartilage becomes dissected resulting in cartilage flaps, which may remain attached or become loose and fall into the joint space. In Greater Swiss Mountain Dogs most of these cases occur in the shoulder joints and occasionally in elbows and hocks. Except for very mild cases without flap development, the clinical signs are persistent or intermittent lameness. The dog may be stiff after resting and the lameness is usually aggravated by exercise. It is diagnosed by x-rays, and treatment depends on the severity of the case. Mild cases without cartilage flaps may be treated and heal with several weeks of rest and treatment with medication and supplements. Many cases require surgery to remove the flaps and loose fragments, and scraping and smoothing of the defective surface. Surgical repair of the shoulder usually has excellent results, surgical results involving other sites are not as predictable.

Heavier dogs such as the Greater Swiss Mountain Dogs tend to have shorter lifespans than medium- and small-sized dogs; longevity is inversely related to breed size. Two websites list the life expectancy for Greater Swiss Mountain Dogs at 10 to 11 years; another lists it as 8-10 years. A survey by the US breed club shows a median lifespan of 6.75 years. Dog lifespans may vary in different countries, even in the same breed.

Kennel Club and Pet Registry Recognition

The Grosser Schweizer Sennenhund, or Greater Swiss Mountain Dog, is recognised internationally by the Fédération Cynologique Internationale (FCI). They are in Group 2, Section 3 Swiss Mountain and Cattle Dogs; standards are dated March 25, 2003. The first standard was published not before February 5, 1939.

- The American Kennel Club (AKC) fully recognized the breed in 1995, and classifies them in the Working Group.
- The Canadian Kennel Club recognized the breed in 2006, and also places the breed in the Working Group.
- The United Kennel Club recognized the breed in 1992; they place the breed in the Guardian Dog Group.
- The Kennel Club, based in the United Kingdom, classifies the Greater Swiss Mountain Dog in the Working Group.

- The Continental Kennel Club (CKC) lists the Greater Swiss Mountain Dog and provides minimal information about the breed.
- The America's Pet Registry Inc. (APRI) does have a classified ad section for Greater Swiss Mountain Dogs.
- The American Canine Registry (ACR) lists the Greater Swiss Mountain Dog as an acceptable breed under their American Canine Registry section.
- As of May 2010 the breed is not recognised by the New Zealand Kennel Club or the Australian National Kennel Council.

The Greater Swiss Mountain Dog is considered the oldest of the Swiss breeds. It is the largest of the four Sennenhund breeds; all four have the same colours and markings but are different sizes.

Evolutionary hierarchy suggests breeds should genetically cluster into groups sharing recent common ancestry. A genetic clustering algorithm could not easily distinguish between the obviously related pairs of Greater Swiss Mountain Dog and the Bernese Mountain Dog.

The four breeds of Sennenhund, with the original breed name followed by the most popular English version of the breed name, and their size:

- Grosser Schweizer Sennenhund, Greater Swiss Mountain Dog. Males range between 25.5 to 28.5 inches (65 to 72 cm) at the shoulder and females range between 23.5 to 27 in (60 to 69 cm) at the shoulder. There is no standard for weight in the Greater Swiss Mountain Dog; males tend to weigh between 100 to 140 lb (45 to 64 kg) and females weigh between 80 to 115 lb (36 to 52 kg).
- Berner Sennenhund, Bernese Mountain Dog. This is the only one of the four with a long coat; it is the second-largest with males at 25 to 27.5 in (63 to 70 cm) high and 90 to 130 lb (41 to 59 kg). Females are 23 to 26 in (58 to 66 cm) tall and weigh 75 to 100 lb (34 to 45 kg).
- Appenzeller Sennenhund, Appenzeller Mountain Dog. Males are 22 to 23 in (56 to 58 cm) tall and weighs 49 to 70 lb (22 to 32 kg). Females are 18 to 20 in (46 to 51 cm) tall.
- Entlebucher Sennenhund, Entlebucher Mountain Dog. Males are 17 to 21 in (43 to 53 cm) tall, and females are 16 to 20 in (41 to 51 cm). They weigh 55 to 66 lb (25 to 30 kg).

Similar Breeds

In addition to the three breeds mentioned in the previous section, Greater Swiss Mountain Dogs are related to other mountain dogs: Boxers, Bullmastiffs, Doberman Pinschers, Great Danes, Great Pyrenees, Komondors, Kuvaszes and Mastiffs. The breed probably contributed to the development of the St. Bernard and the Rottweiler.

Komondor

The Komondor (Hungarian plural *komondorok*) is a large white-coloured Hungarian breed of livestock guardian dog with a long, corded coat. They are sometimes referred to as mop dogs. The Komondor is an old-established powerful dog breed that has a natural guardian instinct to guard livestock and other property. The Komondor was mentioned for the first time in 1544 in a Hungarian codex. The Komondor breed has been declared one of Hungary's national treasures, to be preserved and protected from modification.

The Komondor is a large dog (many are over 30 inches tall), making this one of the largest common breeds of dog, or a molosser. The body is covered by a heavy, matted, corded coat. The dogs have robust bodies, strongly muscled, with long legs and a short back, with the tails carried low. The body, seen sideways, forms a prone rectangle. The length of body is slightly longer than the height at the withers, approximately 104 per cent of the height at withers.

The Komondor has a broad head with the muzzle slightly shorter than half of the length of the head, with an even and complete scissor bite. Nose and lips are always black. People unfamiliar with the breed are often surprised by how quick and agile the dogs are.

The minimum height of female Komondors is 25.5 inches (65 cm) at the withers, with an average height of 27.5 inches (70 cm). The minimum height of male Komondors is 27.5 inches (70 cm) with an average height of 31.5 inches (80 cm). No upper height limit is given. Komondor females on average weigh between 88-110 lb (40-50 kg) and Komondor males weigh on average between 110-132 lb (50-60 kg).

The Komondor's coat is a long, thick, strikingly corded white coat, about 20-27 cm long (the heaviest amount of fur in the canine world), which resembles dreadlocks or a mop. The puppy coat is soft and fluffy. However, the coat is wavy and tends to curl as the puppy matures. A fully mature coat is formed naturally from the soft undercoat and the coarser outer coat combining to form tassels, or cords and will take around two years to form. Some help is needed in separating the cords so the dog does not turn into one large matted mess. The length of the cords increases with time as the coat grows. Shedding is very minimal with this breed, contrary to what one might think (once cords are fully formed). The only substantial shedding occurs as a puppy before the dreadlocks fully form. The Komondor is born with only a white coat, unlike the similar-looking Puli, which can be white, black, or sometimes grayish. However, a working Komondor's coat may be discoloured by the elements, and may appear off-white if not washed regularly. Traditionally the coat protected the Komondor from wolves' bites, as the bites were not able to penetrate the thick coat. The coat of the Komondor takes about two and a half days to dry after a bath.

The Komondor's temperament is like that of most livestock guarding dogs; it is calm and steady when things are normal, but in case of trouble, the dog will fearlessly defend its charges. It was bred to think and act independently and make decisions on his own.

It is affectionate with its family, and gentle with the children and friends of the family. Although wary of strangers, they can accept them when it is clear that no harm is meant, but is instinctively very protective of its family, home and possessions. The Komondor is good with other family pets but is intolerant to trespassers and teasing, and is not a good dog for city life. The dog is vigilant, will rest in the daytime, keeping an eye on the surroundings, but at night is constantly moving, patrolling the place, moving up and down around the whole area. The dogs usually knock down intruders and keep them down until the owner arrives. Hungarian Komondor breeders used to say that an intruder may be allowed to enter the property guarded by a Komondor, but he will not be allowed to come out again.

The breed has a natural guardian instinct and ability to guard livestock. An athletic dog, the Komondor is fast and powerful and will leap at a predator to drive it off or knock it down. It can be used successfully to guard sheep against wolves or bears. The Komondor is one breed of livestock guardian dog which has seen a vast increase in use as a guardian of sheep and goats in the United States to protect against predators such as coyotes, cougars, bears, and other predators.

Training

Due to the Komondor's size, power, speed and temperament, a lack of obedience training, which should start from a young age (4-8 months), can result in danger to others. Komondors generally take well to training if started early. A Komondor can become obstinate when bored, so it is imperative that training sessions be upbeat and happy. Praise is a must, as are consistent and humane corrections. Once a Komondor gets away with unfriendly or hostile behaviour, it will always think such behaviour is appropriate. Therefore, consistent corrections even with a young puppy are necessary to ensure a well-adjusted adult. Socialization is also extremely important. The Komondor should be exposed to new situations, people and other dogs as a puppy. Because it is a natural guard dog, a Komondor that is not properly socialized may react in an excessively aggressive manner when confronted with a new situation or person.

Given the proper environment and care, a Komondor is a responsible, loving dog. They are devoted and calm without being sluggish. As in any breed, there is quite a range of personalities, so your needs should be outlined clearly to your breeder. An experienced breeder can try to identify that personality which would be happier as an independent livestock dog, or that which wants more to please and would make a good obedience dog or family pet. Adolescence can be marked by changes in a Komondor's temperament, eating habits, trainability and general attitude. Many Komondors are "late bloomers," not fully mature until nearly three years of age. Komondors do not suffer many hereditary problems. Perhaps because the breed has descended from centuries of hardy working stock, Komondors have few genetically linked problems. In particular, there is no evidence of the retinal eye problems found in other breeds, nor is there dwarfism or hereditary blood disorders.

Hip Dysplasia

As in all large breeds (and some small ones) there is some hip dysplasia, though the incidence is about 12 per cent of all radiographs submitted to the OFA.

Eyes

There are two eye disorders found in the breed. Entropion is indicated by the curling inwards of either the upper or lower eyelid. This lid deformity causes the lashes to rub against the cornea causing lacerations and infections. More recently, juvenile cataracts have been documented. The Canine Eye Registration Foundation, CERF, located at Purdue University, evaluates eye exams and assigns a CERF number to it if the dog's eyes are free from genetic problems.

Vitamin B_{12} Deficiency

Rarely, Komondors may have an autosomal recessive gene which prevents absorption of Vitamin B_{12}. Prompt diagnosis is key, as the condition is easily treated with semimonthly B_{12} injections.

Bloat

There is some indication of bloat, a life-threatening condition. The incidence of bloat is no greater than with any other large breeds. To possibly help to avoid bloat do not feed soon before or after any exercise.

Parasites

External parasites can be a problem due to the heavy coat. As with any long-haired dog, a skin check should be part of a regular grooming routine. If fleas or ticks are found, aggressive measures are in order. 'Spot-ons', shampoos and powders work well, but great care should be observed as it is easy to miss a spot where the fleas can hide. Owners should check anti-flea and tick preparations carefully with a veterinary surgeon as the Komondor can be extremely sensitive to some of these products. Be wary of over-the-counter treatments as these are often too weak to effectively treat infestation, others can cause severe reactions if dosed incorrectly. It is recommended to spot-test the coat before dipping as some flea dips have been known to discolour the white coat. Flea collars can also discolour the hair beneath them, so look for a white or transparent one.

Ears

Ear care should also be routine. As Komondors have ears which prevent air circulation, it is especially necessary to keep them clean and hair-free. Some ear canals are more hairy than others, but commercial powders, cleansing fluids and plucking of the hair can greatly reduce infections.

Feet

Thick hair grows between the pads of the feet which also requires maintenance. This hair can pick up burrs, or become a source of irritation and infection when wet. For the health and comfort of the dog, this hair should be cut out with an electric clipper or scissors to keep mats from forming between the foot pads.

Vaccinations

As in all breeds one should be careful that a Komondor have the proper vaccines against rabies, distemper, canine parvovirus, etc. Dogs should also be checked periodically for worms and other internal parasites. Like all stock guard dogs Komondors are usually extremely sensitive to anesthetics. These drugs should always be administered to effect, never by weight.

English Mastiff

The English Mastiff, referred to by virtually all Kennel Clubs simply as the Mastiff, is a breed of large dog perhaps descended from the ancient Alaunt through the Pugnaces Britanniae. Distinguishable by enormous size, massive head, and a limited range of colours, but always displaying a black mask, the Mastiff is noted for its gentle temperament. The lineage of modern dogs can be traced back to the early 19th century, and the modern type was stabilised in the 1880s. Following a period of sharp decline, the Mastiff has increased its worldwide popularity.

With a massive body, broad skull and head of generally square appearance, it is the largest dog breed in terms of mass. Though the Irish Wolfhound and Great Dane are taller, they are not nearly as robust.

The body is large with great depth and breadth, especially between the forelegs, causing these to be set wide apart. The AKC standard height (per their website) for this breed is 30 inches (76 cm) at the shoulder for males and 27.5 inches (70 cm) (minimum) at the shoulder for females. A typical male can weigh 150-250 pounds (68-110 kg), a typical female can weigh 120-200 pounds (54-91 kg).

Coat Colour Standards

The former standard specified the coat should be short and close-lying (though long haired Mastiffs, called 'Fluffies', are occasionally seen) and the colour is apricot-fawn, silver-fawn, fawn, or dark fawn-brindle, always with black on the muzzle, ears, and nose and around the eyes.

The colours of the Mastiff coat are differently described by various kennel clubs, but are essentially fawn or apricot, or those colours as a base for black brindle. A black mask should occur in all cases. The fawn is generally a light "silver" shade, but may range up to a golden yellow. The apricot may be a slightly reddish hue up to a deep, rich red. The brindle markings should ideally be heavy, even and clear stripes, but may actually be light, uneven, patchy, faint or muddled. Pied Mastiffs occur rarely. Other non-standard colours include black, blue brindle, and chocolate mask. Some Mastiffs have a heavy shading caused by dark hairs throughout the coat or primarily on the back and shoulders. Brindle is dominant over solid colour. Apricot is dominant over fawn, though that dominance may be incomplete. Most of the colour faults are recessive, though black is so rare in the Mastiff that it cannot be certain if it is recessive, or a mutation that is dominant.

The greatest weight ever recorded for a dog was an English Mastiff, 343 pounds (156 kg), was from England named Aicama Zorba of La Susa, although claims of larger dogs exist. According to the 1989 edition of the Guinness Book of Records, in March 1989, when he was 7 years old, Zorba stood 35 inches (89 cm) at the shoulder and was 8.25 feet (251 cm) from the tip of his nose to the tip of his tail, about the size of a small donkey. After 2000, the Guinness Book of World Records stopped accepting largest or heaviest pet records.

The Mastiff breed has a desired temperament, which is reflected in all formal standards and historical descriptions. Though calm and affectionate to its master, it is capable of protection. If an unfamiliar person approaches near the Mastiff's perceived territory or its master, ideally, it would protect its master. If the approaching person is perceived as a threat, the Mastiff may take immediate defensive action by placing itself between its master and using a "warning growl" although some will actually hide behind their master and issue their intimidating growl from there. Mastiffs, even fearless ones, will rarely attack an intruder or perceived threat (unless severely provoked) and instead will generally pin the individual until a human they know arrives and tells them it is ok. Mastiffs are good natured, calm, easygoing, and surprisingly gentle for their size. They are a very sensitive breed, as such harsh training methods and discipline are not recommended. It is a well-mannered house pet, requiring minimal daily exercise and activity. The Mastiff is typically an extremely loyal breed, exceptionally devoted to its family and good with children and small dogs and is often described by owners as 'their giant teddybear'.

The Mastiff is a particularly large dog demanding correct diet and exercise. Excessive running is not recommended for the first two years of the dog's life. However, regular exercise must be maintained throughout the dog's life in order to discourage slothful behaviour and to prevent a number of health problems. A soft surface is recommended for the dog to sleep on in order to prevent the development of calluses, arthritis, and hygroma (an acute inflammatory swelling). Due to the breed's large size, puppies may potentially be smothered or crushed by the mother during nursing. A whelping box, along with careful monitoring can prevent such accidents. The average lifespan of the Mastiff is about 7 years although it's not uncommon for some to live to 10-11 years.

Major problems can include hip dysplasia and gastric torsion. Minor problems include obesity, osteosarcoma, and cystinuria. Problems only occasionally found include cardiomyopathy, allergies, vaginal hyperplasia, cruciate ligament rupture, hypothyroidism, OCD, entropion, progressive retinal atrophy (PRA), and persistent pupillary membranes (PPM).

The Pugnaces Britanniae (Latin) was the name given by the Romans to the original English Mastiff.

The origin of the term 'Mastiff' is not clear. Many claim that it evolved from the Anglo-Saxon word 'masty', meaning 'powerful'. Other sources, like the Oxford English dictionary, say the word originated from the Old French word *mastin* (Modern French *mâtin*), the word being itself derived from Vulgar Latin *ma(n)suetinus* 'tame', see Classical Latin *mansuetus* with same meaning.

In 1570, Conrad Heresbach, in *Rei Rusticae Libri Quatuor*, referred to "the Mastie that keepeth the house". Heresbach was writing in Latin; his work was translated a few years later into English by Barnabe Googe as *Foure Bookes of Husbandrie*. This work is adapted from *De Re Rustica* by 1st century Roman writer Columella, which highlights the Roman connection, but it has been speculated the Mastiff is descended from dogs brought to Britain by the Phoenicians in the 6th century BC. From Roman to Medieval times, these dogs were used in the blood sports of bear-baiting, bull-baiting, dog fighting, and lion-baiting. Dogs known as Bandogs, who were tied (bound) close to houses, were of Mastiff type. They were described by John Caius in 1570 as vast, huge, stubborn, ugly, and eager, of a heavy and burdensome body. Throughout its history, the Mastiff has contributed to the development of a number of dog breeds.

When in 1415 Sir Peers Legh was wounded in the Battle of Agincourt, his Mastiff stood over and protected him for many hours through the battle. The Mastiff was later returned to Legh's home and was the foundation of the Lyme Hall Mastiffs. Five centuries later this pedigree figured prominently in founding the modern breed. Other aristocratic seats where Mastiffs are known to have been kept are Elvaston Castle (Charles Stanhope, 4th Earl of Harrington and his ancestors) and Chatsworth House. The owner of the Chatsworth Mastiffs (which were said to be of Alpine stock) was William Cavendish, 5th Duke of Devonshire, known to his family as *Canis*. Mastiffs were also kept at Hadzor Hall, owned by members of the Galton family, famous for industrialists and scientists, including Charles Darwin.

Some evidence exists that the Mastiff first came to America on the Mayflower, but the breed's documented entry to America did not occur until the late 19th century.

In 1835, the Parliament of the United Kingdom implemented an Act called the Cruelty to Animals Act 1835, which prohibited the baiting of animals. This may have led to decline in Mastiffs used for this purpose, but Mastiffs continued to be used as guards for country estates and town businesses. Organised breeding began in the 19th century, when J.W.(John Wigglesworth)Thompson sought out a bitch, Dorah, from John Crabtree, the head gamekeeper of Kirklees Hall, whose dogs were often held in the name of his employer, Sir George Armitage. Dorah was descended in part from animals owned by Thompson's grandfather, Commissioner Thompson, at the beginning of the century, as well as a Mastiff of the Bold Hall line, recorded from 1705, one purchased from canal boat men and another caught by Crabtree in a fox trap. J.W. Thompson's first stud dog Hector came from crossing a bitch, Juno, bought from animal dealer Bill George, to a dog, Tiger, owned by a Captain Fenton.

Neither of these had any pedigree, as was normal for the period. Between 1830 and 1850 he bred the descendants of these dogs and some others to produce a line with the short, broad head and massive build he favoured. In 1835, T.V.H.Lukey started his operations by breeding an Alpine Mastiff bitch of the Chatsworth line, Old Bob-Tailed Countess (bought from dog dealer Bill White), to Pluto, a large black Mastiff of unknown origin belonging to the Marquis of Hertford. The result was a bitch called Yarrow, who was mated to Couchez, another Alpine Mastiff belonging (at the time) to White and later mated to a brindle dog also in White's possession. Lukey produced animals that were taller but less massive than Thompson's. After 1850, Thompson and Lukey collaborated, and the modern Mastiff was created, though animals without pedigree or of dubious pedigree continued to be bred from into the 20th century.

Another important contribution to the breed was made by a dog called Lion, owned by Captain Garnier. He bought two Mastiffs from the previously mentioned dealer Bill George. The bitch, Eve, bought by George at Leadenhall Market, was old enough to be gray-muzzled, but of good type; the dog, Adam, was of reputed Lyme Hall origin, but bought at Tattersalls and suspected by Garnier of containing a "dash of Boarhound", an ancestral form of Great Dane. Garnier took them to the United States with him and brought back their puppy, Lion. He was bred to Lukey's Countess to produce Governor, the source of all existing Mastiff lines. (Lion was also mated to Lufra, a Scottish Deerhound, and their puppy Marquis appears in the pedigrees of both Deerhounds and Irish Wolfhounds.)

In the 1880s soundness was sacrificed for type (widely attributed to the short-headed but straight-stifled Ch. Crown Prince), and subsequently, the Mastiff lost popularity but gained a consistency of type. In the USA particularly, Mastiffs declined steadily through the 1890s and the early 20th century. From 1906 to 1918, only 24 Mastiffs were registered in the United States, none American bred after 1910. By the time the First World War ended, other than for a few imports, the breed was extinct outside of Great Britain.

History After the First World War

In 1918, a dog called Beowulf, bred in Canada from British imports Priam of Wingfied and Parkgate Duchess, was registered by the AKC, starting a slow re-establishment of the breed in North America. Priam and Duchess, along with fellow imports Ch Weland, Thor of the Isles, Caractacus of Hellingly and Brutus of Saxondale, ultimately contributed a total of only two descendants who would produce further offspring, Buster of Saxondale and Buddy. There were, however, a number of other imports in the period between the wars and in the early days of the Second World War, and those whose descendants survive were 12 in number, meaning the North American contribution to the gene pool after 1945 consists of 14 Mastiffs. In the British Isles, virtually all breeding stopped due to the rationing of meat. After the war, such puppies as were produced mostly succumbed to canine distemper, for which no vaccine was developed until 1950. Only a single bitch puppy produced by the elderly stock that survived the war reached maturity, Nydia of Frithend, and her sire had to be declared a Mastiff by the Kennel Club, as his parentage was unknown, and he was thought by some to be a Bullmastiff. After the war, animals from North America, prominently from Canada, were imported. Therefore all Mastiffs in the late 1950s were descended from Nydia and the 14 Mastiffs previously mentioned. It has been alleged that the Mastiff was bred with other more numerous giant breeds such as Bullmastiffs and St. Bernards, as these were considered close relatives to the Mastiff. In 1959, a Dogue de Bordeaux, Fidelle de Fenelon, was imported from France to the USA, registered as a Mastiff, and entered the gene pool. Since that time, the breed has gradually been restored in Britain, has reached 28th most popular breed in the USA, and is now found worldwide.

Extract from Abraham Fleming's translation of John Caius's description, dated 1570, of the 'Mastiue or Bandogge'.

"This kinde of Dogge called a Mastyue or Bandogge is vaste, huge, stubborne, ougly, and eager, of a heuy and burthenous body, and therefore but of litle swiftnesse, terrible, and frightfull to beholde, and more fearce and fell then any Arcadian curre (notwithstãding they are sayd to hane their generation of the violent Lyon.) They are called Villatici, because they are appoynted to watche and keepe farme places and coutry cotages sequestred from commõ recourse, and not abutting vpon other houses by reason of distaunce, when there is any feare conceaued of theefes, robbers, spoylers, and night wanderers. They are seruiceable against the Foxe and the Badger, to drive wilde and tame swyne out of Medowes, pastures, glebelandes *(church lands)* and places planted with fruite, to bayte and take the bull by the eare, when occasion so requireth. One dogge or two at the vttermost, sufficient for that purpose be the bull neuer so monsterous, neuer so fearce, neuer so furious, neuer so stearne, neuer so vntameable. For it is a kinde of dogge capeable of courage, violent and valiaunt, striking could feare into the harts of men, but standing in feare of no man, in so much that no weapons will make him shrincke, nor abridge his boldnes. Our Englishe men (to th' intent that theyr dogges might be the more fell and fearce) assist nature with arte, vse, and custome, for they teach theyr dogges to baite the Beare, to baite the

Bull and other such like cruell and bloudy beastes (appointing an ouerseer of the game) without any collar to defend theyr throtes, and oftentimes they traine them vp in fighting and wrestling with a man hauing for the safegarde of his lyfe, eyther a Pikestaffe, a clubbe, or a sworde and by vsing them to such exercises as these, theyr dogges become more sturdy and strong. The force which is in them surmounteth all beleefe, the fast holde which they take with their teeth exceedeth all credit, three of them against a Beare, fowre against a Lyon are sufficient, both to try masteryes with them and vtterly to ouermatch them".

Extract from Barnaby Googe's 1577 translation of Conrad Heresbach's description of the Bandog for the house:

"First, the Mastie that keepeth the house. For this purpose you must provide you such a one as hath a large and mightie body, a great shrill voyce, that both with his barking he may discover, and with his sight dismaye the theefe, yea, being not seene, with the horror of his voice put him to flight. His stature must be neither long nor short, but well set ; his head, great; his eyes, sharp and fiery, either browne or grey; his lippes, blackish, neither turning up nor hanging too much down; his mouth black and wide; his neather jaw, fat, and coming out of it on either side a fang appearing more outward than his other teeth; his upper teeth even with his neather, not hanging too much over, sharpe, and hidden with his lippes; his countenance, like a lion; his brest, great and shag hayrd; his shoulders, broad; his legges, bigge; his tayle, short; his feet, very great. His disposition must neither be too gentle nor too curst, that he neither faune upon a theefe nor flee upon his friends; very waking; no gadder abroad, nor lavish of his mouth, barking without cause; neither maketh it any matter though he be not swifte, for he is but to fight at home, and to give warning of the enemie."

Sydenham Edwards (1800), wrote in the *Cynographia Britannica*, London: C. Whittingham:

"What the Lion is to the Cat the Mastiff is to the Dog, the noblest of the family; he stands alone, and all others sinking before him. His courage does not exceed its temper and generosity and in attachment he equals the kindest of his race. His docility is perfect; the teasing of the smaller kinds will hardly provoke him to resent, and I have seen him down with his paw the Terrier or cur that has bit him, without offering further injury. In a family he will permit the children to play with him and will suffer all their little pranks without offence. The blind ferocity of the bulldog will often wound the hand of the master who assists him to combat, but the Mastiff distinguishes perfectly, enters the field with temper, and engages the attack as if confident of success: if he overpowers, or is beaten, his master may take him immediately in his arms and fear nothing. This ancient and faithful domestic, the pride of our island, uniting the useful, the brave and the docile, though sought by foreign nations and perpetuated on the continent, is nearly extinct where he was probably an aborigine, or is bastardized by numberless crosses, everyone of which degenerate from the invaluable character of the parent, who was deemed worthy to enter the Roman amphitheatre and in the presence of the masters of the world, encounter the pard and assail even the lord of the savage tribes, whose courage was sublimed by torrid suns, and found none gallant enough to oppose him on the deserts of Zaara or the plains of Numidia."

Famous English Mastiffs

- 'Crown Prince', progenitor of the modern breed, owned by psychiatrist L. Forbes Winslow.
- 'Cash', owned by Trevor Dwyer-Lynch ('Patrick' from Coronation Street), also appeared in one episode of the show.
- 'Hercules' (a.k.a. 'the Beast'), from the film *The Sandlot* (played by Ch. Mtn. Oaks Gunner)
- 'Goliath' (a.k.a. 'the Great Fear'), from the film *The Sandlot 2.*
- 'Carlo' from 'The Adventure of the Copper Beeches', a Sherlock Holmes story.
- 'Kazak', owned by Winston Niles Rumfoord, a wealthy space traveler in Kurt Vonnegut's novel *The Sirens of Titan*.
- 'Moss' and 'Jaguar', of the Japanese series *Ginga: Nagareboshi Gin* and its sequel *Ginga Densetsu Weed*.
- 'Mason The Mastiff', in the 2007 film *Transformers*.
- 'Leo', owned by Richard Ansdell, R.A., and the model for his painting 'The Poacher', aka 'The Poacher At Bay'.
- 'Rocky' (Ch Sterling's Against All Odds) appeared in the 'Leech Trapper' episode of the TV series *Dirty Jobs*.
- 'Lady Marton', owned by Victorian industrialist Henry Bolckow, and claimed by some to have been a St. Bernard.
- 'Chupadogra' A.K.A 'Buster' is an elderly English Mastiff, voiced by Sam Elliott from in the 2010 film, *Marmaduke*.
- 'Lenny' is a brindled English Mastiff from the 2009 movie, *Hotel for Dogs*.

Neapolitan Mastiff

The Neapolitan Mastiff, Italian Mastiff, (Mastino Napoletano in Italian) is a large, ancient dog breed. This massive breed is often used as a guard and defender of family and property due to their protective instincts and their fearsome appearance. The breed is reported to have been used to fight alongside the Roman Legions, by having bladed and spiked leather harnesses tied to their backs and being trained to run under the bellies of enemy horses, to disembowel them.

According to the American Kennel Club (AKC) standards , male Neapolitan Mastiffs should measure 26-31 inches (66-79 cm) at the withers, weighing between 130 and 155 pounds (60-70 kg), while females should be 24-29 inches (61-74 cm) and weigh between 110 and 130 pounds (50-60 kg). Body length should be 10-15 per cent more than that of the height.

Temperament

The Neapolitan Mastiff is fearless and extremely protective of its home and family. They prefer to be with their family and to remain in and around the home at all times. The Neapolitan Mastiff rarely barks unless under provocation, renowned for sneaking up on intruders as opposed to first alerting them of their presence.

Neopolitan Mastiffs, as a breed, are extremely intelligent dogs with a tendency to be independent thinkers. They learn quickly, which is both good *and* bad, since this guardian breed needs extensive proper socialization to learn to accept strangers, especially within the home; without proper early socialization and training, these dogs are likely to become aggressive towards strangers and unfamiliar dogs. Like with other breeds, forceful training methods, 'alpha roles', and a general 'dominance' mentality will not work with these dogs, especially since it is difficult to try to physically dominate a dog that is as large as an adult; if you want a well mannered dog, prevent problems before they happen by using positive training methods, beginning socializing early, and continuing socializing throughout life.

The Neapolitan Mastiff is not a breed for most people, and certainly not a dog for beginners. Neapolitans must be well socialized with people, especially children, as Neos are large, powerful dogs and do not always know their own strength. Additionally, young children have young friends, and even with extensive socialization and training, Neapolitans will be wary of strangers and protective of their family, which can be disastrous for small children.

Additional protection training is unnecessary because they are natural guard dogs and always have been.

As with every breed, obedience training is very important. The Mastino is very tolerant of pain due to the breed's early fighting background and the fact the skin is loose on the body, so it is important to routinely check for health problems, as a Neo may not behave differently when injured or ill. They also are renowned for drooling especially after drinking or if they get excited. Their temperament and protective instincts are noticeably sharper as compared to allied 'heavy molosser' breeds such as the Dogue de Bordeaux, the English Mastiff, the Mastín Españ~ol etc. and therefore they have been used as a breed component in the development of many modern protection breeds such as the Swinford Bandog (also known as the American Bandog Mastiff) and others. This breed is not particularly dog-aggressive, but males are known to be very dominant and, at times, confrontational.

The Neo has some specific health concerns. The most common is Cherry eye. Others include:

- Hip dysplasia
- Ectropion
- Entropion
- Elbow dysplasia
- Progressive retinal atrophy
- Hypothyroidism
- Cardiomyopathy
- Bloat
- Skin infections between skin folds called Pyoderma
- Anesthetic Sensitivity

Additionally, Neos do not do well in hot weather, and are prone to heatstroke. Like most giant breeds, the Neapolitan Mastiff is not particularly long-lived, averaging 7 to 9 years, however, with a proper biologically appropriate diet, safe exercise, and proper weight maintenance, there is no reason that the average Neo cannot live beyond that.

When it comes to exercise, Neapolitans are not a very active breed as their energy tends to be short lived and their weight causes stress to their joints when excessive. However, they can and will have short, extremely powerful bursts of energy.

The Neapolitan Mastiff is one of the Molosser type of dogs, which probably descend from a common stock; whether this was the Molossus attested in antiquity is controversial.

Despite centuries of popularity throughout Europe, this type of dog was almost lost after World War II. Soon after the war, Italian painter Piero Scanziani established a breeding kennel to turn the mastiff-type dogs of Italy into a formal breed which was then named the Neapolitan Mastiff and English Mastiff was used to help in this process.

Newfoundland (Dog)

The Newfoundland is a breed of large dog. Newfoundlands can be black, brown, gray, or black and white. They were originally bred and used as a working dog for fishermen in the Dominion of Newfoundland, now part of Canada. They are known for their giant size, tremendous strength, calm dispositions, and loyalty. Newfoundland dogs excel at water rescue/ lifesaving due to their muscular build, thick double coat, webbed feet, and innate swimming abilities.

Newfoundlands ('Newfs', 'Newfies') have webbed feet and a water-resistant coat. Males weigh 60-70 kg (130-150 lb), and females 45-55 kg (100-120 lb), placing them in the 'Giant' weight range. Some Newfoundland dogs have been known to weigh over 90 kg (200 lb). The largest Newfoundland on record weighed 120 kg (260 lbs) and measured over 6 feet from nose to tail, ranking it among the biggest Molossers. They may grow up to 22-28 inches tall at the shoulder.

The American Kennel Club (AKC) standard colours of the Newfoundland dogs are: black, brown, gray, and landseer (black or brown head and white and black or brown body); The Kennel Club (KC) permits only black, brown, and landseer; the Canadian Kennel Club (CKC) permits are only black and landseer.

The Landseer is named after the artist Sir Edwin Henry Landseer, who featured them in many of his paintings. AKC, CKC, and KC all treat Landseer as part of the breed. Fédération Cynologique Internationale (FCI) consider the Landseer to be a separate breed; others consider it only a Newfoundland colour variation.

The Newfoundland's extremely large bones give it mass, while its large musculature gives it the power it needs to take on rough ocean waves and powerful tides. These dogs have great lung capacity for swimming extremely long distances, and a thick, oily and waterproof double coat which protects them from the chill of icy waters. The droopy lips and jowls make the dog drool.

In the water, the dog's massive webbed paws give it maximum propulsion. The swimming stroke is not an ordinary dog paddle. Unlike other dogs, the Newfoundland moves its limbs in a down-and-out motion, which can be seen as a modified breaststroke. This gives it more power with every stroke.

The Newfoundland dog is legendary for its calm and docile nature and its strength. It is for this reason that this breed is known as "the gentle giant". International kennel clubs generally describe the breed as having a sweet temper. It typically has a deep loud bark, is easy to train if started young, makes a fine guardian or watchdog. It is exceptionally good with children, giving it the nickname 'the nanny dog'. The breed was memorialized in 'Nana', the beloved dog guardian in *Peter Pan*.

The Newfoundland dog is also extremely good with other animals. Its caring and gentle nature comes out in play and interaction with humans and animals alike. As with any breed, the Newfoundland can have dominance issues, but this is unusual for the breed.

There are several health problems associated with Newfoundlands. Newfoundlands are prone to hip dysplasia (a malformed ball and socket in the hip joint). They also get Elbow dysplasia, and cystinuria (a hereditary defect that forms calculi stones in the bladder). Another genetic problem is subvalvular aortic stenosis. This is a common heart defect in Newfoundlands involving defective heart valves. SAS can cause sudden death at an early age.

The Newfoundland shares many characteristics with other mastiffs, such as the St. Bernard and English mastiff, including short, stout legs, massive heads with very broad snouts, a thick bull neck, and a very sturdy bone structure. In fact, many St. Bernard Dogs have Newfoundland Dog ancestry. Newfoundlands were brought and introduced to the St. Bernard breed in the 18th century when the population was threatened by an epidemic of distemper. They share many characteristics of many Mountain dog breeds such as the Great Pyrenees.

The Newfoundland breed originated in Newfoundland, and is descended from a breed indigenous to the island known as the lesser Newfoundland, or St. John's Dog. The mastiff characteristics of the Newfoundland are likely a result of breeding with mastiffs brought to the island by Portuguese fishermen beginning in the 16th century.

The speculation that Newfoundlands may be partly descended from big black bear dogs introduced by the Vikings in 1001 A.D. is based more in romance than in fact.

By the time colonization was permitted in Newfoundland in 1610, the distinct physical characteristics and mental attributes had been established in the Newfoundland breed. In the early 1880s, fishermen and explorers from Ireland and England traveled to the Grand Banks of Newfoundland, where they described two main types of working dog. One was heavily built, large with a longish coat, and the other medium-sized in build – an active, smooth-coated water dog. The heavier breed was known as the Greater Newfoundland, or Newfoundland. The smaller breed was known as the Lesser Newfoundland, or St. John's Dog. The St. John's Dog became the founding breed of the modern retrievers, including the Labrador Retriever. Both breeds were used as working dogs to pull fish nets, with the Greater Newfoundland also being used to haul carts, and other equipment.

Because of that, they were part of the foundation stock of the Leonberger (which excelled at water rescue and was imported by the Canadian government for that purpose); and the now extinct Moscow Water Dog, a failed attempt at creating a lifesaving dog by the Russian state kennel — the unfortunate outcross with the Caucasian Ovcharka begat a biting and not a rescuing dog.

Many tales have been told of the courage displayed by Newfoundlands in adventuring and lifesaving exploits. Over the last two centuries, this has inspired a number of artists, who have portrayed the dogs in paint, stone, bronze and porcelain. One famous Newfoundland was a dog named Seaman, who accompanied American explorers Lewis and Clark on their expedition.

The breed prospered in the United Kingdom, until 1914 and again in 1939, when its numbers were almost fatally depleted by wartime restrictions. Since the 1950s there has been a steady increase in numbers and popularity, despite the fact that the Newfoundland's great size and fondness for mud and water makes it unsuitable as a pet for many households.

During the Discovery Channel's second day of coverage of the AKC Eukanuba National Championship on December 3, 2006, anchor Bob Goen reported that Newfoundlands exhibit a very strong propensity to rescue people from water. Goen stated that one Newfoundland alone once aided the rescue of 63 shipwrecked sailors. Today, kennel clubs across the United States host Newfoundland Rescue Demonstrations, as well as offering classes in the field.

An unnamed Newfoundland is credited for saving Napoleon Bonaparte in 1815. During his famous escape from exile on the island of Elba, rough seas knocked Napoleon overboard. A fisherman's dog jumped into the sea, and kept Napoleon afloat until he could reach safety.

In 1828, Ann Harvey of Isle aux Morts, her father, her brother, and a Newfoundland Dog named Hairyman saved over 160 Irish immigrants from the wreck of the brig Dispatch.

In the early 20th century, a dog that is thought to have been a Newfoundland saved 92 people who were on a sinking ship in Newfoundland during a blizzard. The dog retrieved a rope thrown out into the turbulent waters by those on deck, and brought the rope to shore to people waiting on the beach. A breeches buoy was attached to the rope, and all those aboard the ship were able to get across to the shore.

In 1995, a 10-month old Newfoundland named Boo saved a hearing-impaired man from drowning in the Yuba River in Northern California. The man fell into the river while dredging for gold. Boo noticed the struggling man as he and his owner were walking along the river. The Newfoundland instinctively dove into the river, took the drowning man by the arm, and brought him to safety. According to Janice Anderson, the Newfoundland's breeder, Boo had received no formal training in water rescue.

Further evidence of Newfoundlands' ability to rescue or support life saving activities was cited in a recent article by the BBC. The breed continues in that role today, along with the Leonberger, Labrador Retriever and Golden Retriever dogs; they are used at the Italian School of Canine Lifeguard.

"The man they had got now was a jolly, light-hearted, thick-headed sort of a chap, with about as much sensitiveness in him as there might be in a Newfoundland puppy. You might look daggers at him for an hour and he would not notice it, and it would not trouble him if he did".

"Newfoundland dogs are good to save children from drowning, but you must have a pond of water handy and a child, or else there will be no profit in boarding a Newfoundland".

"A man is not a good man to me because he will feed me if I should be starving, or warm me if I should be freezing, or pull me out of a ditch if I should ever fall into one. I can find you a Newfoundland dog that will do as much".

"Near this spot are deposited the remains of one who possessed Beauty without Vanity, Strength without Insolence, Courage without Ferocity, and all the Virtues of Man, without his Vices. This Praise, which would be unmeaning Flattery if inscribed over human ashes, is but a just tribute to the Memory of Boatswain, a Dog." George Gordon, Lord Byron, Epitaph to a Dog.

"That boat, Rover by name, which, though now in strange seas, had often pressed the beach of Captain Delano's home, and, brought to its threshold for repairs, had familiarly lain there, as a Newfoundland dog; the sight of that household boat evoked a thousand trustful associations..."

"Your fatuous specialist is now beginning to rebuke 'secondrate' newspapers for using such phrases as 'to suddenly go' and 'to boldly say'. I ask you, Sir, to put this man out without interfering with his perfect freedom of choice between 'to suddenly go', to go suddenly" and 'suddenly to go'. Set him adrift and try an intelligent Newfoundland dog in his place."

- **Adam – Seaward's Blackbeard** – 1984 Best in Show winner at the Westminster Dog Show.
- **Boatswain** - pet of English poet Lord Byron and the subject of his poem Epitaph to a Dog.
- **Bilbo** - lifeguard at Sennon cove beach in Cornwall.
- **Brumus** - Robert F. Kennedy's dog.
- **Brutus** - first dog to complete the Appalachian Mountain Club's 'Winter 48', climbing all 48 peaks in one calendar winter.
- **Carlo** - Emily Dickinson's dog.
- **Faithful** - First dog of President Ulysses S. Grant.
- **Frank** - Unofficial mascot of the Orphan Brigade during the American Civil War.
- **Gander** - the Mascot of the Royal Rifles of Canada who was killed in action at the Battle of Hong Kong when he carried a grenade away from wounded soldiers. For this he was awarded the PDSA Dickin Medal retroactively in 2000.
- **Hairy Man** - The dog who helped Ann Harvey and her father and brother rescue 163 people from a shipwreck.
- **Josh – Darbydale's All Rise Pouchcove** – 2004 Best in Show winner at the Westminster Dog Show.
- **Luath** - Landseer Newfoundland pet of J. M. Barrie and the inspiration for 'Nana', the Darling children's nurse in Peter Pan.
- **Pluto** - pet of the Croatian operatic soprano Ilma de Murska, which used to dine at table with her and was trained to eat a cooked fowl from a place setting without dripping gravy on the tablecloth. Pluto lived in the 1860s.

- **Rigel** - pet of first officer William Murdoch aboard the Titanic. Murdoch went down with the ship but Rigel swam for three hours next to a lifeboat until it was rescued by the Carpathia. Rigel is renowned as a hero alerting the ship's captain of the weakened survivors before the ship hit them. Rigel was adopted by crewman Jonas Briggs.
- **Robber** - dog of Richard Wagner who accompanied him on his flight from his creditors from Riga on a fishing boat, which inspired the opera *The Flying Dutchman.*
- **Russ** - last dog of Richard Wagner, buried at the feet of his master in the composer's tomb in the park of Villa Wahnfried in Bayreuth, under his own plaque: "Here rests and watches Wagner's Russ."
- **Sable Chief** - mascot of Royal Newfoundland Regiment.
- **Swansea Jack** - Famous Welsh rescue dog.
- **Seaman** - companion of explorer Meriwether Lewis.
- **Thunder** - Nadeau's family dog.

Famous Fictional Newfoundlands

- **Carl** - pet of Teddy Armstrong of *Anne of Windy Poplars,* by Lucy Maud Montgomery.
- **Crusoe** - main character of *The Dog Crusoe,* by R.M. Ballantine.
- **Jakob** - hero and one of the main characters in the 1977 Slovenian movie *Sreca na vrvici.*
- **Lou** - companion to Officers Mahoney and Shtulman in the 1985 movie *Police Academy 2.*
- **Mother Teresa** - major canine character in the movie *Must Love Dogs.*
- **Nana** - The 'nurse' dog of Wendy, John and Michael in J.M. Barrie's 'Peter Pan'.
- **Pilot** - pet of Edward Fairfax Rochester in Charlotte Brontë's classic novel *Jane Eyre* (1847).
- **Pollux** - pet of Lieutenant William Babbington in Patrick O'Brian's novel *Desolation Island.*
- **Rollo** - Effi and Geert Von Instetten's dog in *Effi Briest,* by Theodor Fontane.
- **Sirius** - hero and companion of Maggie in *Star in the Storm* by Joan Hiatt Harlow.
- **Sonar** - The naval mascot, was 'recruited' into the Canadian Forces Maritime Command in 2010 as part of the Canadian navy's centennial celebrations.
- **Tiger** - companion of Arthur Gordon Pym in *The Narrative of Arthur Gordon Pym of Nantucket,* a novel by Edgar Allan Poe (1838).

Rottweiler

The Rottweiler is a medium to large size breed of domestic dog that originated in Rottweil, Germany. The dogs were known as 'Rottweil butchers' dogs' (German: *Rottweiler Metzgerhund*) because they were used to herd livestock and pull carts laden with butchered meat and other products to market. Some records indicate that earlier Rottweilers may have also been used for hunting, although the modern Rottweiler has a relatively low hunting instinct.

The Rottweiler was employed in its traditional roles until the mid-19th century when railroads replaced droving for getting livestock to market. While still used in herding, Rottweilers are now also used in search and rescue, as guide dogs for the blind, as guard or police dogs, and in other roles.

Although a versatile breed used in recent times for many purposes, the Rottweiler is primarily known as one of the oldest herding breeds. A multi-faceted herding and stock protection dog, it is capable of working all kinds of livestock under a variety of conditions.

The breed's history dates to the Roman Empire. In those times, the Roman legion travelled with their meat on the hoof and required the assistance of working dogs to herd the cattle. One route the army travelled was through Württemberg and on to the small market town of Rottweil. The principal ancestors of the first Rottweilers during this time are believed to be the Roman droving dog, local dogs the army met on its travels, and dogs with molosser appearance coming from England and the Netherlands.

This region was eventually to become an important cattle area, and the descendants of the Roman cattle dogs proved their worth in both driving and protecting the cattle from robbers and wild animals. Rottweilers were said to have been used by travelling butchers at markets during the Middle Ages to guard money pouches tied around their necks. However, as railroads became the primary method for moving stock to market, the breed had declined so much that by 1900 there was only one female to be found in the town of Rottweil.

The build up to World War I saw a great demand for police dogs, and that led to a revival of interest in the Rottweiler. During the First and Second World Wars, Rottweilers were put into service in various roles, including as messenger, ambulance, draught, and guard dogs.

Deutscher Rottweiler-Klub (DRK, *German Rottweiler Club*), the first Rottweiler club in Germany, was founded January 13, 1914, and followed by the creation of the Süddeutscher Rottweiler-Klub (SDRK, *South German Rottweiler Club*) on April 27, 1915 and eventually became the IRK (International Rottweiler Club). The DRK counted around 500 Rottweilers, and the SDRK 3000 Rottweilers. The goals of the two clubs were different. The DRK aimed to produce working dogs and did not emphasize the morphology of the Rottweiler.

The various German Rottweiler Clubs amalgamated to form the Allgemeiner Deutscher Rottweiler Klub (ADRK, *General German Rottweiler*

Club) in 1921. This was officially recorded in the register of clubs and associations at the district court of Stuttgart on January 27, 1924. The ADRK is recognised worldwide as the home club of the Rottweiler.

In 1935 the Rottweiler was officially recognized by the American Kennel Club. In 1936, Rottweilers were exhibited in Britain at Crufts. In 1966, a separate register was opened for the breed. In fact, in the mid 1990s, the popularity of the Rottweiler reached an all time high with it being the most registered dog by the American Kennel Club.

Head

The skull is of medium length, broad between the ears. The forehead line is moderately arched as seen from the side, with the occipital bone well developed without being conspicuous. The stop is well defined.

The Rottweiler nose is well developed, more broad than round, with relatively large nostrils and always black. The muzzle should appear neither elongated nor shortened in relation to the cranial region. The nasal bridge is broad at the base and moderately tapered.

The lips are black and close fitting with the corner of the mouth not visible. The gums should be as dark as possible.

Both the upper and lower jaws are strong and broad. According to the FCI Standard Rottweilers should have strong and complete dentition (42 teeth) with scissor bite, the upper incisors closely overlapping the lower incisors.

The zygomatic arches should be pronounced. The eyes should be of medium size, almond-shaped and dark brown in colour. The eyelids are close fitting.

The ears are medium-sized, pendant, triangular, wide apart, and set high on the head. With the ears laid forward close to the head, the skull appears to be broadened.

The skin on the head is tight fitting overall. When the dog is alert, the forehead may be slightly wrinkled.

Neck

The neck is strong, of fair length, well muscled, slightly arched, clean, free from throatiness.

Body

The back is straight, strong and firm. The loins are short, strong and deep. The croup is broad, of medium length, and slightly rounded, neither flat nor falling away. The chest is roomy, broad and deep (approximately 50% of the shoulder height) with a well-developed forechest and well sprung ribs. The flanks are not tucked up.

Tail

Natural bob tailed ('stumpy') or if present the tail was historically docked. Docking is banned in many countries, but remains legal in others, notably the USA and New Zealand. According to the FCI Standard an undocked Rottweiler tail is "level in extension of the upper line; at ease it may be hanging".

Limbs

When seen from the front, the front legs are straight and not placed close to each other. The forearm, seen from the side, stands straight and vertical. The slope of the shoulder blade is about 45°. The shoulders are well laid back. The upper arm is close fitting to the body. The forearm is strongly developed and muscular. Pasterns are slightly springy, strong but not steep. The front feet are round, tight and well arched, the pads hard, nails are short, black and strong.

When seen from behind, the rear legs are straight and not too close together. When standing free, obtuse angles are formed between the dog's upper thigh and the hip bone, the upper thigh and the lower thigh, and the lower thigh and metatarsal. The upper thigh is moderately long, broad and strongly muscled. The lower thigh is long, strongly and broadly muscled, sinewy. The hocks are sturdy, well angulated, not steep. The hind feet are slightly longer than the front feet. Toes are strong, arched, as tight as the front feet.

Gait

The Rottweiler is a trotting dog. In movement the back remains firm and relatively stable. Movement is harmonious, steady, full of energy and unrestricted, with good stride.

Coat

The coat consists of a top coat and an undercoat. The top coat is of medium length, coarse, dense and flat. The undercoat must not show through the top coat. The hair is a little longer on the hind-legs.

Rottweilers living in hot climates may have acclimatised and may be missing the undercoat.

Rottweiler coats tend to be low maintenance, although they experience heavy shedding prior to their seasons (females) or seasonally (males).

Size

Technically a 'medium/large' breed, according to the FCI standard the Rottweiler stands 61 to 69 cm (24"-27") at the withers for males, 56 to 63 cm (22"-25") for females, and the weight must be between 50 to 58 kg (110-130 lbs) for males and between 40-48 kg (90-105 lbs) for females. Weight must be relative to height.

According to the FCI Standard, the Rottweiler is good-natured, placid in basic disposition, very devoted, obedient, biddable and eager to work. Their appearance is natural and rustic, their behaviour self-assured, steady and fearless. They react to their surroundings with great alertness. The American Kennel Club says it is basically a calm, confident and courageous dog with a self-assured aloofness that does not lend itself to immediate and indiscriminate friendships. A Rottweiler is self-confident and responds quietly and with a wait-and-see attitude to influences in its environment. It has an inherent desire to protect home and family, and is an intelligent dog of extreme hardness and adaptability with a strong willingness to work, making them especially suited as a companion, guardian and general all-purpose dog.

Rottweilers are a powerful breed with well-developed genetic herding and guarding instincts. As with any breed, potentially dangerous behaviour in Rottweilers usually results from irresponsible ownership, abuse, neglect, or lack of socialization and training. However, the exceptional strength of the Rottweiler is an additional risk factor not to be neglected. It is for this reason that breed experts recommend that formal training and extensive socialization are essential for all Rottweilers. According to the AKC, Rottweilers love their owners and may behave in a clownish manner toward family and friends, but they are also protective of their territory and do not welcome strangers until properly introduced. Obedience training and socialization are musts.

The breed has received some negative publicity. In the US, in a 1997 report by the CDC, the Rottweiler was listed as the second most likely breed of dog named in fatal human attacks, following Pit Bulls, although at approximately half the rate of the Pit Bull. Breed-specific bite rates are not known, and less responsible owners being drawn to certain breeds may be a factor. Dog related human fatalities need to be considered in the context that there are fewer than 30 dog related fatalities in the United States each year out of approximately 4.7 million bite incidents, from a total dog population estimated by the American Pet Products Association at 77.5 million dogs. A 2008 study surveying breed club members found that while Rottweilers were average in aggressiveness (bites or bite attempts) towards owners and other dogs, it indicated they tend to be more aggressive than average towards strangers. This aggression appears unrelated to the fear of the dog, but is correlated with watchdog and territorial instincts.

According to the American Kennel Club Rottweilers have a natural gathering style with a strong desire to control. They generally show a loose-eye and have a great amount of force while working well off the stock. They make much use of their ability to intimidate.

The Rottweiler often carries the head on an even plane with the back or carries the head up but with the neck and shoulders lowered. Some females lower the entire front end slightly when using eye. Males also do this when working far off the stock in an open field. This is rarely seen in males when working in confined spaces such as stock yards.

The Rottweiler has a reasonably good natural balance, force-barks when necessary, and when working cattle uses a very intimidating charge. There is a natural change in forcefulness when herding sheep. When working cattle it may use its body and shoulders and for this reason should be used on horned stock with caution.

The Rottweiler, when working cattle, searches out the dominant animal and challenges it. Upon proving its control over that animal it settles back and tend to its work.

Some growers have found that Rottweilers are especially suited to move stubborn stock that simply ignore Border Collies, Kelpies, and others. Rottweilers use their bodies to physically force the stubborn animal to do its bidding if necessary.

When working with sheep the Rottweiler shows a gathering/fetching style and reams directions easily. It drives sheep with ease.

In some cases Rottweilers have begun herding cattle without any experience at all.

If worked on the same stock for any length of time the Rottweiler tends to develop a bond with the stock and will become quite affectionate with them as long as they do as it says.

Rottweilers are a relatively healthy, disease-free breed. As with most large breeds, hip dysplasia can be a problem. For this reason the various Rottweiler breed clubs have had x-ray testing regimes in place for many years. Osteochondritis Dissecans, a condition affecting the shoulder joints, can also be a problem due to the breed's rapid growth rate. A reputable breeder will have the hips and elbows of all breeding stock x-rayed and read by a recognised specialist, and will have paperwork to prove it.

They will also have certificates that their breeding animals do not have entropion or ectropion and that they have full and complete dentition with a scissor bite.

As with any breed, hereditary conditions occur in some lines. Because of recent overbreeding, cancer has become one of the leading causes of early death in Rottweilers. For unknown reasons, Rottweilers are more susceptible than other breeds to become infected with parvovirus, a highly contagious and deadly disease of puppies and young dogs. Parvovirus can be easily prevented by following a veterinarian's recommended vaccine protocol.

If overfed or under exercised, Rottweilers are prone to obesity. Some of the consequences of obesity can be very serious, including arthritis, breathing difficulties, diabetes, heart failure, reproductive problems, skin disease, reduced resistance to disease and overheating caused by the thick jacket of fat under the skin.

Media Portrayal

The portrayal of Rottweilers as evil dogs in several fictional films and TV series, most notably in *The Omen*, and negative press has added to their negative publicity. This has led to Rottweilers being banned in some municipalities, and they are sometimes targeted as dangerous dogs by legislation, such as in the Netherlands, Poland, Portugal and the Republic of Ireland. However, the Dutch law has since been changed as of 2008. On the other hand, not all mainstream media has portrayed the breed in a negative light: for example, a gentler side of the Rottweiler's personality was observed in the movie *Lethal Weapon 3* where a Rottweiler guarding a gun smuggling operation was placated by the main character, played by Mel Gibson, with dog treats. The dog was subsequently rescued and *de facto* adopted by the protagonist. Also, in the HBO series Entourage a Rottweiler named Arnold is a dear pet of the main characters. Cujo the loveable family dog and voice of the official website in the TV series *Kath and Kim*, is played by National Rottweiler Council (Australia) Champion and Dual Champion (Tracking) Goodiesway Basko (AI) CDX ET TSDX PT (pet name 'Polo').

The hero of the picture book Good Dog, Carl and its sequels is a Rottweiler, and quite favorably portrayed as a gentle, attentive, protective and intelligent guardian of his family members. In the Fox TV series *Human Target*, a Rottweiler named Carmine (played by Simba) is the loyal pet of main character Christopher Chance that Chance adopted after his original owner was killed. Carmine was likely named after Carmine Infantino, one of the developers of the original comic book series for Human Target.

In an event widely reported by the media, a two-year-old UK Rottweiler named Jake owned by Liz Maxted-Bluck was recognised for his bravery by the RSPCA. The dog was out walking with his owner when they heard screams. Jake chased off a man as he molested a woman on Hearsall Common, Coventry, in July 2009. He located the attacker and his victim in thick scrub, chased off the attacker, led his owner to the scene, then stood guard over the victim until police arrived. The attacker was convicted of serious sexual assault and jailed for four years. Jake was nominated by police for the bravery award and medallion after the incident. Det Con Clive Leftwich, from Coventry police station, said: "From our point of view Jake the Rottweiler stopped a serious sexual assault from becoming even worse."

St. Bernard (Dog)

The St. Bernard is a breed of very large working dog from the Italian and Swiss Alps, originally bred for rescue. The breed has become famous through tales of alpine rescues, as well as for its large size.

The St. Bernard is a large dog. The average weight of the breed is between 140 and 264 lb (64-120 kg) or more and the approximate height at the withers is 27½ inches to 35½ inches (70 to 90 cm). The coat can be either smooth or rough, with the smooth coat close and flat. The rough coat is dense but flat, and more profuse around the neck and legs. The coat is typically a red colour with white, or sometimes a mahogany brindle with white. Black shading is usually found on the face and ears. The tail is long and heavy, hanging low with the end turned up slightly. The dark eyes should have naturally tight lids, with "haws only slightly visible". Sometimes the eyes, brown usually, can be icy blue, nearly white.

The ancestors of the St. Bernard share a history with the Sennenhunds, also called Swiss Mountain Dogs or Swiss Cattle Dogs, the large farm dogs of the farmers and dairymen of the Swiss Alps, which were livestock guardians, herding dogs, and draft dogs as well as hunting dogs, search and rescue dogs, and watchdogs. These dogs are thought to be descendants of molosser type dogs brought into the Alps by the ancient Romans, and the St. Bernard is recognized internationally today as one of the Molossoid breeds.

The earliest written records of the St. Bernard breed are from monks at the hospice at the Great St Bernard Pass in 1707, with paintings and drawings of the dog dating even earlier.

The most famous St. Bernard to save people at the pass was Barry (sometimes spelled Berry), who reportedly saved somewhere between 40 and 100 lives. There is a monument to Barry in the Cimetière des Chiens, and his body was preserved in the Natural History Museum in Berne.

The classic St. Bernard looked very different from the St. Bernard of today due to cross-breeding. Severe winters from 1816 to 1818 led to increased numbers of avalanches, killing many of the dogs used for breeding while they were performing rescues. In an attempt to preserve the breed, the remaining St. Bernards were crossed with Newfoundlands brought from the Colony of Newfoundland in the 1850s, and so lost much of their use as rescue dogs in the snowy climate of the alps because the long fur they inherited would freeze and weigh them down.

The Swiss St. Bernard Club was founded in Basel on March 15, 1884. The St. Bernard was the very first breed entered into the Swiss Stud Book in 1884, and the breed standard was finally approved in 1888. Since then, the breed has been a Swiss national dog.

Naming

The name 'St. Bernard' originates from traveller's hospice on the often treacherous St. Bernard Pass in the Western Alps between Switzerland and Italy, where the name was passed to the local dogs. The pass, the lodge, and the dogs are named for Bernard of Menthon, the 11th century monk who established the station.

'St. Bernard' wasn't in widespread use until the middle of the 19th century. The dogs were called 'Saint Dogs', 'Noble Steeds', 'Alpenmastiff', or 'Barry Dogs' before that time. They were also used for rescuing people in the Alps.

Related Breeds

The breed is strikingly similar to the English Mastiff and Newfoundland. This can be attributed to a common shared ancestry with the Alpine Mastiff and the Tibetan Mastiff. It is suspected that these breeds were used to redevelop each other to combat the threat of their extinction after World War II.

The four Sennenhund breeds, the Grosser Schweizer Sennenhund (Greater Swiss Mountain Dog), the Berner Sennenhund, (Bernese Mountain

Dog), the Appenzeller Sennenhund, (Appenzeller), and the Entlebucher Sennenhund (Entlebucher Mountain Dog) are similar in appearance and share the same location and history, but are tricolour rather than red and white.

St. Bernards share many characteristics of many Mountain dog breeds.

Kennel Club Recognition

The St. Bernard is recognised internationally by the Fédération Cynologique Internationale as a Molosser in Group 2, Section 2. The breed is recognised by The Kennel Club (UK), the Canadian Kennel Club, and the American Kennel Club in the Working Dog breed group. The United Kennel Club (US) places the breed in the Guardian Dog Group. The New Zealand Kennel Club and the Australian National Kennel Council place the breed in the Utility Group.

St. Bernard dogs are no longer used for alpine rescues, but do participate in a variety of dog sports including carting and weight pulling.

The very fast growth rate and the weight of a St. Bernard can lead to very serious deterioration of the bones if the dog does not get proper food and exercise. Many dogs are genetically affected by hip dysplasia or elbow dysplasia. Osteosarcoma (bone cancer) has been shown to be hereditary in the breed. They are susceptible to eye disorders called entropion and ectropion, in which the eyelid turns in or out. The breed standard indicates that this is a major fault. The breed is also susceptible to epilepsy and seizures, a heart disease called dilated cardiomyopathy, and eczema.

Due to the likelihood of health problems in later years, the average lifespan for a St. Bernard is around 8 years. A few St. Bernards may live beyond 10 years, but this is highly unusual.

St. Bernards, like all very large dogs, must be well socialized with people and other dogs in order to prevent fearfulness and any possible aggression or territoriality. The biggest threat to small children is being knocked over by this breed's larger size. Overall they are a loyal and affectionate breed, and if socialized are very friendly and are occasionally avoided because of their slobber.

Due to its large adult size, it is essential that proper training and socialization begin while the St. Bernard is still a puppy, so as to avoid the difficulties that normally accompany training large animals. An unruly St. Bernard may present problems for even a strong adult, so control needs to be asserted from the beginning of the dog's training. While generally not as aggressive as dogs bred for protection, a St. Bernard may bark at strangers, and their size makes them good deterrents against possible intruders.

Record Size

St. Bernards were exported to England in the mid-19th century, where they were bred with mastiffs to create an even larger dog. Plinlimmon, a famous St. Bernard of the time, was measured at 95 kg (210 lbs) and 87.5 cm

($34^1/_2$ins), and was sold to an American for $7000. Commercial pressure encouraged breeding ever larger dogs until "the dogs became so gross that they had difficulties in getting from one end of a show ring to another".

An 1895 New York Times report mentions a St. Bernard named Major F. who, if the claims are true, would be the longest dog in history. Another St. Bernard named Benedictine V Schwarzwald Hof (Pierson, Michigan - USA) also reached 315 lbs, which earned a place in the 1981 edition of the Guinness Book of World Records.

In Media

St. Bernards are often portrayed, especially in old live action comedies such as *Swiss Miss*, the TV series *Topper*, and classic cartoons, wearing small barrels of brandy around their necks. The brandy was supposedly used to warm the victims that the dogs found. The monks of the St. Bernard Hospice deny that any St. Bernard has ever carried casks or small barrels around their necks; they believe that the origin of the image is an early painting. The monks did keep casks around for photographs by tourists.

A *Punch* magazine cartoon from 1949 depicts a man with a St. Bernard and several puppies, all of which are wearing neck casks. The man explains, "Of course, I only breed them for the brandy."

A frequent joke in old MGM and Warner Brothers shorts is to depict the dogs as compulsive alcoholics who engage in frequent nips from their own casks.

The 1981 Stephen King novel *Cujo* portrays a rabid and crazed St. Bernard that terrorizes the residents of the fictional town of Castle Rock, Maine.

The 1992 comedy film *Beethoven* features a large, friendly but troublesome St. Bernard and, in later sequels, his mate and their brood of unruly pups. According to the producers of the sequel Beethoven's 2nd, the St. Bernards used in the film grew so fast during filming that over 100 St. Bernard puppies were cast to portray the sequel's four puppies (Tchaikovsky, Chubby, Dolly, and Mo) and a mother St Bernard name Missy.

In the book *Rascal*, the main character puts forth the myth that St. Bernards drool because they carried flasks of brandy for travellers for dozens of generations. Never were they allowed any, and to this day every St. Bernard is born drooling for brandy. The main character does not give his St. Bernard any brandy.

Famous St. Bernards

- Bamse, a Norwegian dog honoured for exploits during World War II memorial statue in Montrose, Scotland where he died in 1944.
- Båtsman, a St. Bernard in Astrid Lindgren's story *Vipå Saltkråkan.*
- Barry, famous Alpine rescue dog.
- Beethoven (From the movie series of the same name).
- Bernie, mascot of the Colourado Avalanche.
- Bernie 'Saint' Bernard, mascot of the Siena Saints.

- Bolivar a/k/a Bornworthy and Bernie, Donald Duck's non-anthropomorphic pet, and Bolivar's son, Behemoth.
- Buck, from Jack London's *The Call of the Wild*, is half St. Bernard.
- Cujo, the rabid dog from the book *Cujo* and film of the same name.
- George, from the 1972 movie George! and its 1972-74 spinoff TV Series.
- Gumbo, team mascot for the New Orleans Saints.
- Gumbo, Bradley Brannings pet dog on *EastEnders*.
- Little Cicero and Big Alexander from the MGM cartoon short, Little Cicero.
- Nana, in the Disney and Columbia Pictures *Peter Pan* movies (but a Newfoundland in J.M. Barrie's original play and novel).
- Neil, the martini-slurping St. Bernard of George and Marion Kerby in *Topper*.
- Porthos, J.M. Barrie's dog.
- Schnorbitz, on-stage partner of British comedian Bernie Winters during his later career.
- Schotzie & Schotzie '02', beloved pets and mascots of Cincinnati Reds' owner Marge Schott.
- Wallace (currently Wallace VI), mascot of The Canadian Scottish Regiment (Princess Mary's).

The famous Barry found a small boy in the snow and persuaded the boy to climb on his back, and then carried the boy to safety.

A St Bernard is often credited with being the dog that helped save Manchester United, currently one of the world's largest football clubs, from financial ruin. The legend goes that in 1902 when the club owed sizable debts, the then captain Harry Stafford was showing off his prized St Bernard at a fund-raiser for the club when he was approached by a wealthy brewery owner, J.H.Davis, who enquired to buy the dog. Harry Stafford refused the offer but managed to convince him to buy the club thus saving Manchester United from going bankrupt.

Samoyed (dog)

The Samoyed dog takes its name from the Samoyedic peoples of Siberia. An alternate name for the breed, especially in Europe, is Bjelkier. These nomadic reindeer herders bred the fluffy, white dogs to help with the herding, to pull sleds when they moved.

Size

Males typically weigh between 23-30 kg (50-65 lbs), while females typically weigh 17-25 kg (40-55 lbs). AKC Standard: 21-23.5 inches (53-60 cm) at the shoulder for males, 19-21 inches (48-53 cm) for females. UK Kennel Club Standard: 51-56 cm (20-22 inches) for males, 46-51 cm (18-20 inches) for females.

Eyes

Samoyed eyes are usually black or brown and are almond in shape. Blue or other colour eyes can occur but are not allowed in the show ring.

Ears

Samoyed ears are thick and covered with fur, triangular in shape, and erect. They are almost always white but can occasionally have a light brown tint, usually around the tips of ears.

The Samoyed tail is one of the breed's more distinguishing features. Like the Alaskan Malamute, their tail is carried curled over their backs; however, unlike the Malamute, the Samoyed tail is held actually touching the back. It should not be a tight curl or held "flag" like, it should be carried lying over the back and to one side. In cold weather, Samoyeds may sleep with their tails over their noses to provide additional warmth. Almost all Samoyeds will allow their tails to fall when they are relaxed and at ease, as when being stroked or while eating, but will return their tails to a curl when more alert.

NZKC Standard: Tail: Long and profuse, carried over the back when alert; sometimes dropped when at rest.

UK Kennel Club Standard: Tail: Long and Profusely coated, carried over the back and to side when alert, sometimes dropped when at rest.

Samoyeds have a dense, double layer coat. The topcoat contains long, coarse, and straight guard hairs, which appear white but have a hint of silver colouring. This top layer keeps the undercoat relatively clean and free of debris. The under layer, or undercoat, consists of a dense, soft, and short fur that keeps the dog warm. The undercoat is typically shed heavily once or twice a year, and this seasonal process is sometimes referred to as "blowing coat". This does not mean the Samoyed will only shed during that time however; fine hairs (versus the dense clumps shed during seasonal shedding) will be shed all year round, and have a tendency to stick to cloth and float in the air. The standard Samoyed may come in a mixture of biscuit and white colouring, although pure white and all biscuit dogs are common. Males typically have larger ruffs than females.

Samoyeds' friendly disposition makes them poor guard dogs; an aggressive Samoyed is rare. With their tendency to bark, however, they can be diligent watch dogs, barking whenever something approaches their territory. Samoyeds are excellent companions, especially for small children or even other dogs, and they remain playful into old age. When Samoyeds become bored they may begin to dig. With their sled dog heritage, a Samoyed is not averse to pulling things, and an untrained Samoyed has no problem pulling its owner on a leash rather than walking alongside. Samoyeds were also used to herd reindeer. They will instinctively act as herd dogs, and when playing with children, especially, will often attempt to turn and move them in a different direction. The breed is characterized by an alert and happy expression which has earned the nicknames 'Sammy smile' and 'Smiley dog'.

Samoyeds can compete in dog agility trials, carting, obedience, showmanship, flyball, tracking, mushing and herding events. Herding instincts and trainability can be measured at noncompetitive herding tests. Samoyeds exhibiting basic herding instincts can be trained to compete in herding trials.

Samoyeds can be affected by a genetic disease known as 'Samoyed Hereditary Glomerulopathy', a renal disease. The disease is known to be caused by an X-linked dominant faulty allele and therefore the disease is more severe in male Samoyeds. Carrier females do develop mild symptoms after 2-3 months of age, but mostly do not go on to develop renal failure. The disease is caused by a defect in the structure of the type-IV collagen fibrils of the glomerular basement membrane. As a consequence, the collagen fibrils of the glomerular basement membrane are unable to form cross-links, so the structural integrity is weakened and the membrane is more susceptible to "wear-and-tear" damage. As the structure of the basement membrane begins to degenerate, plasma proteins are lost in the urine and symptoms begin to appear. Affected males appear healthy for the first 3 months of life, but then symptoms start to appear and worsen as the disease progresses: the dog becomes lethargic and muscle wastage occurs, as a result of proteinuria. From 3 months of age onwards, a reduced glomerular filtration rate is detected, indicative of progressive renal failure. Death from renal failure usually occurs by 15 months of age.

Also known as Hereditary nephritis, it is caused by a nonsense mutation in codon 1027 of the COL4A5 gene on the X chromosome (glycine to stop codon), which is similar to Alport's syndrome in humans. The disease is simply inherited X-linked dominant, with males generally having more severe symptoms than females. Clinically, proteinuria is found in both sexes from the age of three to four months; in dogs older than this, renal failure in combination with more or less pronounced hearing loss occurs swiftly and death at the age of 8 to 15 months is expected. In heterozygous females, the disease develops slowly. The disease can be treated to slow down the development by use of cyclosporine A and ACE inhibitors, but not be stopped.

As yet there is no genetic screening test available for Samoyed Hereditary Glomerulopathy. If a carrier female is mated with a healthy stud dog, the female offspring have a 50 per cent chance of being carriers for the disease, and any male offspring have a 50 per cent chance of being affected by the disease.

For the Samoyeds in the veterinary literature several breed-specific hereditary diseases are described:

- *Diabetes mellitus similar but not identical to human Type I (insulin deficiency):* The disease occurs in middle-aged Samoyeds, the mean age at diagnosis is seven years. The cause is a chronic inflammation of the pancreas and/ or autoimmune destruction of beta cells of islets of Langerhans. Moreover, in affected dogs autoantibodies were found to insulin. Currently, several genetic markers are discussed as possible causes.
- *Progressive retinal atrophy (PRA)* caused by a frameshift mutation in the RPRG locus of the X chromosome. The disease leads to a slowly progressive loss of vision, which eventually leads to blindness. The first symptoms appear between two and five years of age. The disease corresponds to the X-linked PRA type 3 in humans.
- *Short legs in conjunction with eye abnormalities:* Due to a genetic defect at the COL2A1 locus occurs on disproportionate dwarfism with short limbs in connection with cataracts, malformations of the retina and/or retinal detachment, liquefaction of the vitreous and a persistent hyaloid artery. The malformations of the retina are dominant (ie before coming in heterozygous dogs), the other symptoms are recessive, so only come to expression in homozygous affected dogs. A connection with Opticin is not.
- *Pulmonary stenosis* occurs more frequently in Samoyeds in comparison with other breeds. The disease can cause shortness of breath, cardiac arrhythmias and tiring on motion and increases the risk of congestive heart failure.
- *Hip dysplasia* is also a concern for Samoyeds.
- *Eye problems* such as cataracts and glaucoma and other retinal problems.
- The breed can also be affected by *Sebaceous adenitis*, an uncommon idiopathic autoimmune skin disease.

Life expectancy is about 12-15 years.

The Samoyed was used for sledding, herding, guarding and keeping their owners warm.

Researcher believed that the use of sled dogs was the only effective way to explore the north and used Samoyeds on his polar expeditions. His plan to feed the weaker dogs to the stronger ones as they died during the expedition ultimately consumed nearly all of his dogs.

Researcher used a team of sled dogs led by a Samoyed named Etah on the first expedition to reach the South Pole.

Recent DNA analysis of the breed has led to the Samoyed being included amongst the fourteen most ancient dog breeds, along with Siberian Huskies, Alaskan Malamutes, the Chow Chow, and 10 others of a diverse geographic background. The first Samoyed was brought to United States by fur traders in 1906. The Samoyeds have been bred and trained for at least 3000 years. Like the former two other dog breeds, the Samoyed also has a wolf-like appearance, and has also sometimes crossbred to wolves to produce a wolf-dog hybrid.

Shed Samoyed fur is sometimes used as an alternative to wool in knitting, with hypoallergenic properties and a texture similar to angora. The fur is sometimes also used for the creation of artificial flies for fly fishing. Samoyed fur sweaters have been reported to handle temperatures well below freezing.

Famous Samoyeds to:

- *Kaifas* and *Suggen*, the lead dogs for Fridtjof Nansen's North Pole expedition.
- *Etah*, the lead dog for Roald Amundsen's expedition to the South Pole, the first to reach the pole.
- *Soichiro* is the name of a Samoyed that belonged to one of the main characters in the popular Japanese anime, *Maison Ikkoku*. He was featured prominently throughout most of the series, and became a major character in his own right, often serving as comic relief. He was given the name 'Snowy' by his owner, but instead began responding to her husband's name.
- Samoyeds serve as the sled dogs of Stone Fox in the book of the same name.
- *Xiah Junsu*, member of South Korean boy band JYJ, owns a Samoyed named Xiaky (which translates as 'Xiah's dog').
- *Mush* was the name of the Samoyed dog owned by Karen Carpenter of the popular music group The Carpenters.
- *Denis Leary* owned a Samoyed named 'Little Bastard'.

Siberian Husky

The Siberian Husky is a medium-size, wolf-like, dense-coat working dog breed that originated in eastern Siberia. The breed belongs to the Spitz genetic family. It is recognisable by its thickly furred double coat, sickle tail, erect triangular ears, and distinctive markings.

Huskies are an active, energetic, and resilient breed whose ancestors came from the extremely cold and harsh environment of the Siberian Arctic. Siberian Huskies were bred by the Chukchi of Northeastern Asia to pull heavy loads long distances through difficult conditions. The dogs were imported into Alaska during the Nome Gold Rush and later spread into the United States and Canada. They were initially sent to Alaska and Canada as sled dogs but rapidly acquired the status of family pets and show dogs.

The Siberian Husky, Samoyed, and Alaskan Malamute are all breeds directly descended from the original 'sled dog'. The DNA analysis confirms that this is one of the oldest breeds of dog. The term 'husky' is a corruption of the nickname 'Esky' once applied to the Eskimos and subsequently to their dogs.

Breeds descending from the Eskimo dog were once found throughout the Northern Hemisphere from Siberia to Canada, Alaska, Greenland, Labrador, and Baffin Island.

With the help of Siberian Huskies, entire tribes of people were able not only to survive, but to push forth into *terra incognita.* Admiral Robert Peary of the United States Navy was aided by this breed during his expeditions in search of the North Pole.

Dogs from the Anadyr River and surrounding regions were imported into Alaska from 1908 (and for the next two decades) during the gold rush for use as sled dogs, especially in the 'All-Alaska Sweepstakes,' a 408-mile (657 km) distance dog sled race from Nome to Candle and back. Smaller, faster and more enduring than the 100- to 120-pound (45 to 54 kg) freighting dogs then in general use, they immediately dominated the Nome Sweepstakes. Leonhard Seppala, the foremost breeder of Siberian Huskies of the time, participated in competitions from 1909 to the mid 1920s.

On 3rd February, 1925 Gunnar Kaasen was first in the 1925 serum run to Nome to deliver diphtheria serum from Nenana over 600 miles to Nome. This was a group effort by several sled dog teams and mushers, with most of the run covered by Leonhard Seppala. The Iditarod Trail Sled Dog Race commemorates this famous delivery. The event is also loosely depicted in the 1995 animated film *Balto,* as the name of Gunnar Kaasen's lead dog in his sled team was named Balto, although unlike the real dog, Balto the character was portrayed as half wolf in the film. In honor of this lead dog a bronze statue was erected at Central Park in New York City. The plaque upon it is inscribed.

Dedicated to the indomitable spirit of the sled dogs that relayed antitoxin six hundred miles over rough ice, across treacherous waters, through Arctic blizzards from Nenana to the relief of stricken Nome in the winter of 1925. Endurance; Fidelity; Intelligence.

In 1930 the last Siberians were exported as the Soviet government closed the borders of Siberia to external trade. The same year saw recognition of the Siberian Husky by the American Kennel Club. Nine years later the breed was first registered in Canada. Today's Siberian Huskies registered in North America are largely the descendants of the 1930 Siberia imports and of Leonhard Seppala's dogs. Seppala owned a kennel in Nenana before moving to New England, where he became partners with Elizabeth Ricker. The two co-owned the Poland Springs kennel and began to race and exhibit their dogs all over the Northeast.

As the breed was beginning to come to prominence, in 1933 Navy Rear Admiral Richard E. Byrd brought about 50 Siberian Huskies with him on an expedition in which Byrd hoped to journey around the 16,000-mile coast of Antarctica. Many of the dogs were trained at Chinook Kennels in New Hampshire. Called Operation Highjump, the historic trek proved the worth of the Siberian Husky due to its compact size and greater speeds. Siberian Huskies also served in the United States Army's Arctic Search and Rescue Unit of the Air Transport Command during World War II.

As the breed was beginning to come to prominence, in 1933 Navy Rear Admiral Richard E. Byrd brought about 50 Siberian Huskies with him on an expedition in which Byrd hoped to journey around the 16,000-mile coast of Antarctica. Many of the dogs were trained at Chinook Kennels in New Hampshire. Called Operation Highjump, the historic trek proved the worth of the Siberian Husky due to its compact size and greater speeds. Siberian Huskies also served in the United States Army's Arctic Search and Rescue Unit of the Air Transport Command during World War II.

Siberian Huskies share many outward similarities with the Alaskan Malamute as well as many other Spitz breeds such as the Samoyed, which has a comparable history to the Huskies. They come in a variety of colours and patterns, usually with white paws and legs, facial markings, and tail tip. The most common coats are black and white, copper-red and white, gray and white, pure white, and the rare 'Agouti' coat, though many individuals have blondish or piebald spotting. Striking masks, spectacles, and other facial markings occur in wide variety. They tend to have a wolf-like appearance.

The American Kennel Club describes the Husky's eyes as 'an almond shape, moderately spaced and set slightly obliquely'. The eyes of a Siberian Husky are ice-blue, dark blue, amber, or brown. In some individual dogs, one eye may be brown and the other blue (complete heterochromia), or one or both eyes may be 'parti-coloured', that is, half brown and half blue (partial heterochromia). All of these eye colour combinations are considered acceptable by the American Kennel Club.

Coat

The Siberian Husky's coat is thicker than that of most breeds of dogs, comprising two layers: a dense undercoat and a longer topcoat of short, straight guard hairs. It protects the dogs effectively against harsh Arctic winters, but the coat also reflects heat in the summer. It is able to withstand temperatures as low as -50°C to - 60°C. The undercoat is often absent during shedding. Their thick coats require weekly grooming, although they do not often shed. Long guard hair is not desirable and is considered a fault.

Nose

Show-quality dogs are preferred to have neither pointed nor square noses. The nose is black in gray dogs, tan in black dogs, liver in copper-coloured dogs, and may be flesh-coloured in white dogs. In some instances, Siberian Huskies can exhibit what is called 'snow nose' or 'winter nose'. This condition is called hypopigmentation in animals. 'Snow nose' is acceptable in the show ring.

Tail

Husky tails are furry and fluffy in order to provide warmth for their face and nose during cold winter nights. Huskies are also known for their uniquely identifiable 'curled' or 'sickle' tails.

Size

The breed standard indicates that the males of the breed are ideally between 21 and 23.5 inches (53 and 60 cm) tall at the withers and weighing between 45 and 60 pounds (20 and 27 kg). Females are smaller, growing to between 20 to 22 inches (51 to 56 cm) tall at the withers and weighing between 35 to 55 pounds (16 to 25 kg).

The Siberian Husky has been described as a behavioural representative of the domestic dog's forebear, the wolf, exhibiting a wide range of its ancestors' behaviour. They are known to howl rather than bark. If the dog is well trained it can make a great family pet. The frequency of kenneled Siberian Huskies, especially for racing purposes, is rather high, as attributed through the history of the breed in North America. They are affectionate with people, but independent. A fifteen-minute daily obedience training class will serve well for Siberian Huskies. Siberians need consistent training and do well with a positive reinforcement training programme. They rank 45th in Stanley Coren's *The Intelligence of Dogs,* being of average working/obedience intelligence. They tend to run because they were at first bred to be sled dogs. Owners are advised to exercise caution when letting their Siberian Husky off the leash as the dog could be miles away before looking around and realizing their owner is nowhere in sight. They are excellent 'escape artists' as well and have been known to climb chain-link fences and find other ways of escaping a confined area. They also get bored easily, so playing with toys or throwing the ball at least once a day is essential. Failure to give them the attention or proper exercise they need can result in unwanted behaviour, such as excessive howling, marking, chewing on furniture, or crying.

Intelligence

Siberian Huskies are highly intelligent, which allows them to excel in obedience trials, though many clubs would like to keep the Husky's instinct by doing sled-racing. However, because of their intelligence, they can easily become bored and may stop listening to commands. Many dog trainers usually attempt to avoid this behaviour by keeping them busy with new activities. Also due in part to their intelligence, Huskies tend to be very observant on the actions of people around them and have been known to mimic common household activities such as turning on lights with their paws and opening doors with their canines. Some undesirable behaviours they can exhibit include opening refrigerators (and eating the food inside), climbing fences or digging tunnels in the backyard to escape. These behaviours can be prevented if the dog is given enough activity to occupy it. Huskies require both mental and physical stimulation for optimum health.

Health

Siberian Huskies, with proper care, have a typical lifespan ranging from twelve to fifteen years. Health issues in the breed are mainly genetic such as seizures and defects of the eye (juvenile cataracts, corneal dystrophy, and progressive retinal atrophy). Hip dysplasia is not often found in this breed; however, as with many medium or larger-sized canines, it can occur. The Orthopedic Foundation for Animals currently has the Siberian Husky ranked 148th out of a possible 153 breeds at risk for hip dysplasia, with only two percent of tested Siberian Huskies showing dysplasia.

Siberian Huskies used for sled racing may also be prone to other ailments, such as gastric disease, bronchitis or bronchopulmonary ailments ('ski asthma'), and gastric erosions or ulcerations.

Working Siberians

Siberian Huskies are still used as sled dogs in sled dog racing. Siberians are still popular in races restricted to purebreds and are faster than other pure sled dog breeds such as the Samoyed and the slower but much stronger Alaskan Malamute. Today the breed tends to divide along lines of 'racing' Siberians and 'show' Siberians. Racing Siberians tend to have more leg to enable them more reach when running. Show Siberians tend to be a bit smaller.

Apart from sled racing, they are very popular for recreational mushing and are also used for skijoring (one to three dogs pulling a skier) and European ski-hi. A few owners use them for dog-packing and hiking.

Standard Schnauzer

The Standard Schnauzer is the original breed of the three breeds of Schnauzer, and despite its wiry coat and general appearance, is not related to the British terriers. Rather, its origins are in old herding and guard breeds of Europe. Generally classified as a working or utility dog, this versatile breed is a robust, squarely built, medium-sized dog with aristocratic bearing. It has been claimed that it was a popular subject of painters Sir Joshua Reynolds, Albrecht Dürer and Rembrandt, but actual proof remains elusive.

Standard Schnauzers are either salt-and-pepper or black in colour, and are known for exhibiting many of the 'ideal' traits of any breed. These include high intelligence, agility, alertness, reliability, strength and endurance. This breed of dog has been very popular in Europe, specifically Germany where it originated. The breed was first exhibited at a show in Hanover in 1879, and since then have taken top honors in many shows including the prestigious "Best in Show at Westminster Kennel Club" in the United States in 1997.

In the Middle Ages, schnauzer-type dogs of medium size were developed from herding, ratting and guardian breeds in Western Europe. A dog of the peasant farmer for centuries, with the advent of dog showing in the 19th century they finally captured the interest of German dog fanciers, who began to standardize their look and temperament for the show ring.

In the earliest days of the show schnauzer, puppies from a single litter could be classified as either German Pinschers (short haired puppies) or schnauzers (long-coated wire-haired puppies), dependent only on coat length. And before the original German Pincher breed was wiped out during WWI (it has since been brought back from different stock) the pepper-and-salt coat that is the trademark of the Standard Schnauzer breed in North America could be seen in the German Pincher (called the *silberpinsch*), attesting to the close relationship between the two breeds in modern times. It was also in the late 19th century that the medium-sized schnauzer was developed into three different breeds/sizes: the Miniature, the Standard (the original), and the Giant.

Speaking on the more distant origins of the breed, writers from the late 19th century proposed that the grey Wolfspitz and black German pudles contributed to the early development of the schnauzer, though this has yet to be confirmed through genetic work.

The three schnauzer breeds take their name from one of their kind, a medium-sized show dog named 'Schnauzer', who won at the 1879 Hanover Show in Germany. The word *Schnauzer* (from the German word for 'snout', recalling the long hair on the muzzle) appeared for the first time in 1842 when used as a synonym for the Wire-haired *Pinscher* (the name under which the breed first competed at dog shows). The schnauzer was first imported into the United States in the early 1900s.

In modern history, the Standard Schnauzer has taken on a variety of roles. The Red Cross used the dogs for guard duty during World War I. Both German and (in one documented instance) American police departments have put the dogs to work as well. Several Standard Schnauzers have been used in the USA for drug and bomb detection, and also as search-and-rescue dogs.

The current Standard Schnauzer excels at obedience, agility, tracking, herding, therapy work and, in Germany, schutzhund. Despite being a popular pet in Europe, the Standard Schnauzer has never gained wide popularity in North America. For the past 20 years, the American Kennel Club has registered only ~540 Standard Schnauzer puppies a year (compared with ~100,000 Labrador Retreiver puppies each year).

Distinguished by their long beards and eyebrows, Standard Schnauzers are always pepper and salt or less commonly black in colour, with a stiff and wiry hair coat on the body similar to that of other wirehaired breeds. Their hair will perpetually grow in length without properly shedding, but contrary to popular belief Standard Schnauzers are not hypo-allergenic and they all shed to some degree. The more wiry - and correct and weather-resistant - the coat, the more that the coat will shed, though the hair dropped from a single dog is said to be nearly unnoticeable.

Twice a year, when most other breeds of dog are shedding their coat, a Schnauzer's coat will become dull and relatively easy to pull out and is said to have 'blown'. At this point the coat can be stripped or pulled out by hand and a new wire coat will re-grow in its place. Stripping is not painful for the dog and can be performed at any stage of hair growth although it is easier to do when the coat is 'blown'.

Alternatively, the coat can be regularly clipped with shears. Clipping as opposed to stripping results in a loss of the wiry texture and some of the fullness of the coat. Dogs with clipped fur no longer 'blow' their coat but the coat loses its wiry texture and becomes soft. The fur of clipped dogs tends to be more prone to tangling and knots, particularly when long, and is duller in colour than that of stripped coats. In the case of the salt and pepper Schnauzers, the characteristic banded colour of the hair is completely lost when maintained through clipping; each shaft of hair becomes entirely gray rather than being banded with multiple shades of gray, white, and black.

Clipping is most common in the US as it can be difficult to locate a professional willing to hand strip as the process is quite labor intensive. In Europe it is very uncommon to see a wire-coated dog which is clipped. It may not be possible to hand strip a poor quality coat, i.e. one that is soft in texture, but soft coats, while relatively common in pet quality Miniature Schnauzers, is not a widespread problem in Standards.

Regardless of whether the body of the coat is stripped or clipped the 'furnishings' or longer hair on the legs and face must be scissored or clipped regularly and require daily brushing to remain free of potentially painful mats. Whether a Schnauzer is stripped or clipped, his coat requires a great deal of grooming. In most cases this means an owner must either take care to learn the required grooming - for which the dog's breeder should be a great resource - or the owner must take their dog in for regular, often expensive, trips to a grooming salon.

Inside the US and Canada, ears and tail and dewclaws are typically docked as a puppy. Veterinarians or experienced breeders will cut tails and dewclaws between 3 and 7 days of age. Tails are traditionally docked to around three vertebrae. Ear cropping is usually performed at about 10 weeks of age in a veterinary clinic. Many breeders inside North America have begun to crop only those puppies retained for show purposes, or those puppies whose owners request it. There is still somewhat of a bias against natural ears in the North American show ring. However, there is a growing sentiment among breeders and judges that both ear types are equally show-worthy, and many North American show breeders enjoy both cropped and natural eared dogs in their kennels. However, unlike in Europe, the majority of North American breeders believe that the choice of whether to cut ears and/or tails should continue to remain with the breeders and owners. Outside of North America, most Standard Schnauzers retain both their natural ears and tail as docking is now prohibited by law in many countries.

The smallest of the working breeds, the Standard schnauzer makes loyal family dog with guardian instincts. Most will protect their home from uninvited visitors with a deep and robust bark. Originally a German farmdog, they adapt well to any climatic condition, including cold winters. In general, they typically are good with children and were once known in Germany as 'kinderwachters'. If properly trained and socialized early to different ages, races, and temperaments of people, they can be very patient and tolerant in any situation. Like other working dogs, Standard Schnauzers require a fairly strong-willed owner that can be consistent and firm with training and commands.

Standard Schnauzers also widely known to be intelligent and easy to train. They have been called 'the dog with a human brain', and in Stanley Coren's book The Intelligence of Dogs, they are rated 18th out of 80 breeds on the ability to learn new commands and to obey known commands. Standard Schnauzers are extremely versatile, excelling at dog sports such as agility, obedience, tracking, Disc dog, Flyball and herding. Members of the breed have been used in the last 30 years in the United States as for bomb detection, search and rescue, and skin and lung cancer-detection.

Like most working dogs, Standard Schnauzers will be rambunctious until about the age of two; and lots of exercise will keep them busy. Owners must be prepared to mentally and physically stimulate their Schnauzer every day, even into their old age. Like other high-intelligence breeds, a bored Schnauzer is a destructive Schnauzer.

According to the Standard Schnauzer Club of America, "The Standard Schnauzer is considered a high-energy dog. They need ample exercise not only for physical well-being, but also for emotional well-being. The minimum amount an adult dog should get is the equivalent of a one long walk a day. This walk should be brisk enough to keep the dog at a steady trotting pace in order to keep the dog in prime physical condition. The Standard Schnauzer puppy is constantly exploring, learning and testing his limits. As adults, they are always ready for a walk in the woods, a ride in the car, a training session or any other activity that allows them to be with their owner. This is a breed that knows how to be on the alert, even when relaxing by the feet of their owner.

Overall, the Standard Schnauzer is a very healthy breed. The 2008 health survey done by the Standard Schnauzer Club of America revealed that roughly only 1 per cent of dogs surveyed had serious health issues. The final, full report can be found here but a general summary is as follows:

- Data were collected for 10-15 per cent of eligible dogs;
- Median life span was 12.9 years;
- Only a few serious diseases were noted;
- Potentially serious conditions affect less than 1 per cent of dogs;
- Apparent progress has been made in reducing the incidence of hip dysplasia.

The two major hereditary within the breed are: hip dysplasia and hereditary eye disease. Both problems can be tested for and identified in breeding stock before they pass the trait onto the next generation, so the Standard Schnauzer Club of America recommends that every kennel test their breeding stock for hip and eye problems before breeding and to breed only healthy animals.

However, it is entirely up to breeders whether they choose to health test their animals and whether they choose use animals for breeding despite knowing they have tested positive for carrying a genetic disease. The SSCA also encourages all potential buyers to ask their breeder for up to date OFA and CERF certifications of the parent dogs before buying a puppy.

The cost of OFA testing is relatively high (about US$ 150-200 per dog per year) and born directly by breeders. OFA testing is not required for AKC registration of breeding stock or their offspring so the benefits of a good OFA test scores are more indirect and long range for individual breeders while a poor results represent a direct negative impact. Responsible buyers looking to buy from responsible breeders should only choose puppies from a litter where both parents have current OFA test certificates and scores of 'excellent', 'good', 'fair'.

The Canine Eye Registration Foundation is a registry for purebred breeding stock who have been certified free of any hereditary eye disease: results for this test can also be found at the OFA website. Dogs must be examined by an approved veterinarian who checks for the presence of heritable eye diseases. Testing is less inexpensive (about 20-40 USD) than OFA examinations but, like OFA testing, must be done annually to remain valid.

Famous Schnauzers

From the AKC: "Rembrandt painted several Schnauzers, Lucas Cranach the Elder shows one in a tapestry dated 1501, and in the 18th century one appears in a canvas of the English painter Sir Joshua Reynolds. In the marketplace of Mechlinburg, Germany, is a statue of a hunter dating from the 14th century, with a Schnauzer crouching at his feet which conforms very closely to the present-day show Standard.

- George, the cancer-sniffing Schnauzer, has received much acclaim.
- Tramp, the street-wise mutt from Lady and the Tramp is most likely a Schnauzer-mix.
- Blu, Franklin's pet blue dog in *Monica's Gang*.
- Colin, dog in the UK comedy series *Spaced*, became a regular feature in the middle of the first series.

Errol Flynn had two Standard Schnauzers. His first, 'Arno', was very well known in the tabloids of the day and was, according to Flynn biographers, loved by the actor more than any human being in his life. Arno was a constant presence on the movie set and on Flynn's yacht, 'Sirocco'. One night, the dog fell overboard and drowned, and Flynn mobilized the Coast Guard in a search. A gossip columnist, Jimmy Fidler, wrote a scathing piece on the dog's death and Flynn, enraged, tracked him down in a nightclub and beat him senseless. Flynn later obtained another standard, 'Moody', which—like Arno before him—accompanied the actor onto all his movie sets.

Tibetan Mastiff

The Tibetan Mastiff (Do-khyi) is an ancient breed and type of domestic dog (*Canis lupus familiaris*) originating with nomadic cultures of Central Asia.

The Tibetan Mastiff also known as Do-khyi (variously translated as 'home guard', 'door guard', 'dog which may be tied', 'dog which may be kept'), reflects its use as a guardian of herds, flocks, tents, villages, monasteries, and palaces, much as the old English ban-dog (also meaning tied dog) was a dog tied outside the home as a guardian. However, in nomad camps and in villages, the Do-khyi is traditionally allowed to run loose at night and woe be unto the stranger who walks abroad after dark.

'Bhote Kukur' in Nepali means Tibetan Dog. In Mandarin Chinese, the name is (Zang'Ao), which literally means Tibetan Mastiff or Tibetan 'big ferocious dog'. In Mongolia it is called 'bankhar', meaning 'guard dog'. But there is another type of Mastiff in Mongolia, called Mongolian Mastiff (Mongol Bankhar) which is bigger than Tibetan Mastiff and have darker colour. The molosser type with which the modern Tibetan Mastiff breed is purportedly linked was known across the Ancient world by many names.

Note that the name Tibetan 'mastiff' is a misnomer. This dog is not a true mastiff, and first got that name when someone observed that it looked like a mastiff ... A better name for the dog would be 'Tibetan mountain dog' or, to include the same dogs on the periphery of Tibet: 'Himalayan mountain dog'.

There is also some controversy pro and con over the idea that the so-called Tibetan mastiff is a molosser.

Currently, some breeders differentiate between two 'types' of Tibetan Mastiff: The Do-khyi and the 'Tsang-khyi'. The 'Tsang-khyi' (which, to a Tibetan, means only 'dog from Tsang') is also referred to as the 'monastery type', described as generally taller, heavier, more heavily boned, with more facial wrinkling and haw than the 'Do-khyi' or 'nomad type'. Both 'types' are often produced in the same litter.

Males can reach heights up to 31+ inches (80+cm) at the withers, although the standard for the breed is typically in the 25 to 28 inch (61 to 72 cm) range. The heaviest TM on record may be one weighing over 130 kg (286.6 Lbs) but dogs bred in the West are more typically between 140 lb (64 kg) to 180 lb (82 kg)—especially if they are in good condition and not overweight. The enormous dogs being produced in some Western and some Chinese kennels would have 'cost' too much to keep fed to have been useful to nomads; and their questionable structure would have made them well-nigh useless as livestock guardians.

The Tibetan Mastiff is considered a primitive breed. It typically retains the instincts which would be required for it to survive in Tibet, including canine pack behaviour. In addition, it is one of the few primitive dog breeds that retains a single oestrus per year instead of two, even at much lower altitudes and in much more temperate climates than its native climate. This characteristic is also found in wild canids such as the wolf. Since its oestrus usually takes place during late fall, most Tibetan Mastiff puppies are born between December and January.

Its double coat is long, subject to climate, and found in a wide variety of colours, including solid black, black & tan, various shades of gold/'blonde', blue/gray, chocolate brown, red, the rarest being solid white.

The coat of a Tibetan Mastiff lacks the unpleasant 'big-dog smell' that affects many large breeds. The coat, whatever its length or colour(s), should shed dirt and odors. Although the dogs shed somewhat throughout the year, there is generally one great 'molt' in late winter or early spring and sometimes another, lesser molt in the late summer or early fall. (Sterilization of the dog or bitch may dramatically affect the coat as to texture, density, and shedding pattern.)

Tibetan Mastiffs are shown under one standard in the West, but separated by the Indian breed standard into two varieties: Lion Head (smaller; exceptionally long hair from forehead to withers, creating a ruff or mane) and Tiger Head (larger; shorter hair).

Temperament

The native type of dog, which still exists in Tibet and the Himalayas (in Bhutan, Nepal, and North India), and the Westernized purebred breed can vary in temperament—but so can dogs of identical breeding, within the same litter, raised in the same household. Elizabeth Schuler states, "The few individuals that remain in Tibet are ferocious and aggressive, unpredictable in their behaviour, and very difficult to train. But the dogs bred by the English are obedient and attached to their masters." However, other observers have found the dogs remaining in Tibet to be quite approachable under the right circumstances—and some Western-bred dogs to be completely unapproachable.

Some Western and Asian breeders are seeking to create a replica of the legendary dog which they identify as the 'true Tibetan Mastiff' or 'Tsang-khyi'. Some breeders appear to select primarily for appearance (great size, profuse coat, heavy wrinkling, jowls, haw) while others also select for 'soft' temperament (in the West) and fierce temperament (in Asia where the dogs' 'ferocity' is much vaunted and encouraged).

As a flock guardian dog in Tibet and in the West, it is tenacious in its ability to confront predators the size of wolves and leopards. As a socialized, more domestic dog, it can thrive in a spacious, fenced yard with a canine companion, but it is generally not an appropriate dog for apartment living. The Western-bred dogs are generally more easy-going, although somewhat aloof with strangers coming to the home. Through hundreds of years of selective breeding for a protective flock and family guardian, the breed has been prized for being a nocturnal sentry, keeping would-be predators and intruders at bay, barking at sounds throughout the night. Leaving a Tibetan Mastiff outside all night with neighbors nearby is not recommended. They often sleep during the day to be more active, alert and aware at night.

Like all flock guardian breeds, they are intelligent and stubborn to a fault, so obedience training is recommended (although only mildly successful with some individuals) since this is a strong-willed, powerful breed. Socialization is also critical with this breed because of their reserved nature with strangers and guardian instincts. They are excellent family dogs—for the right family. Owners must understand canine psychology and be willing and able to assume the primary leadership position. Lack of consistent, rational discipline can result in the creation of dangerous, unpredictable dogs (although this is true of virtually every dog breed).

Newspaper reports have suggested that a pair of these Mastiffs have killed tigers while guarding sheep in the highlands of Nepal.

Life Expectancy

Unlike most large breeds, its life expectancy is long, some 10-14 years. The breed has fewer genetic health problems than many breeds, but cases can be found of hypothyroidism, entropion, ectropion, skin problems including allergies, autoimmune problems including demodex, missing teeth, malocclusion (overbite or underbite), cardiac problems, epilepsy, progressive retinal atrophy (PRA), cataract, and small ear canals with a tendency for infection. As with most large breeds, some will suffer with elbow or hip dysplasia, although this has not been a major problem in the Tibetan Mastiff. Another concern includes canine inherited demyelinative neuropathy (CIDN), a rare inherited neural disease that appeared in one bloodline in the early 1980s.

Canine Hip Dysplasia (CHD) takes many forms, e.g., the femoral head ('ball') may not fit well into the acetabulum ('socket'); the ligament connecting the two may be lax, allowing dislocation; there may be no femoral head at all. Not all forms cause clinical signs. Very active, well-muscled dogs with no femoral heads may show no impairment. Their owners may be unaware of their dogs' 'hip dysplasia' unless/until there is a reason to x-ray the hips.

As with all dog breeds, hip dysplasia is caused by the interaction of genes and environment. Inheritance of CHD appears to be polygenic, i.e., it is caused by more than one gene. Mode of inheritance (dominant, recessive, dominant with incomplete penetrance, etc.) has not been determined but may be different in different breeds. Rapid growth and weight gain in puppies may trigger or exacerbate a genetic tendency to all sorts of skeletal problems. Many TM breeders recommend against feeding 'puppy food' and especially against feeding 'large-breed' puppy food, as these concoctions may contain too many calories, leading to fat puppies. Some breeders and owners believe that supplementation with Vitamin C may prevent the development of CHD even in dogs with the genes for it.

Canine Inherited Demyelinative Neuropathy is an inherited condition that appeared in one of the prominent lines of Tibetan Mastiffs in the early 1980s. CIDN affect the peripheral nervous system. Nerve fibers are unable to transmit impulses from the spinal cord to the muscles because of the breakdown of the myelin sheath. Starting at approximately six weeks of age, affected pups begin to lose the ability to walk or even stand. Progression of the condition can take anywhere from a few days to two weeks.

Because this condition is inherited as a simple autosomal recessive, it is virtually impossible to completely eliminate it from the gene pool. One known carrier was bred to over 30 times, producing at least 134 direct descendants. Many descendants of this dog are still being bred so there is always the risk—however slim—of producing more affected puppies. Breeders need to be cautious about pairing up any two descendants of this dog.

Hypothyroidism is fairly common in Tibetan Mastiffs, as it is in many large 'Northern' breeds. TMs should be tested periodically throughout their lives using a complete thyroid 'panel'. (Simple T2/T4 testing is virtually useless.) However, because the standard thyroid levels were established using domestic dog breeds, test results must be considered in the context of what is 'normal' for the breed, not what is normal across all breeds. Many TMs will have 'low' thyroid values but no clinical symptoms. Vets—and owners—differ on the relative merits of medicating dogs who 'test low' but are completely asymptomatic. Some researchers think that asymptomatic hypothyroidism may have been adaptive in the regions of origin for many breeds, since less nutrition is required for the dog to stay in good condition. Therefore, attempts to eliminate 'low thyroid' dogs from the TM gene pool may have unintended consequences for the breed.

In affected dogs, symptoms may include decreased activity and playing, increased sleeping, weight gain, poor skin and coat condition such as flaking and scaling, a 'yeasty' smell to the coat, frequent ear infections, and negative changes in temperament. Fortunately, this condition is easily treated by the use of daily thyroid supplementation.

Osteochondritis Dessicans is a skeletal defect in which the cartilage lifts off the bone, becomes thickened and cracked, causes inflammation and pain, and in severe cases degeneration of the joint. This conditions strikes males more than females. Keeping an affected puppy lean may help but surgery may be required to relieve pain.

Panosteitis is inflammation of the bones that strikes young dogs. The animal will become lame in one leg and then the inflammation will shift to a different leg. This is one condition that corrects itself over time, and only pain medication is needed.

Hypertrophic Osteodystrophy (*HOD*) is a condition that affects young large breed dogs. It is very painful and prognosis is fair to poor. due to recurring episodes of the condition. Clinical signs of HOD include fever, lack of appetite, and depression. Lameness may vary from mild to severe. With multiple limbs affected, the dog may be reluctant to stand or walk. HOD may be mistaken for Panosteitis without proper diagnosis.

Treatment is only supportive. Intravenous fluids are usually required to keep the patient hydrated. Nutritional support is provided with a feeding tube if the dog refuses to eat for five or more days. Pain is controlled with narcotics and NSAIDs. Antibiotics are used if the dog has signs of pneumonia or other bacterial infections. If the bones become twisted due to growth plate damage, corrective surgery may be indicated. Because the distemper vaccination has been implicated, inoculation should be delayed until the pet has been in remission for a couple of months.

Ear Infections can be serious and the dog should be taken to the vet if you see it shaking its head or scratching more than normal. Tibetan Mastiffs have pendant ears, making them more prone to ear infections. The vet needs to determine the cause, and may prescribe antibiotics and/or ear drops. Some ear infections are contagious to other dogs if they involve mites or some bacteria.

This is an ancient breed. It has been theorized that an early Tibetan dog is the ancestor to all Molossuses breeds, although this is disputed by some experts. A study at Nanjing Agricultural University's Laboratory of Animal Reproductive Genetics and Molecular Evolution in Nanjing, China, found that while most common dog breeds genetically diverged from the wolf approximately 42,000 years ago, the Tibetan Mastiff genetically diverged from the wolf approximately 58,000 years ago. They share many characterisitcs of many Mountain dog breeds.

Many Tibetan Mastiff breeders and owners (and their web sites) claim that Marco Polo encountered the large Tibetan dogs in his travels and described them as "tall as a donkey with a voice as powerful as that of a lion." However, reading of Polo's works does not support this. In fact, other travels told Marco Polo about these enormous dogs—and about unicorns and other exotic creatures.

In the early 19th century, King George IV owned a pair of TMs, and there were enough of the breed in England in 1906 to be shown at the 1906 Crystal Palace show. However, during the war years, the breed lost favor and focus and nearly died out in England.

After 1980, the breed began to gain in popularity worldwide. Although the breed is still considered somewhat uncommon, as various registries and show organisations (FCI, AKC) began to recognize the breed, more and more active breeders have arisen. Initially the breed suffered because of the limited gene pool from the original stock, but today's reputable breeders work hard at reducing the genetic problems through selective breeding and the international exchange of new bloodlines.

It was reported in September 2009 that a Chinese woman spent more than 4 million yuan to buy an 18 month old purebred male Tibetan Mastiff, which she named Yangtze No. 2. In December 2010, a buyer from Dalian paid 16 million yuan (almost US$2.5 million) for a slightly less than one-year-old puppy. In March 2011, a red Tibetan mastiff was reported to have been sold to a 'coal baron' from northern China for 10 million yuan.

CHAPTER 17
Dog Behaviour

Dog behaviour refers to the collection of behaviours by the domestic dog, *Canis lupus familiaris*, and is believed to be influenced by genetic, social, situational and environmental causes. The domestic dog is a subspecies of the grey wolf, and shares many of its behavioural characteristics. Although there are important and distinct differences between dogs and wolves, contemporary views of dog behaviour are heavily influenced by research on wild wolves.

The social unit of dogs is the pack. From research on wolf packs that are formed in captivity, the pack has traditionally been thought of as a tightly knit group composed of individuals that have earned a ranking in a linear hierarchy, and within which there is intense loyalty. It is believed that dogs were able to be domesticated by and succeed in contact with human society because of their social nature. According to this traditional belief, dogs generalize their social instincts to include humans, in essence 'joining the pack' of their owner/handler. However, much of this traditional view is based on findings from grey wolf packs that are formed of unrelated animals in captivity, and thus may not apply to natural wolf packs, natural dog packs, or dogs incorporated into a human household. Research in packs formed in the wild indicates that wolves form a family group, including a breeding pair and their offspring. In these familial packs, the terms 'dominance', and 'submission' are less useful than 'parent', and 'offspring', and bring with them a number of misconceptions. While the majority of research to date indicates that domestic dogs conform to a hierarchy around an Alpha-Beta-Omega structure, domestic dogs, like their wild wolf counterparts, also interact in complex hierarchical ways.

The existence and nature of personality traits in dogs have been studied (15,329 dogs of 164 different breeds) and five consistent and stable 'narrow traits' identified, described as playfulness, curiosity/fearlessness, chase-proneness, sociability and aggressiveness. A further higher-order axis for shyness–boldness was also identified.

Dr. David Mech of the University of Minnesota, who has studied wolves in their natural habitat, claims that much of what is widely believed about wolf packs is mistaken. From observations of wolf packs on Ellesmere Island over more than a decade, he claims that natural wolf packs are not at all similar to those formed in captivity by unrelated wolves. He attributes many of the misconceptions about wolf packs to generalizations from these unnatural packs in captivity, and equates this to erroneous inferences we might draw from generalizing human behaviour from studying refugee camps.

Dr. Mech argues that the natural wolf pack is typically a family, with a breeding pair of adult wolves and their offspring. In such cases, the terms 'alpha' and 'dominant' are less appropriate than 'parent'. Of course, the parent wolves are both 'alpha' and 'dominant' (by definition), but he argues that these terms are misleading because they imply that a pack of wolves typically include multiple families and that the members assume a place in a linear hierarchy. A wolf pack should not be seen as a tribe of individuals who have an established place in a hierarchy until a younger dog usurps the role. Rather, a wolf pack should be seen as a family unit, with young wolves of age dispersing into new territories of their own, to find other wolves and begin their own family units.

Mech also states that dominance is rare in wild wolves, and does not arise from sexual competition. Because young wolves usually disperse before age two, and almost always before age three, there is little sexual tension within a pack. Instead of 'dominance' and 'submission', he uses the terms 'assertiveness' and 'passiveness' to reflect the role of the wolf in the pack. Dominant breeding pairs led the pack most of the time (71%), and initiated most new behaviours (70%). Leadership behaviour in subordinate pack members tended to be followed by dispersion.

It is believed by some that dogs establish a dominance hierarchy through aggressive play and roughhousing along a continuum of dominance and submission, although the concept of social hierarchies in dogs is unproven and controversial. It is important for successful socialization that puppies participate with their littermates in learning to relate to other dogs. Dogs learn to successfully relate to other dogs by keeping the peace, rather than by constantly fighting to reestablish this hierarchy.

Although dogs are commonly characterized in terms of their dominance (e.g., 'Fido is the alpha'), there is some controversy as to whether dominance is a stable personality trait.

In wild wolf packs, displays of dominance have been observed to include 'licking up', which involves essentially begging for food; 'pinning', in which the dominant dog appears to threaten another, which shows submission by rolling over; 'standing over'; territorial marking; and more passive expressions of body language, including holding the tail and ears erect, looking directly at other dogs, circling and sniffing other dogs, growling if the other dog moves.

Submissive displays mirror dominant displays and include adopting a posture that is physically lower than other dogs, such as crouching, rolling over on the back and exposing the abdomen, lowering the tail (sometimes to the point of tucking it between the legs), flattening of the ears, averting the gaze, nervously licking or swallowing, dribbling of urine, and freezing or fleeing when other dogs are encountered.

In wolves, recent research has indicated that dominant behaviours have been misinterpreted as personality traits that determine the inidividual's place in a linear hierarchy in the pack. In contrast, Mech (see recent research, below) argues that packs are family units, and that the 'alpha' of a pack does not change through struggles for dominance. Rather, he argues that the family unit serves to raise the young, which then disperse to pair up with other dispersed wolves to form a breeding pair, and a pack of their own. This model undermines the popular conception of dominance in wolf social behaviour.

Research on canine familiaris has also questioned whether dominance is a personality trait. Svartberg and colleagues (2002) gathered behavioural data from 15,000 dogs of 164 breeds in attempt to identify major personality traits. In an approach similar to those used in humans, the authors performed a factor analysis of their data, and identified five major traits: 'Playfulness', 'Curiosity/Fearlessness', 'Chase-proneness', 'Sociability', 'Aggressiveness'. A similar analysis by Goddard and Beilharz (1985) revealed two major factors in social behaviour: 'Confidence', and 'Aggression–dominance'.

These studies suggest that dominance, per se, may not be a personality trait. Rather, underlying personality traits such as aggressiveness, confidence and curiosity may affect the prevalence of dog behaviours that are viewed as dominant.

Research has shown that there are individual differences in the interactions between dogs and their human masters that have significant effects on dog behaviour. For instance, Topal and colleagues (1997) have shown that the type of relationship between dog and master, characterized as either *companionship* or *working relationship*, significantly affected the dog's performance on a cognitive problem-solving task. They speculate that companion dogs have a more dependent relationship with their owners, and look to them to solve problems. In contrast, working dogs are more independent.

Dogs value the companionship of the others in their "pack" and are sometimes distressed if they are separated from it. Typical reactions when a dog is separated from the pack are barking, howling, digging, and chewing. These activities may distress humans when they need to leave dogs alone for a period of time. However, this behaviour, called *separation anxiety*, can be overcome with training, or at least decreased to the point where it becomes manageable. If young puppies are habituated to periods alone from an early age, this can normally be prevented entirely. Dogs are also crepuscular, meaning their natural period of peak activity is dawn and dusk, and may be content to rest during the day and night (because of this trait, domestic dogs are more likely to show barking and chewing activity at times when people are leaving to or returning from work.). Some owners struggling to deal with this problem resort to devocalization, a controversial practice considered cruel by animal advocates and outlawed in many countries.

From a young age, dogs engage in play with one another. Dog play is made up primarily of mock fights. It is believed that this behaviour, which is most common in puppies, is training for important behaviours later in life. Research on puppy play has shown that puppies do not engage equally in both dominant and submissive roles in fights; rather, puppies will tend to start play fights with weaker puppies they believe they can dominate. Additionally, puppies will intervene in play engaged by other pairs. In these situations, the puppies overwhelmingly aid the dominant dog. Puppies do not show reciprocity in interventions, suggesting that they prefer to be dominant in a fight, and are being opportunistic in the short-term. In the long-term, intervention may aid the puppies in learning coordination.

A common behaviour among domesticated dogs is chasing their own tails. Researchers are not completely certain why dogs chase their own tail, however some research studies found a link between tail-chasing and high cholesterol. A study found that when dogs experience an increase in activity of hormones tied to the 'fight or flight' response, it causes dogs to chase their tails more often.

CHAPTER 18

Role of Dogs in Religions

Dogs (*Canis lupus familiaris*), which are humankind's first and most common domestic animals, have played a role in many religious traditions.

Dogs have a major religious significance among the Hindus in Nepal and in the Mithilanchal part of India. The dogs are worshipped as a part of a five-day Tihar festival that falls roughly in November every year. In Hinduism, it is believed that the dog is a messenger of *Yama*, the god of death, and dogs guard the doors of Heaven.This is a day when the dog is worshipped by applying *tika* (the holy vermilion dot), incense sticks and garlanded generally with marigold flower. Sarama, the bitch of the gods, is described as the mother of all dogs.

The dog (*Shvan*) is also the vahana or mount of the Hindu god Bhairava.

Mesopotamia

There is a temple in Isin, Mesopotamia, named é-ur-gi7-ra which translates as 'dog house' Enlilbani, a king from the Old Babylonian First Dynasty of Isin, commemorated the temple to the goddess Ninisina. Although there is a small amount of detail known about it, there is enough information to confirm that a dog cult did exist in this area. Usually, dogs were only associated with the Gula cult, but there is some information, like Enlilbani's commemoration, to suggest that dogs were also important to the cult of Ninisina, as Gula was another goddess who was closely associated to Ninisina. More than 30 dog burials, numerous dog sculptures, and dog drawings were discovered when the area around this Ninisina temple was excavated. In the Gula cult, the dog was used in oaths and was sometimes referred to as a divinity.

The Ancient Egyptians are often more associated with cats in the form of Bastet, yet here too dogs are found to have a sacred role and figure as an important symbol in religious iconography. At the cemetery at Abydos a portion was reserved for dogs, near the graves of women, archers and dwarves.

Dogs were associated with Anubis, the jackal headed god of the underworld. At times throughout its period of being in use the Anubieion catacombs at Saqqara saw the burial of dogs.

In Zoroastrianism, the dog is regarded as an especially beneficent, clean and righteous creature, which must be fed and taken care of. The dog is praised for the useful work it performs in the household, but it is also seen as having special spiritual virtues. A dog's gaze is considered to be purifying and to drive off Daevas (demons). It is also believed to have a special connection with the afterlife: the Chinwad Bridge to Heaven is said to be guarded by dogs in Zoroastrian scripture, and dogs are traditionally fed in commemoration of the dead. *Ihtiram-i sag*, 'respect for the dog', is a common injunction among Iranian Zoroastrian villagers.

Detailed prescriptions for the appropriate treatment of dogs are found in the Vendidad (a subdivision of the Zoroastrian holy scripture Avesta), especially in chapters 13, 14 and 15, where harsh punishments are imposed for harm inflicted upon a dog and the faithful are required to assist dogs, both domestic and stray, in various ways; often, help or harm to a dog is equated with help and harm to a human. The killing of a dog ('a shepherd's dog, or a house-dog, or a Vohunazga [i.e. stray] dog, or a trained dog') is considered to lead to damnation in the afterlife. A homeowner is required to take care of a pregnant bitch that lies near his home at least until the puppies are born (and in some cases until the puppies are old enough to take care of themselves, namely six months). If the homeowner does not help the bitch and the puppies come to harm as a result, "he shall pay for it the penalty for wilful murder", because "Atar (Fire), the son of Ahura Mazda, watches as well (over a pregnant bitch) as he does over a woman". It is also a major sin if a man harms a dog by giving it bones that are too hard and become stuck in its throat, or food that is too hot, so that it burns its throat. Giving bad food to a dog is as bad as serving bad food to a human. The believers are required to take care of a dog with a damaged sense of smell, to try to heal it "in the same manner as they would do for one of the faithful" and, if they fail, to tie it lest it should fall into a hole or a body of water and be harmed.

Both according to the Vendidad and in traditional Zoroastrian practice, dogs are allotted some funerary ceremonies analogous to those of humans. In the Vendidad, it is stated that the spirits of a thousand deceased dogs are reincarnated in a single otter ('water dog'), hence the killing of an otter is a terrible crime that brings drought and famine upon the land and must be atoned either by the death of the killer or by the killer performing a very long list of deeds considered pious, including the healing of dogs, raising of puppies, paying of fines to priests, as well as killing of animals considered noxious and unholy (cats, rats, mice and various species of reptiles, amphibians, and insects).

Sagdid is a funeral ceremony in which a dog is brought into the room where the body is lying so that it can look on it. 'Sagdid' means 'dog sight' in the Middle Persian language of Zoroastrian theological works. There are various spiritual benefits thought to be obtained by the ceremony. It is believed that the original purpose was to make certain that the person was really dead, since the dog's more acute senses would be able to detect signs of life that a human might miss. A 'four-eyed' dog, that is one with two spots on its forehead, is preferred for sagdid.

The traditional rites involving dogs have been under attack by reformist Zoroastrians since the mid 19th century, and they had abandoned them completely by the late 20th century. Even traditionalist Zoroastrians tend to restrict such rites to a significant extent nowadays (late 20th - early 21st century).

Chinese Tradition

The dog is one of the 12 animals honored in Chinese astrology. The second day of the Chinese New Year is considered to be the birthday of all dogs and Chinese people often take care to be kind to dogs on that day.

Christianity

A dog is mentioned in the deuterocanonical Book of Tobit, faithfully accompanying Tobias, Tobit's son and the angel Raphael on their journeys.

Jesus told the story of the poor man Lazarus, whose sores were licked by street dogs. This has traditionally been seen as showing Lazarus's wretched situation. However, some modern commentators have pointed out that the dogs' saliva, which contains lysozyme (an enzyme with antibacterial qualities), could have beneficial effects on the sores.

The Catholic Church recognizes Saint Roch (also called Saint Rocco), who lived in the early 14th century in France, as the patron saint of dogs. It is said that he caught the black plague while doing charitable work and went into the forest, expecting to die. There he was befriended by a dog which licked his sores and brought him food, and he was able to recover. The feast day of Saint Roch, August 16, is celebrated in Bolivia as the 'birthday of all dogs'.

Saint Guinefort was the name given to a dog who received local veneration as a saint at a French shrine from the thirteenth to the twentieth centuries.

A black and white dog is sometimes used as an informal symbol of the Dominican order of friars, religious sisters and nuns. This stems from a Latin pun: though the order's name is actually the Friars Preachers (*Ordus Praedicatorum* - order of preachers), it is generally called the Dominicans (after St. Dominic, their founder): *Domini canes* in Latin means "the dogs/ hounds of the Lord."

Islam

The majority of both Sunni and Shi'a Muslim jurists consider dogs to be ritually unclean. It is uncommon for practising Muslims to have dogs as pets.

There are a number of traditions concerning Muhammad's attitude towards dogs. He said that the company of dogs, except as helpers in hunting, herding, and home protection, voided a portion of a Muslim's good deeds. On the other hand, he advocated kindness to dogs and other animals.

Another source that supports the kind treatment of dogs in Islam is seen with the narration by Abu Huraira Volume 3, Book 40, Number 551. He narrated that the Prophet said, "While a man was walking he felt thirsty and went down a well, and drank water from it. On coming out of it, he saw a dog panting and eating mud because of excessive thirst. The man said, 'This (dog) is suffering from the same problem as that of mine.' So, he (went down the well), filled his shoe with water, caught hold of it with his teeth and climbed up and watered the dog. Allah thanked him for his (good) deed and forgave him. *The people asked "O Allah's Apostle! Is there a reward for us in serving (the) animals?"* He replied: Yes, there is a reward for serving any animate (living being).

Additionally many Muslim theologians have argued that the dog is not an unclean animal based on the inclusion of a dog among the Seven Sleepers as recorded in the 18th verse of the 18th chapter of the *Qur'an*, which reads:

> Thou wouldst have deemed them awake, whilst they were asleep, and We turned them on their right and on their left sides: their dog stretching forth his two fore-legs on the threshold: if thou hadst come up on to them, thou wouldst have certainly turned back from them in flight, and wouldst certainly have been filled with terror of them.

Atheism and Criticism of Religion

The Ancient Greek philosopher and critic of social mores Diogenes of Sinope was recorded as living with many dogs, seeing their freedom from self-consciousness and sincere enjoyment of simple physical pleasure to be admirable role models.

In an article in the *New York Times Magazine* atheist Natalie Angier quoted Frans de Waal, a primatologist at Emory University:

> "I've argued that many of what philosophers call moral sentiments can be seen in other species. In chimpanzees and other animals, you see examples of sympathy, empathy, reciprocity, a willingness to follow social rules. Dogs are a good example of a species that have and obey social rules; that's why we like them so much, even though they're large carnivores".

In 1808 the English poet Lord Byron expressed similar thoughts in his famous poem *Epitaph to a Dog*:

But the poor dog, in life the firmest friend,
The first to welcome, foremost to defend,
Whose honest heart is still his master's own,
Who labours, fights, lives, breathes for him alone,
Unhonored falls, unnoticed all his worth,
Denied in heaven the soul he held on earth –
While man, vain insect! hopes to be forgiven,
And claims himself a sole exclusive heaven.

CHAPTER 19

Dogs Bark

A bark is a noise most commonly produced by dogs and puppies. Other animals that make this noise include wolves and quolls. *Woof* is the most common representation in the English language for this sound (especially for large dogs). Other transliterations include the onomatopoeic *ruff, arf, au au, yip* (for small dogs), and *bow-wow*.

Although dogs are descended from the wolf, *Canis lupus*, their barking constitutes a significant difference from their parent species. Although wolves do bark, they do so only in specific situations. According to Coppinger and Feinstein, dogs bark in long, rhythmic stanzas but adult wolf barks tend to be brief and isolated. Compared with wolves, dogs bark frequently and in many different situations.

It has been suggested that the reason for the difference lies in the dog's domestication by humans. An increased tendency to bark could have been useful to humans to provide an early warning system. Domestication has altered the physical appearance of dogs. Dogs present a striking example of neoteny, the retention of juvenile characteristics in the adults. They are similar to young wolves in many of their mannerisms and physical features, such as large heads, flat faces, large eyes, submissiveness and vocalizing – all of which are exhibited in wolf puppies.

Individual dogs bark for a variety of reasons. They may bark to attract attention, to communicate a message, or to express excitement. Statistical analysis has revealed that barks can be divided into different subtypes based on context and that individual dogs can be identified by their barks. Disturbance barks tend to be harsh, low frequency, and unmodulated, whereas isolation and play barks tend to be tonal, higher frequency, and modulated. Barks are often accompanied by body movements as part of a broader package of dog communication.

Warning Bark

A warning will usually start out as a low, quiet, but ferociously noticeable growl before escalating into something of a howling bark. This type of reaction is most typically seen in domesticated animals in response to a perceived territorial intrusion. The dog may also bare its teeth if it feels immediately threatened.

Also most monkeys make this type of barking noise when communicating with other monkeys or to scare off larger animals.

Alarm Barking

It is a dog's attempt to be alert, attentive, and informative to its human 'pack', as regarding unusual events. This kind of barking is known as 'alarm barking', and is common within a variety of breeds. It does not signify aggression, and (although often associated with unusual noises intruding on the dog's 'territory') is not the same as territoriality type barking. It may take the form of just one or a few barks, or it may give rise to sustained barking until the dog sees that some action has been taken. Alarm barking is more likely to arise when a dog can hear, but not see the source of, some noise. Examples of sounds which commonly cause alarm barking include doorbells, cars, noises from adjacent dwellings, and the like. It is a behavior that tends to develop with age and maturity, and also can be related to whether there are others around who might need to be informed of such events - often an alarm barker will remain quiet if alone and there is nobody to 'tell'.

Many dogs can self-develop actions that serve themselves if they need something. This is commonly done along with a form of action. Example, a dog may nudge its bowl and bark if it is hungry, or it may nudge its owner and bark if it wants some form of attention such as petting.

Nuisance-barking dogs sound off for no particular reason. The electric collars deliver an irritating shock of adjustable intensity when a vibration sensor in the collar detects barking. The citronella collar releases a spray of the plant-based fragrance when a microphone in the collar senses barking. For the eight dogs that wore both types of collars (one shepherd mix did not complete the study), all owners found the citronella collar to be effective in reducing or stopping nuisance barking and most preferred the fragrance spray. Four out of eight owners said electric shocks had no effect on their dogs—they kept on barking. The citronella collars were not without problems. One dog owner complained that citronella oil stained the upholstery when the couch-potato pooch barked. 'One owner thought the scent was preferable to her dog's body odor'.

Canine barking can be a nuisance to neighbours, and is a common problem dog owners or their neighbours may face. (Many dogs can bark at 100 dBA. Even at 17.5 yards away and with the dog outside a closed window, the noise level of a barking dog can be well over the level that causes psychological distress. Different kinds of barking often require different kinds of approach to reduction.

Common approaches are as follows:

- Attempting to understand, and if possible eliminate, the causes of barking.
- Using positive training methods to correct the behaviour. Dogs may bark from anxiety or stress, so punishment can often cause problems by reinforcing a cycle of bad behaviour. Positive approaches can include:
  - *Repeated exposure* to stimuli whilst calming the dog and persuading it to remain quiet.
  - *Distraction* as the stimulus happens, through treats, praise, or similar.
  - *Reshaping* via clicker training (a form of operant conditioning) or other means to obtain barking behaviour on command, and then shaping the control to gain command over silence.

Seeking professional advice from local organizations, dog trainers, or veterinarians.

Use of a mechanical device such as a bark collar. There are several types. all of which use a collar device that produces a response to barking that the dog notices:

- *Citrus spray ('citronella')* - Dogs as a rule do not like citrus. At the least, it is very noticeable and disrupts the pattern through surprise. These collars spray citrus around the dog's muzzle when it barks. (Sometimes these devices make a "hissing" noise before spraying, as an additional deterrent.
- *Sonic/ultrasonic (including vibration)* - These collars produce a tone which humans may or may not be able to hear, in response to barking. Over time, the sound becomes annoying or distracting enough to deter barking.
- *Electrical* - These collars produce a mild stinging or tingling sensation in response to a bark. It is important that such devices have a failsafe mechanism and shut off after a certain time, to prevent ongoing operation.
- *Combination and escalation devices* - Many sound and/or electrical collars have combination or escalation systems. A combination system is one that (for example) uses both sound and spray together. An escalation device is one that uses quiet sounds, or low levels of output, rising gradually until barking ceases. Escalation devices are effective since they 'reward' the dog for stopping sooner by not having 'all-or-nothing' action, so the dog can learn to react by stopping before much happens.

Different bark collars have been both praised, and criticised, and some are considered inhumane by various people and groups. Electrical devices especially come under criticism by people who consider them torturous and akin to electrocution. However most Societies for the Prevention of Cruelty to Animals agree that in a last resort even an electric collar is better than euthanasia if it comes to an ultimatum, for a stubborn dog that will not stop any other way. It is generally agreed that understanding the communication and retraining by reward is the most effective and most humane way.

Surgical Debarking

The controversial surgical procedure known as 'debarking' is a veterinary procedure for modifying the voice box so that a barking dog will make a significantly reduced noise. It is considered a last resort by some owners, on the basis that it is better than euthanasia, seizure, or legal problems if the matter has proven incapable of being reliably corrected any other way.

Debarking is illegal in Europe and opposed by many animal welfare organizations.

Woof is the conventional representation in the English language of the barking of a dog. As with other examples of onomatopoeia or imitative sounds, other cultures 'hear' the dog's barks differently and represent them in their own ways. Some of the equivalents of 'woof' in other European and Asian languages are as follows:

- English - woof, woof; ruff, ruff; arf, arf (large dogs and also the sound of sea lions); yap, yap; yip, yip (small dogs), bow wow.
- Afrikaans - blaf, blaf; woef, woef; keff, keff (small dogs).
- Albanian - ham, ham.
- Arabic - hau, hau; how how.
- Armenian -haf, haf.
- Basque - au, au; txau, txau (small dogs); zaunk, zaunk (large dogs); jau, jau (old dogs).
- Balinese - kong, kong.
- Bengali - gheu, gheu; bhao, bhao.
- Bulgarian - bau-bau ; jaff, jaff.
- Brazilian Portuguese - au au.
- Burmese - woke, woke.
- Catalan - bau, bau; bub, bub.
- Chinese, Cantonese - wow, wow (??).
- Chinese, Mandarin - wang, wang.
- Croatian - vau, vau.
- Czech - haf, haf; □tek (the bark itself).
- Danish - vov, vuf.
- Dutch - waf, waf; woef, woef.
- Esperanto - boj, boj.
- Estonian - auh, auh.
- Finnish - hau, hau; vuh, vuh; rauf, rauf.
- French - waouh, waouh; ouahn, ouahn; vaf, vaf; wouf, wouf; wouaf, wouaf; jappe jappe.

- German - wuff, wuff; wau, wau; rawrau, rawrau.
- Greek - ghav, ghav (?aß, ?aß).
- Hebrew - hav, hav; hau, hau.
- Hindi - bow, bow.
- Hungarian - vau, vau.
- Icelandic - voff, voff.
- Indonesian - guk, guk.
- Irish - amh, amh.
- Italian - bau, bau.
- Japanese - wan-wan ; kyan-kyan.
- Korean - meong, meong (??, pronounced).
- Latvian - vau, vau.
- Lithuanian - au, au.
- Macedonian - av, av.
- Malay - gong, gong ("menggonggong" means barking).
- Marathi - bhu, bhu; bho, bho.
- Norwegian - voff, voff or boff.
- Persian - vogh, vogh.
- Polish - hau, hau.
- Portuguese - au, au; ão-ão (nasal diphthong); béu-béu (toddler language); cain-cain (whining).
- Romanian - ham, ham; hau, hau.
- Russian - gav, gav.
- Serbian - av, av.
- Sinhala - buh, buh.
- Slovak - haf, haf; hau, hau.
- Slovene - hov, hov.
- Spanish - guau-guau; gua, gua; jau, jau.
- Swedish - voff, voff; vov, vov; bjäbb, bjäbb.
- Tagalog - aw, aw; baw, baw.
- Tamil - wal wal.
- Thai - (hoang, hoang); (bog bog).
- Turkish - hev hev; hav, hav.
- Ukrainian - (hau, hau); (dzyau, dzyau).
- Urdu - bow bow.
- Vietnamese - gâu gâu; ng ng.
- Welsh - wff, wff.

Compared to most domestic dogs, the bark of a dingo is short and monosyllabic. During observations, the barking of Australian dingoes was shown to have a relatively small variability; sub-groups of bark types, common among domestic dogs, could not be found. Furthermore, only 5 per cent of the observed vocalisations were made up of barking. Australian dingoes bark only in swooshing noises or in a mixture atonal/tonal. Also, barking is almost exclusively used for giving warnings. Warn-barking in a homotypical sequence and a kind of "warn-howling" in a heterotypical sequence has also been observed. The bark-howling starts with several barks and than fades into a rising and ebbing howl and is probably, similarly to coughing, used to warn the puppies and members of the pack. Additionally, dingoes emit a sort of "wailing" sound, which they mostly use when approaching a water hole, probably to warn already present dingoes. According to the present state of knowledge, it is not possible to get Australian dingoes to bark more frequently by making them asosciate with other domestic dogs. However Alfred Brehm reported a dingo that completely learned the more "typical" form of barking and knew how to use it, while its brother did not. Whether dingoes bark or bark-howl less frequently in general is not sure.

The now extinct Hare Indian dog of northern Canada was not known to bark in its native homeland, though puppies born in Europe learned how to imitate the barking of other dogs. When hurt or afraid, it howled like a wolf, and when curious, it made a sound described as a growl building up to a howl.

The Basenji of central Africa produces an unusual yodel-like sound, due to its unusually shaped larynx. This trait also gives the Basenji the nickname 'Barkless Dog'.

Many animals communicate via various vocalizations. While there is not a precise, consistent and functional acoustic definition for barking, researchers may classify barks according to several criteria. University of Massachusetts Amherst researchers identified volume, pitch, tonality, noise, abrupt onset and pulse duration are amongst the criteria that can be used to define a bark.

Besides dogs and wolves, other canines like coyotes and jackals can bark. Their barks are quite similar to those of wolves and dogs. The bark of a dingo is short and monosyllabic.

The warning bark of a fox sounds much like a dog's, but generally the vocalisation of foxes is higher and more drawn out than barks of other canids.

There are also non-canine species with vocalizations that could be described as barking. Because the Muntjac's alarm call resembles a dog's bark, they are sometimes known as Barking deer. Eared seals are also known to bark. Prairie dogs employ a complex form of communication that involves barks and rhythmic chirps. A wide variety of bird species produce vocalizations that include the canonical features of barking, especially when avoiding predators.

CHAPTER 20

Police Dog

A police dog, often referred to as a 'K-9 dog' in some areas (which is a homophone of canine), is a dog that is trained specifically to assist police and other law-enforcement personnel in their work. One commonly used breed is the German Shepherd, although now Belgian Malinois are popular dogs to use. In many jurisdictions the intentional injuring or killing of a police dog is a felony, subjecting the perpetrator to harsher penalties than those in the statutes embodied in local animal cruelty laws, just as an assault on a human police officer is often a more serious offense than the same assault on a non-officer. A growing number of law-enforcement organizations outfit dogs with ballistic vests, and some make the dogs sworn officers, with their own police badges and IDs. Furthermore, a police dog killed in the line of duty is often given a full police funeral.

Roles of police dogs include:

- **Public order enforcement dog:** The traditional image of a police dog is one used to enforce public order by chasing and holding suspects, or detaining suspects by the threat of being released, either by direct apprehension or a method known as Bark and Hold. German Shepherd Dogs and Belgian Malinois are most commonly used because of their availability however other dog breeds have also contributed, such as Dutch Shepherds, Rottweilers, Boxers, Doberman Pinschers Giant Schnauzers, American Pit Bull Terriers, and American Staffordshire Terriers.
- **Search and rescue dog (SAR):** This dog is used to locate suspects or find missing people or objects. Bloodhounds are often used for this task.
- **Detection dog or explosive-sniffing dog:** Some dogs are used to detect illicit substances such as drugs or explosives which may be carried on a person in their effects. In many countries, Beagles are used in airports to sniff the baggage for items that are not permitted; due to their friendly nature and appearance, the Beagle does not worry most passengers.

- **Cadaver dogs:** Some dogs are trained in detecting the odor of decomposing bodies. Dogs' noses are so sensitive that they are even capable of detecting bodies that are under running water Pioneering work was done by Dr. Debra Komar (University of Alberta) in Association with the RCMP Civilian Search Dog Association in this area. The result was the development of training techniques that resulted in near 100 per cent accuracy rates. Her research has been published in the Journal of Forensic Anthropology.

Popular Breeds

- Argentine Dogo (protect the officer, attack dog, sniff out bombs, sniff out drugs, sniff out food).
- German Shepherd (protect the officer, attack dog, ground based tracking and air based tracking, locating human remains, locating drugs, locating EODs, locating evidence).
- Dutch Shepherd (protect the officer, attack dog).
- Belgian Malinois (protect the officer, attack dog, locating EODs).
- Boxer (protect the officer, attack dog).
- Labrador Retriever (sniff out bombs, sniff out drugs).
- Doberman Pinscher (protect the officer, attack dog).
- Springer Spaniel (sniff out bombs, sniff out drugs).
- Bloodhound (Odor Specific ID, trackings, sniff out bombs, sniff out drugs, locating evidence).
- Beagle (sniff out bombs, sniff out drugs, sniff out food).
- Rottweiler .(protect the officer, attack dog).
- Giant Schnauzer (protect the officer, attack dog).

Official use of police dogs was recognized as being of value on the European Continent as early as 1859, with the Belgium Police in Ghent using dogs to officially patrol with the night shift.

Germany, France, Austria and Hungary soon followed with dogs becoming an accepted part of the official police establishment. The dogs employed at this time were hard aggressive animals that could inspire fear, protect their handler against attackers and be prepared to tackle courageously anyone found lurking in the ill-lit streets or open spaces. The breeds most commonly used by the end of the nineteenth century in these countries were Belgian & German Shepherds, Boxers, Dobermans and Airedales (imported from England).

The first major step forward in the development of the modern police dog came in the 1890s in Germany where serious attempts had been made to introduce recognised training programmes for the dogs purchased by the police, army and customs authorities. Rapid progress was made in the field of dog training with the development of the German Shepherd Dog as a breed and the formation on the 22nd of April 1899 of the Verein für Deutsche

Schäferhunde or SV (The German Shepherd Dog Society). In 1903 the SV staged civilian police dog trials that encompassed control, criminal work and nose work exercises. The police authorities were not convinced dogs were cost effective. The primary object of the police dog at this time was still seen as that of deterrent.

Belgium

The Belgian Canine Support Group is part of the country's federal police. It has 35 dog teams. Some dogs are trained to detect drugs, human remains, hormones or fire accelerants. About a third are tracker dogs trained to find or identify living people. These teams are often deployed to earthquake areas to locate people trapped in collapsed buildings. The federal police's explosive detector dogs are attached to the Federal Police Special Units.

Netherlands

The Dutch Mounted Police and Police Dog Service (DLHP) is part of the *Korps landelijke politiediensten* (KLPD; National Police Services Agency) and supports other units with horse patrols and specially trained dogs. The DLHP's dogs are trained to recognize a single specific scent. They specialize in identifying scents (identifying the scent shared by an object and a person), narcotics, explosives and firearms, detecting human remains, locating drowning people and fire accelerants.

The KLPD is just one of the 26 police regions in the Netherlands. Every other region has its own K-9 unit. For example, the K-9 unit of the regional police Amsterdam-Amstelland has 24 patroldog handlers and 6 specialdog handlers and 4 instructors. The unit has 24 patroldogs, 3 explosives/firearms dogs, 3 active narcotic dogs, 2 passive narcotic dogs, 2 scent identifying dogs, 1 crime scene dog and 1 USAR dog. They work on a 24/7 basis, every shift (07:00-15:00/15:00-23:00/23:00-07:00 local time), has a minimum of 2 patroldog handlers on patrol. The special dog handlers work only in the dayshift or after a call.

United Kingdom

Documented evidence exists from the Middle Ages showing that money was set aside in towns and villages to pay for the upkeep of bloodhounds to be used by parish constables to track down outlaws and criminals. In fact, during the reign of King Henry I, documents showing the staffing levels of the Royal Palaces refer to the appointment of a constable who, with the aid of a marshal, 'shall maintain the stables, kennels and mews, and be responsible for protecting and policing the whole court'.

During the twelfth and thirteenth centuries, the forces of law and order were employed by the Barons and landowners to protect their privileges. Restrictions were placed upon the right to own a dog. Divided into three classes, small dogs, which were unlikely to be a threat to hunting, were unrestricted. Dogs that had natural hunting instincts, such as greyhounds and spaniels were barred altogether, and larger breeds were only allowed if used for security purposes and if their claws were removed. Constables used these larger breeds such as the bloodhounds more for their own protection than the ability to apprehend villains. A point worthy of note is that the bloodhounds of those times were described as "unreliable, bad-tempered and savage" but even then displayed an uncanny ability to track through the marshes and bogs which bordered the highways of that time.

In Scotland bloodhounds became known as 'Slough dogs' and it is from this name that the word "Sleuth", usually applied to a detective, is derived. By the beginning of the nineteenth century, people were leaving the rural areas to move into the larger cities and towns. Large country estates were breaking down into smaller units, and with this change came the decline in the popularity of the dog as a hunter and enforcer of the law. At about this point in history, people of all classes began to treat their dogs as domestic pets rather than working animals, and size and appearance became as important as temperament and working ability.

The period of the Napoleonic Wars saw extreme outbreaks of violence and lawlessness in England and the existing forces of law & order, the parish constables and the Bow Street Runners were overwhelmed. As a result private associations were formed to help combat crime. Night watchmen were employed to guard premises with many of these individuals provided with firearms and dogs to protect themselves from the criminal elements. In 1829 Sir Robert Peel established London's Metropolitan Police, the first professional body to police the whole metropolitan area. From 1835 onwards, police forces were set up in the larger boroughs and cities, as well as in the counties, so that by the end of the century, professional policemen were policing the whole country.

One of the first real attempts to use dogs to aid police in the detection of crime and the apprehension of a criminal was in 1888 when two bloodhounds were used in a simple tracking test set by the then Commissioner of the Metropolitan (London) Police, Sir Charles Warren with a view to using them in the hunt for the Victorian murderer, Jack the Ripper. The results were far from satisfactory, with one of the hounds biting the Commissioner and both dogs later running off requiring a police search to find them.

The attitude in the UK was very much the same as that of continental Europe in the early 20th century; dogs were considered beneficial as long as they did not cost money or require special training, an attitude that still appears to be prevalent in many police departments around the world today. In 1914 official authority was granted for 172 constables in the Metropolitan (London) Police to take their own dogs on patrol with them, a motley crew of sheepdogs, retrievers, collies, terriers, spaniels, mongrels and even one Pomeranian.

In 1908, the North Eastern Railway police who used Airedales to put a stop to theft from the docks in Hull formed the first recognised UK Police

Dog Section. By 1910 the British Transport Commission Police had taken over, experimenting with other breeds such as Labradors, Dobermans and finally, the German Shepherd or Alsatian as it was then known.

After the 1914-1918 war, despite the success of the transport police dogs the police authorities in the UK continued to show a lack of interest in the use of dogs as an aid to police work. On the continent, however, dogs were being used for a variety of purposes with organised dog training centres being set up in various locations. In 1934 a committee was set up to investigate the whole question surrounding the use of police dogs in the UK. An interesting excerpt from *The Times* dated 15 January 1938 gives an interesting insight into the thinking of senior police officers of the time in regard to the use of dogs. Colonel Hoel Llewellyn, Chief Constable of Wiltshire was quoted as follows:

> "A good dog with a night duty man is as sound a proposition as you can get. The dog hears what the constable does not, gives him notice of anyone in the vicinity, guards his master's bicycle to the death, and remains mute unless roused. He is easily trained and will go home when told to do so with a message in his collar".

Bearing in mind that this was a statement from a pro-dog man of the times, is it any wonder that the authorities failed to understand the true worth of the dog in the role of law enforcement for a number of years to come.

In order to establish the best breed to be employed as a police service dog, the 1934 committee set up an experimental Home Office dog training school in Washwater, near Newbury, adjoining Lord Carnarvon's Highclere Estate. It concluded that a multi-purpose dog, trained to carry out all disciplines, was not possible, and that tracking and other work would have to be divided. The committee reported in 1937 that the experiments at the dog training school showed that the best breed of dog for following a scent was the bloodhound, and the best breed of dog for general patrol purposes was the Labrador. Experiments had been done in crossing Fell Hounds to Labradors and Otter Hounds to Bloodhounds, but both sets of crosses left something to be desired. As a result of the committee's conclusions, recommendations were made that Chief Constables 'consider' the use of dogs in police work, and it was once again left to the individual chief police officer to decide the worth of employing dogs in his respective police force. In 1938 two specially trained black Labradors were introduced into the Metropolitan Police as general patrol or 'utility' dogs, however, they were transferred in 1940 to the Cheshire Constabulary. With the outbreak of the Second World War, any further efforts to introduce dogs into a policing role in the UK were abandoned.

The end of the Second World War brought a crime wave to the shores of the UK, generally attributed to the presence of returning servicemen. It also brought the appointment of Chief Constable of the Surrey Constabulary to Sir Joseph Simpson K.B.E., a man who had a lifelong interest in gundogs and who saw clearer than most the possibilities of adapting the natural abilities and qualities of the dog to the specialist requirements of the police service. By good fortune, the Surrey Constabulary also employed an officer who had taken part in many of the unrewarding experiments to try and prove the value of the trained dog in police work; his name was Sergeant Harry Darbyshire.

This liaison set in motion the first positive effort to convince the Home Office and Police Forces throughout the UK of the true worth of a well-trained dog. With Darbyshire's enthusiasm and idea's and Simpson leadership and influence, the Surrey police headquarters at Mountbrown in Guildford became the epicentre of breeding and training of the modern police dog. Within a short space of time the Surrey police dogs were touring the country giving demonstrations to other police forces, whilst at the same time, Sir Joseph Simpson was bringing his influence to bear on the Kennel Club and other senior police officers. Slowly, they began to understand and appreciate the potential value of the police service dog.

After a careful study of the work carried out by Harry Darbyshire, Sir Joseph Simpson reached a number of important conclusions on which further developments and progress were to be based. The most far-reaching of these was to discard the accepted notion that all police dogs should be divided into two classes, tracking dogs and criminal work patrol dogs. The evidence pointed to the fact that some breeds of dogs were capable of being trained to carry out both disciplines. He also concluded that there should be a more rigorous selection process when accepting dogs for police work, the first step towards the notion that the police service should breed their own animals in an attempt to produce the ideal police dog.

1946 also saw the formation of a small dog section within the Metropolitan Police, an important event in itself as the Metropolitan Police, serving the capital city and with the largest deployment of manpower has always been an influential component in the policing tactics of the UK as a whole. Six Labradors were purchased from Yorkshire farmers and deployed in South London, quickly proving their worth when on their first night on patrol they were used in the arrest of two American servicemen after a purse snatch. In 1948 a new breed of police dog was used on the streets of London for the first time, the Alsatian Wolf Dog, later to be known as the Alsatian or German Shepherd Dog had arrived. The first of this breed in London was called 'Smokey' and such was the impression that he made, that a further twelve Alsatians together with another seven Labradors were purchased. The Metropolitan Police Dog Section was growing so rapidly that a central dog training school was established at Imber Court and by 1950 the total number of trained dogs in the force numbered 90.

The popularity of the police dog was being echoed all over the UK with police forces both large and small employing dogs and handlers on their strength and setting up dog training schools to cater for the ever increasing number of dogs being used.

The value of the police dog has been recognised by all to such an extent that there are over 2500 police dogs employed amongst the various police forces in the UK with the German Shepherd still the most popular breed for general purpose work with the Belgian Shepherd Malinois catching up fast, proven when a Belgian Malinois female called Metpol Kairo Demi bred by Steve Dean of the Metropolitan Police, handled by PC Graham Clarke won the 2008 National Police Dog Trials with the highest score ever recorded.

All British police dogs, irrespective of the discipline they are trained in, must be licensed to work operationally. To obtain the license they have to pass a test at the completion of their training, and then again every year until they retire, which is usually at about the age of 8 when the majority settle into a life as a family pet with their handler. The standards required to become operational are laid down by the Association of Chief Police Officers (ACPO) sub-committee on police dogs and are reviewed on a regular basis to ensure that training and licensing reflects the most appropriate methods & standards.

Many British police services now source the majority of their replacement dogs from within specialized police dog breeding programmes designed to ensure that the dogs are bred with strong working ethics & health as a priority. The Metropolitan Police has the largest police dog breeding programme in the UK supplying not only the capital city, London, but many other parts of the UK & the world with police service dogs.

USSR and Successor States (Russia, Ukraine, etc.)

Police patrolling on foot have long sporadically used attack dogs, generally exceptionally big German Shepherds, bred to weigh at least 35 kg and generally 40+ kg. These are kept on a leash at all times and required to wear muzzles, removed only when needed to pursue and detain suspects. They are trained to remain calm, docile, and unfazed by crowds and noise, retaining a perfect calm on public transportation. Such dogs may react to any and all stimuli only if ordered to do so. They are a common sight in cities and are rarely if ever perceived as unnerving by the general public.

Crime scene investigation units and patrols seeking dangerous fugitives have also been known to use dogs for tracking. Interestingly enough, these units also use German Shepherds, which were chosen as the all-purpose police and army breed. These practices have remained common in most of the Soviet Union's successor states.

Guard Dog

A guard dog, an attack dog or watch dog is a dog used to guard against, and watch for, unwanted or unexpected people or animals. The dog is discriminating so that it does not annoy or attack familiar people.

Both guard dogs and watchdogs bark loudly to alert their owners of an intruder's presence and scare away the intruder. The watch dog's function ends here; a guard dog is capable of attacking or restraining the intruder. For example, livestock guardian dogs are often large enough and strong enough to attack and drive away livestock predators such as wolves. Some breeds (such as Keeshonden) are excellent watchdogs but not excellent guard dogs because they bark loudly to alert their masters of intruders but are not given to assertive behavior. Similarly, even very small but attentive dogs (among a few other species) may function well as watchdogs.

The following pedigree breeds are the best at watch dog barking:

- Miniature schnauzer
- West Highland white terrier
- Scottish terrier
- Doberman pinscher
- German shepherd
- Rottweiler

If the risk is from human intruders, a suitable dog can be simply trained to be aggressive towards unrecognized humans and then tethered or enclosed unsupervised in an area the owner wishes to protect when he is not around (such as at night); the stereotypical 'junkyard dog' is a common example of this. Other guard dogs intended for police or more supervised work are trained to bite, restrain and release an intruder only on the specific commands of its handler—as in Schutzhund or K9 Pro Sports training.

Many of the now prominent guardian breeds such as Rottweilers started as farm dogs types but then developed over many years into guard breeds. Some breeds, such as the Weimaraner and Rhodesian Ridgeback, were originally bred for hunting, but their large intimidating look and territorial instincts have helped them evolve into guard dogs in today's society. Others like Dobermans were specifically bred as guard dogs. Many of the below breeds have a greater amount of molossoid or mastiff DNA. This is confirmed by a DNA study done on >270 pure breed dogs. The study suggests that in the distant past thirteen ancient breeds broke off early on after which a group of mastiff style dogs were developed.

These dogs are grouped with the mastiffs Great Dane and Irish wolfhound. The Irish wolfhound (a traditional hunting guardian breed) has evidence that its population was nearly wiped out 200 years ago and its existing members descend from a very small group of dogs and thus it is a rebuilt breed, but evidently out of somewhat different building blocks. Some people think that the Irish wolfhound contributed to the Great Dane.

The St. Bernard is also somewhat different from the mastiffs and is not in the molossoid group; however, the Swiss mountain dogs are. The Moscow Watchdog thus probably inherits its guarding ability not from the St. Bernard but from its other major contributor, the Caucasian Ovcharka (no evidence other than speculation and the known breed characteristics). Great Danes are odd because they are not in the molossoid group and traditionally behaved as though they should be.

The original Saint Bernard was used for alpine rescue in the Saint Bernard Pass by the monks. An avalanche killed off many of the dogs used for breeding. The Saint Bernards had to be bred with larger dogs such as mastiffs, which give it the large size and the guard dog instinct that the Saint Bernard has today.

It is claimed that female dogs tend to make better personal guardians than males, due to maternal instincts, but males are considered better for guarding property because of their greater territorial instinct. Female protection dogs are much easier to train and learn at a faster rate. Less independent, they are adept at integrating into their new family and swiftly blend into any situation they are consigned to.

The Jindo dog is widely used in civilian and military in South Korea.

The German Shepherd dog is widely used by the Metropolitan Police Force and private security companies in the UK.

List of breeds commonly used as guard dogs

- American Bulldog
- Anatolian Shepherd (US and UK) or Kangal Dog
- Armenian Gampr dog
- Belgian Shepherd Dog (Malinois)
- Black Russian Terrier (Russia)
- Boerboel (South Africa)
- Boxer
- Bullmastiff
- Cane Corso (Italy)
- Chow Chow (China)
- Doberman Pinscher
- Dogue de Bordeaux
- English mastiff
- Fila Brasileiro (Brazil)
- German Shepherd
- Giant Schnauzer
- Komondor (Hungary)
- Korean Jindo (Korea)
- Kunming Wolfdog (In Asian nations)
- Kuvasz
- Leonberger
- Pit bull
- Puli

- Rhodesian Ridgeback (Africa)
- Rottweiler
- Shar Pei
- Sharr Mountain Dog (Macedonia)
- Tibetan Mastiff

List of other guard dog breeds:

- Akita Inu (Japan)
- Alano Español (Spain)
- Argentine Dogo (Argentina)
- Australian Cattle dogs (Australia)
- Bandog (USA)
- Beauceron (France)
- Bouvier des Flandres (Belgium)
- Bull Terrier (England)
- Bully Kutta (Pakistan)
- Cão de Castro Laboreiro (Portugal)
- Canis Panther (USA)
- Caucasian Ovcharka (Georgia)
- Ciobanesc de Bucovina (Romania)
- Danish Broholmer (Denmark)
- Dogo Guatemalteco (Guatemala)
- Dutch Shepherd Dog (Netherlands)
- Fila Brasileiro (Brazil)
- Great Dane (Germany)
- Great Pyrenees (France)
- Greater Swiss Mountain Dog (Switzerland)
- Gull Dong (Pakistan)
- Gull Terr (Pakistan)
- Hovawart (Germany)
- Icelandic Sheepdog (Iceland)
- Karelian Bear Dog (Finland)
- Mioritic (Romania)
- Moscow Watchdog (Russia)
- Mucuchies (Venezuela)
- Neapolitan Mastiff (Italy)
- Perro de Presa Canario (Canary Islands)
- Pariah Dog (India)
- Perro de Presa Mallorquin (aka: Ca de Bou)
- Saint Bernard (Switzerland)
- Schipperke (Belgium)

- Shiloh Shepherd (USA)
- Swinford (USA)
- Tibetan Mastiff (Tibet, Mongolia)
- Weimaraner (Germany)

Note: Some are not AKC, UKC, recognized and a few are not FCI recognized, but all at least have their own breed club.

Rare Breeds

- Antebellum Bulldog (USA)
- Black Russian Terrier (Russia)
- Boerboel (South Africa)
- Caucasian Ovcharka (Russia)
- Chippiparai (India)
- Combai (India)
- Formosan Mountain Dog (Taiwan)
- Jindo dog (South Korea)
- Kanni (India)
- Rajapalayam (dog) (India)

Livestock Guardian Dog

A livestock guardian dog (LGD) is a domesticated canine used to defend livestock against predators. LGDs are commonly referred to as 'sheep dogs' since they most often have guarded flocks of sheep, but most are capable of guarding other species of livestock. They are classified as pastoral dogs. Unlike herding dogs (also often called 'sheepdogs') such as the Border Collie, an LGD does not control the movement of the flock with predatory actions causing bunching. Instead, LGDs tend to blend into the flock and generally ignore the individual animals in favor of keeping an eye out for potential threats. While bunching behavior is observed, it is the livestock that tend to bunch around the guarding dogs, especially on open range when predators are near.

The dogs are introduced to livestock as puppies so they 'imprint' on the animals. This imprinting is thought to be largely olfactory and occurs between 3 and 16 weeks of age. An LGD raised with sheep will generally not be an effective guardian of cattle or goats and one raised with cattle will not be an effective guardian of goats or sheep. The imprinting is critical because LGDs tend to behave in a non-predatory and protective way only with animal species they have been raised with. Proper socialization and instinct, not training, are key to rearing an effective LGD. Bonding LGDs to cattle is more difficult than bonding them to the smaller livestock species. However, the practice of bonding guarding dogs to cows is becoming more common, especially in places such as the American West where the reintroduction of predators has conflicted with cattle herds in areas where predation had been rare. There are even trials underway to protect penguins.

In Namibia in Southwest Africa, Anatolians are used to guard goat herds from cheetahs, and are typically imprinted between seven and eight weeks of age. Impoverished Namibian farmers often came into conflict with predatory cheetahs; now, Anatolians usually are able to drive off cheetahs with their barking and displays of aggressions.

LGDs are generally large and protective, which can make them less than ideal for urban or even suburban living. Nonetheless, despite their size, they can be gentle, make good companion dogs, and are often protective towards children. If introduced to a family as a pup, most LGDs are as protective of their family as a working guard dog is of its flock. In fact, in some communities where LGDs are a tradition, the runt of a litter would often be kept or given as a household pet or simply kept as a village dog without a single owner.

Anywhere from one to five dogs may be placed with a flock or herd depending on its size, the type of predators, their number, and the intensity of predation. If predators are scarce, one dog may be adequate though range operations usually require two dogs. Both male and female LGDs have proved to be equally effective in protecting of livestock. However, in regions where dogs were used in annual transhumance migrations, males were often used exclusively as LGDs since pregnant females and newborn pups would likely perish on the long journeys.

The three qualities most sought after in LGDs are trustworthiness, attentiveness and protectiveness—trustworthy in that they do not roam off and are not aggressive with the livestock, attentive in that they are situationally aware of threats by predators, and protective in that they will attempt to drive off predators. Dogs, being social creatures with differing personalities, will take on different roles with the herd and among themselves: most sticking close to the livestock, others tending to follow the shepherd or rancher when one is present, and some drifting farther from the livestock. These differing roles are often complementary in terms of protecting livestock, and experienced ranchers and shepherds sometimes encourage these differences by adjustments in socialization technique so as to increase the effectiveness of their group of dogs in meeting specific predator threats. LGDs that follow the livestock closest assure that a guard dog is on hand if a predator attacks, while LGDs that patrol at the edges of a flock or herd are in a position to keep would-be attackers at a safe distance from livestock. Those dogs that are more attentive tend to alert those that are more passive but perhaps also more trustworthy or less aggressive with the livestock.

While LGDs have been known to fight to the death with predators, in most cases predator attacks are prevented by a display of aggressiveness. LGDs are known to drive off predators that physically they would be no match for, such as bears and even lions. With the reintroduction of predators into natural habitats in Europe and North America, environmentalists have come to appreciate LGDs because they allow sheep and cattle farming to coexist with predators in the same or nearby habitats. Unlike trapping and poisoning, LGDs seldom kill predators; instead, their aggressive behaviors tend to condition predators to seek unguarded (thus, non-farm animal) prey. For instance, in Italy's Gran Sasso National Park, where LGDs and wolves have coexisted for centuries, older, more experienced wolves seem to 'know' the LGDs and leave their flocks alone.

CHAPTER 21
Sniffer Dog

Sniffer dog is a dog that is trained to and works at using its senses (almost always the sense of smell) to detect substances such as explosives, illegal drugs, or blood. Hunting dogs that search for game and search dogs that search for missing humans are generally not considered detection dogs. There is some overlap, as in the case of human remains detection dogs (sometimes called cadaver dogs), trained to detect human remains. They are also used for drug raids to find where the drugs are.

In the state of California, dogs are trained to detect the Quagga Mussel on boats at public boat ramps, as it is a invasive species. Sniffer dogs have also been enlisted to find bumblebee nests. The Bumblebee Conservation Trust has trained a springer spaniel to detect the colonies, assisting them with the conservation of threatened species. Some prisons have dogs trained to detect illicit cell phones in prison cells.

Detection dogs have been trained to search for many substances, including:

- Plants, animals, produce, and other agricultural items (used by customs services to detect possible invasive species such as Quagga mussel).
- Cancer.
- Polycarbonate optical discs such as DVDs (used to search for bootleg recordings).
- Crime evidence.
- Currency.
- Drugs.
- Diabetes.
- Bed bugs.
- Explosives.
- Mobile phones (as contraband in prisons).
- Firearms.

- Human remains.
- Mold.
- Termites.

One notable quality of detection dogs is that they are able to discern individual scents even when the scents are combined or masked by other odors. In one case at an Australian prison, a detection dog foiled an attempt to smuggle drugs that had been hidden in a woman's bra and smeared with coffee, pepper and Vicks Vapo-rub. A sniffer dog can detect blood even if it has been scrubbed off surfaces. In one case, a sniffer dog sniffed a drop of blood on a wall although an attempt had been made to scrub it off. It was so small that it couldn't be seen without a microscope.

Criticism of Drug Detection Dogs

Their use has been criticized as allowing the police to conduct searches without cause, in a manner that is unregulated, and for being used to target adults carrying drugs for personal use rather than commercial purposes. They have been criticized as a form of show-policing, motivated more by the state's desire to be seen to be doing something than any serious attempt to respond to the dangers of drug use.

Problems exist with detection dogs in that they can be trained to indicate the presence of drugs when none exist and the dog, of course, cannot be called to testify. Officers sometimes attempt to intimidate drivers into consenting to a search by saying that a detection dog is on the way, whether one is really on the way or not.

In 2001 the Australian state of New South Wales introduced legislation to provide police with powers to use drug detection dogs without a warrant in public places such as licensed venues, music festivals and public transport. The legislation was reviewed by the NSW Ombudsman who in 2006 handed down a report highly critical of the use of dogs for drug detection. The report stated that prohibited drugs were found in only 26 per cent of searches following an indication by a drug sniffer dog. Of these, 84 per cent were for small amounts of cannabis deemed for personal use. The report also found that the legislation was ineffective at detecting persons in supply of prohibited drugs, with only 0.19 per cent of indications ultimately leading to a successful prosecution for supply.

Bed bug detection dogs are specially trained by handlers to identify the scent of bed bugs.

With the increased focus on green pest management and integrated pest management, bed bug detection dogs are gaining popularity in North America. Dogs are a safer alternative to pesticide use as a management strategy. If operators can find out exactly where bed bugs are located, they can minimize the area that needs to be sprayed. Dogs smell in parts per trillion, something a human cannot do, and detect bed bugs through all life cycle phases from eggs to nymphs to adults.

Bed bug detection dogs are relatively new. The National Entomology Scent Detection Canine Association, states that there are over 100 dogs currently working in the U.S., but this number is increasing, while the International Forensic Detection Canine Association based in the US, estimates well over 200 and counting. IFEDCA, founded by a Certified Master Trainer, Bill Whitstine, also estimates that the need for bed bug dogs far outweighs the supply. Bill Whitstine was the first trainer to train and certify bed bug detection dogs in the United States and has an estimated 150 dogs internationally.

Bed bug detection dogs are a viable and scientifically-proven alternative to traditional methods of pest detection. A 2008 report by the University of Kentucky Department of Entomology endorsed bed bug detection dogs by stating that the "reliability of the dogs has been impressive provided they are properly trained." Scientists at the university reviewed studies on the dogs and concluded that although expensive for operators, canine detection dogs were promising.

Bed bug detection is complicated by the fact that the insects can hide almost anywhere. Bed bug detection dogs solve this problem because they are small and agile, finding bugs in places humans cannot such as wall voids, crevices and furniture gaps.

With the increase in global travel and shared living accommodations, bed bugs have become more prevalent. The U.S. Environmental Protection Agency held a bed bug summit in April 2009 to address the ongoing problem of bed bugs and how to eradicate them. The certification of bed bug detection dogs was discussed.

Guide Dog

Guide dogs (also called seeing-eye dogs) are assistance dogs trained to lead blind and visually impaired people around obstacles.

Although the dogs can be trained to navigate various obstacles, they are partially (red-green) colour blind and are not capable of interpreting street signs. The human half of the guide dog team does the directing, based upon skills acquired through previous mobility training. The handler might be likened to an aircraft's navigator, who must know *how* to get from one place to another, and the dog is the pilot, who gets them there safely.

In several countries, guide dogs, along with most service and hearing dogs, are exempt from regulations against the presence of animals in places such as restaurants and public transportation.

References to guide dogs date at least as far back as the mid-16th century; the second line of the popular verse alphabet 'A was an Archer' is most commonly 'B was a Blind-man/Led by a dog' In the 19th century verse novel *Aurora Leigh* by Elizabeth Barrett Browning, the title character remarks "The blind man walks wherever the dog pulls/And so I answered".

The first guide dog training schools were established in Germany during World War I, to enhance the mobility of returning veterans who were blinded in combat. The United States followed suit in 1929 with The Seeing Eye in Nashville, Tennessee (relocated in 1931 to Morristown, New Jersey). One of the founders of The Seeing Eye was America's first guide dog owner, Nashville resident Morris Frank. Frank was trained with Buddy, a German Shepherd, in Switzerland in 1928.

The first guide dogs in Great Britain were German Shepherds. Three of these first were Judy, Meta, and Folly, who were handed over to their new owners, veterans blinded in World War I, on 6 October 1931. Judy's new owner was Musgrave Frankland. In 1934 The Guide Dogs for the Blind Association in Great Britain began operation.

Important studies on the behavior and training methods of guide dogs were done in 1921s and 1930s by Jakob von Uexküll and Emanuel Georg Sarris. They studied the richness of guide dogs and introduced advanced methods of dog training.

Early on, trainers began to recognize which breeds produced dogs most appropriate for guide work; today, Golden Retrievers, Labradors, and German Shepherds are most likely to be chosen , though by no means does this mean other breeds, such as Yorkshire Terriers, Poodles, Collies, Vizslas, Dobermans, Rottweilers, Boxers, Papillons, Border Collies, Australian Shepherds and Airedale Terriers, are not.

Crosses such as Golden Retriever/Labrador (which are popular due to both breeds' known intelligence, work-ethic, and early maturation) and Labradoodles (Labrador/Poodles bred to provide dogs with less shedding for those with allergies to hair or dander) are also common.

Despite regulations or rules that deny access to animals in restaurants and other public places, in many countries, guide dogs and other types of assistance dogs are protected by law, and therefore may accompany their handlers most places that are open to the public. Laws and regulations vary worldwide:

- In the United States, the Americans with Disabilities Act prohibits any business, government agency, or other organization that provides access to the general public from barring guide dogs. However, religious organizations are not required to provide such access. The Fair Housing Act requires that landlords allow tenants to have guide dogs in residences that normally have a *No Pets* policy and no extra fees may be charged for such tenants. Whether guide dogs in training have the same rights or not usually falls on each individual state government.
- In most South American countries and Mexico, guide dog access depends solely upon the goodwill of the owner or manager. In more tourist-heavy areas, guide dogs are generally welcomed without problems. In

Brazil, however, a 2006 federal decree requires allowance of guide dogs in all public and open to public places. The Brasília Metro has developed a programme which trains guide dogs to ride it.

- In Europe, the situation varies. Some countries have laws that govern the entire country and sometimes the decision is left up to the respective regions.
- In Australia, the Disability Discrimination Act 1992 protects guide dog handlers. Each state and territory has its own laws, which may differ slightly.
- In Canada, guide dogs are allowed anywhere that the general public is allowed.
- In South Korea, it is illegal to deny access to guide dogs in any areas that are open to the public. Violators are fined for no more than two million won.

CHAPTER 22

Working Dog

Working dog, is a type of pastoral dog that either has been trained in herding or belongs to breeds developed for herding. Their ability to be trained to act on the sound of a whistle or word of command is renowned throughout the world.

In Australia, New Zealand and the United States herding dogs are known as *working dogs* irrespective of their breeding. Some herding breeds work well with any kind of animals; others have been bred for generations to work with specific kinds of animals and have developed physical characteristics or styles of working that enhance their ability to handle these animals. Commonly mustered animals include cattle, sheep, goats and reindeer, although it is not unusual for poultry to be handled by dogs.

The term 'herding dog' is sometimes erroneously used to describe livestock guardian dogs, whose primary function is to guard flocks and herds from predation and theft, and they lack the herding instinct. Although herding dogs may guard flocks their primary purpose is to move them; both herding dogs and livestock guardian dogs may be called 'sheep dogs'.

In general terms when categorizing dog breeds, herding dogs are considered a subcategory of working dogs, but for conformation shows they usually form a separate group.

Australia has the world's largest cattle stations and sheep stations and some of best-known herding dogs, such as the Koolie, Kelpie, Red and Blue Heelers are bred and found there.

All herding behavior is modified predatory behavior. Through selective breeding, man has been able to minimize the dog's natural inclination to treat cattle and sheep as prey while simultaneously maintaining the dog's hunting skills, thereby creating an effective herding dog.

Dogs can work other animals in a variety of ways. Some breeds, such as the Australian Cattle Dog, typically nip at the heels of animals (for this reason they are called *heelers*) and the Cardigan Welsh Corgi and the Pembroke

Welsh Corgi were historically used in a similar fashion in the cattle droves that moved cattle from Wales to the Smithfield Meat Market in London but are rarely used for herding today.

Other breeds, notably the Border Collie, get in front of the animals and use what is called *strong eye* to stare down the animals; they are known as *headers*. The *headers* or fetching dogs keep livestock in a group. They consistently go to the front or head of the animals to turn or stop the animal's movement. The *heelers* or driving dogs keep pushing the animals forward. Typically, they stay behind the herd. The Australian Kelpie and Australian Koolie use both these methods and also run along the backs of sheep so are said to head, heel, and back. Other types such as the Australian Shepherd, English Shepherd and Welsh Sheepdog are *moderate* to *loose eyed*, working more independently. The New Zealand Huntaway uses its loud, deep bark to muster mobs of sheep. German Shepherd Dogs and Briards are historically *tending* dogs, who act as a 'living fence', guiding large flocks of sheep to graze while preventing them from eating valuable crops and wandering onto roads.

Herding instincts and trainability can be measured when introducing a dog to livestock or at noncompetitive herding tests. Individuals exhibiting basic herding instincts can be trained to compete in herding trials.

The competitive dog sport in which herding dog breeds move animals around a field, fences, gates, or enclosures as directed by their handlers is called a *sheepdog trial, herding test* or *stockdog trial* depending on the area. Such events are particularly associated with hill farming areas, where sheep range widely on largely unfenced land. These trials are popular in the United Kingdom, Ireland, South Africa, Chile, Canada, the USA, Australia, New Zealand and other farming nations, and have occasionally even become primetime television fare.

In the US, regular events are run by the United States Border Collie Handler's Association, Australian Shepherd Club of America, American Kennel Club and many others.

- Come-bye or just bye - go to the left of the stock, or clockwise around them.
- Away to me, or just away or 'way - go to the right of the stock, or counterclockwise around them.
- Stand - stop, although when said gently may also mean just to slow down.
- Wait, (lie) down or sit - stop.
- Steady or take time - slow down.
- Cast - gather the stock into a group. Good working dogs will cast over a large area.
- Find - search for stock. A good dog will hold the stock until the shepherd arrives. Some will bark when the stock have been located.

- Get out or get back - move away from the stock. Used when the dog is working too close to the stock, potentially causing the stock stress. Occasionally used as a reprimand.
- Hold - keep stock where they are.
- Bark or speak up - bark at stock. Useful when more force is needed, and usually essential for working cattle and sheep.
- Look back - return for a missed animal.
- In here - go through a gap in the flock. Used when separating stock.
- Walk up, walk on or just walk - move in closer to the stock.
- That'll do - stop working and return to handler.

These commands may be indicated by a hand movement, whistle or voice. There are many other commands that are also used when working stock and in general use away from stock. Herding dog commands are generally taught using livestock as the modus operandi. Urban owners without access to livestock are able to teach basic commands through herding games.

These are not the only commands used: there are many variations. When whistles are used, each dog usually has a different set of commands to avoid confusion when more than one dog is being worked at one time.

Herding Dogs as Pets

Herding dogs are often chosen as family pets. The collie breeds including the Bearded Collie and Border Collie are well known. Although they make good family dogs and show dogs they are at their best when they have a job to do. These dogs have been bred as working dogs and need to be active. They retain their herding instincts and may sometimes nip at people's heels or bump them in an effort to 'herd' their family, and may need to be trained not to do so. Their activity level and intelligence makes them excellent canine athletes. The Shetland Sheepdog, Rough Collie, Smooth Collie and Old English Sheepdog are more popular as family companion dogs.

Sled Dog

Sled dogs, known also as sleigh man dogs, sledge dogs, or sleddogs, are highly trained types of dogs that are used to pull a dog sled, a wheel-less vehicle on runners also called a sled or sleigh, over snow or ice, by means of harnesses and lines.

Sled dogs have become a popular winter recreation and sport in North America and Europe; sled dogs are now found even in such unlikely places as Germany and Japan. Several distinct dog breeds are used as sled dogs, however, dog drivers have a long history of using other breeds or crossbreeds as sled dogs. There are two main qualities that are expected in sled dogs: endurance and speed. Racing sled dogs will travel up to an average 20 mph (32 km/h) over distances up to 25 mi (40 km). Although these dogs are very helpful, the origins of this arrangement are unknown.

Dog power has been utilized for hunting and travel for hundreds of years. As far back as the 10th century these dogs were contributing to human culture.

Dog sled teams are put together with great care. Putting a dog sled team together involves picking leader dogs, point dogs, swing dogs and wheel dogs. The lead dog is very treasured, and seldom will mushers ever let these dogs out of their sight. Indeed, trained lead dogs become part of the family household. Important too is to have powerful wheel dogs to pull the sled out from the snow. Point dogs (optional) are located behind the leader dogs, swing dogs between the point and wheel dogs, and team dogs are all other dogs in between the wheel and swing dogs and are selected for their endurance, strength and speed as part of the team.

Several distinct dog breeds are in common use as sled dogs, although any sized breed may be used to pull a sled. Purebred sled dog breeds range from the well-known Siberian Husky and Alaskan Malamute to rarer breeds such as the Mackenzie River Husky or the Canadian Eskimo Dog (Canadian Inuit Dog). Dog drivers, however, have a long history of using other breeds or crossbreeds as sled dogs. In the days of the Gold Rush in Yukon, mongrel teams were the rule, but there were also teams of Foxhounds and Staghounds. Today the unregistered hybridized Alaskan Husky is preferred for dogsled racing, along with a variety of crossbreeds, the German Shorthaired Pointer often being chosen as the basis for cross breeding. From 1988 through 1991, a team of Standard Poodles competed in the Iditarod Trail Sled Dog Race.

Sled dogs are expected to demonstrate two major qualities in their work (apart from basic physical capability to pull the sled). Endurance is needed to travel the distances demanded in dogsled travel, which may be anything from 5 to 80 mi (8 to 129 km) or more a day. Speed is needed to travel the distance in a reasonable length of time. Over longer distances, average traveling speed declines to 10 to 14 mph (16 to 23 km/h). In poor trail conditions, sled dogs can still usually average 6 or 7 mph (9.7 or 11 km/h). Sled dogs have been known to travel over 90 mi (145 km) in a 24 hour period while pulling 85 lb (39 kg) each.

Sled dogs pull various sorts of sleds, from the small 25 lb (11 kg) sprint-racing sleds, through the larger plastic-bottomed distance racing toboggan sleds, to traditional ash, freighting sleds and the trapper's high-fronted narrow toboggan. Sled dogs are also used to pull skiers, kicksleds and to draw wheeled rigs when there is no snow. They have even been used to pull kick scooters in places where there is a lack of snow, a sport known as dog scootering. Modern teams are usually hitched in tandem, with harnessed pairs of sled dogs pulling on tug lines attached to a central gangline. Trappers in deep snow conditions using the toboggan will hitch their dogs in single file with traces on either side of the line of dogs. Dog teams of some Inuit are run in 'fan hitch', each dog having its own tow line tied directly to the sled.

Sled Dog Breeds

- A typical sled dog breed, such as the Greenland Dog, has a very dense double coat, wide padded feet, erect ears, a curled tail, wedge-shaped head, and a muscular build.
- Alaskan Husky is not a breed, but a category or type of dog.
- Alaskan Malamute was originally bred to be used as an Alaskan sled dog. It is generally a large and domesticated dog.
- Canadian Inuit Dog is an Arctic breed and is considered to be the oldest and rarest of the remaining purebred indigenous domestic canines.
- Chinook is a rare New England sled dog breed of "in-between" type, neither a sprinter nor an endurance freighter; the original lead dog 'Chinook' on whom the breed is based was a mixture from working sled dog lines and of a more mastiff-type build than most sled dogs, and the breed varies in appearance much more than most sled dog breeds and often superficially resembles a yellow German Shepherd Dog mix.
- Eurohound is a crossbred dog, a mix between the Alaskan Husky and the Pointer. It has both the Alaskan Husky's sledding ability and the Pointer's enthusiasm and athleticism. It is one of the most formidable sprint-racing sled dogs in the world.
- Greenland Dog is a large breed of husky-type dog kept as a sled dog and also used for hunting polar bear and seal.
- Greyster sled dog type bred in Norway.
- Labrador Husky was bred as a strong, fast, working sled dog and originated in Canada.
- Mackenzie River Husky is built for heavy freighting in single file through deep snow. Less a specific breed than a certain set of varieties of sled dog types from a specific geographic area, a mix of Arctic and subarctic sled dogs.
- Sakhalin Husky is rarely used and usually lives in Japan.
- Samoyed is a pure or mostly-white spitz that was used for herding reindeer as well as pulling sleds.
- Seppala Siberian Sleddog is active and energetic, sharing the same ancestral base as the Siberian Husky.
- Siberian Husky originated in Siberia. They were originally meant to be sled dogs, but nowadays are mainly family pets and show dogs.
- Tamaskan Dog originated in Finland and bred to look like wolves. N bred specifically for (though still capable of) sledding work, it excels agility, obedience, and working trials.
- Utonagan and Northern Inuit Dog are bred to resemble wolves, but are mixes between the Alaskan Malamute, German Shepherd, and Siberian Husky.

There were ten distinct husky breeds differentiated by region, height/weight and colour: the Husky proper (recognised by the American Kennel Club under the name of Eskimo), the Alaskan Malamute, the Toganee, the Mackenzie River Husky, the Timber-Wolf Dog, the West Greenland Husky, the East Greenland Husky, the Baffinland Husky, the Chuchi (recognised by the American Kennel Club as the Siberian Husky), and the Ostiak.

The *Husky* or *Eskimo* dog is rare outside of the Northwest Territories. These are mostly used by trappers, explorers, Eskimos and Indians; the Hudson Bay traders, Royal Canadian Mounted Police, lumber-jacks, doctors, priests and others generally use what the Indians call the *white* dogs, or crossbred dogs which are half Husky and half Hound, Great Dane, Newfoundland or any other type that is handy.

The *Toganee* and *Mackenzie River Dogs* were closely related to the true Husky and sometimes interbred. The Toganee had longer legs while the Mackenzie River Dog had a longer coat. The Timber-Wolf Dog of the Yukon basin was a first-cross between the true Husky and the timber-wolf and used as a leader or 'king' dog. The Baffinland Husky differed from the true Husky in having a black coat with white markings. The West Greenland Husky and the slightly smaller East Greenland Husky both had timber-wolf blood and were sometimes crossed with the Baffinland Husky. The East Greenland Husky (also called the Angmagssalik Husky) was considered the oldest and least diluted type. The comparatively small Ostiak or West Siberian Husky was used not only for sled hauling but also in hunting elk, bear and wolf. The tenth recognised type was the Chuchi (Siberian Husky) first imported into Alaska in 1909.

Therapy Dog

A therapy dog is a dog trained to provide affection and comfort to people in hospitals, retirement homes, nursing homes, schools, people with learning difficulties, and stressful situations, such as disaster areas.

Therapy dogs come in all sizes and breeds. The most important characteristic of a therapy dog is its temperament. A good therapy dog must be friendly, patient, confident, gentle, and at ease in all situations. Therapy dogs must enjoy human contact and be content to be petted and handled, sometimes clumsily.

A therapy dog's primary job is to allow unfamiliar people to make physical contact with it and to enjoy that contact. Children in particular enjoy hugging animals; adults usually enjoy simply petting the dog. The dog might need to be lifted onto, or climb onto, an individual's lap or bed and sit or lie comfortably there. Many dogs contribute to the visiting experience by performing small tricks for their audience or by playing carefully structured games.

Gun Dog

Gun dogs, also gundogs or bird dogs, are types of dogs developed to assist hunters in finding and retrieving game, usually birds. Gun dogs are divided into three primary types: Retrievers, flushing dogs, and pointing breeds. Some kennel clubs define a Gundog Group for gundogs, while other kennel clubs include them in the Sporting Group. The three most popular types are: Spaniel, Golden Retriever and Labrador.

Upon reaching the field, the handler often will *cast* or direct the dog in a wide circle. Experienced dogs will search the edges of the field knowing that birds are usually found there. This wide run helps to burn off the dog's initial exuberance and may help the dog establish its bearings and form a "background" upon which game smells will be processed. The dog then begins working back and forth, starting near the hunter and slowly ranging out. The dog repeats this process as the hunters move through the field. How far a handler allows the dog to range is a matter of personal preference. When a pair of dogs work as a team, one works close in while the other ranges out in larger circles. If either dog becomes birdy, the other dog works its way over to assist. Good bird dogs are alert to their handlers and to the disposition of other dogs in the field. They should readily comply if the handler casts them to an area of particular interest, such as a brush pile or shuck of corn.

When game is detected, a dog freezes, either pointing or crouching. If other dogs are present, they also freeze, "honoring" the first dog's point. The pointing dog remains motionless until the hunters are in position. Handlers give the command *whoa*, instructing the dog to remain still. What happens next depends on the dog's training. Some trainers train the dog to stay motionless while the hunter steps forward and flushes the game. Other trainers direct the dog to flush the game with a command such as *get it!* Pointing dogs excel on covey type birds such as bobwhite, quail, and grouse as these birds will hold in position well, allowing the hunter to approach and get into position.

If a bird is downed, the dogs are instructed to search for and retrieve it with the command *dead bird*, or simply *dead*.

When hunting upland game flushing dogs (spaniels and retrievers) work much more closely with the hunter. Flushers will not cover the same amount of ground as a pointing dog as the flusher must be kept within shotgun distance. Flushing dogs are often used on birds that run from the hunter. On such birds as pheasant, an aggressive flush is necessary to spring the bird to wing. Flushing dogs excel on these types of bird because they do not point the birds, giving them little time for escape on the ground. Pointing breeds are used on such birds, but must be well trained to know when the bird pointed has moved.

Once a bird has been flushed, the dog will sit or 'hup' to watch the flight of the bird and mark the fallen birds for retrieval. The dog which does this successfully is referred to as steady to wing and shot. Steadiness is the hallmark of the finished spaniel.

When a bird is shot, the dog should mark where it fell and wait until given the command to retrieve. Once commanded, the dog will race to the point of fall, pick up the bird, and return it to the handler.

Retrievers

Retrievers are typically used when waterfowl hunting although they can also be employed in hunting upland birds as well. Since a majority of waterfowl hunting employs the use of small boats in winter conditions retrievers are expected to remain sitting calmly and quietly until sent to retrieve. As birds move into range a well trained retriever will watch and follow the handler's gun as he shoots, marking and remembering each bird that is downed. This is called 'marking off the gun', and the downed birds are called 'marks'. Once the shooting has ceased the handler commands the dog to retrieve each bird that has been downed. If a dog did not see the bird fall, a retriever takes direction from the handler, who can use hand and whistle signals to guide the dog to the unseen downed bird. This is called a 'blind' retrieve. During a typical day of shooting it is not uncommon for additional birds to be downed while the dog is performing a retrieve. Retrievers are taught to ignore these 'diversions' until the current retrieve has been completed. Also at times multiple dogs are used on a hunt and retrievers are also taught to 'honour' another dog's retrieve by remaining calm and quiet while the other dog is working.

CHAPTER 23

Dogs in Warfare

Dogs in warfare have a long history starting in ancient times. From 'war dogs' trained in combat to their use as scouts, sentries and trackers, their uses have been varied and some continue to exist in modern military usage.

War dogs were used by the Egyptians, Greeks, Persians, Sarmatians, Alans, Slavs, Britons, and the Romans. The Molossian 'Canis Molossus' dog of Epirus was the strongest known to the Romans, and was specifically trained for battle. However, when fought against the broad-mouthed, powerful mastiff of Britannia, they were outmatched. The Romans exported many of this breed of mastiff to Rome and then disseminated them over the known world. Often war dogs would be sent into battle with large protective spiked metal collars and coats of mail armor. The Romans had attack formations made entirely of dogs. Native Americans also used dogs, though not on this scale.

During the Late Antiquity, Attila the Hun used giant Molosser dogs in his campaigns. Gifts of war dog breeding stock between European royalty were seen as suitable tokens for exchange throughout the Middle Ages. Other civilizations used armored dogs to defend caravans or attack enemies. The Spanish conquistadors used armoured dogs that had been trained to kill and disembowel when they invaded the land controlled by South American natives. The British used dogs when they attacked the Irish and the Irish in turn used Irish Wolfhounds to attack invading Norman knights on horseback. Two wolfhounds, or even a single one were often capable of taking a mounted man in armour off his horse, where the lightly armed handler would finish him off if necessary.

Later on, Frederick the Great used dogs as messengers during the Seven Years' War with Russia. Napoleon would also used dogs during his campaigns. Dogs were used up until 1770 to guard naval installations in France.

The first official use of dogs for military purposes in the United States was during the Seminole Wars. The American Pit Bull Terrier was used in the American Civil War to protect, send messages, and as mascots in American World War I propaganda and recruiting posters.

The use of dogs in warfare has been common even in many early civilizations. As warfare has progressed, their purposes have changed greatly. Some examples are:

- 628 BC: The Lydians deployed a separate battalion of fighting dogs.
- 525 BC: Cambyses II used huge fighting dogs against Egyptian spearmen and archers.
- 490 BC: Battle of Marathon: A brave fighting dog was immortalized in a mural.
- 385 BC: Siege of Mantineia: Fighting dogs cut off enemy reinforcements.
- 101 BC: Battle of Vercellae: Large Cimbri dogs led by women defended their wagon forts.
- 1525: Henry VIII exported 400 mastiffs to support Spain.
- 1580: Elizabeth I sent 800 fighting dogs to fight in the Desmond Rebellions.
- 1799: Napoleon assembled large numbers of fighting dogs in front of his reserves.
- 1914: The Belgian Army used carabiniers, strong-muscled Bouvier des Flandres to haul heavy machine guns to the front.
- 1914-1918: Dogs were used by international forces to deliver vital messages.
- 1941-1945: The Soviet Union used dogs strapped with explosives to destroy invading German tanks.
- 1943-1945: The United States Marine Corps used dogs, donated by their American owners, in the Pacific theater to help take islands back from Japanese occupying forces. During this period the Doberman Pinscher became the official dog of the U.S.M.C.; however, all breeds of dogs were eligible to train to be 'war dogs of the Pacific'. Of the 549 dogs that returned from the war, only 4 could not be detrained and returned to civilian life. Many of the dogs went home with their handlers from the war.
- 1966-1973: Approximately 5,000 US war dogs served in the Vietnam War (the US Army did not retain records prior to 1968); about 10,000 US servicemen served as dog-handlers during the war, and the K9 units are estimated to have saved over 10,000 human lives. 232 military working dogs and 295 US servicemen working as dog handlers were killed in action during the war. It is estimated that about 200 Vietnam War dogs survived the war to be assigned at other US bases outside the US. The remaining canines were euthanized or left behind.
- 1979-1988: The Soviet Union again used dogs, this time in the Soviet war in Afghanistan.

- 2011: United States Navy SEALs used a Belgian Malinois war dog named Cairo in Operation Neptune Spear, in which Osama bin Laden was killed.

Dogs have been used for many different purposes. Different breeds were used for different things, but always met the demands of the handlers. Many roles for dogs in war are obsolete and no longer practised.

In ancient times, dogs, often large ancient mastiff type breeds, would be strapped with armor and spiked collars, and sent into battle to attack the enemy. This strategy was used by various civilizations, such as the Romans and the Greeks. This approach has been largely abandoned in modern day militaries due to the fact that modern weapons would allow the dogs to be killed almost immediately, as on Okinawa when U.S. soldiers quickly eliminated a platoon of Japanese soldiers and their dogs.

Another programme attempted during World War II was suggested by a Swiss citizen living in Santa Fe, New Mexico. William A. Prestre proposed using large dogs to kill Japanese soldiers. He convinced the military to lease an entire island in the Mississippi to house the training facilities. There the army hoped to train as many as two million dogs. The idea was to begin island invasions with landing craft releasing thousands of dogs against the Japanese defenders, then followed up by troops as the Japanese defenders scattered in confusion. One of the biggest problems encountered was getting Japanese soldiers to train the dogs with, as few Japanese soldiers were being captured. Eventually, Japanese-American soldiers volunteered for the training. The biggest problem was the dogs; either they were too docile, did not respond to training teaching them to rush across beaches, or were terrified by shellfire. After millions of dollars were spent, the programme was abandoned.

About the time World War I broke out, many Europeans used dogs to pull small carts. Many European armies adapted the process for military use.

The Belgian Army used dogs to pull their Maxim Guns and other supplies or wounded in their carts. The French had 250 dogs at the start of World War I. The Dutch army copied the idea and had hundreds of dogs trained and ready by the end of World War I (the Netherlands remained neutral).

The Soviet army also used dogs to drag wounded men to aid stations during WWII. The dogs were well-suited to transporting loads over snow and through craters.

Dogs were often used to carry messages in battle. They would be turned loose to move silently to a second handler. This required a dog which was very loyal to *two* masters, otherwise the dog would not deliver the message on time, or at all. Some messenger dogs also performed other communication jobs, such as pulling telephone lines from one location to another.

Mascots

Dogs were often used as unit mascots for military units. The dog in question might be an officer's dog, an animal that the unit chose to adopt, or one of their canines employed in another role as a working dog. Some naval dogs such as Sinbad and Judy were themselves enlisted service members.

Some units also chose to employ a particular breed of dog as their standard mascot, with new dogs replacing the old when it died or was retired. The presence of a mascot was designed to uplift morale, and many were used to this effect in the trenches of World War I.

In World War II, dogs took on a new role in medical experimentation, as the primary animals chosen for medical research. The animal experimentation allowed doctors to test new medicine without risking human lives, though these practices came under more scrutiny after the war. The United States' government responded by proclaiming these dogs as heroes.

The Cold War sparked a heated debate over the ethics of animal experimentation in the U.S., particularly aimed at how canines were treated in World War II. In 1966, major reforms came to this field with the adoption of the Laboratory Animal Welfare Act.

Many dogs were used to locate mines. They did not prove to be very effective under combat conditions. Marine mine detecting dogs were trained using bare electric wires beneath the ground surface. The wires shocked the dogs, teaching them that danger lurked under the dirt. Once the dog's focus was properly directed, dummy mines were planted and the dogs were trained to signal their presence.

While the dogs effectively found the mines, the task proved so stressful for the dogs they were only able to work between 20 and 30 minutes at a time. The mine detecting war dogs anticipated random shocks from the heretofore friendly earth, making them extremely nervous. The useful service life of the dogs was not long. Experiments with lab rats show that this trend can be very extreme, in some tests rats even huddled in the corner to the point of starvation to avoid electric shock.

This is the result of variable schedule operant conditioning. Rather than shocking the entire ground surface, the electric shock components should be placed directly over the mine detonation area. This would teach the dogs and mice that only sections of ground over mines are dangerous, not all of the ground.

Dogs have historically also been used in many cases to track fugitives and enemy troops, overlapping partly into the duties of a scout dog, but use their olfactory skill in tracking a scent, rather than warning a handler at the initial presentation of a scent.

Some dogs are trained to silently locate booby traps and concealed enemies such as snipers. The dog's keen senses of smell and hearing would make them far more effective at detecting these dangers than humans. The best scout dogs are described as having a disposition intermediate to docile tracking dogs and aggressive attack dogs.

Scout dogs were used in World War II, Korea, and Vietnam by the United States to detect ambushes, weapon caches, or enemy fighters hiding underwater, with only reed breathing straws showing above the waterline. The US operated a number of scout dog platoons (assigned on a handler-and-dog team basis to individual patrols) and had a dedicated dog training school in Fort Benning, Georgia.

One of the earliest military-related uses, sentry dogs were used to defend camps or other priority areas at night and sometimes during the day. They would bark or growl to alert guards of a stranger's presence. During the Cold War, the American military used sentry dog teams outside of nuclear weapons storage areas. A test programme was conducted in Vietnam to test sentry dogs, launched two days after a successful Vietcong attack on Da Nang Air Base (July 1, 1965).

Forty dog teams were deployed to Vietnam for a four month test period, with teams placed on the perimeter in front of machine gun towers/bunkers. The detection of intruders resulted in a rapid deployment of reinforcements. The test was successful, so the handlers returned to the US while the dogs were reassigned to new handlers. The Air Force immediately started to ship dog teams to all the bases in Vietnam and Thailand.

The buildup of American forces in Vietnam created large dog sections at USAF Southeast Asia (SEA) bases. 467 dogs were eventually assigned to Bien Hoa, Bien Thuy, Cam Ranh Bay, Da Nang, Nha Trang, Tuy Hoa, Phu Cat, Phan Rang, Tan Son Nhut, and Pleiku Air Bases. Within a year of deployment, attacks on several bases had been stopped when the enemy forces were detected by dog teams. Captured Vietcong told of the fear and respect that they had for the dogs. The Vietcong even placed a bounty on lives of handlers and dogs. The success of sentry dogs was determined by the lack of successful penetrations of bases in Vietnam and Thailand. It is estimated by the United States War Dogs Association that war dogs saved over 10,000 U.S. lives in Vietnam. Sentry Dogs were also used by the Army, Navy, and Marines to protect the perimeter of large bases.

Contemporary dogs in military roles are also often referred to as police dogs, or in the United States as a Military Working Dog (MWD), or K-9. Their roles are nearly as varied as their ancient cousins, though they tend to be more rarely used in front-line formations. As of 2011, 600 U.S. Military dogs were actively participating in the conflicts in Iraq and Afghanistan.

Traditionally, the most common breed for these police-type operations has been the German Shepherd; in recent years there has been a shift to smaller dogs with keener senses of smell for detection work, and more resilient breeds such as the Belgian Malinois and Dutch Shepherd for patrolling and law enforcement. All MWDs in use today are paired with a single individual after their training. This person is called a handler. While a handler usually won't stay with one dog for the length of either's career, usually a handler will stay partnered with a dog for at least a year, and sometimes much longer.

In the 1970s the US Air Force used over 1,600 dogs worldwide. Today, personnel cutbacks have reduced USAF dog teams to approximately 530, stationed throughout the world. Many dogs that operate in these roles are trained at Lackland Air Force Base, the only United States facility that currently trains dogs for military use.

Change has also come in legislation for the benefit of the canines. Prior to 2000, older war dogs were required to be euthanized. Thanks to a new law, retired military dogs may now be adopted, one noteable case 17:38, 9 July 2011 (UTC) of which of which was Lex, a working dog whose handler was killed in Iraq.

There are numerous memorials dedicated to war dogs, including March Field Air Museum in Riverside, California; the Infantry School at Fort Benning, Georgia; at the Naval Facility, Guam, with replicas at the University of Tennessee College of Veterinary Medicine in Knoxville; the Alfred M. Gray Marine Corps Research Center in Quantico, Virginia; and the Alabama War Dogs Memorial at the USS Alabama Battleship Memorial Park in Mobile, Alabama.

Law Enforcement

As a partner in everyday military police work, dogs have proved versatile and loyal officers. Police dogs can chase suspects, track them if they are hidden, and guard them when they are caught. They are trained to respond viciously if their handler is attacked, and otherwise not to react at all unless they are commanded to do so by their handler. Many police dogs are also trained in detection as well.

Drug and Explosives Detection

Both MWDs and their civilian counterparts provide service in drug detection, sniffing out a broad range of psychoactive substances despite efforts at concealment. Provided they have been trained to detect it, MWDs can smell small traces of nearly any substance, even if it is in a sealed container. Dogs trained in drug detection are normally used at ports of embarkation such as airports, checkpoints, and other places where there is high security and a need for anti-contraband measures.

MWDs can also be trained to detect explosives. As with narcotics, trained MWDs can detect minuscule amounts of a wide range of explosives, making them useful for searching entry points, patrolling within secure installations, and at checkpoints. These dogs are capable of achieving over a 98 per cent success rate in bomb detection.

Intimidation

The use of Military Working Dogs on prisoners by the United States during recent wars in Afghanistan and Iraq has been very controversial.

Iraq War: The U.S. has used dogs to intimidate prisoners in Iraqi prisons. In court testimony following the revelations of Abu Ghraib prisoner abuse, it was stated that Col. Thomas M. Pappas approved the use of dogs for interrogations. Pvt. Ivan L. Frederick testified that interrogators were authorized to use dogs and that a civilian contract interrogator left him lists of the cells he wanted dog handlers to visit. "They were allowed to use them to ... intimidate inmates", Frederick stated.

Two soldiers, Sgt. Santos A. Cardona and Sgt. Michael J. Smith, were then charged with maltreatment of detainees, for allegedly encouraging and permitting unmuzzled working dogs to threaten and attack them. Prosecutors have focused on an incident caught in published photographs, when the two men allegedly cornered a naked detainee and allowed the dogs to bite him on each thigh as he cowered in fear.

Guantanamo Bay: It is believed that the use of dogs on prisoners in Iraq was learned from practices at Guantanamo Bay Naval Base. The use of dogs on prisoners by regular U.S. forces in Guantanamo Bay Naval Base was prohibited by Donald Rumsfeld in April 2003. A few months later following revelations of abuses at Abu Ghraib prison, including use of dogs to terrify naked prisoners; Rumsfeld then issued a further order prohibiting their use by the regular U.S. forces in Iraq.

Retirement

Traditionally, as in World War II, US military working dogs (war dogs) were returned home after the war; to their former owners or new adopted ones. The Vietnam War was different in that US war dogs were designated as expendable equipment and were either euthanized or turned over to an allied army prior to the US departure from South Vietnam.

Due to lobbying efforts by veteran dog handlers from the Vietnam War Congress approved a bill allowing veteran US military working dogs to be adopted after their military service. In 2000, President Bill Clinton signed a law that allowed these dogs to be adopted , making the Vietnam War the only American war in which US war dogs never came home.

Military Working dogs continue to serve as sentries, trackers, Search and rescue, scouts, and mascots. Retired working dogs are often adopted as pets or Therapy dogs.

Iraq War: The U.S. has used dogs to intimidate prisoners in Iraq. Citing court testimony following the revelations of Abu Ghraib prisoner abuse, it was reported that Colonel Thomas M. Pappas approved the use of dogs for interrogations. [illegible] testified that [illegible] authorized the use of dogs and [illegible] civilian contract interrogators [illegible] the [illegible] dog handlers [illegible]. They were allowed to use dogs [illegible] interrogation [illegible] muzzled.

Two soldiers, Sgt. Santos A. Cardona and Sgt. Michael J. Smith were then charged with maltreatment of detainees, for allegedly encouraging and permitting their unmuzzled working dogs to threaten and attack them. They [illegible] photographs [illegible] when the two [illegible] dog [illegible] and allowed the dogs to [illegible] as he cowered in fear.

[illegible] it is believed that the use of dogs [illegible] in Iraq was learned from [illegible] Guantanamo [illegible]. The use of dogs on prisoners [illegible] in Guantanamo Bay [illegible] had been prohibited by Donald Rumsfeld in April 2003. A few months later, following revelations of abuses at Abu Ghraib prison, [illegible] use of dogs to terrify naked prisoners, [illegible] embarrassing [illegible] by the [illegible] in Iraq.

Retirement

Traditionally, [illegible] World War II, [illegible] military working dogs were returned home after the war, to their former owners or new adopted ones. The Vietnam War was different in that US war dogs were [illegible] as expendable equipment and were either euthanised or turned over to an allied army prior to the US departure from South Vietnam.

Due to a lobbying effort by Vietnam dog handlers [illegible] from the Vietnam War, Congress approved a bill allowing [illegible] military working dogs to be adopted after their military service. In 2000 President Bill Clinton signed [illegible] allowing these dogs to be adopted, making the Vietnam War the only American war in which US war dogs never came home.

Military working dogs continue to [illegible] explosives, drugs and [illegible]. Retired working dogs are often adopted [illegible].

Bibliography

Adler, Leonore Loeb, Helmut E. Adler (2004). "Ontogeny of Observational Learning in the Dog (Canis Familiaris)". *Developmental Psychobiology* 10 (3): 267-271.

Burnam, John C. (2006). *Dog Tags of Courage: Combat Infantrymen and War Dog Heros in Vietnam*. Lost Coast Press. ISBN 978-1-882897-88-9.

Burnam, John C. (2008). *A Soldier's Best Friend; Scout Dogs and their Handlers in the Vietnam War*. Sterling Publishing. ISBN 978-1-4027-5447-0.

Christine, Mlot (June 28, 1997). "Stalking the Ancient Dog". Retrieved 04/20 2008. "When We Became An Agricultural Society, What We Needed Dogs for Changed Enormously, and a Further and Irrevocable Division [Between Dogs and Wolves] Occurred at that point."

Davis SJM and FR Valla, *Evidence for Domestication of the Dog 12,000 Years Ago in the Natufian of Palestine,* Nature 276, 608-610 (7 December 1978).

Dyer, Walter A. (2006). *Pierrot the Carabinier: Dog of Belgium*. Meadow Books. ISBN 1846850363.

Gould, Stephen Jay (1993). *Eight Little Piggies: Reflections in Natural History*. New York: W.W. Norton & Company. ISBN 0393311392.

Heidenberger, E, Unshelm J, E (Feb 1990). "Changes in the Behaviour of Dogs After Castration" (in German). *Tierärztliche Praxis* 18 (1): 69-75. ISSN 0303-6286. PMID 2326799.

Katcher, A.H.; Wilkins, G.G. (2006). "The Centaur's Lessons: Therapeutic Education Through Care of Animals and Nature Study". In Fine, Aubrey H.. *Handbook on Animal-assisted Therapy: Theoretical Foundations and Guidelines for Practice*. Amsterdam: Elsevier/Academic Press. pp. 153-77. ISBN 0-12-369484-1.

Klütsch, CFC, Seppälä EH, Lohi H, Fall T, Hedhammar Å, Uhlén M, Savolainen P (2010) Regional Occurrence, High Frequency But Low Diversity of Mitochondrial DNA Haplogroup d1 Suggests a Recent Dog-wolf Hybridization in Scandinavia. Animal Genetics, online early.

Kruger, K.A. & Serpell, J.A. (2006). Animal-assisted Interventions in Mental Health: Definitions and Theoretical Foundations, In Fine, A.H. (Ed.), Handbook on Animal-assisted Therapy: Theoretical Foundations and Guidelines for Practice. San Diego, CA, Academic Press: 21-38. ISBN 0123694841.

Kubinyi, E., Topal, J., & Miklosi, A. (2003). "Dogs (Canis Familiaris) Learn Their Owners Via Observation in a Manipulation Task". *Journal of Comparative Psychology* 117 (2): p. 156.

Mahlow, Jane C. (1999). "Estimation of the Proportions of Dogs and Cats that are Surgically Sterilized". *Journal of the American Veterinary Medical Association (Excerpt Quoted by Spayusa.org)* 215: 640-643. Retrieved 30 November 2006. "Although the Cause of Pet Overpopulation is Multifaceted, Failure of Owners to Spay and Castrate Their Animals is a Major Contributing Factor".

McGreevy, P.D., and W.F. Nicholas, Some Practical Solutions to Welfare Problems in Pedigree Dog Breeding, Animal Welfare, 1999, Vol. 8, 329-331.

Morey, Darcy. *Dogs: Domestication and the Development of a Social Bond* (Cambridge University Press; 2010) p. 384; Uses Zooarchaeology to Explores Ties Between Humans and Canines Over the Past 15,000 Years with a Focus on the New World and Arctic regions.

Richardson, E.H. (1920). *British War Dogs; Their Training and Psychology*. London: Skeffington.

Rohan, Jack (2006). *Rags, The Dog Who Went to War*. Liskeard: Diggory Press. ISBN 978-1846853647.

Srivastava, AK, Sardana V, Prasad K, Behari M (March 2004). "Diagnostic Dilemma in Flaccid Paralysis Following Anti-rabies Vaccine". *Neurol India* 52 (1): 132-3.

Scott, John Paul; Fuller, John L. (1974). *Dog Behaviour: The Genetic Basis* (2, Illustrated ed.). University of Chicago Press.

Serpell James, *The Domestic Dog: Its Evolution, Behaviour, and Interactions with People*, pp. 10-12. Cambridge University Press, 1995.

Whitridge-Smith, Bertha (2006). *Only A Dog: The True Story of a Dog's Devotion to His Master During World War*. Lightning Source. ISBN 978-1846853654.

Wood, E.S.; R.M. Franklin (2005). *Captain Loxley's Little Dog And Lassie The Life-saving Collie: Hero Dogs of the First World War Associated With The Sinking of H.M.S. Formidable*. Burgress Hill: Diggory Press. ISBN 978-1905363131.

Index